Mac OS X Lion

FOR

DUMMIES®

by Bob "Dr. Mac" LeVitus

WILEY

John Wiley & Sons, Inc.

Mac OS X Lion For Dummies®

Published by
John Wiley & Sons, Inc.
111 River Street
Hoboken, NJ 07030-5774

www.wiley.com

WILEY

About the Author

Bob LeVitus, often referred to as "Dr. Mac," has written or co-written 60 popular computer books, including *iPhone For Dummies*, *iPad For Dummies*, *Incredible iPad Apps For Dummies*, *Incredible iPhone Apps For Dummies*, and *Dr. Mac: The OS X Files* for John Wiley & Sons, Inc.; *Stupid Mac Tricks* and *Dr. Macintosh* for Addison-Wesley; and *The Little iTunes Book* and *The Little iDVD Book* for Peachpit Press. His books have sold more than a million copies worldwide.

Bob has penned the popular Dr. Mac column for the *Houston Chronicle* since 1996 and has been published in dozens of computer magazines over the past 15 years. His achievements have been documented in major media around the world. (Yes, that was him juggling a keyboard in *USA Today* a few years back!)

Bob is known for his expertise, trademark humorous style, and ability to translate techie jargon into usable and fun advice for regular folks. Bob is also a prolific public speaker, presenting more than 100 Macworld Expo training sessions in the U.S. and abroad, keynote addresses in three countries, and Macintosh training seminars in many U.S. cities. (He also won the Macworld Expo MacJeopardy World Championship three times before retiring his crown.)

Bob is considered a leading authority on Apple technology. From 1989 to 1997, he was a contributing editor/columnist for *MacUser* magazine, writing the Help Folder, Beating the System, Personal Best, and Game Room columns at various times.

In his copious spare time, Bob heads up a team of expert technical consultants who do nothing but provide technical help and training to Mac, iPhone, and iPad users via telephone, e-mail, and/or a unique Internet-enabled remote control software, which allows the team to see and control your Mac no matter where in the world you may be.

If you're having problems with your Mac, you ought to give them a try. You'll find them at www.boblevitus.com or 408-627-7577.

Prior to giving his life over to computers, LeVitus spent years at Kresser/Craig/D.I.K. (a Los Angeles advertising agency and marketing consultancy) and its subsidiary, L & J Research. He holds a BS in marketing from California State University.

Dedication

For the sixtieth time, this book is dedicated to the love of my life, my wife and best friend, Lisa, who taught me almost everything I know about almost everything I know except computers.

And, as always, it's also dedicated to my kids, Allison and Jacob, who love their Apple gadgets almost as much as I love them (my kids, not Apple gadgets).

Author's Acknowledgments

Thanks to my super-agent, Carole "Swifty" McClendon. We've been together more than 20 years and you're *still* a treasure.

Special thanks to everyone at Apple who helped me turn this book around in record time: Keri Walker, Monica Sarkar, Janette Barrios, Greg (Joz) Joswiak, and all the rest. I couldn't have done it without you.

Big-time thanks to the gang at Wiley: Bob "Is it done yet?" Woerner, Linda "Whipcracker IX" Morris, Andy "The Big Boss Man" Cummings, Barry "Still no humorous nickname" Pruett, my technical editor Dennis R. Cohen, who did a rocking job as always, and all the others.

Thanks also to my family and friends for putting up with me during my all-too-lengthy absences during this book's gestation. And thanks to Saccone's Pizza, Rudy's BBQ, Taco Cabana, Sodastream, and Five Guys for sustenance.

And finally, thanks to you, gentle reader, for buying this book.

Publisher's Acknowledgments

We're proud of this book; please send us your comments at http://dummies.custhelp.com. For other comments, please contact our Customer Care Department within the U.S. at 877-762-2974, outside the U.S. at 317-572-3993, or fax 317-572-4002.

Some of the people who helped bring this book to market include the following:

Acquisitions and Editorial

Project Editor: Linda Morris

Executive Editor: Bob Woerner

Copy Editor: Linda Morris

Technical Editor: Dennis Cohen

Editorial Manager: Jodi Jensen

Editorial Assistant: Amanda Graham

Sr. Editorial Assistant: Cherie Case

Cartoons: Rich Tennant
(www.the5thwave.com)

Composition Services

Project Coordinator: Sheree Montgomery

Layout and Graphics: Samantha K. Cherolis, Joyce Haughey, Corrie Socolovitch

Proofreaders: Lindsay Amones, Kathy Simpson

Indexer: Infodex Indexing Services, Inc.

Publishing and Editorial for Technology Dummies

Richard Swadley, Vice President and Executive Group Publisher

Andy Cummings, Vice President and Publisher

Mary Bednarek, Executive Acquisitions Director

Mary C. Corder, Editorial Director

Publishing for Consumer Dummies

Kathy Nebenhaus, Vice President and Executive Publisher

Composition Services

Debbie Stailey, Director of Composition Services

Table of Contents

Introduction *1*

About This Book 1
What You Won't Find in This Book 2
Conventions Used in This Book 2
Foolish Assumptions 3
How This Book Is Organized 3
Icons Used in This Book 5
Where to Go from Here 5

Part 1: Introducing OS X Lion: The Basics *7*

Chapter 1: Mac OS X Lion 101 (Prerequisites: None). **9**

Gnawing to the Core of OS X 10
A Safety Net for the Absolute Beginner (Or Any User) 11
    Turning the dang thing on 12
    What you should see on startup 12
    Shutting down properly 16
    A few things you should definitely NOT do with your Mac 16
    Point-and-click boot camp 18
Not Just a Beatles Movie: Help and the Help Menu 19

Chapter 2: The Desktop and Windows and Menus (Oh, My)! **23**

Touring the Finder and Its Desktop 24
Anatomy of a Window 25
    Top o' the window to ya! 28
    A scroll new world 28
    (Hyper)Active windows 30
Dialog Dealie-Boppers 31
Working with Windows 32
    Opening and closing windows 33
    Resizing windows and window panes 33
    Moving windows 34
    Shuffling windows 34
Menu Basics 35
    The ever-changing menu bar 36
    Contextual menus: They're sooo sensitive 36
    Recognizing disabled options 38
    Navigating submenus 39
    Underneath the Apple menu tree 39
    Using keyboard shortcut commands 41

Chapter 3: Have It Your Way 45

Introducing System Preferences 45
Putting a Picture on the Desktop 47
Setting Up a Screen Saver 49
Putting Widgets on the Dashboard 51
    Translation 54
    Flight Tracker 54
Giving Buttons, Menus, and Windows a Makeover 55
Adjusting the Keyboard, Mouse, Trackpad, and Other Hardware ...58
    Keyboard 58
    Mouse 62
    Bluetooth 64
    Trackpad (notebook Macs only) 65
Styling Your Sound 67
    Changing sound effects 68
    Choosing output options 68
    Choosing input options 68

Chapter 4: What's Up, Dock? 69

A Quick Introduction to Your Dock 69
    The default icons of the Dock 70
    Trash talkin' 73
    Opening application menus in the Dock 74
    Reading Dock-icon body language 76
    Opening files from the Dock 77
Customizing Your Dock 78
    Adding Dock icons 78
    Removing an icon from the Dock 80
    Resizing the Dock 81
    What should you put in YOUR Dock? 82
    Setting your Dock preferences 83

Chapter 5: The Finder and Its Desktop 89

Introducing the Finder and its Minions: The Desktop and Icons ...89
    Figuring out what an icon is 90
    Identifying your Finder icons in the wild 90
Aliases: Greatest Thing Since Sliced Bread 92
    Creating aliases 94
    Deleting aliases 95
    Hunting down an alias's parent 96
    Introducing the Desktop 96
    Bellying up to the toolbar 98
The View(s) from a Window 101
    Moving through folders fast in Column view 101
    Perusing in Icon view 103

Finder on the Menu 107
   The actual Finder menu 107
   Like a road map: The current folder's pop-up menu 109
   Going places with the Go menu 110
Customizing Finder Windows 112
   Adding folders to the Sidebar 113
   Setting Finder preferences 114
Digging for Icon Data in the Info Window 116

Part II: Lion Taming (Or "Organization for Smart People") 121

Chapter 6: The Care and Feeding of Files and Folders 123
Understanding the Mac OS X Folder Structure 124
   Understanding nested folders 125
   From the top: The Computer folder 126
   Peeking into the Applications folder 127
   Finding fonts (and more) in the public Library folder 127
   Let it be: The System folder 129
   The usability of the Users folder 129
   There's no place like Home 130
   Your personal Library card 132
Saving Your Document Before It's Too Late 134
   Stepping through a basic Save or Save a Version 135
   Versions could be the new Save As 139
Open Sez Me 142
   With a Quick Look 144
   With drag-and-drop 146
   When your Mac can't open a file 146
   With the application of your choice 147
Organizing Your Stuff in Folders 149
   Files versus folders 149
   Organizing your stuff with subfolders 150
   Creating new folders 153
   Navigating with spring-loaded folders 153
   Smart Folders 154
Shuffling Around Files and Folders 157
   Comprehending the Clipboard 157
   Copying files and folders 158
   Pasting from the Clipboard 160
   Moving files and folders 160
   Selecting multiple icons 161
   Playing the icon name game: Renaming icons 163
   Compressing files 164
   Getting rid of icons 164

Chapter 7: Timesaving Tools **165**

Finding Files and Folders Faster 165
Using the Search box in Finder windows 166
Using the Spotlight menu and window 168
Finding files by other attributes 170
Exposé Yourself to Mission Control's Spaces 171
The painless Mission Control pane 172
Hot corners! 174
Spaces from 30,000 feet (An overview) 175
Getting around in Space(s) 178
Launchpad: The Place for Applications 180
Customizing Your Launchpad 181

Chapter 8: Dealing with Disks **183**

Comprehending Disks 184
Some disks need to be formatted first 185
Moving and copying disk icons 185
Surprise: Your PC Disks Work, Too! 186
Burning CDs and DVDs 187
Burning on the fly 188
Creating a burn folder 192
Getting Disks out of Your Mac 193

Chapter 9: Organizing Your Life **195**

Keeping Track with iCal 196
Navigating iCal views 196
Creating calendars 198
Grouping calendars 199
Deleting a calendar or group 200
Creating and managing events 200
To do or not to do: Setting reminders 203
Are you available? 204
Stickies 205

Part III: Do Unto Lion: Getting Things Done *207*

Chapter 10: Internet-Working **209**

Getting Connected to the Internet 210
Setting up your modem 210
Your Internet service provider and you 211
Plugging in your Internet-connection settings 212

Browsing the Web with Safari..214
    Navigating with the toolbar buttons 215
    Bookmarking your favorite pages................................216
    What's on your reading list?..218
    Using the terrific Top Sites page................................219
    Simplifying surfing with RSS feeds.............................221
    Searching with Google...222
    Checking out Help Center 225
Communicating via iChat 225
    Chit-chatting with iChat 226
    Chatting with audio and video 227
    Remote Screen Sharing: Remarkable and superbly satisfying.....229
Video Calls with FaceTime 231

Chapter 11: E-Mail Made Easy.............................233
Keeping Contacts Handy with Address Book 233
    Adding contacts 234
    Importing contacts from other programs...................236
    Creating a basic group 236
    Setting up a Smart Group (based on contact criteria).................237
    The Views are lovely 238
    Sending e-mail to a contact or group 239
Sending and Receiving E-Mail with Mail 240
    Setting up Mail...241
    Composing a new message...242
    A quick overview of the toolbar.................................244
    Working with stationery 245
    Checking your mail 246
    Dealing with spam...248
    Changing your preferences 248
    Mail rules rule..249
    Mailboxes smart and plain 250
    Sign here, please 253
    Take a (Quick) look and (Slide) show me some photos 255

Chapter 12: The Musical Mac 257
Introducing iTunes 257
Working with Media 260
    Adding songs 261
    Adding movies and videos...263
    Adding podcasts 263
    Learning from iTunes U...264
    Listening to Internet radio..264

All About Playlists 266
    Creating a regular playlist...266
    Working with smart playlists 267
    Burning a playlist to CD 268
    Looking at two specific playlists.................................269
Backing Up Your iTunes Media...271

Chapter 13: The Multimedia Mac **275**
Watching Movies with DVD Player....................................275
Playing Movies and Music in QuickTime Player................278
Viewing and Converting Images and PDFs in Preview.........279
Importing Media 280
    Downloading photos from a camera 281
    Downloading DV video from a camcorder....................283

Chapter 14: Words and Letters.............................**285**
Processing Words with TextEdit.......................................285
    Creating and composing a document 287
    Working with text..288
    Adding graphics to documents....................................290
Font Mania...292
    Types of fonts...292
    Managing your fonts with Font Book 293
    Installing fonts manually..294

Part 1V: Making This Lion Your Very Own.....................*295*

Chapter 15: Publish or Perish: The Fail-Safe Guide to Printing.....**297**
Before Diving In 297
Ready: Connecting and Adding Your Printer.....................298
    Connecting your printer 298
    Setting up a printer for the first time 299
    One last thing: Printer sharing...................................302
Set: Setting Up Your Document with Page Setup 303
Print: Printing with the Print Sheet.................................305
    Printing a document 305
    Choosing among different printers..............................306
    Choosing custom settings...307
    Saving custom settings..310
Preview and PDF Options 310
Just the Fax 313

Chapter 16: Sharing Your Mac and Liking It 315

Introducing Networks and File Sharing 316
Portrait of home-office networking.................................... 317
Three ways to build a network 318
Setting Up File Sharing... 321
Access and Permissions: Who Can Do What 322
Users and groups and guests 323
Creating users 324
Mac OS X knows best: Folders shared by default............... 331
Sharing a folder or disk by setting permissions 332
Useful settings for permissions.. 337
Unsharing a folder 340
Connecting to a Shared Disk or Folder on a Remote Mac.............. 340
Changing Your Password 344
Changing your account password on your Mac 344
Changing the password of any account but your own
on your Mac 345
Changing the password for your account on
someone else's Mac 346
Five More Types of Sharing... 346
DVD or CD Sharing.. 347
Screen Sharing.. 347
Printer Sharing.. 348
Scanner Sharing.. 348
Web Sharing.. 348
Internet Sharing.. 348
Bluetooth Sharing 350

Chapter 17: Features for the Way You Work .351

Talking and Listening to Your Mac 351
Talking to your Mac.. 352
Listening to your Mac read for you 357
Automatic Automation.. 359
AppleScript 360
Automator... 361
A Few More Useful Goodies... 364
App Store 364
Universal Access 364
Energy Saver... 367
Bluetooth 369
Ink 369
Automatic Login (Users & Groups System Preferences pane) 369
Boot Camp 370

Part V: The Care and Feeding of Your Lion 373

Chapter 18: Safety First: Backups and Other Security Issues 375

Backing Up Is (Not) Hard to Do 376
    Backing up with Lion's excellent Time Machine.......................... 376
    Backing up by using the manual, brute-force method 380
    Backing up by using commercial backup software 380
Why You Need Two Sets of Backups 381
Non-Backup Security Concerns 382
    About viruses and other malware 383
    Firewall: Yea or nay?.. 385
    Install recommended software updates 388
Protecting Your Data from Prying Eyes.. 389
    Blocking or limiting connections 389
    Locking down files with FileVault 390
    Setting other options for security.. 391

Chapter 19: Utility Chest 393

Calculator 393
Activity Monitor 394
AirPort Utility 396
Audio MIDI Setup 396
ColorSync Utility 396
DigitalColor Meter 398
Disk Utility 398
    First Aid tab 398
    Erase tab 398
    Partition tab... 399
    RAID tab 400
    Restore tab 400
Grab... 401
Grapher 402
Keychain Access 402
Migration Assistant 404
System Information 404
Terminal.. 404

Chapter 20: Troubleshooting Mac OS X 407

About Startup Disks and Booting 407
    They call it a prohibitory sign for a reason 408
Recovering with Recovery HD 410
    Step 1: Run First Aid 411
    Step 2: Safe Boot into Safe Mode... 413

Step 3: Zapping the PRAM..414
Step 4: Reinstalling Mac OS X...415
Step 5: Things to try before taking your Mac in for repair..........415
If Your Mac Crashes at Startup..416

Part VI: The Part of Tens.................................... 419

Chapter 21: Almost Ten Ways to Speed Up Your Mac Experience...421

Use Those Keyboard Shortcuts...421
Improve Your Typing Skills...423
Resolution: It's Not Just for New Year's Anymore 423
A Mac with a View — and Preferences, Too 425
Get a New, Faster Model...426
You Can Never Have Too Much RAM!......................................427
Get an Accelerated Graphics Card 427
Get a New Hard Drive...427
Get a Solid State Drive (SSD) 429

Chapter 22: Ten Ways to Make Your Mac Better by Throwing Money at It 431

RAM...431
Backup Software and/or Hardware 432
A Better Monitor (Or a Second One).....................................432
A Fast Internet Connection...433
Games...433
Multimedia Titles...434
Some Big Honking Speakers with a Subwoofer.....................434
A New Mouse and/or Keyboard 434
A MacBook or MacBook Pro 435

Chapter 23: Ten (Or So) Great Websites for Mac Freaks 437

MacFixIt...437
Macworld...438
The Mac Observer..438
CNET Downloads (formerly VersionTracker)..........................439
MacInTouch...439
Alltop...439
Apple Support and Knowledge Base.....................................440
Ramseeker 441
Other World Computing 442
EveryMac.com..442
Inside Mac Games 442
dealmac..442
Dr. Mac Consulting 443

Appendix: Installing or Reinstalling
Mac OS X Lion (Only If You Have To) *445*

How to Install (or Reinstall) Mac OS X 446
Getting Set Up with Setup Assistant 447

Index *451*

Introduction

You made the right choice twice: OS X Lion and this book.

Take a deep breath, and get ready to have a rollicking good time. That's right. This is a computer book, but it's going to be fun. What a concept! Whether you're brand spanking new to the Mac or a grizzled old Mac vet, I guarantee that reading this book to discover the ins and outs of OS X Lion will make everything easier. Wiley, Inc. (the publisher of this book), couldn't say as much on the cover if it weren't true!

About This Book

This book's roots lie with my international best seller *Macintosh System 7.5 For Dummies,* an award-winning book so good that now-deceased Mac cloner Power Computing gave away a copy with every Mac clone it sold. *OS X Lion For Dummies* is the latest revision and has been, once again, completely updated to include all the OS X goodness in Lion. In other words, this edition combines all the old, familiar features of previous editions — but is once again updated to reflect the latest and greatest offering from Apple as well as feedback from readers.

Why write a *For Dummies* book about Lion? Well, Lion is a big, somewhat complicated personal-computer operating system. So I made *OS X Lion For Dummies* a not-so-big, not-very-complicated book that shows you what Lion is all about without boring you to tears, confusing you, or poking you with sharp objects.

In fact, I think you'll be so darned comfortable that I wanted the title to be *OS X Lion Without Discomfort,* but the publishers wouldn't let me. Apparently, we *For Dummies* authors have to follow some rules, and using *For Dummies* and *OS X Lion* in this book's title are among them.

And speaking of *dummies,* remember that it's just a word. I don't think you're dumb — quite the opposite! My second choice for this book's title was *OS X Lion For People Smart Enough to Know They Need Help with It,* but you can just imagine what Wiley thought of that. ("C'mon, that's the whole point of the name!" they insisted. "Besides, it's shorter our way.")

Anyway, the book is chock-full of information and advice, explaining everything you need to know about OS X in language you can understand — along with timesaving tips, tricks, techniques, and step-by-step instructions, all served up in generous quantities.

What You Won't Find in This Book

Another rule we *For Dummies* authors must follow is that our books cannot exceed a certain number of pages. (Brevity is the soul of wit, and all that.) So I wish I could have included some things, but they didn't fit. Although I feel confident you'll find everything you need to know about OS X Lion in this book, some things bear further looking into, including these:

- **Information about some of the applications (programs) that come with OS X Lion:** An installation of OS X Lion includes roughly 70 separate applications, mostly located in the Applications folder and the Utilities folder within it. I'd love to walk you through each one of them, but that would have required a book a whole lot bigger, heavier, and more expensive than this one.

  This book is, first and foremost, about using OS X, so I brief you on the small handful of bundled applications essential to using OS X Lion and keep the focus there — namely, iCal, Address Book, Mail, Safari, TextEdit, and the like, as well as important utilities you may need to know how to use someday.

  For what it's worth, many books cover the applications that come with OS X Lion as well as applications commonly bundled with Lion on a new Mac, such as iLife; the one my publisher suggested I recommend is *OS X Lion All-in-One For Dummies,* written by Mark L. Chambers, which is (by sheer coincidence, of course) also published by Wiley.

- **Information about Microsoft Office, iLife, iWork, Adobe Photoshop, Quicken, and most other third-party applications:** Okay, if all the gory details of all the bundled (read: *free*) OS X Lion applications don't fit here, I think you'll understand why digging into third-party applications that cost extra was out of the question.

- **Information about programming for the Mac:** This book is about *using* OS X Lion, not writing code for it. Dozens of books cover programming on the Mac, most of which are two or three times the size of this book.

Conventions Used in This Book

To get the most out of this book, you need to know how I do things and why. Here are a few conventions I use in this book to make your life easier:

- When I want you to open an item in a menu, I write something like "Choose File⇨Open," which means, "Pull down the File menu and choose the Open command."

- Stuff you're supposed to type appears in bold type, **like this.**

- ✔ **Sometimes an entire a sentence is in boldface, as you see when I present a numbered list of steps. In those cases, I leave the bold off what you're supposed to type,** like this.

- ✔ Web addresses, programming code (not much in this book), and things that appear on-screen are shown in a special monofont typeface, `like this`.

- ✔ For keyboard shortcuts, I write something like ⌘+A, which means to hold down the ⌘ key (the one with the little pretzel and/or symbol on it) and then press the A key on the keyboard. If you see something like ⌘+Shift+A, that means to hold down the ⌘ and Shift keys while pressing the A key. Again, for absolute clarity, I never refer to the ⌘ key with the symbol. I reserve that symbol for the menu (Apple menu). For the Command key, I use only the ⌘ symbol. Got it? Very cool.

Foolish Assumptions

Although I know what happens when you make assumptions, I've made a few anyway. First, I assume that you, gentle reader, know nothing about using OS X — beyond knowing what a Mac is, that you want to use OS X, that you want to understand OS X without having to digest an incomprehensible technical manual, and that you made the right choice by selecting this particular book.

And so I do my best to explain each new concept in full and loving detail. Maybe that's foolish, but . . . oh well.

Oh, and I also assume that you can read. If you can't, ignore this paragraph.

How This Book Is Organized

OS X Lion For Dummies is divided into six logical parts, numbered (surprisingly enough) 1 through 6. By no fault of mine, they're numbered using those stuffy old Roman numerals, so you see I–VI where you (in my humble opinion) ought to see Arabic numbers 1–6. It's another rule that *For Dummies* authors have to follow, I think.

Anyway, it's better if you read the parts in order, but if you already know a lot — or think you know a lot — feel free to skip around and read the parts that interest you most.

Part I: Introducing OS X Lion: The Basics: This first part is very, very basic training. From the mouse to the Desktop, from menus, windows, and icons to the snazzy-but-helpful Dock, it's all here. A lot of what you need to know to navigate the depths of OS X safely (and sanely) and perform basic tasks can be found in this part. And although old-timers might just want to skim it, newcomers should probably read every word. Twice.

Part II: Lion Taming (or "Organization for Smart People"): In this part, I build on the basics of Part I and really get you revving with your Mac. Here, I cover additional topics that every Mac user needs to know, coupled with some hands-on, step-by-step instructions. The part starts with a closer look at ways you can organize your files and folders, followed by a chapter about using removable media (which means *ejectable discs* — mostly CDs and DVDs). Last, but certainly not least, is a chapter about all the Lion applications (such as iCal, Address Book, and Mail) that help you keep your digital life organized.

Part III: Do Unto Lion: Getting Things Done: This part is chock-full of ways to do productive stuff with your Mac. In this section, you discover the Internet first — or at least how to get it working on your Mac and what to do with it after you do. Next, you look at the digital-media side of things with chapters about music, video, games, and digital photos. Finally, you look at Lion's built-in tools for writing — namely, TextEdit and fonts.

Part IV: Making This Lion Your Very Own: Here, I get into the nitty-gritty underbelly of making OS X Lion work the way you want it to work. I start with the ins and outs of printing under OS X. Then I move on to somewhat more advanced topics, such as file sharing, creating and using multiple user accounts (and why you might want to), and the lowdown on numerous OS X Lion features — Text to Speech, speech recognition, automation, and more — that can make your computing experience even more pleasant.

Part V: The Care and Feeding of Your Lion: This part starts with a chapter about backups and security, which not only stresses the importance of backing up your data, but also shows you how to do it almost painlessly. Then I introduce you to a handful of useful utilities included with Lion, and explain when and how to use them. Finally, I tell you how to avoid most disasters, as well as what to do in the unlikely event that a major mishap does occur.

Part VI: The Part of Tens: Finally, it's The Part of Tens, which might have started life as a Letterman rip-off but does include heaping helpings of tips, optional software, great Mac web sites, and hardware ideas.

Appendix: Last, but certainly not least, I cover installing OS X Lion in the appendix. The whole process has become quite easy with this version of the system software, but if you have to install Lion yourself, it would behoove you to read this helpful appendix first.

Icons Used in This Book

Little round pictures (icons) appear off to the left side of the text throughout this book. Consider these icons miniature road signs, telling you a little something extra about the topic at hand. Here's what the different icons look like and what they all mean.

Look for Tip icons to find the juiciest morsels: shortcuts, tips, and undocumented secrets about Lion. Try them all; impress your friends!

When you see this icon, it means that this particular morsel is something that I think you should memorize (or at least write on your shirt cuff).

Put on your propeller-beanie hat and pocket protector; these parts include the truly geeky stuff. It's certainly not required reading, but it must be interesting or informative, or I wouldn't have wasted your time with it.

Read these notes very, very, very carefully. (Did I say *very?*) Warning icons flag important cautionary information. The author and publisher won't be responsible if your Mac explodes or spews flaming parts because you ignored a Warning icon. Just kidding. Macs don't explode or spew (with the exception of a few choice PowerBook 5300s, which won't run Lion anyway). But I got your attention, didn't I? I'll tell you once again: It is a good idea to read the Warning icons *very carefully.*

These icons represent my ranting or raving about something that either bugs me or makes me smile. When I'm ranting, imagine foam coming from my mouth. Rants are required to be irreverent, irrelevant, or both. I try to keep them short, more for your sake than mine.

Well, now, what could this icon possibly be about? Named by famous editorial consultant Mr. Obvious, this icon highlights all things new and different in OS X Lion.

Where to Go from Here

Go to a comfortable spot (preferably not far from a Mac) and read the book.

The first few chapters of this book are where I describe the basic everyday things that you need to understand to operate your Mac effectively. If you're new to Macs and OS X Lion, start there.

Even though OS X Lion is somewhat different from previous Mac operating systems, the first part of the book is so basic that if you've been using a Mac for long, you might think you know it all — and okay, you might know most of it. But hey! Not-so-old-timers need a solid foundation. So here's my advice: Skip the stuff you know; you'll get to the better stuff faster.

I didn't write this book for myself. I wrote it for you — and would love to hear how it worked for you. So please send me your thoughts, platitudes, likes and dislikes, and any other comments. You can send snail mail in care of Wiley, but it takes a long time to reach me that way, and I just don't have time to respond to 99.9 percent of it. If you want a response, your best bet is to send e-mail to me directly at Lion4Dummies@boblevitus.com. I appreciate your feedback, and I *try* to respond to all reasonably polite e-mail within a few days.

Did this book work for you? What did you like? What didn't you like? What questions were unanswered? Did you want to know more about something? Did you want to find out less about something? Tell me! I have received more than 100 suggestions about previous editions, most of which are incorporated here. So keep up the good work!

So what are you waiting for? Go — enjoy the book!

Part I
Introducing OS X Lion: The Basics

The 5th Wave   By Rich Tennant

"He saw your MacBook and wants to know if he can check out the new OS X features."

In this part . . .

Because I believe it's important to crawl before you walk, in this part, you get a look at the most basic of basics — such as how to turn on your Mac. Next, I acquaint you with the Mac OS X Finder, with its Desktop, windows, icons, and menus (oh my)! Then you find out how to make this cat your own by customizing your work environment to suit your style. After that is a date with the Dock. And last but certainly not least, you discover ways you can use the Finder to make life with Lion ever so much easier.

So get comfortable, roll up your sleeves, fire up your Mac if you like, and settle down with Part I, a delightful little section I like to think of as "The Hassle-Free Way to Get Started with OS X Lion."

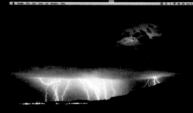

Mac OS X Lion 101
(Prerequisites: None)

....

In This Chapter

▶ Understanding what an operating system is and is not

▶ Turning on your Mac

▶ Getting to know the startup process

▶ Turning off your Mac

▶ Avoiding major Mac mistakes

▶ Pointing, clicking, dragging, and other uses for your mouse

▶ Getting help from your Mac

....

*C*ongratulate yourself on choosing Mac OS X, which stands for *Macintosh Operating System X* — that's the Roman numeral *ten,* not the letter *X* (pronounced *ten,* not *ex*). You made a smart move because you scored more than just an operating-system upgrade. Mac OS X Lion includes several new features that make using your Mac easier and dozens of improvements that help you do more work in less time.

In this chapter, I start at the very beginning and talk about Mac OS X in mostly abstract terms; then I move on to explain what you need to know to use Mac OS X Lion successfully.

If you've been using Mac OS X for a while, some of the information in this chapter might seem hauntingly familiar; some features that I describe haven't changed from earlier versions of Mac OS X. But if you decide to skip this chapter because you think you have all the new stuff figured out, I assure you that you'll miss at least a couple of things that Apple didn't bother to tell you (as if you read every word in Mac OS X Help — the only user manual Apple provides — anyway!).

Tantalized? Let's rock.

If you're about to upgrade to Lion from an earlier version of Mac OS X, I feel obliged to mention a major pitfall to avoid: One very specific misplaced click, done while installing your new OS, *could erase every file on your hard drive.* The Appendix describes this situation in full and loving detail, and it contains other important information about installing Lion that can make upgrading a more pleasant experience.

Gnawing to the Core of OS X

The operating system (that is, the *OS* in *Mac OS X*) is what makes a Mac a Mac. Without it, your Mac is a pile of silicon and circuits — no smarter than a toaster.

"So what does an operating system do?" you ask. Good question. The short answer is that an operating system controls the basic and most important functions of your computer. In the case of Mac OS X and your Mac, the operating system

- Manages memory
- Controls how windows, icons, and menus work
- Keeps track of files
- Manages networking
- Does housekeeping (No kidding!)

Other forms of software, such as word processors and web browsers, rely on the operating system to create and maintain the environment in which they work their magic. When you create a memo, for example, the word processor provides the tools for you to type and format the information. In the background, the operating system is the muscle for the word processor, performing crucial functions such as the following:

- Providing the mechanism for drawing and moving the on-screen window in which you write the memo
- Keeping track of a file when you save it
- Helping the word processor create drop-down menus and dialogs for you to interact with
- Communicating with other programs
- And much, much more (stuff that only geeks could care about)

So, armed with a little background in operating systems, take a gander at the next section before you do anything else with your Mac.

The Mac advantage

Most of the world's personal computers use Microsoft Windows. But you're among the lucky few to have a computer with an operating system that's intuitive, easy to use, and (dare I say?) fun. If you don't believe me, try using Windows for a day or two. Go ahead. You probably won't suffer any permanent damage. In fact, you'll really begin to appreciate how good you have it. Feel free to hug your Mac. Or give it a peck on the disc-drive slot. Just try not to get your tongue caught.

As someone once told me, "Claiming that the Macintosh is inferior to Windows because most people use Windows is like saying that all other restaurants serve food that's inferior to McDonald's."

We might be a minority, but Mac users have the best, most stable, most modern all-purpose operating system in the world, and here's why: Unix, on which Mac OS X is based, is widely regarded as the best industrial-strength operating system on the planet. For now, just know that

being based on Unix means that a Mac running OS X will crash less often than an older Mac or a Windows machine, which means less downtime. Being Unix-based also means far fewer viruses and malicious software. But perhaps the biggest advantage OS X has is that when an application crashes, it doesn't crash your entire computer, and you don't have to restart the whole computer to continue working.

By the way, with the advent of Intel-powered Macs a few years ago, you can now run Windows natively. That's right — you can now install and run Microsoft Windows on any Mac powered by an Intel processor, as described in Chapter 17. Don't let that Unix stuff scare you. It's there if you want it, but if you don't want it or don't care (like most of us), you'll rarely even know it's there. In fact, you'll rarely (if ever) see the word *Unix* again in this book. As far as you're concerned, Unix under the hood means your Mac will just run and run and run without crashing and crashing and crashing.

One last thing: As I mention in the introduction (I'm repeating it here only in case you normally don't read introductions), Mac OS X Lion comes with more than 50 applications. Although I'd love to tell you all about each and every one, I have only so many pages at my disposal. If you need more info on the programs I don't cover, may I (again) recommend *Mac OS X Lion All-in-One For Dummies,* written by Mark L. Chambers, or *iLife All-in-One For Dummies,* written by my old friends Tony Bove and Cheryl Rhodes (both from Wiley).

A Safety Net for the Absolute Beginner (Or Any User)

In the following sections, I deal with the stuff that Mac OS X Help doesn't cover — or doesn't cover in nearly enough detail. If you're a first-time Macintosh user, please, *please* read this section of the book carefully; it could save your life. Okay, okay, perhaps I'm being overly dramatic. What I mean to say is that reading this section could save your *Mac* or your sanity. Even if you're an experienced Mac user, you might want to read this section. Chances are you'll see at least a few things you might have forgotten that will come in handy now that you've been reminded of them.

Turning the dang thing on

Okay. This is the big moment — turning on your Mac! Gaze at it longingly first, and say something cheesy, such as "You're the most awesome computer I've ever known." If that doesn't turn on your Mac (and it probably won't), keep reading.

Apple, in its infinite wisdom, has manufactured Macs with power buttons on every conceivable surface: on the front, side, and back of the computer itself and even on the keyboard or monitor.

So if you don't know how to turn on your Mac, don't feel bad; just look in the manual or booklet that came with your Mac. It's at least one thing that the documentation *always* covers.

 These days, most Macs have a power-on button near the keyboard (notebooks) or the back side (iMacs). It usually looks like the little circle thingie you see in the margin.

 Don't bother choosing Help⇨Mac Help, which opens the Help Viewer program. It can't tell you where the switch is. Although the Help program is good for finding out a lot of things, the location of the power switch isn't among them. If you haven't found the switch and turned on the Mac, of course, you can't access Help anyway. (D'oh!)

What you should see on startup

When you finally do turn on your Macintosh, you set in motion a sophisticated and complex series of events that culminates in the loading of Mac OS X and the appearance of the Mac OS X Desktop. After a small bit of whirring, buzzing, and flashing (meaning that the operating system is loading), OS X first tests all your hardware — slots, ports, disks, random-access memory (RAM), and so on. If everything passes, you hear a pleasing musical tone and see the tasteful gray Apple logo in the middle of your screen, along with a small spinning-pinwheel cursor somewhere on the screen. Both are shown in Figure 1-1.

Here are the things that might happen when you power up your Mac:

> ✔ **Fine and dandy:** Next, you might or might not see the Mac OS X login screen, where you enter your name and password. If you do, press Return or Enter (after you type your name and password, of course), and away you go.

Figure 1-1: This is what you'll see if everything is fine and dandy when you turn your Mac on.

If you don't want to have to type your name and password every time you start or restart your Mac (or even if you do), check out Chapter 17 for the scoop on how to turn the login screen on or off.

Either way, the Desktop soon materializes before your eyes. If you haven't customized, configured, or tinkered with your Desktop, it should look pretty much like Figure 1-2. Now is a good time to take a moment for positive thoughts about the person who convinced you that you wanted a Mac. That person was right!

Figure 1-2: The Mac OS X Lion Desktop after a brand-spanking-new installation of OS X.

✔ **Blue/black/gray screen of death:** If any of your hardware fails when it's tested, you might see a blue, black, or gray screen.

Some older Macs played the sound of a horrible car wreck instead of the chimes, complete with crying tires and busting glass. It was exceptionally unnerving, which might be why Apple doesn't use it anymore.

The fact that something went wrong is no reflection on your prowess as a Macintosh user. Something is broken, and your Mac may need repairs. If this is happening to you right now, check out Chapter 20 to try to get your Mac well again.

If your computer is under warranty, dial 1-800-SOS-APPL, and a customer-service person can tell you what to do. Before you do anything, though, skip ahead to Chapter 20. It's entirely possible that one of the suggestions there can get you back on track without your having to spend even a moment on hold.

✔ **Prohibitory sign (formerly known as the flashing-question-mark disk):** Most users eventually encounter the prohibitory sign shown in the left margin (which replaced the flashing question-mark-on-a-disk icon and flashing folder icon back in Mac OS X Jaguar). This icon means that your Mac can't find a startup disk, hard drive, network server, or DVD-ROM containing a valid Macintosh operating system. See Chapter 20 for ways to ease your Mac's ills.

✔ **Kernel panic:** You shouldn't see this very often, but you might occasionally see a block of text in four languages, including English, as shown in Figure 1-3. This means that your Mac has experienced a *kernel panic,* the most severe type of system crash. If you restart your Mac and see this message again, look in Chapter 20 for a myriad of possible cures for all kinds of ailments, including this one.

> You need to restart your computer. Hold down the Power button for several seconds or press the Restart button.
>
> Veuillez redémarrer votre ordinateur. Maintenez la touche de démarrage enfoncée pendant plusieurs secondes ou bien appuyez sur le bouton de réinitialisation.
>
> Sie müssen Ihren Computer neu starten. Halten Sie dazu die Einschalttaste einige Sekunden gedrückt oder drücken Sie die Neustart-Taste.
>
> コンピュータを再起動する必要があります。パワーボタンを数秒間押し続けるか、リセットボタンを押してください。

Figure 1-3: If this is what you're seeing, things are definitely *not* fine and dandy.

How do you know which version of the Mac OS your computer has? Simple:

1. **Choose About This Mac from the menu (the menu with the symbol in the top-left corner of the menu bar).**

   The About This Mac window pops up on your screen, as shown in Figure 1-4. The version you're running appears just below *Mac OS X* in the center of the window. Version 10.7 is the release we know as *Lion.*

   If you're curious or just want to impress your friends, Mac OS X version 10.6 was called Snow Leopard; 10.5 was known as Leopard; 10.4 as Tiger; 10.3 as Panther; 10.2 as Jaguar; 10.1 as Puma; and 10.0 as Cheetah.

2. **Click the More Info button to launch the System Information application.**

This app shows you much more information, including bus speed, number of processors, caches, installed memory, networking, storage devices, and much more. You can find more about this useful program in Chapter 19.

Figure 1-4: See which version of Mac OS X you're running.

The legend of boot

Boot this. *Boot* that. "I *booted* my Mac and. . . ." or "Did it *boot?*" and so on. Talking about computers for long without hearing the *boot* word is nearly impossible.

But why *boot*? Why not *shoe* or *shirt* or even *shazam?*

Back in the very olden days — say, 1958 or a little earlier — starting a computer required you to toggle little manual switches on the front panel, which began an internal process that loaded the operating system. The process became known as *bootstrapping* because if you toggled the right switches, the computer would "pull itself up by its bootstraps." This phrase didn't take long to transmogrify into *booting* and finally to *boot.*

Over the years, *booting* has come to mean turning on almost any computer or even a peripheral device, such as a printer. Some people also use it to refer to launching an application ("I booted Excel").

So the next time one of your gearhead friends says the b-word, ask whether he knows where the term comes from. Then dazzle him with the depth and breadth of your (not-quite-useful) knowledge!

Shutting down properly

Turning off the power without shutting down your Mac properly is one of the worst things you can do to your poor Mac. Shutting down your Mac improperly can really screw up your hard drive, scramble the contents of your most important files, or both.

If a thunderstorm is rumbling nearby, or you're unfortunate enough to have rolling blackouts where you live, you might *really* want to shut down your Mac. (See the next section, where I briefly discuss lightning and your Mac.)

To turn off your Mac, always use the Shut Down command on the menu or shut down in one of these kind-and-gentle ways:

- ✔ Press the Power key once and then click the Shut Down button in the Are You Sure You Want To Shut Down Your Computer Now? dialog.

- ✔ On keyboards that don't have a Power key, press Control+Eject instead — and then click the Shut Down button that appears in the Are You Sure You Want To Shut Down Your Computer Now? dialog.

You can use a handy keyboard shortcut when the Shut Down button (or any button, for that matter) is highlighted in blue and pulsating slightly. Pressing the Return or Enter key is the same as clicking that button.

The Are You Sure You Want To Shut Down Your Computer Now? dialog sports a new check-box option in Mac OS X Lion: Reopen Windows When Logging Back in. If you check this box, your Mac will start back up with the same windows (and applications) that were open when you shut down or restarted. I think it's pretty darn sweet! I'm happy to report that Lion is full of such nice little improvements.

Most Mac users have been forced to shut down improperly more than once without anything horrible happening, of course — but don't be lulled into a false sense of security. Break the rules one time too many (or under the wrong circumstances), and your most important files *will* be toast. The *only* time you should turn off your Mac without shutting down properly is when your screen is completely frozen or when your system crashed due to a kernel panic and you've already tried everything else. (See Chapter 20 for what those "everything else"s are.) A really stubborn crash doesn't happen often — and less often under OS X than ever before — but when it does, forcing your Mac to turn off and then back on might be the only solution.

A few things you should definitely NOT do with your Mac

In this section, I cover the bad stuff that can happen to your computer if you do the wrong things with it. If something bad has already happened to you — I know . . . I'm beginning to sound like a broken record — see Chapter 20.

Eternally yours . . . *now*

Mac OS X is designed so that you never have to shut it down. You can configure it to sleep after a specified period of inactivity. (See Chapter 17 for more info on the Energy Saver features of OS X.) If you do so, your Mac will consume very little electricity when it's sleeping and will usually be ready to use (when you press any key or click the mouse) in less than a minute. On the other hand, if you're not going to be using it for a few days, you might want to shut it down anyway.

Note: If you leave your Mac on constantly, and you're gone when a lightning storm or rolling blackout hits, your Mac might get wasted. So be sure you have adequate protection — say, a decent surge protector designed specifically for computers — if you decide to leave your Mac on and unattended for long periods. See the section "A few things you should definitely NOT do with your Mac," elsewhere in this chapter, for more info on lightning and your Mac. Often as not, I leave it on when I'm on the road so that I can access it from my laptop via remote screen sharing. So because OS X is designed to run 24/7, I don't shut it down at night unless the night happens to be dark and stormy.

✔ **Don't unplug your Mac when it's turned on.** Very bad things can happen, such as having your operating system break. See the preceding section, where I discuss shutting down your system properly.

Note that this warning doesn't apply to laptops as long as their battery is at least partially charged. As long as there's enough juice in the battery to power your Mac, you can plug and unplug its power adapter to your heart's content.

✔ **Don't use your Mac when lightning is near.** Here's a simple life equation for you: Mac + lightning = dead Mac. 'Nuff said. Oh, and don't place much faith in inexpensive surge protectors. A good jolt of lightning will fry the surge protector right along with your computer — as well as possibly frying your modem, printer, and anything else plugged into it. Some surge protectors can withstand most lightning strikes, but those warriors aren't the cheapies that you buy at your local computer emporium. Unplugging your Mac from the wall during electrical storms is safer and less expensive. (Don't forget to unplug your external modem, network hubs, printers, and other hardware that plugs into the wall as well; lightning can fry them too.)

For laptops, disconnect the power adapter and all other cables (because whatever those cables are connected to could fry, and fry your laptop right along with it). That said, you could use your laptop during a storm, if you like. Just make sure that it's 100 percent wireless and cableless if you do.

✔ **Don't jostle, bump, shake, kick, throw, dribble, or punt your Mac, especially while it's running.** Your Mac contains a hard drive that spins at 4,200 revolutions per minute (rpm) or more. A jolt to a hard drive while it's reading or writing a file can cause the head to crash into the disk, which can render many — or all — files on it unrecoverable. Ouch!

✓ **Don't forget to back up your data!** If the stuff on your hard drive means anything to you, you must back it up. Not *maybe. Must.* Even if your most important file is your last saved game of Bejeweled, you still need to back up your files. Fortunately, Mac OS X Lion includes an awesome backup utility called Time Machine. (Unfortunately, you need either an external hard drive or an Apple Time Capsule device to take advantage of it.) So I beg you: Please read Chapter 18 now, and find out how to back up before something horrible happens to your valuable data!

I *strongly* recommend that you read Chapter 18 sooner rather than later — preferably before you do any significant work on your Mac. Dr. Macintosh says, "There are only two kinds of Mac users: those who will not lose data and those who will." Which kind do you want to be?

✓ **Don't kiss your monitor while wearing stuff on your lips.** For obvious reasons! Use a soft cloth and/or OmniCleanz display cleaning solution (I love the stuff, made by RadTech; www.radtech.us) to clean your display.

Point-and-click boot camp

Are you new to the Mac? Just figuring out how to move the mouse around? Now is a good time to go over some fundamental stuff that you need to know for just about everything you'll be doing on the Mac. Spend a few minutes reading this section, and soon you'll be clicking, double-clicking, pressing, and pointing all over the place. If you think you have the whole mousing thing pretty much figured out, feel free to skip this section. I'll catch you on the other side.

Still with me? Good. Now for some basic terminology:

✓ **Point:** Before you can click or press anything, you have to *point* to it. Place your hand on your mouse, and move it so that the cursor arrow is over the object you want — like on top of an icon or a button.

✓ **Click:** Also called *single click.* Use your index finger to push the mouse button all the way down and then let go so the button produces a satisfying clicking sound. (If you have one of the new optical Apple Pro mice, you push down the whole thing to click.) Use a single-click to highlight an icon, press a button, or activate a check box or window.

In other words, first you point and then you click — *point and click,* in computer lingo.

✓ **Double click:** *Click twice* in rapid succession. With a little practice, you can perfect this technique in no time. Use a double click to open a folder or to launch a file or application.

- **Control+click:** Hold down the Control key while single-clicking. Control+clicking is the same as right-clicking a Windows system and displays a menu (called a *contextual menu*) where you Control+clicked. In fact, if you're blessed with a two-or-more-button mouse such as the Apple Magic Mouse, you can right-click and avoid having to hold down the Control key.

- **Drag:** *Dragging* something usually means you have to click it first and hold down the mouse button. Then you move the mouse on your desk or mouse pad so that the cursor and whatever you select move across the screen. The combination of holding down the button and dragging the mouse is usually referred to as *clicking and dragging*.

- **Choosing an item from a menu:** To get to Mac OS menu commands, you must first open a menu and then pick the option you want. Point at the name of the menu you want with your cursor, press the mouse button down, and then drag downward until you select the command you want. When the command is highlighted, finish selecting by letting go of the mouse button.

If you're a longtime Mac user, you probably hold down the mouse button the whole time between clicking the name of the menu and selecting the command you want. You can still do it that way, but you can also click the menu name to open it, release the mouse button, drag down to the item you want to select, *and then click again.* In other words, OS X menus stay open after you click them, even if you're not holding down the mouse button. After you click a menu to open it, you can even type the first letter (or letters) of the item to select it and then execute that item by pressing the spacebar or the Return or Enter key.

A menu remains open until you click something else.

Go ahead and give it a try . . . I'll wait.

The terms listed above apply to all Mac laptop, desktop, and tower systems. If you use a MacBook, MacBook Pro, or Apple Magic Trackpad, however, there are a few more terms — such as *tap, swipe, rotate, pinch,* and *spread* — you'll want to add to your lexicon. You can read all about them in full and loving detail in Chapter 3.

Not Just a Beatles Movie: Help and the Help Menu

One of the best features about all Macs is the excellent built-in help, and Mac OS X Lion doesn't cheat you on that legacy: This system has online help in abundance. When you have a question about how to do something, the Help Center is the first place you should visit (after this book, of course).

Clicking the Help menu reveals the Search Help field at the top of the menu and the Mac Help item, which opens the Mac Help window, as shown in Figure 1-5.

Figure 1-5: Mac Help is nothing if not helpful.

The keyboard shortcut for Help appears on the Help menu as ⌘+?, but you really need to press ⇧+⌘+? to open Help through the keyboard.

Just so you know, this is the only shortcut I can think of in which the menu doesn't display an up arrow (⇧+⌘+?) to let you know that you need to press Shift.

You can find out much more about keyboard shortcuts in Chapter 3.

To use Mac Help, simply type a word or phrase in either Search field — the one in the Help menu itself or the one near the top of the Help window on the right side — and then press Return or Enter. In a few seconds, your Mac provides you one or more articles to read, which (theoretically) are related to your question. Usually. If you type **menus** and press Return, for example, you get 17 help topics, as shown in Figure 1-6.

As long as your Mac is connected to the Internet, search results include articles from Apple's online support database by default. Click the magnifying-glass icon to the left of the Search field, as shown in Figure 1-6, if you want to disable this feature.

I can't think of any reason why you'd want to disable this useful feature, but I want you to know that you can if you like.

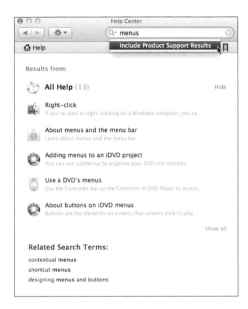

Figure 1-6: You have questions? Mac has answers.

Although you don't have to be connected to the Internet to use Mac Help, you do need an Internet connection to get the most out of it. (Chapter 10 can help you set up an Internet connection, if you don't have one.) That's because OS X installs only certain help articles on your hard drive. If you ask a question that those articles don't answer, Mac Help connects to Apple's web site and downloads the answer (assuming that you have an active Internet connection). These answers are the Support Articles, denoted by a plus sign (as shown at the bottom of the window in Figure 1-6, earlier in this chapter). Click one of these entries, and Help Viewer retrieves the text over the Internet. Although this can sometimes be inconvenient, it's also quite smart. This way, Apple can update the Help system at any time without requiring any action from you.

Furthermore, after you've asked a question and Mac Help has grabbed the answer from the Apple web site, the answer remains on your hard drive forever. If you ask for it again — even at a later date — your computer won't have to download it from the Apple web site again.

Finally, here's a cool feature I like to call *automatic visual help cues.* Here's how they work:

1. **Type a word or phrase in the Help menu's Search field.**

2. **Select any item that has a menu icon to its left (such as the Secure Empty Trash item in Figure 1-7).**

   The automatic visual cue — an arrow — appears, pointing at that command in the appropriate menu.

Figure 1-7: If you choose an item with a menu icon, an arrow points to that item in context.

Safari | Stickies | System Preferences | TextEdit | Time Machine | Ut | Stickies | System Preferences | TextEdit | Time Machine | Utilities

2

The Desktop and Windows and Menus (Oh, My)!

In This Chapter

▶ Checking out the parts of a window

▶ Dealing with dealie-boppers in windows

▶ Resizing, moving, and closing windows

▶ Getting comfortable with menu basics

This chapter introduces important features of Mac OS X, starting with the first thing you see when you log in: the Finder and its Desktop. After a quick look around the Desktop, you get a look into two of its most useful features: windows and menus.

Windows are (and have always been) an integral part of Macintosh computing. Windows in the Finder (or, as a PC user would say, "on the Desktop") show you the contents of the hard drive, optical drive, flash (thumb) drive, network drive, disk image, and folder icons; windows in applications do many things. The point is that windows are part of what makes your Mac a Mac; knowing how they work — and how to use them — is essential.

Menus are another quintessential part of the Macintosh experience. The latter part of this chapter starts you out with a few menu basics. As needed, I direct you to other parts of the book for greater detail. So relax and don't worry. By the end of this chapter, you'll be ready to work with windows and menus in any application that uses them (and most applications, games excluded, do).

Touring the Finder and Its Desktop

The Finder is the program that creates the Desktop, keeps track of your files and folders, and is always running. Just about everything you do on your Mac begins and ends with the Finder. It's where you manage files, store documents, launch programs, and much more. If you ever expect to master your Mac, the first step is to master the Finder and its Desktop. Check out the default Mac Finder and Desktop for Mac OS X Lion in Figure 2-1.

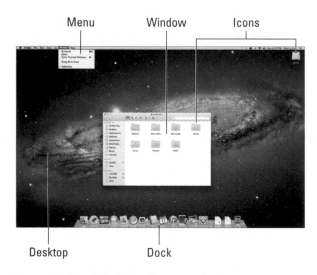

Figure 2-1: The default Lion Finder and Desktop.

The Finder is the center of your Mac OS experience, so before I go any further, here's a quick description of its most prominent features:

✔ **Desktop:** The Desktop is the area behind the windows and the Dock, where your hard-drive icon (ordinarily) lives. The Desktop isn't a window, yet it acts like one. Like a folder window or drive window, the Desktop can contain icons. But unlike most windows, which require a bit of navigation to get to, the Desktop is a great place for things you use a lot, such as folders, applications, or particular documents.

Some folks use the terms *Desktop* and *Finder* interchangeably to refer to the total Macintosh environment you see after you log in — the icons, windows, menus, and all that other cool stuff. Just to make things confusing, the background you see on your screen — the picture behind your hard-drive icon and your open windows — is *also* called the Desktop. In this book, I refer to the application you use when the

Desktop is showing as the *Finder.* When I say *Desktop,* I'm talking about the picture background behind your windows and the Dock, which you can use as a storage place for icons if you want.

To make things even more confusing, the Desktop is a full-screen representation of the icons in the Desktop folder inside your Home folder. Don't panic — this is all explained in more detail in Chapter 6.

✔ **Dock:** The Dock is the Finder's main navigation shortcut tool. It makes getting to frequently used icons easy, even when you have a screen full of windows. Like the Desktop, the Dock is a great place for things you use a lot, such as folders, applications, or particular documents. Besides putting your frequently used icons at your fingertips, it's almost infinitely customizable; read more about it in Chapter 4.

✔ **Icons:** Icons are the little pictures you see in your windows and even on your Desktop. Most icons are containers for things you work with on your Mac, such as programs and documents, which are also represented by — you guessed it — icons.

✔ **Windows:** Opening most icons (by double-clicking them) makes a window appear. Windows in the Finder show you the contents of hard-drive and folder icons, and windows in applications usually show you the contents of your documents. In the sections that follow, you can find the full scoop on Lion windows, which may be different from Mac windows in previous OS releases.

✔ **Menus:** Menus let you choose to do things, such as create new folders; duplicate files; cut, copy, or paste text; and so on. I introduce menu basics later in this chapter; you find details about working with menus for specific tasks throughout this book.

Whereas this section offers a basic introduction to the Finder and Desktop, Chapter 5 explains in detail how to navigate and manage your files in the Finder. You find out how to use the Finder toolbar, navigate folders and subfolders, and switch among views, among other things. But before you start using the Finder, it helps to know the basics of working with windows and menus; if these Mac features are new to you, I suggest that you read all of this chapter and pay special attention to Chapter 5 later.

Anatomy of a Window

Windows are a ubiquitous part of using a Mac. When you open a folder, you see a window. When you write a letter, the document that you're working on appears in a window. When you browse the Internet, web pages appear in a window . . . and so on.

For the most part, windows are windows from program to program. You'll probably notice that some programs (Adobe Photoshop or Microsoft Word, for example) take liberties with windows by adding features (such as pop-up menus) or textual information (such as zoom percentage or file size) in the scroll-bar area of a document window.

Don't let it bug you; that extra fluff is just window dressing (pun intended). Maintaining the window metaphor, many information windows display different kinds of information in different *panes,* or discrete sections.

And so, without further ado, the following list gives you a look at the main features of a typical Finder window (as shown in Figure 2-2). I discuss these features in greater detail in later sections of this chapter.

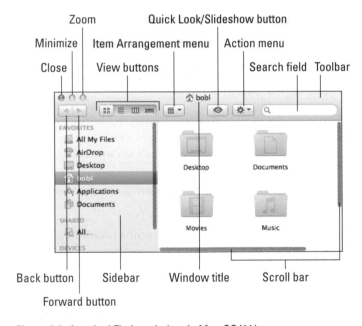

Figure 2-2: A typical Finder window in Mac OS X Lion.

If your windows don't look exactly like the one shown in Figure 2-2, don't be concerned. You can make your windows look and feel any way you like. As I explain later in this section, moving and resizing windows are easy tasks. Chapter 3 explains how to customize certain window features. Chapter 5 focuses on ways you can change a window's view specifically when you're using the Finder.

Meanwhile, here's what you see (clockwise from top left):

✔ **Close, Minimize, and Zoom (gumdrop) buttons:** Shut 'em, shrink and place 'em in the Dock, and make 'em grow.

✔ **View buttons:** Choose among four exciting views of your window: Icon, List, Column, and Cover Flow. Find out more about views in Chapter 5.

✔ **Item Arrangement menu:** Click this little doohickey to arrange this window's icons by Kind, Application, Date Modified, Date Created, Date Last Opened, Date Added, Size or Label.

✔ **Quick Look/Slideshow button:** Gives you a quick peek at the contents of the selected item. If more than one item is selected, it gives you a quick peek at one item and Next and Previous buttons so you can view the others slide-show style.

✔ **Action button:** This button is really a pop-up menu of commands you can apply to currently selected items in the Finder window.

✔ **Window title:** Shows the name of the window. ⌘+click the name of the window to see a pop-up menu with the complete path to this folder (try it).

✔ **Search field:** Type a string of characters here, and Mac OS X Lion digs into your system to find items that match by filename or document contents (yes, words within documents).

✔ **Toolbar:** Buttons for frequently used commands and actions.

✔ **Icon Resizer:** Use this slide control to change the size of the icons in this window. (Note that this control appears on windows only in the Icon view, which you find out all about in Chapter 5.)

✔ **Scroll bars:** Use the scroll bars for moving around a window.

✔ **Sidebar:** Frequently used items live here.

✔ **Forward and Back buttons:** These buttons take you to the next or previous folder displayed in this particular window.

If you're familiar with web browsers, the Forward and Back buttons in the Finder work exactly the same way. The first time you open a window, neither button is active. But as you navigate from folder to folder, these buttons remember your breadcrumb trail so you can quickly traverse backward or forward, window by window. You can even navigate this way from the keyboard by using the shortcuts ⌘+[for Back and ⌘+] for Forward.

The Forward and Back buttons remember only the other folders you've visited that appear in *that* open window. If you've set a Finder Preference so that a folder always opens in a new window — or if you forced a folder to open in a new window, which I describe in a bit — the Forward and Back buttons won't work. You have to use the modern, OS X–style window option, which uses a single window, or the buttons are useless.

Kudos to Apple for fixing something I ranted about in previous editions of this book. In Snow Leopard and earlier releases of Mac OS X, if you hid the toolbar, the Sidebar was also hidden, whether you liked it or not. Conversely, if you wanted to see the toolbar, you'd have to see the Sidebar as well. Lion gives you the flexibility to show or hide them independently in its View menu, as you'll soon see (in Chapter 5).

Top o' the window to ya!

Take a gander at the top of a window — any window. You see three buttons in the top-left corner and the name of the window in the top center. The three buttons (called *gumdrop buttons* by some folks because they look like, well, gumdrops) are officially known as Close, Minimize, and Zoom, and their colors (red, yellow, and green, respectively) pop off the screen. Here's what they do:

- **Close (red):** Click this button to close the window.

- **Minimize (yellow):** Click this button to minimize the window. Clicking Minimize appears to close the window, but instead of making it disappear, Minimize adds an icon for the window in the Dock. To view the window again, click the Dock icon for the window that you minimized. If the window happens to be a QuickTime movie, the movie continues to play, albeit at postage-stamp size, in its icon in the Dock. (I discuss the Dock in Chapter 4.)

- **Zoom (green):** Click this button to make the window larger or smaller, depending on its current size. If you're looking at a standard-size window, clicking Zoom *usually* makes it bigger. (I say *usually* because if the window is larger than its contents, clicking this button shrinks the window to the smallest size that can completely enclose the contents without scrolling.) Click the Zoom button again to return the window to its previous size.

A scroll new world

Yet another way to see more of what's in a window or pane is to scroll through it. Scroll bars appear at the bottom and right sides of any window or pane that contains more stuff — icons, text, pixels, or whatever — than you can see in the window. Figure 2-3, for example, shows two instances of the same window: Dragging the scroll bar on the right side of the front window reveals the items above DVD Player and FaceTime and below iDVD and Image Capture, which you see in the expanded window in the background. Dragging the scroll bar on the bottom of the window reveals items to the left and right, such as Dictionary, iChat, GarageBand, and iPhoto.

Simply click and drag a scroll bar to move it up or down or side to side.

Scroll areas

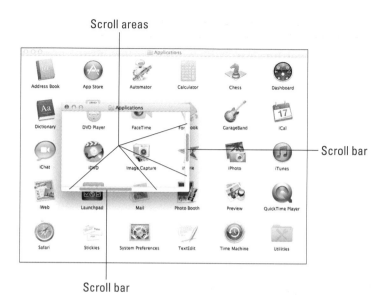

Scroll bar

Scroll bar

Figure 2-3: The same window twice; in the front window, you use the scroll bars to see the hidden icons that are visible in the back window.

If your scroll bars don't look exactly like the ones in Figure 2-3 or work as described below, don't worry. These are System Preferences you can configure to your heart's desire, but you'll have to wait until Chapter 3 to learn how.

Here are some ways you can scroll in a window:

- ✔ **Click a scroll bar and drag.** The content of the window scrolls proportionally to how far you drag the scroll bar.

- ✔ **Click in the scroll bar area but don't click the scroll bar itself.** The window scrolls either one page up (if you click above the scroll bar) or down (if you click below the scroll bar). You can change a setting in your General System Preferences pane to cause the window to scroll proportionally to where you click.

For what it's worth, the Page Up and Page Down keys on your keyboard function the same way as clicking the grayish scroll bar area (the vertical scroll bar only) in the Finder and many applications. But these keys don't work in every program; don't become too dependent on them. Also, if you've purchased a mouse, trackball, or other pointing device that has a scroll wheel, you can scroll vertically in the active (front) window with the scroll wheel or press and hold the Shift key to scroll horizontally. Alas, this horizontal scrolling-with-the-Shift-key works in Finder windows, but not in all applications. For example, it works in Apple's TextEdit application, but not in Microsoft Word.

✔ **Use the keyboard.** In the Finder, first click an icon in the window and then use the arrow keys to move up, down, left, or right. Using an arrow key selects the next icon in the direction it indicates — and automatically scrolls the window, if necessary. In other programs, you might or might not be able to use the keyboard to scroll. The best advice I can give you is to try it — either it'll work or it won't.

✔ **Two-finger swipe (on a trackpad):** If you have a notebook with a trackpad or use a Magic Trackpad, just swipe the pad with two fingers to scroll in a window.

(Hyper)Active windows

To work within a window, the window must be *active*. The active window is always the frontmost window, and inactive windows always appear behind the active window. Only one window can be active at a time. To make a window active, click it anywhere — in the middle, on the title bar, or on a scroll bar. It doesn't matter where you click, with one proviso: You can't click the red, yellow, or green gumdrop buttons or the clear Hide/Show button of an inactive window to activate it.

Look at Figure 2-4 for an example of an active window in front of an inactive window (the Applications window and the Utilities window, respectively).

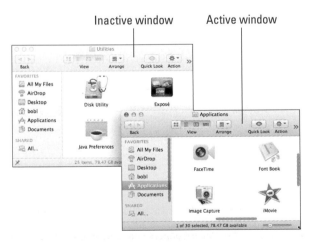

Figure 2-4: An active window in front of an inactive window.

The following is a list of the major visual cues that distinguish active from inactive windows:

✔ **The active window's title bar:** The Close, Minimize, and Zoom buttons are red, yellow, and green. The inactive windows' buttons are not.

This is a nice visual cue — colored items are active, and gray ones are inactive. Better still, if you move your mouse over an inactive window's gumdrop buttons, they light up in their usual colors so you can close, minimize, or zoom an inactive window without first making it active. Neat!

✔ **Other buttons and scroll bars in an active window:** They're bright. In an inactive window, these features are grayed out and more subdued.

✔ **Bigger and darker drop shadows in an active window:** They grab your attention more than those of inactive windows.

Dialog Dealie-Boppers

Dialogs are special windows that pop up over the active window. You generally see them when you select a menu item that ends in an ellipsis (...).

Dialogs can contain a number of standard Macintosh features (I call them *dealie-boppers*), such as radio buttons, pop-up menus, tabs, text-entry fields, and check boxes. You see these features again and again in dialogs. Take a moment to look at each of these dealie-boppers in Figure 2-5.

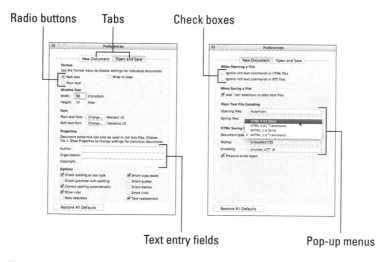

Figure 2-5: This window offers most dealie-boppers you're ever likely to encounter.

✔ **Radio buttons:** *Radio buttons* are so named because, like the buttons on your car radio (if you have a very old car), only one at a time can be active. (When they're active, they appear to be pushed in, just like the old radio buttons.) Radio buttons always appear in a group of two or more; when you select one, all the others are automatically deselected.

Here's a nifty and undocumented shortcut: You can usually select check boxes and radio buttons by clicking their names (instead of the buttons or boxes).

✓ **Tabs:** When a dialog contains more information than can fit in a single window, the info is divided among tabs. In Figure 2-5, the New Document tab is selected on the left, and the Open and Save tab is selected on the right.

✓ **Pop-up menus:** These menus are appropriately named because that's what they do: They pop up when you click them. In Figure 2-5, the Document Type menu has been clicked and is popped up; the five other pop-up menus — Opening Files, Saving Files (mostly obscured by the popped-up Document Type menu), Styling, and Encoding — are unclicked and unpopped.

You can always recognize a pop-up menu because it appears in a slightly rounded rectangle and has a double-ended arrow symbol (or a pair of triangles, if you like) on the right.

Have you figured out yet what radio buttons, tabs, and pop-up menus have in common? *Hint:* All three enable you to make a single selection from a group of options. (Well, okay, that was more of an answer than a hint.)

✓ **Text-entry fields:** In text-entry fields, you type text (including numbers) from the keyboard. In Figure 2-5, the Width, Height, Author, Organization, and Copyright options are text-entry fields.

✓ **Check boxes:** The last dealie-bopper that you see frequently is the check box. In a group of check boxes, you can select as many options as you like. Check boxes are selected when they contain a check mark, and they're deselected when they're empty, as shown in Figure 2-5.

Some applications have *tri-state* check boxes (and no, I'm not talking geography here). These special check boxes are empty when nothing in the group is selected, sport an *x* when everything in the group is selected, and sport a minus sign (–) when *some* items in the group are selected and some are not. This type of check box is often used for the Custom Install screen of Mac OS X installers.

Working with Windows

In the following sections, I give you a closer look at windows themselves: how you move them, size them, and use them. And although Mac OS X windows are similar to windows you've used in other versions of Mac OS, they have some new wrinkles.

If you're relatively new to the Mac, you might want to read this section while sitting at your computer, trying the techniques as you read them. You might find it easier to remember something you read if you actually do it. If you've been using your Mac for a while, you've probably figured out how windows work by now.

Opening and closing windows

To start peering into windows on your Mac, first you need to know how to open and close them. When you're working in the Finder, you can choose the following commands from the File menu. Note that you'll probably find similar commands on the File menu of programs other than the Finder.

You'll use many of these commands frequently, so it would behoove you to memorize the keyboard shortcuts. If you're not sure how keyboard shortcuts work, check out "Using keyboard shortcut commands," later in this chapter.

- **New Finder Window (⌘+N):** Opens a new Finder window. In other programs, ⌘+N might open a new document, project, or whatever that program helps you create.

- **Open (⌘+O):** Opens the selected item, be it an icon, a window, or a folder.

- **Close Window (⌘+W):** Closes the active window. If no windows are open or if no window is selected, the Close Window command is grayed out and can't be chosen. Or if you prefer, you can close a window by clicking the red Close button in the top-left corner.

If you hold down the Option key with the File menu open, the Close Window command changes to Close All. This very useful command enables you to close all open Finder windows. But it shows up only when you press the Option key; otherwise, it remains hidden.

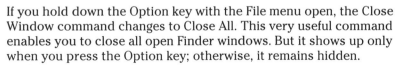

Note that several other commands in the File menu transmogrify when you press the Option key. It would be off topic to get into them here, but here's a tip: Press the Option key, and browse all the Finder menus. At least a dozen useful commands appear only if the Option key is pressed. Press it early and often for hidden (often time-saving) commands.

Resizing windows and window panes

If you want to see more (or less) of what's in a window, just hover the pointer over any edge or corner and drag. When the cursor turns into a little double-headed arrow, as shown in Figure 2-6, click and drag to resize the window.

Display windows, like those in the Finder, frequently consist of multiple panes. If you look at Figure 2-6, the line divides the blue Sidebar to the left of it and the actual contents of the window to the right. When your mouse pointer hovers over the resizing area of this bar, the cursor changes to a vertical bar (or it could be horizontal if the panes are one above the other) with little arrows pointing out of both sides, as shown in the margin and Figure 2-6.

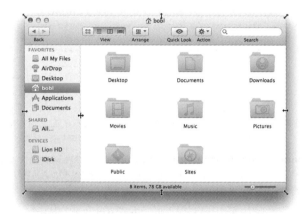

Figure 2-6: Hover over any corner or edge; when the arrow cursor appears, click and drag to resize the window.

When you see this cursor, you can click and drag anywhere in the dividing line that separates the Sidebar from the rest of the window. Doing so resizes the two panes relative to each other; one gets larger and one gets smaller.

Moving windows

To move a window, click anywhere in a window's title bar (or anywhere in the gray part of a display window, except on a button, menu, search field, or scroll bar) and drag the window to wherever you want it. The window moves wherever you move the mouse, stopping dead in its tracks when you release the mouse button.

Shuffling windows

I've already spent plenty of pages giving you the scoop on how to work with windows. But wait; there's more . . . the commands on the Window menu provide tools you can use to manage your windows. (Refer to Figure 2-1.) Here is a brief look at each of the items on the Window menu (and if you're unfamiliar with menus and keyboard shortcuts, I explain how they work later in this chapter):

✔ **Minimize (⌘+M):** Use this command to minimize the active Finder window to the Dock and unclutter your Desktop. It's the same as clicking the yellow gumdrop button.

✔ **Zoom:** This command does the same thing as the green gumdrop button. If you've forgotten what the green gumdrop does already, just turn back a few pages to the "Anatomy of a Window" section and read it again.

✔ **Cycle Through Windows (⌘+'):** Each time you choose this command or use the keyboard shortcut for it, a different window becomes active. So if you have three windows — call 'em Window 1, Window 2, and Window 3 — and you're using Window 1, this command deactivates Window 1 and activates Window 2. If you choose it again, the command deactivates Window 2 and activates Window 3. Choose it one more time, and it deactivates Window 3 and reactivates Window 1.

This command actually has been available in several earlier versions of Mac OS X, but only as a keyboard shortcut. Mac OS X 10.5 Leopard marked the first time it appeared in a Finder menu.

✔ **Bring All to Front:** In Mac OS X Lion, windows from different applications interleave. For example, you can have (from front to back) a Finder window, a Microsoft Word window, an Adobe Photoshop window, another Microsoft Word window, and another Finder window. Choosing Bring All to Front while the Finder is the active application enables you to have both of the Finder windows in this example move in front of those belonging to Word and Photoshop.

If you want to bring all the windows belonging to the Finder (or any other program, for that matter) to the front at the same time, you can also click the appropriate Dock icon (the Finder, in this case).

If you hold down the Option key when you pull down the Window menu, Minimize Window changes to Minimize All, and the Zoom command changes to Zoom All.

✔ **Other items:** The remaining items on the Window menu are the names of all currently open Finder windows. Click a window's name to bring it to the front.

Menu Basics

Mac menus are often referred to as *pull-down menus*. To check out the Mac OS X menus, click the Finder button in the Dock to activate the Finder and then look at the top of your screen. From left to right, you see the Apple menu, the Finder menu, and six other menus. To use an OS X menu, click its name to make the menu appear and then pull (drag) down to select a menu item. Piece of cake!

Ever since Mac OS 8, menus stay down after you click their names until you either select an item or click outside the menu's boundaries.

The ever-changing menu bar

Before you start working with OS X menus, you really, really should know this about menus in general: *They can change unexpectedly.* Why? Well, the menus you see on the menu bar at the top of the screen always reflect the program that's active at the time. When you switch from the Finder to a particular program — or from one program to another — the menus change immediately to match whatever you switched to.

Figure 2-7 shows the menu bars for the Finder, TextEdit, and Preview applications.

Figure 2-7: Menu bars change to reflect the active application.

An easy way to tell which program is active is to look at the application menu — it's the leftmost menu with a name, just to the right of the menu. When you're in the Finder, of course, the application menu reads *Finder*. But if you switch to another program (by clicking its icon in the Dock or by clicking any window associated with the program) or launch a new program, that menu changes to the name of the active program.

When you have an application open, the commands on the menu change, too — but just a little bit. What makes this cool is that you have access to some standard application menu items whether you're running Mail or Safari. For example, most (but not all) applications have Cut, Copy, and Paste commands in their Edit menus, and Open, Save, and Print commands in their File menus. You can find much more about commands for applications in Part III, which explains how applications that come with Mac OS X Lion can help you get things you want to do done.

Contextual menus: They're sooo sensitive

Contextual menus are, as the name implies, context-sensitive; they list commands that apply only to the item that is currently selected. Contextual menus might be available in windows, on icons, and in most places on the Desktop.

To use them, you either hold down the Control key and click — which you can call a *Control+click* to sound cool to your Mac friends — or, if your mouse has two or more buttons, *right-click*.

Most Mac laptops let you click the trackpad using two fingers to simulate a *right-click* or *Control+click*. If this doesn't work for you, make sure the Secondary Click check box is enabled in the Two Fingers section of the Trackpad System Preference pane.

Actions appear in contextual menus only if they make sense for the item that you Control+click or right-click. (That's why people call 'em *contextual!* They stick to the immediate context.) Figure 2-8 shows the contextual menu that appears when you Control+click (or right-click) a document icon on the left and the contextual menu for the Desktop on the right.

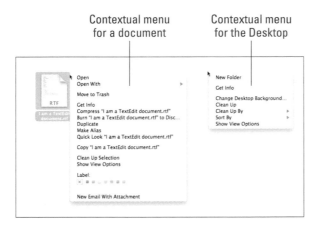

Figure 2-8: Only relevant items appear in a contextual menu.

Contextual menus are also available in most applications. Open your favorite app and try Control+clicking to find out whether those menus are there. In most cases, using a contextual menu is a quick way to avoid going to the menu bar to choose a command. In some programs — such as iMovie, iTunes, and many more — contextual menus are the *only* way to access some commands.

To make the Finder-related contextual menus available to users who didn't have the foresight to purchase this book, Apple added the Actions button to the toolbar. As a result, people who don't know about Control+clicking or right-clicking (or have only one free hand) can access most contextual menus by clicking the Actions button and displaying its contextual menu. You, on the other hand, gentle reader, know how to get at these commands without having to run your mouse all the way up to the Action button in the toolbar, plus a handful of commands appear in the Control+click/right-click contextual menu that don't appear in the Actions button/menu.

I'm a big fan of multibutton mice, and contextual menus are a huge reason for this preference. Fortunately, Apple now includes multibutton mice with all its desktop computers (except the Mac Mini, which doesn't include a mouse, keyboard, or monitor). If you have an older Mac with a single-button mouse, you might want to replace that mouse with one that offers you at least two buttons. With a multibutton mouse, you need only one hand to access these beautiful little contextual menus.

Get in the habit of Control+clicking (or right-clicking or two-finger clicking) items on your screen. Before you know it, using contextual menus will become second nature to you.

Recognizing disabled options

Menu items that appear in black on a menu are currently available. Menu items that aren't currently available are grayed out, meaning that they're disabled for the time being. You can't select a disabled menu item.

In Figure 2-9, the File menu on the left is pulled down while nothing is selected in the Finder; this is why many of the menu items are disabled (in gray). These items are disabled because an item (such as a window or icon) must be selected for you to use one of these menu items. For example, the Show Original command is grayed out because it works only if the selected item is an alias. On the right side of Figure 2-9, I selected a document before I pulled down the menu; notice that many of the formerly disabled commands are enabled when an icon is selected.

Figure 2-9: File menu with nothing selected (left) and with a document icon selected (right); the disabled items are grayed out.

Navigating submenus

Some menu items have more menus attached to them, and these are called *submenus* — menus that are subordinate to a menu item. If a menu has a black triangle to the right of its name, it has a submenu.

To use a submenu, click a menu name once (to drop the menu down) and then slide your cursor down to any item with a black triangle. When the item is highlighted, move your mouse to the right just slightly. The submenu should pop out of the original menu's item, as shown in Figure 2-10.

Figure 2-10: The Apple menu's Recent Items selection, with its submenu popped out.

Underneath the Apple menu tree

On the far left side of the menu bar sits a little , which, if you click it, actually displays a menu. No matter what application is active, the menu is always available in the top-left corner of your menu bar.

From top to bottom, the menu gives you a number of options, including the following:

- **About This Mac:** Choose this item to see what version of Mac OS X you're running, what kind of Mac and processor you're using, how much memory your Mac has, and the name of your Startup Disk. The window that appears also sports a Get Info button that will launch Apple System Information; there, you can find out more than you'll probably ever want or need to know about your Mac's hardware and software.

If you click the version number in this window, it changes to the *build number* (Apple's internal tracking number for versions). If you click the build number in this window, it changes to the serial number of your Mac. Finally, if you click the serial number of your Mac in this window, it changes to the version number again. This interesting effect is shown in Figure 2-11.

✔ **Software Update:** If you're connected to the Internet, choose this item to have your Mac check with the mothership (Apple) to see whether any updates are available for OS X or its included applications (or even for Apple-branded peripheral devices, such as the iPod or iPhone).

✔ **System Preferences:** Choose this item to open the System Preferences window (which I discuss further in Chapter 3 and elsewhere).

✔ **Dock (submenu):** This lets you mess with options for the Dock. Scour Chapter 4 for more info on the Dock.

✔ **Recent Items:** This lets you quickly access applications, documents, and servers you've used recently, as shown in Figure 2-10.

✔ **Force Quit:** Use this option only in emergencies. What's an emergency? Use it when an application becomes recalcitrant or otherwise misbehaves, or refuses to quit when you say Quit.

Memorize the keyboard shortcut for Force Quit (⌘+Option+power button). Sometimes a program gets so badly hosed that you can't click anywhere and other keyboard shortcuts won't do anything at all. It doesn't happen often; neither does it happen to everyone. If it should happen to you, calmly press the magic key combo you memorized (⌘+Option+power button), and the Force Quit Applications dialog (usually) appears. Click the name of the program that's acting up and then click the Force Quit button or press the Return or Enter key to make balky application stop balking.

The reason Force Quit should be used only in an emergency is that if you use it on an application that's working fine and have any unsaved documents, your work since the last time you saved the file will be blown away.

Figure 2-11: Click the Version, build, or serial number to cycle through these three informative items in this window.

Or not. Lion introduces Auto Save and Versions, which you'll hear more about in Chapter 6, so if the app you're using supports these new features, you shouldn't lose any (or at least not much) of your work regardless of when you last saved.

✏ **Shut Down options:** The commands here can tell your Mac to Force Quit when a program freezes or otherwise becomes recalcitrant: Sleep, Restart, Shut Down, or Log Out. See Chapter 1 for details about turning off your Mac.

Using keyboard shortcut commands

Most menu items, or at least the most common ones, have *keyboard shortcuts* to help you quickly navigate your Mac without having to haggle so much with the mouse. Using these key combinations activates menu items without using the mouse; to use them, you press the Command (⌘) key and then press another key (or keys) without releasing the ⌘ key. Memorize the shortcuts that you use often.

Some people refer to the Command key as the *Apple key*. That's because on many keyboards, that key has both the pretzel-like Command-key symbol (⌘) and an Apple logo () on it. To avoid confusion, I always refer to ⌘ as the Command key.

Here are five things to know that will give you a handle on keyboard shortcuts:

✏ **Keyboard shortcuts are shown in menus.** For example, Figure 2-9 shows that the keyboard shortcut for the Close Window command appears on the menu after the words Close Window: ⌘+W. Any menu item with one of these pretzel-symbol+letter combinations after its name can be executed with that keyboard shortcut. Just hold down the ⌘ key and press the letter shown in the menu — N for New Finder Window, F for Find, and so on — and the appropriate command executes.

✏ **Capital letters don't mean that you have to press Shift as part of the shortcut.** Although the letters next to the ⌘ symbol in the Finder menus are indeed capitals, they just identify the letter on the keyboard. For example, if you see ⌘+P, just hold down the ⌘ key and then press P. Some programs have keyboard combinations that require the use of ⌘ and the Shift key, but those programs tell you so by calling the key combination something like ⇧+⌘+S or ⇧+⌘+O. (Look at the Empty Trash shortcut in Figure 2-12 to see one of these up-facing arrows in its natural environment.)

A very few (usually older) programs indicate when you need to use the Shift key by using the word *Shift* rather than the ⇧ symbol.

✔ **Recognize the funky-looking Option-key symbol.** You'll see one other symbol sometimes used in keyboard shortcuts: It represents the Option key (sometimes abbreviated in keyboard shortcuts as *Opt* and, on some keyboards, also labeled *Alt*). Check it out next to the Hide Others command, shown in Figure 2-12.

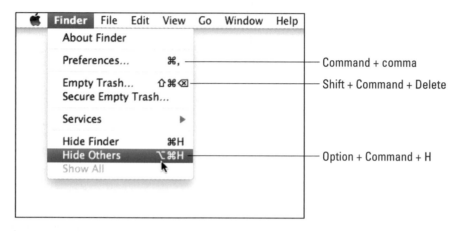

Figure 2-12: Some keyboard shortcuts, such as Hide Others, use the Option (⌥) key in combination with the Command (⌘) key.

What this freakish symbol means in the Finder menu item (Hide Others in Figure 2-12) is that if you hold down both the Option and ⌘ keys as you press the H key, all applications other than the Finder will be hidden.

✔ **Okay, there was more than one more symbol.** Occasionally, you'll see a caret (^) used as the symbol for the Control key.

✔ **If it makes sense, it's probably a shortcut.** Most keyboard shortcuts have a mnemonic relationship with their names. For example, here are some of the most basic keyboard shortcuts:

Command	*Mnemonic Keyboard Shortcut*
New Finder Window	⌘+N
New Folder	⇧+⌘+N
Open	⌘+O
Get Info	⌘+I
Select All	⌘+A
Copy	⌘+C
Duplicate	⌘+D

More menus 4 U

If you like the menus you've seen so far, have I got a treat for you: Mac OS X Lion includes 24 additional special-purpose menus, known as Menu Extras, that you can install if you like. Some — including Sound, Displays, Battery, and others — can be enabled from the appropriate System Preferences pane. But the easiest way is to open the Menu Extras folder (`System/Library/CoreServices/ Menu Extras`) and double-click each Menu Extra you want to install.

The following figure shows a handful of Menu Extras installed in the menu bar.

If you install a Menu Extra and later decide that you don't need or want it in your menu bar, hold down the ⌘ key and drag it off the menu bar; it disappears with a satisfying poof.

3

Have It Your Way

In This Chapter

▶ Making it just the way you like it with System Preferences

▶ Beautifying your Lion with a Desktop background and screen saver

▶ Working with those wonderful Dashboard widgets

▶ Customizing hardware and keyboard shortcuts

▶ Setting up for superb sound

*E*veryone works a bit differently, and everyone likes to use the Mac in a particular way. In this chapter, you find out how to tweak various options so everything is just the way you like it. The first things most people like to do are set their background and screen saver and populate the Dashboard with handy widgets. You can begin with that stuff, but keep in mind that you can do much more.

You can change the colors in windows, the standard font, and more if you like. Your Mac lets you choose how on-screen elements behave and how your hardware — such as the keyboard, mouse, and any wireless Bluetooth gadgets — interacts with your Mac.

Introducing System Preferences

You should start by becoming familiar with System Preferences, which appear on the Apple () menu and in the Dock.

The following steps explain how to move around the System Preferences window, no matter what you're trying to tweak:

1. **Open the System Preferences window, shown in Figure 3-1.**

   You can do this in at least three different ways:

   - Choose ➪ System Preferences.
   - Open the System Preferences icon in your Applications folder.
   - Click the System Preferences icon on your Dock.

Figure 3-1: The System Preferences window is where you change your on-screen world.

2. **Click any of the icons in the System Preferences window.**

   The bottom part of the window changes to reflect the options for whichever icon you click. When this happens, I call the bottom part of the window a *pane*. So, for example, when you click the General icon in the System Preferences window, the bottom part of the window becomes the General System Preference pane.

3. **When you finish working with a System Preference pane, click the Show All button to return to the window with icons for all available System Preference panes, or press ⌘+L.**

   Or, if you want to work with a different System Preference pane, you can choose it from the View menu, as shown in Figure 3-2. Also notice that you can navigate to the next or previous pane you've viewed with the Back and Forward buttons below the red and yellow gumdrops (shortcuts ⌘+[and ⌘+], respectively). Back and Forward commands also appear on the View menu.

   You can get rid of the categories altogether and display the icons in alphabetical order. As a bonus, it makes the System Preferences window roughly 25 percent smaller on-screen. To do so, choose View➪Organize Alphabetically. The categories disappear; the window shrinks; and the icons are alphabetized, as shown in Figure 3-2. To switch from alphabetical view back to category view, choose View➪Organize by Categories.

Figure 3-2: The View menu and the System Preferences window, organized alphabetically.

System Preferences is actually an application; you can find it in the Applications folder. The menu item and Dock icon are merely shortcuts that open the System Preferences application. The actual files for preferences panes are stored in the Preference Panes folder, inside the Library folder in the System folder. If you choose to install third-party preference panes, they should go either in the Preference Panes folder in the Library folder at the top level of your startup disk (if you want them to be available to all users) or in the Preference Panes folder in the Library inside your Home folder (if you want to keep them to yourself). Don't sweat this technical stuff too much; most System Preferences panes come with an installer that puts them in the proper folder for you.

One last general tip before we work with an actual System Preferences pane: If you press System Preferences' icon in the Dock, a menu that looks almost exactly like the View menu in Figure 3-2 pops up and lets you open a specific System Preferences pane without first seeing the System Preferences window. If you know which System Preferences pane you need, this shortcut is often the fastest way to get to it.

Putting a Picture on the Desktop

Figure 3-3 shows my Desktop with a beautiful black-and-white background picture of lightning striking a distant city. (If you want a reminder of what the default Desktop background looks like, refer to Figure 3-2.)

Here's how you can change your Desktop picture if you care to:

Figure 3-3: My beautified Desktop.

1. **From the Desktop, choose ⇨System Preferences.**

   Or Control+click the Desktop itself and choose Change Desktop Background from the contextual menu. Then you can skip to Step 3.

   The System Preferences window appears.

2. **Click the Desktop & Screen Saver icon.**

   The Desktop & Screen Saver Preferences pane appears, as shown in Figure 3-4.

Figure 3-4: Choosing a Desktop picture from the Plants folder.

3. **Click a folder in the column on the left and then click a picture in the area on the right.**

   In Figure 3-4, I'm clicking a picture called Petals, one of the items in the Plants folder.

You have at least three other ways to change your Desktop picture:

✔ Drag a picture file from the Finder onto the *image well* (the little rectangular picture to the left of the picture's name).

✔ Choose the Pictures Folder in the list of folders on the left side of the Desktop & Screen Saver System Preference pane and then choose a folder by using the standard Open File dialog. That folder then appears in the list; you can use any picture files it contains for your Desktop picture.

   If you don't know how to choose a folder that way, see Chapter 5.

✔ Click one of the iPhoto Albums items in the column on the left side of the Desktop & Screen Saver System Preferences pane.

One last thing before moving on: Although I love having a beautiful Desktop picture, from this point forward, I use a plain white Desktop (obtained by clicking Solid Colors in the list and then clicking the white color swatch). The plain Desktop makes it easier for you to see fine details in this book's figures.

Setting Up a Screen Saver

Mac OS X comes with several screen-saver modules. To set up your screen saver, follow these steps:

1. **Open System Preferences, click the Desktop & Screen Saver icon, and then click the Screen Saver tab to see the options shown in Figure 3-5.**

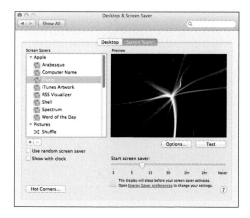

Figure 3-5: The Screen Saver tab of the Desktop and Screen Saver System Preferences pane.

2. **In the Screen Savers column on the left side of the pane, choose a screen saver option that interests you.**

   If you can't decide, you can choose the Use Random Screen Saver check box to have your Mac choose a new screen saver at random each time the screen saver kicks in.

3. **(Optional) To see what the chosen module looks like in action, click the Test button; then press any key or click anywhere to end the test.**

4. **After you've chosen a screen saver, drag the Start Screen Saver slider to the number of minutes you want the Mac to wait before activating the screen saver.**

   If you see the yellow Alert icon below the slider, as shown in Figure 3-5, click the words in blue (Energy Saver preferences), which causes the Energy Saver pane to replace the Desktop and Screen Saver pane. Drag the Computer Sleep slider to a value higher than the number of minutes you selected in step 4. Click the Back button when you're done to return to the Desktop and Screen Saver pane.

5. **Choose the Show with Clock check box to display a digital clock along with the screen saver.**

6. **(Optional) Click the Hot Corners button to choose which corner of your screen activates the screen saver and which disables it.**

   If you enable this option, when you move your cursor to the chosen corner of the screen, you activate or disable the screen saver until you move the cursor elsewhere.

   Note that hot corners are optional and are turned off by default.

7. **When you're done, close the Desktop & Screen Saver pane.**

You can require a password to wake your Mac from sleep or a screen saver. To do so, follow these steps:

1. **Open System Preferences, click the Security and Privacy icon, and then click the General tab at the top of the System Preferences pane.**

2. **Choose the Require Password after Sleep or Screen Saver Begins check box.**

3. **Choose a length of time from the drop-down menu between the words** *Password* **and** *After,* **which contains options such as immediately, 15 minutes, and 4 hours.**

   From now on, you must supply the user account password to wake up your computer. (User accounts and passwords are discussed in Chapter 16 and the Appendix.)

If you like screen savers and effects, you can find plenty more available at your favorite downloadable software repository. (My favorite is www.version

tracker.com.) Many are free, but some cost a few bucks. Some of those, such as Marine Aquarium in Figure 3-6 (from www.serenescreen.com), are even worth paying for.

Figure 3-6: This lifelike screen saver features fish you never need to feed.

Putting Widgets on the Dashboard

 Dashboard offers a way-cool set of *widgets,* Apple's name for the mini-applications that live inside the Dashboard layer. You see, Dashboard takes over your screen when you invoke it (as shown in Figure 3-7) by clicking Dashboard's Dock icon or pressing its keyboard shortcut: F4 on newer Mac keyboards or F12 (or fn+F12) on almost any Mac keyboard. In Figure 3-7, Dashboard is shown with just a few of its default widgets: Calculator, Weather, World Clock, and Calendar.

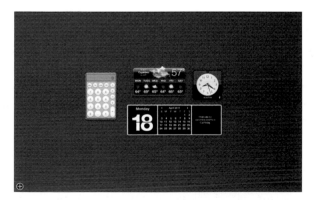

Figure 3-7: Dashboard lives in its own gray overlay layer, hiding all Finder and application windows.

Widgets are small, single-function applications that work only within Dashboard. Some widgets talk to applications on your hard drive, such as Address Book and iCal. Other widgets — such as Flight Tracker, Stocks, Movies, and Weather — gather information for you via the Internet.

The following tips can help you work with widgets:

✏ **Each time you invoke Dashboard,** widgets that were open the last time you used it will be on your screen.

✏ **To close an open widget,** click the encircled X in its top-left corner. If you don't see an X, press the Option key and move the cursor over the widget, and you will.

✏ **To configure most widgets:** Move your cursor over the bottom-right corner of a widget, and click the little *i*-in-a-circle that appears (as it does with the Clock widget in Figure 3-7). The widget then flips around so you can see its backside where the configuration options reside. So, for example, the Clock widget allows you to choose your region and city, and the Weather widget gives you choices that include your City, State, or Zip Code; Fahrenheit or Celsius; and whether to include lows in the six-day forecast (as shown in Figure 3-8). When you finish configuring a widget, click the Done button, which is usually (but not always) in the bottom-right corner; doing so flips the widget around again.

Not all widgets can be configured. For example, the iCal and Calculator widgets have no options to configure. If a little *i*-in-a-circle doesn't appear when you hover over the bottom-right corner of a widget with your cursor (or hovering while pressing the Option key), that widget has no options to configure.

✏ **To access widgets other than the four on your screen by default,** click the Open button (the large encircled plus sign shown earlier in the bottom-left corner of Figure 3-7) to open the Widget Bar, shown at the bottom of Figure 3-8.

When the Widget Bar is open, every widget on-screen displays an encircled X in its top-left corner; click it to close the widget.

Widget Bar sounds like a trendy watering hole downtown, but I assure you that's it's the official, Apple-sanctioned name for this feature. Really.

✏ **To open a widget window,** click the widget. In Figure 3-8, the Translation widget is open, all set to do my bidding. Or you can click and drag a widget from the Widget Bar to a preferred location on your screen. You can even have more than one instance of the same widget on-screen, such as multiple clocks for different time zones, or multiple weather widgets to show you the weather in multiple cities.

✏ **To see more widgets,** click the tiny arrows on the left and right sides of the Widget Bar (it says *1 of 2* in Figure 3-8, indicating that what you're seeing is the first of two screens of widgets.

Figure 3-8: The Widget Bar (at bottom), Translation widget (top middle), and the backside of the Weather widget (top right).

- ✍ **To move a widget around on your screen,** click almost anywhere on the widget and then drag it to the appropriate location.

- ✍ **To close the Widget Bar,** click the X-in-a-circle displayed on the left of the Manage Widgets button when the Widget Bar is open, as shown in Figure 3-8.

- ✍ **To manage your widgets,** click the Manage Widgets button above the Widget Bar on the left side. The Widget Manager appears in the middle of the screen. In Figure 3-9, for example, I've disabled the Ski Report and Tile Game widgets, which I never use.

  You can manage widgets only if the Widget Bar is open.

  At the bottom of the Widget Manager window is a button titled More Widgets. Clicking it launches your web browser and shows you additional widgets you can download from the Apple website.

- ✍ **To uninstall a third-party widget that you no longer want,** merely open the Widget Manager and click the red minus sign next to its name. Your Mac politely asks whether you want to move this widget to the trash. You do.

Figure 3-9: Widgets with check marks appear in the Widget Bar; widgets without check marks don't.

Finally, to close your Dashboard, either press the same key you pressed to open Dashboard (F4 on newer Mac keyboards, or F12 or fn+F12 on almost any Mac keyboard) or click any item in your Dock.

Because the Dock is hidden when your Dashboard is open, move the cursor to the bottom or the side of the screen (wherever your Dock usually appears), and it magically fades into view.

If you have a trackpad, you can also swipe from left to right with three fingers to switch to your Dashboard.

Think of your Dashboard widgets as being handy-yet-potent miniprograms available at any time with a keystroke or click. Widgets are just so danged cool that I want to give you a quick look at a couple I consider particularly useful. Read on for details.

Translation

The Translation widget could be a lifesaver. You've been able to do this trick on the web for a while, but now you can do it right on your desktop. This widget translates words from one language to another. It offers more than a dozen language choices — including French, German, Spanish, Russian, Dutch, Chinese, and more — and can translate in either direction.

I love the Translation widget so much that sometimes it hurts.

It's fun at parties, too. Try this: Type a paragraph or two of your purplest prose into Translation. Now translate back and forth to any language a few times. Howl when prose written as "It was a dark and stormy night when our heroine met her untimely demise" turns into something like "It was one night dark and stormy where our heroin met an ugly transfer." It doesn't get much better than this, folks. I used to leave my MacBook Pro at home if I wasn't absolutely going to need it. But the Translation widget is so wicked cool and useful that lately I've been taking my MacBook Pro almost everywhere I go, whether I need it or not.

Flight Tracker

Flight Tracker, shown in Figure 3-10, can find flights on most airlines and report the flight's status in real time — a terrific timesaver when you have to meet a flight.

When you have to meet someone's flight, this widget can be a lifesaver. Just open Dashboard every few minutes, and you know exactly what the flight's status is at that moment.

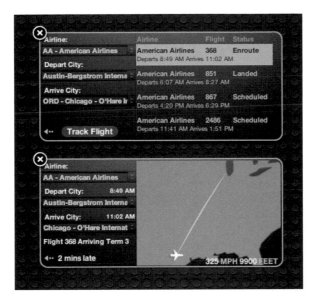

Figure 3-10: Finding a flight (top) and viewing its status (bottom) after clicking the Track Flight button.

This is a really good tip for harried air travelers: You can open more than one instance of a widget. So if you're trying to track *two* flights or want to know the weather in more than one city, just click the appropriate widget in the Widget Bar, and another instance of it appears.

Giving Buttons, Menus, and Windows a Makeover

Computers don't care about appearances, but if you want your Mac to look a bit more festive (or, for that matter, businesslike), you have options in the General pane (see Figure 3-11) at your disposal. To open this pane, choose ⌘⇨System Preferences and then click the General icon.

First up are the general appearance options:

✓ **Appearance pop-up menu:** Use this menu to choose different appearances and change the overall look of buttons, such as the three gumdrop buttons in the top-left corner of most windows, as well as the gumdrop buttons that appear in scroll bars.

Apple, however, in its infinite wisdom, provides only two choices: Blue and Graphite.

✔ **Highlight Color pop-up menu:** From here, you can choose the color that text is surrounded by when you choose it in a document or select an icon. This time, Apple isn't so restrictive: You have eight highlight colors you can choose, plus Other, which brings up a color picker from which you can choose almost any color.

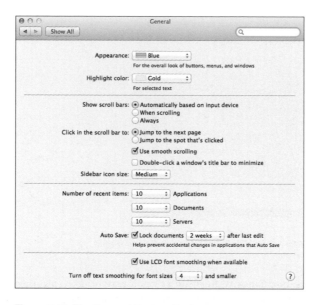

Figure 3-11: The General System Preferences pane.

The next area in the General System Preferences pane enables you to set the behavior of scroll bars and title bars:

✔ The Show Scroll Bars radio buttons let you choose when you wish to see scroll bars on windows. Your choices are Automatically Based on Input Device, When Scrolling, or Always.

✔ The Click in the Scroll Bar To radio buttons give you the option of moving your view of a window up or down by a page (the default) or to the position in the document roughly proportionate to where you clicked in the scroll bar.

An easy way to try these options is to open a Finder window and place it side by side with the General System Preferences pane, as shown in Figure 3-12, reducing the size of the window if necessary to make scroll bars appear. Select an option, observe the behavior of the scroll bars, and then select a different option and observe again.

Choose the Jump to the Spot That's Clicked radio button if you often work with long (multipage) documents. It's quite handy for navigating long documents. And don't forget — the Page Down key does the same thing as choosing the Jump to the Next Page choice, so you lose nothing by choosing Jump to the Spot That's Clicked.

It would be even nicer if all third-party apps supported this feature, but some — including Microsoft Office 2011 — don't behave properly no matter what you choose for this setting.

Figure 3-12: Here's how I try different scroll-bar settings.

> ✔ Selecting the Use Smooth Scrolling check box makes documents more legible while you scroll. Give it a try; if you think it's making your Mac feel sluggish when you scroll, feel free to turn it off.

> ✔ The Double-click a Window's Title Bar to Minimize check box does just what it says when chosen — it shrinks a window to the Dock when you double-click its title bar. For what it's worth, the yellow gumdrop button does exactly the same thing.

The next area in the General pane controls the Number of Recent Items that are remembered and displayed in your ⌘⇨Recent Items submenu. The default is 10, but I like having access to more than 10 applications and documents in my Recent Items submenu, so I crank mine up to 30 and 20, respectively, as you can see in Figure 3-12.

Here's what each pop-up menu means:

> ✔ **Applications:** When you choose to display any number of applications, you can open any application you've used recently from your Recent Items submenu.

> ✔ **Documents:** This setting tells Lion to show specific documents you've opened recently in Recent Items.

> ✔ **Servers:** Determines the number of recently accessed remote computers Lion displays in the Recent Items submenu.

The last item in this section is Restore Windows When Quitting and Re-Opening Apps will do just what it says: Any document windows open when you quit will magically reopen themselves the next time you launch the app.

The final area offers a few options for how your fonts look. The Use LCD Font Smoothing When Available check box makes text look better on most displays. Unless your monitor is a very old tube-type (CRT) display, you probably want to select this box.

The Turn Off Text Smoothing for Font Sizes x and Smaller pop-up menu (where *x* is the pop-up menu setting) does just what it says. Fonts that size and smaller are no longer *antialiased* (smoothed) when displayed.

If you find that type in small font sizes is hard for you to read, try increasing or decreasing this setting.

Adjusting the Keyboard, Mouse, Trackpad, and Other Hardware

No one uses the keyboard and mouse in the same way. Some folks don't use a mouse at all. (You might not even use the keyboard much if you use voice-recognition software or other devices, as I explain in Chapter 16.) If you're using Mac OS X on a notebook, you might have a *trackpad,* that little surface where you move your finger around to control the cursor. Or perhaps you have a Bluetooth-enabled keyboard and mouse so you can hook them up to your Mac wirelessly.

Regardless of what you have, you should give some thought to customizing the way it works so it feels "just right" for you.

The Keyboard, Mouse, and Trackpad System Preferences panes offer several tabs to do just that: let you modify the behavior of your keyboard, mouse, and trackpad in a myriad of ways. So the first thing to do is open the Keyboard preferences pane by choosing ⌘⇨System Preferences and clicking the Keyboard icon.

Keyboard

The Keyboard System Preferences pane has two tabs: Keyboard and Keyboard Shortcuts.

Keyboard tab

On the Keyboard tab, you can adjust your settings in the following ways:

↙ Drag the Key Repeat Rate slider to set how fast a key repeats when you hold it down. This feature comes into play when (for example) you hold down the hyphen (-) key to make a line or the asterisk (*) key to make a divider.

↙ Drag the Delay Until Repeat slider to set how long you have to hold down a key before it starts repeating.

You can type in the box that says Type Here to Test Settings to test your settings before exiting this tab.

If you have a notebook Mac (such as a MacBook, MacBook Pro, or MacBook Air), you also see one or more of these additional features:

↙ **All F1, F2 Keys As Standard Function Keys:** If this check box is selected, the F keys at the top of your keyboard control the active software application.

To use the special hardware features printed on each F key (display brightness, screen mirroring, sound volume, mute, and so on), you have to press the Fn (Function) key before pressing the F key. If the check box is left deselected, you have to press the Fn key if you want to use the F keys with a software application. Got it? Good.

↙ **Illuminate Keyboard in Low Light Conditions:** This check box turns your laptop's ambient keyboard lighting on and off.

↙ **Turn Off When Computer Is Not Used For:** This slide control lets you determine how long the ambient keyboard lighting remains on when your computer isn't in use.

Of course, if your notebook computer doesn't *have* ambient keyboard lighting, as many don't, you don't see the last two items.

Ambient keyboard lighting is a cool feature, but remember that it reduces battery life. My recommendation is to use it only when you really need it.

↙ **Show Keyboard & Character Viewers in the Menu Bar:** This check box adds a new menu for opening either of these useful windows, as shown in Figure 3-13.

Click Emoji in list on the left of the Character Viewer window, as shown in Figure 3-14, to insert whimsical smiley faces and hundreds of other cute images into your documents.

↙ **Input Sources button:** Switches to the Language & Text System Preferences pane's Input Sources tab, where you can to display one or more foreign language keyboards in the Input menu.

Character and Keyboard Viewer menu

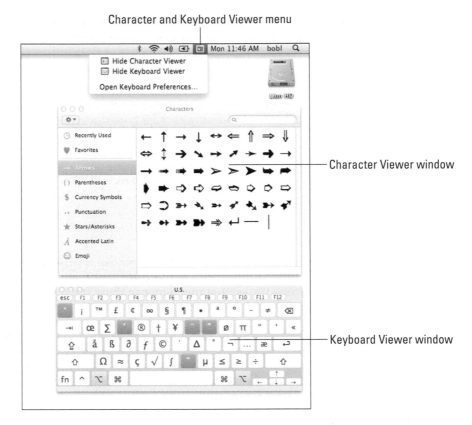

Character Viewer window

Keyboard Viewer window

Figure 3-13: The Keyboard and Character Viewer menu, Character Viewer window, and Keyboard Viewer window in all their glory.

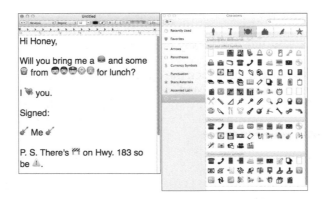

Figure 3-14: To use Emoji in a document, click the character you want, and it instantly appears in the document.

The Input menu and the Keyboard and Character Viewer menu are one and the same. If you select one or more foreign keyboards, it changes from the rather tame icon shown in Figure 3-13 to the flag of the selected keyboard, as shown in the margin (it's the Lithuanian flag, by the way).

✓ **Modifier Keys button:** Lets you change the action performed by the Caps Lock, Control, Option, and Command keys. It's particularly useful if you use a non-Apple keyboard, although it works just fine on Apple keyboards too.

I'm always engaging the Caps Lock key accidentally with my overactive left pinky, so I set *my* Caps Lock key to perform No Action. Now I never type half a sentence in ALL CAPS BECAUSE I ACCIDENTALLY PRESSED THE CAPS LOCK KEY.

Keyboard Shortcuts tab

If you really hate to use your mouse or if your mouse is broken, keyboard shortcuts can be really handy. I tend to use them more on my laptop because I really don't like using the built-in touch-mouse thing (technically, it's a *track-pad,* and I talk more about it in the next section).

I introduce the most commonly used keyboard shortcuts in Chapter 2. You probably don't want to mess with those, but you can assign other commands you use often to just about any key combination you like. By creating your own keyboard shortcuts, you can have whatever commands you need — literally at your fingertips.

Not only can you add, delete, or change keyboard shortcuts for many operating-system functions (such as taking a picture of the screen and using the keyboard to choose menu and Dock items), but you can also add, delete, or change keyboard shortcuts for your applications.

To begin, choose the Keyboard Shortcuts tab in the Keyboard System Preferences pane. Now you can do any or all of the following:

✓ **To change a shortcut,** first click the appropriate application, preference, or feature in the left column. Next, double-click the shortcut you want to change on the right side of the right column (for example, F3 or ⌘+G). The old shortcut becomes highlighted; when it does, press the new shortcut keys you wish to use.

✓ **To add a new shortcut,** click the + button. Choose the appropriate application from the Application pop-up menu, type the exact name of the menu command you want to add in the Menu Title field, and then press the shortcut you want to assign to that command into the Keyboard Shortcut field. If the shortcut you press is in use by another application or preference, a yellow triangular caution symbol appears next to it. It really is that simple.

✓ **To delete a shortcut,** choose it and then click the — button.

The Keyboard Shortcuts tab also offers options for changing the Tab order. The Full Keyboard Access radio buttons control what happens when you press the Tab key in a window or dialog:

- ✔ If you choose the Text Boxes and Lists Only radio button, the Tab key moves the cursor from one text box to the next or from one list item to the next item (usually alphabetically).

- ✔ If you choose the All Controls radio button, you can avoid using the mouse for the most part, if that's your preference.

 When All Controls is selected, the Tab key moves the focus from one item to the next in a window or dialog. So (for example) every time you press the Tab key in an Open File dialog, the focus moves — say, from the Sidebar to the file list to the Cancel button to the icon view button, and so on. Each item is highlighted to show it's selected, and you can activate the highlighted item from the keyboard by pressing the spacebar.

 You can toggle this setting by pressing Control+F7. And if you don't care for Control+F7 as its shortcut, you can change it by clicking Keyboard & Text Input in the left column, double-clicking the Change the Way Tab Moves Focus item in the right column, and then pressing the new shortcut.

Mouse

The Mouse System Preferences pane is where you set your mouse speed and double-click delays.

If you use a notebook Mac, you may see a Mouse icon in the System Preferences application, but unless you have a mouse connected via USB or Bluetooth, it will just sit there searching for a mouse.

Don't be sad. If you use a notebook or an Apple Magic Trackpad, you have something that most iMac, Mac Mini, and Mac Pro users don't have — namely, the System Preferences pane named Trackpad, which I tell you about in a page or two.

The first item in this pane is a check box that's new in Lion: Move Content in the Direction of Finger Movement When Scrolling or Navigating. If scrolling or navigating in windows feels backward to you, try unchecking this box.

Moving right along, here are the features you'll find in the Mouse System Preferences pane (if you have a mouse connected):

- ✔ Move the Tracking Speed slider to change the relationship between hand movement of the mouse and cursor movement on-screen. This slider works just like the slider for trackpads, as I explain in the upcoming section on trackpads.

✔ The Double-Click Speed setting determines how close together two clicks must be for the Mac to interpret them as a double click and not as two separate clicks. Move the slider arrow to the leftmost setting, Very Slow, for the slowest. The rightmost position, Fast, is the fastest setting, which I prefer.

✔ If your mouse has a scroll ball or scroll wheel, you also see a Scrolling Speed slider, which lets you adjust how fast the contents of a window scroll when you use the scroll wheel or ball.

✔ If your mouse has more than one button, you see a pair of Primary Mouse Button radio buttons. These let you choose which button — left or right — you use to make your primary (regular) click. Conversely, the other mouse button (the one you didn't choose) becomes your secondary (Control or right) click.

This is a setting many lefties like to change. Set the primary button as the right button, and you can click with the index finger of your left hand.

Being right-handed, I've done the opposite in Figure 3-15 and set the left button as the primary and the right button as the secondary (Control or right) click.

Notice that I have the center button — the scroll ball, on this particular mouse — set to the Off position. Why? Because I find that I click that button accidentally far too often when I'm trying to scroll.

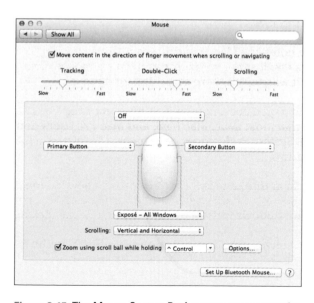

Figure 3-15: The Mouse System Preferences pane set up for a right-hander.

✔ Last but not least, the Zoom Using Scroll Wheel While Holding check box lets you zoom in and out by turning the scroll wheel or ball while holding down a particular key. The default is the Control key, so if you scroll while holding down the Control key, items on-screen get bigger or smaller. Click the arrow to the left of the Options button to open the menu and choose a different modifier key.

The Options button opens a sheet with options for how the screen image moves when you're zoomed in, as well as a check box for smoothing images. See Figure 3-16.

If your Mac is more than a couple of years old, smoothing images might slow it a bit. So if things feel a little sluggish when you zoom in, try clearing this check box.

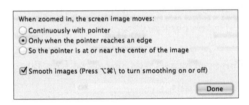

Figure 3-16: Options for zooming.

Changes in the Mouse System Preferences pane take place immediately, so you should definitely play around a little and see what settings feel best for you. You can test the effect of your changes to the Double-Click Speed setting in the Double-Click Here to Test text box just below the slider before you close this Preferences pane.

Bluetooth

Bluetooth is a technology that lets you make wireless connections between your Mac and devices such as Bluetooth mice and phones. You can see a Bluetooth tab in the Mouse System Preferences pane if you're using a Bluetooth mouse. Most Macs manufactured in the past few years have Bluetooth built in; some older models don't.

You configure Bluetooth devices you wish to use with your Mac elsewhere in the Bluetooth System Preferences pane (as described in Chapter 16).

If your Mac does, the Bluetooth tab shows you the battery level of your Bluetooth mouse or keyboard. It also offers a check box to add a Bluetooth status menu to your menu bar and a check box to let Bluetooth devices wake your computer from sleep.

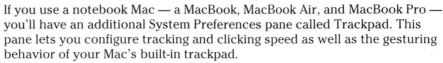

Trackpad (notebook Macs only)

If you use a notebook Mac — a MacBook, MacBook Air, and MacBook Pro — you'll have an additional System Preferences pane called Trackpad. This pane lets you configure tracking and clicking speed as well as the gesturing behavior of your Mac's built-in trackpad.

Note that in 2008, Apple began equipping all its notebooks with a new and improved Multi-Touch trackpad. These features distinguish the new model from its predecessor:

- It's 40 percent larger than the original MacBook Pro and MacBook trackpads.

- It's fabricated from some kind of high-tech glass. So it's even smoother and more touch-friendly than the original trackpads.

- The *whole trackpad* is the click button; you just tap anywhere on it to click.

- It supports multifinger gestures that use up to four fingers at once.

I'm not a huge trackpad fan, but I know many people who love trackpads. If you're among them, Apple's $69 Magic Trackpad can be used with any Mac or PC with Bluetooth. It's also the biggest glass Multi-Touch trackpad yet, nearly 80 percent larger than the MacBook Pro's built-in trackpad. Yes, you can use the Magic Trackpad with your MacBook Pro, and yes, that does mean you have dual trackpads.

If you have an older notebook with the older style of trackpad, you may not see all of the controls listed here:

- Move the **Tracking Speed slider** to change the relationship between finger movement on the trackpad and cursor movement on-screen. A faster tracking-speed setting (moving the slider to the right) sends your cursor flying across the screen with a mere flick of the finger; slower mouse-speed settings (moving the slider to the left) make the cursor crawl across in seemingly slow motion, even when your finger is flying. Set this setting as fast as you can stand it — I like the fastest speed. Try it: You might like it.

- The Double-Click Speed slider determines how close together two clicks must be for the Mac to interpret them as a double click and not as two separate clicks. Move the slider arrow to the leftmost setting (Slow) for the slowest. With this setting, you can double-click at a leisurely pace. The rightmost position (Fast) is the fastest setting, which I prefer. The middle area of the slider represents a double-click speed somewhere in the middle.

✔ The Scrolling Speed slider determines how quickly or slowly pages scroll when you drag two fingers up, down, left, or right on the trackpad.

✔ If you have a pre–Multi-Touch trackpad, you have the following check boxes available, as shown in Figure 3-17:

- Choose the Use Two Fingers to Scroll check box, and when you use two fingers right next to each other and drag up or down on the trackpad, you cause a window's contents to scroll up or down (rather than moving the cursor, as would happen if you did this with a single finger). The Allow Horizontal Scrolling check box just below it causes a window's contents to scroll left or right when you drag two fingers left or right on the trackpad.

- The Zoom While Holding check box lets you zoom in and out by holding down a specific key (the default is the Control key) and dragging two fingers on the trackpad. When you zoom in or out, items on-screen get bigger or smaller. Click the arrow to the left of the Options button to open the menu and choose a different modifier key.

- If you choose the Clicking check box, you can tap your finger on the trackpad once to make your Mac recognize that gesture as a click.

- Choose the Clicking and Dragging check boxes to tap and drag on the trackpad without having to click the trackpad button.

- Choose the Drag Lock check box to keep an item selected after dragging until you tap the trackpad again.

✔ The Trackpad Options check boxes let you tell your laptop to ignore the trackpad while you're typing or when a mouse is connected.

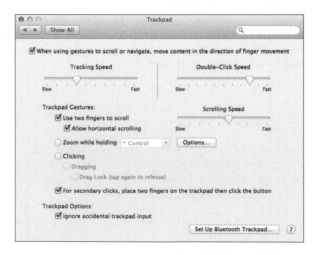

Figure 3-17: The Trackpad System Preferences pane for older trackpads has three sliders and a myriad of check boxes.

If you have one of the new Multi-Touch trackpads, your Trackpad System Preferences pane offers a slightly different set of options for one-, two-, three-, and four-finger gestures (as shown in Figure 3-18): slider controls (top), gesture controls (bottom left), and demonstration movies (bottom right).

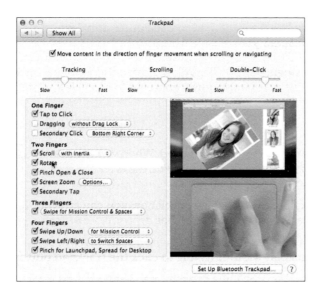

Figure 3-18: The Multi-Touch trackpad System Preferences pane offers controls for one-finger or multifinger gestures.

 To see how a gesture works, just move your cursor over it (you don't even have to click), and a movie demonstrates that gesture on the right side of the window. In Figure 3-18, I'm pointing to the Two Fingers Rotate item on the left; the gesture and what it does are demonstrated in the movie playing on the right. Pretty cool, don't you think?

Styling Your Sound

 Out of the box, Mac OS X Lion comes with a preset collection of beeps and controls. By using the Sound Preferences pane, however, you can change the way your Mac plays and records sound by changing settings on each of its three tabs: Sound Effects, Output, and Input.

Three items appear at the bottom of the Sound pane, no matter which of the three tabs is active:

✔ To make your Mac's volume louder or softer, use the Output Volume slider. You can also change or mute the volume with the designated volume and mute keys found on most Apple keyboards.

✔ Choose the Mute check box to turn off all sound.

✔ Click the Show Volume in Menu Bar check box to add a volume control menu to your menu bar.

A shortcut to the Sound System Preferences pane is to press Option while pressing any of the volume keys (usually the F4 and F5 keys on older laptops and keyboards or the F11 and F12 keys on newer laptops and keyboards).

Changing sound effects

On the Sound Effects tab, choose an alert (beep) sound by clicking its name; set its volume by using the Alert Volume slider control.

You can also specify the output device through which sound effects play (if you have more than one device) by choosing it from the Play Sound Effects Through pop-up menu.

The Play User Interface Sound Effects check box turns on sound effects for actions, such as dragging a file to the Trash.

The Play Feedback When Volume is Changed check box tells your Mac to beep once for each keypress to increase or decrease volume.

Choosing output options

If you have more than one sound-output device (in addition to the built-in speakers), you can choose it here. The Balance slider makes one stereo speaker — left or right — louder than the other.

Choosing input options

If you have more than one sound-input device (in addition to the built-in microphone on many Macs or an iSight camera, which contains its own mic), you can choose it here. The Input Volume slider controls the Input Level (how loud input from that device will be), which is displayed as a row of blue dots. If the dots light up all the way to the right side, your input volume is too loud. Ideally, the input level should light up with about three fourths of the little blue dots — and no more.

What's Up, Dock?

In This Chapter

▶ Getting to know the Dock

▶ Discovering the default Dock icons

▶ Talkin' Trash

▶ Dock icons and their menus

▶ Delving into Dock customization

T he Dock appears at the bottom of your screen by default, providing quick access to your most-often-used applications, documents, and folders.

Many users prefer to have the Dock on the left or right side of the screen instead of at the bottom. You see how to do it (and more) in the coming pages.

Folder icons in the Dock are called *stacks,* and they display a fan, grid, or list of their contents when clicked. Other icons in the Dock open an application or document with one click.

The Dock is your friend. It's a great place to put files, folders, and apps you use a lot so that they're always just a click away.

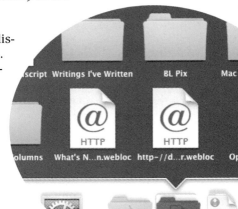

A Quick Introduction to Your Dock

Take a minute to look at the row of icons at the bottom of your display. That row, good friend, is the *Dock* (shown in Figure 4-1), and those individual pictures are known as *icons* (which I discuss in greater detail momentarily).

Figure 4-1: The Dock and all its default icons.

Dock icons are odd ducks; you activate one with a single click. Most other icons in the Finder are *selected* (highlighted) when you single-click and are *opened* only when you double-click them.

So Dock icons are kind of like links on a web page; you need only a single click to open them.

Here's the rundown on what happens when you click Dock icons:

- ✔ If it's **an application icon,** the application opens and becomes active. If the application is already open, it becomes active, which brings it and all its windows to the front.

- ✔ If it's **a document icon,** that document opens in its appropriate application, which becomes the active application. If that application is already open, it becomes the active application with this document in the front.

- ✔ If it's **a folder or disk icon,** a stack with its contents appears so you can pick an item. If you choose Show in Finder from this menu, the folder's window opens in the Finder.

If the item is open already when you click its Dock icon, it becomes active.

The default icons of the Dock

By default, the Dock contains a number of commonly used Mac OS X applications, and you can also store your own applications, files, or folders there. (I show you how to do that in the "Adding Dock icons" section, later in this chapter.)

But first, look at the items you find in a standard Mac OS X Lion Dock. If they aren't familiar to you, they certainly will be as you get to know your Lion.

I admit that I can't do justice to all the programs that come with Mac OS X Lion that aren't, strictly speaking, part of the operating system. Alas, some of the programs in the default Dock are ones you won't be seeing much more of. But I'd hate to leave you wondering what all those icons in the Dock are, so Table 4-1 gives you a brief description of each default Dock icon (moving from left to right on-screen). If additional coverage of an item appears elsewhere in the book, the table tells you where.

To get a quick look at the name of a Dock icon, just move *(hover)* your cursor over any item in the Dock. Like magic, that item's name appears above it (like *Safari* on the left side of Figure 4-5 later in this chapter). And as I describe in the section "Resizing the Dock" (also later in this chapter), you can resize the Dock to make the icons smaller (which also makes them more difficult to see). Hovering the cursor to discover the name of a teeny icon makes this feature even more useful.

Table 4-1		Icons in the Dock	
Icon	*Name*	*What It Is*	*Go Here for More Information*
	Finder	The always-running application that manages the Desktop, files, folders, disks, and more	This chapter, and Chapters 5 and 6
	Launchpad	See all your applications arranged on a grid that looks suspiciously like an iPad or iPhone	This chapter
	Mission Control	See all your windows, applications, and spaces	Chapter 7
	Mac App Store	Where you buy Mac apps from Apple	Chapter 17
	Dashboard	A layer containing small special-use applications called *widgets*	Chapter 3
	Mail	An e-mail program	Chapter 11
	Safari	A web browser	Chapter 10
	FaceTime	A video chat program	Chapter 10

(continued)

Table 4-1 *(continued)*

Icon	Name	What It Is	Go Here for More Information
	Address Book	A contact manager application	Chapter 11
	iCal	Apple's calendar program	Chapter 9
	Preview	Apple's PDF and graphic-viewing program	Chapter 13
	iTunes	An audio and video player and iPod manager (part of the iLife package)	Chapter 12
	Time Machine	Automated data-backup system	Chapter 18
	System Preferences	An application to config-ure the way many aspects of your Mac work	Chapters 3, 15, and 16
	Documents folder (empty)	An empty folder that con-tains files you put in it	Chapter 6
	Downloads folder (empty)	An empty folder that con-tains files you download with Safari	Chapter 10
	Trash	Drag files and folders onto this icon to get rid of them or drag removable discs onto it to eject them.	This chapter

It's likely that your Dock won't look exactly like the one shown in Figure 4-1. If you added icons to your Dock before you installed Lion, for example, you'll see those icons. If you have any of the iLife apps (such as iMovie, iPhoto, and GarageBand) installed, you may see their icons in your Dock. And if you've ever deleted one of the icons shown in Figure 4-1 from your Dock, it won't "come back" when you install Lion.

If you don't understand what I just said or want to make your Dock look exactly like the one shown in Figure 4-1, I have good news: You find out how to do that and much more before the end of this chapter.

Trash talkin'

The *Trash* is a special container where you put the icons you no longer want to hang around on your hard drive(s). Got four copies of *Letter to the Editor re: Bird Waste Issue* on your hard drive? Drag three of them to the Trash. Tired of tripping over old .pdf and .dmg files you've downloaded but no longer need? Drag them to the Trash, too. To put something in the Trash, just drag its icon onto the Trash icon and watch it disappear.

As with other icons, you know that you've connected with the Trash while dragging when the icon is highlighted. And as with other Dock icons, the Trash icon's name appears when you move the cursor over the icon.

Two other ways to put items into the Trash are to select the items you want to dispose of and then choose File➪Move to Trash or press ⌘+Delete.

If you accidentally drag something to the Trash and want it back right now, you can magically put it back where it came from — but only if you act quickly. Immediately after dragging the item(s) to the Trash, choose Edit➪Undo or press ⌘+Z. Don't hesitate; the Undo command is ephemeral and works only until you perform another action in the Finder. In other words, as soon as you do anything else in the Finder, you can no longer undo what you moved to the Trash.

You know how the garbage in the can on the street curb sits there until the sanitation engineers come by and pick it up each Thursday? The Mac OS X Trash works the same way, but without the smell. Items sit in the Trash, waiting for you to empty it. The Trash basket shows you that it has files waiting for you there. As in real life, your unemptied Trash is full of crumpled papers.

- ✔ **To open the Trash and see what's in there,** just click its icon in the Dock. A Finder window called Trash opens, displaying any files it contains.

- ✔ **To retrieve an item that's already in the Trash,** drag it back out, either onto the Desktop or back into the folder where it belongs.

Or use the secret keyboard shortcut: Select the item(s) in the Trash that you wish to retrieve and press ⌘+Delete. This technique has the added benefit of magically transporting the files or folders you select from the Trash back into the folder from which they came. Try it — it's sweet.

> ✔ **To empty the Trash,** when you put something in the Trash, it sits there until you choose Finder⇨Empty Trash or press ⇧+⌘+Delete.
>
> If the Trash window is open, you see an Empty button just below its toolbar on the right. Clicking the button, of course, also empties the Trash.

You can also empty the Trash from the Dock by pressing the mouse button and holding it down on the Trash icon for a second or two, or right- or Control-clicking the Trash icon. The Empty Trash menu item pops up like magic. Move your cursor over it to select it and then release the mouse button.

Think twice before you invoke the Empty Trash command. After you empty the Trash, the files that it contained are (usually) gone forever. My advice: Before you get too bold, read Chapter 18, and back up your hard drive several times. After you get proficient at backups, chances improve greatly that even though the files are technically gone forever from your hard drive, you can get them back if you really want to (at least in theory).

You find out more about the Trash in Chapter 5, so let's leave it at that for now.

Opening application menus in the Dock

Single-clicking an application icon in the Dock launches that application or, if the application is already open, switches you to that application and brings forward all open windows in that application.

But application icons in the Dock — such as iCal, Safari, iTunes, and others — also hide menus containing some handy commands. (Folder icons in the Dock have a different but no less handy menu, which I discuss in a moment.)

You can make application Dock-icon menus appear in two ways:

> ✔ Press and continue to hold down the mouse button.
>
> ✔ Right or Control+click.

If you use a trackpad, a two-finger click will do the trick too.

If an application isn't running, you can use either method to display a menu like the one shown in Figure 4-2.

Figure 4-2: The Options menu for an application icon (iCal) in the Dock.

Choosing Open launches the application; choosing Show in Finder opens the enclosing folder (Applications) and selects the application's icon; choosing Remove from Dock removes that application's icon from the Dock (waiting until after you quit the application if it's running); and Open at Login launches this application automatically every time you log in to this user account. If an application's icon isn't already in the Dock, you see Add to Dock rather than Remove from Dock.

Show Recents is new in Mac OS X Lion. Choose it, and icons for recently used documents appear above the Dock, as shown in Figure 4-3.

Figure 4-3: Hover over an icon (but don't click) to see its full name.

Last but not least, if you press and hold or right- or Control+click an open application's Dock icon, you might see a menu like the ones shown in Figure 4-4.

So there you have it: That's the default Options menu, which is what you'll see for most applications when they aren't open.

When an application *is* running, however, its Dock menu usually looks quite different, as shown in Figure 4-4 (clockwise from top left: Safari, Preview, System Preferences, Mail, and iCal).

Figure 4-4: Press and hold or right- or Control-click an open application's Dock icon, and menus such as these appear.

Some applications — such as iCal, Mail, and System Preferences in Figure 4-4 — provide useful program-specific commands or options.

iTunes (not shown in the figure) has one of my favorite Dock menus, letting me control my music from the Dock with options like Play/Pause, Next Track, Previous Track, Repeat, and Shuffle.

Other programs, including Preview and Safari in Figure 4-4, offer you a list of open windows with a checkmark to indicate the active window.

Finally, the items above the list of open windows for Preview (About Downloads.pdf, Screen Shot 2011-04-11 at 11.24.33 AM, and all the rest in Figure 4-4) are recently used documents.

Reading Dock-icon body language

As you use the Dock or when you're just doing regular stuff on your Mac, the Dock icons like to communicate with you. They can't talk, so they have a few moves and symbols that indicate things you might want to know. Table 4-2 clarifies what's up with your Dock icons.

Table 4-2	What Dock Icons Are Telling You
Icon Movement or Symbol	**What It Means**
The icon moves up and out of its place on the Dock for a moment, as shown in the middle of Figure 4-5.	You single-clicked a Dock icon, and it's letting you know that you activated it.
The icon does a little bouncy dance when that program is open but isn't active (that is, the menu bar isn't showing, and it isn't the frontmost program).	The program desires your attention; give its icon a click to find out what it wants.
A glowing dot appears below its Dock icon, as shown on the right side of Figure 4-5.	This application is open.
An icon that isn't ordinarily in the Dock magically appears.	You see a temporary Dock icon for every program that's currently open on the Dock until you quit that application. The icon appears because you've opened something. When you quit, its icon magically disappears.

Figure 4-5: A raised Dock icon (middle) with before (left) and after (right) shots.

Opening files from the Dock

One useful function of the Dock is that you can use it to open icons easily. The following tips explain several handy ways to open what you need from the Dock:

✔ **You can drag a document icon onto an application's Dock icon.** If the application knows how to handle that type of document, its Dock icon is highlighted, and the document opens in that application. If the application can't handle that particular type of document, the Dock icon isn't highlighted, and you can't drop the document on it.

I'm getting ahead of myself here, but if the application can't handle a document, try opening the document this way: Select the icon and choose File⇨Open With, or right- or Control+click the document icon and use the Open With menu to choose the application you want to open the document with.

If you hold down the Option key, the Open With command changes to Always Open With, which enables you to change the default application for this document permanently.

⤙ **You can find the original icon of any item you see in the Dock by choosing Show in Finder from its Dock menu.** This trick opens the window containing the item's actual icon and thoughtfully selects that icon for you.

Customizing Your Dock

The Dock is a convenient way to get at oft-used icons. By default, the Dock comes stocked with icons that Apple thinks you'll need most frequently (refer to Table 4-1), but you can customize it to contain any icons that you choose, as you discover in the following sections. You also find out how to resize the Dock to fit your new set of icons and how to tell Dock icons what your preferences are.

Adding Dock icons

You can customize your Dock with favorite applications, a document you update daily, or maybe a folder containing your favorite recipes. Use the Dock for anything you need quick access to.

Adding an application, file, or folder to the Dock is as easy as 1-2-3:

1. **Open a Finder window that contains an application, a document file, or a folder you use frequently.**

   You can also drag an icon — including a hard drive icon — from the desktop.

2. **Click the item you want to add to the Dock.**

   As shown in Figure 4-6, I chose the TextEdit application. (It's highlighted.) I use TextEdit all the time to type and edit quick text notes to myself and others, so having its icon in the Dock is very convenient for me.

3. **Drag the icon out of the Finder window and onto the Dock.**

   An icon for this item now appears in the Dock. Note that the Dock item isn't the actual item. That item remains wherever it was — in a window or on the Desktop. The icon you see in the Dock is a shortcut that opens the item. I haven't talked about aliases (known as *shortcuts* in the Windows world) yet, but the icon in the Dock is actually an alias of the icon you dragged onto the Dock.

Furthermore, when you remove an icon from the Dock, as you find out how to do in a moment, you aren't removing the actual application, document, or folder; you're removing only its shortcut from the Dock.

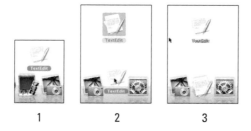

1   2   3

Figure 4-6: Adding an icon to the Dock is as easy as 1–2–3. Just drag the icon onto the Dock.

 Folder, disk, and URL icons must be on the right side of the divider line in the Dock; Application icons must be on the left side of it. Why does the Dock force these rules upon you? I suppose that someone at Apple thinks this is what's best for you; who knows? But that's the rule: apps on the left; folders, disks, and URLs on the right.

 As long as you follow the rule, you can add several items to either side of the divider line at the same time by selecting them all and dragging the group to that side of the Dock. You can delete only one icon at a time from the Dock, however.

Adding a URL to the Dock works slightly differently. Here's a quick way to add a URL to the Dock:

1. **Open Safari, and go to the page with a URL that you want to save on the Dock.**

2. **Click the small icon that you find to the left of the URL in the address bar, and drag it to the right side of the dividing line in the Dock.**

3. **Release the mouse button when the icon is right where you want it.**

   The icons in the Dock slide over and make room for your URL, as shown in Figure 4-7. From now on, when you click the URL icon that you moved to your Dock, Safari opens to that page.

Figure 4-7: Drag the icon from the address bar (top) to the right side of the Dock (middle). The URL appears as a Dock icon (bottom).

If you open an icon that normally doesn't appear in the Dock, and you want to keep its temporary icon in the Dock permanently, you have two ways to tell it to stick around after you quit the program:

- Control+click (or click and hold) and then choose Keep in Dock from the menu that pops up.

- Drag the icon (for an application that's currently open) off and then back to the Dock (or to a different position in the Dock) without letting go of the mouse button.

Removing an icon from the Dock

Removing an item from the Dock is as easy as 1-2 (there is no 3): Just drag its icon out of the Dock, as shown in the top part of Figure 4-8), and it disappears with a cool *poof* animation, as shown in the bottom part of Figure 4-8.

Choosing Remove from Dock from the item's Dock menu is another way to make the item go away.

You can't remove the icon of a program that's running from the Dock until you quit that program. Also, note that by moving an icon out of the Dock, you aren't moving, deleting, or copying the item itself; you're just removing its icon from the Dock. The item is unchanged. The icon is sort of like a library catalog card: Just because you remove the card from the card catalog doesn't mean that the book is gone from the library.

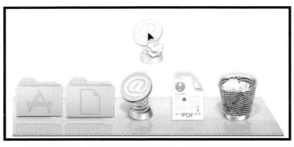

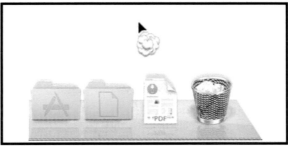

Figure 4-8: To remove an icon, drag it off the Dock, and poof — it's gone.

Resizing the Dock

If the default size of the Dock bugs you, you can make the Dock smaller and save yourself a lot of screen real estate. This space comes in especially handy when you add your own stuff to the Dock.

To shrink or enlarge the Dock (and its icons) without opening the Dock Preferences window, follow these steps:

1. **Make the Sizer appear (as shown in the left margin) by moving your cursor over the dotted line that you find on the right side of the Dock.**

2. **Drag the Sizer down to make the Dock smaller, holding down the mouse button until you find the size you like.**

   The more you drag this control down, the smaller the Dock gets.

3. **To enlarge the Dock again, just drag the Sizer back up.**

   Bam! Big Dock! You can enlarge the Dock until it fills your screen from side to side.

What should you put in YOUR Dock?

Put things in the Dock that you need quick access to and that you use often, or add items that aren't quickly available from menus or the Sidebar. If you like using the Dock better than the Finder window Sidebar (for example), add your Documents, Movies, Pictures, Music, or even your Home folder or hard drive to the Dock.

I suggest adding these items to your Dock:

- ✔ **A word-processing application:** Most people use word-processing software more than any other applications. Just drag the icon for yours to the left side of the Dock, and you're good to go.

   If you don't have a word processor like Microsoft Word or Apple Pages already, give TextEdit a try. It's in every Mac OS X Applications folder, and it's more powerful than you expect from a freebie.

- ✔ **A project folder:** You know — the folder that contains all the documents for your thesis, or all the notes for the biggest project you have at work, or your massive recipe collection . . . whatever. If you add that folder to the Dock, you can access it much quicker than if you have to open several folders to find it.

- ✔ **A special utility or application:** The Preview application is an essential part of my work because I receive a lot of different image files every day. You might also want to add programs (such as AOL), your favorite graphics application (such as Photoshop Elements), or the game you play every afternoon when you think the boss isn't watching.

- ✔ **Your favorite URLs:** Save links to sites that you visit every day — the ones you use in your job, your favorite Mac news sites, or your personalized page from an Internet service provider (ISP). Sure, you can make one of these pages your browser's start page or bookmark it, but the Dock lets you add one or more additional URLs. (Refer to "Adding Dock icons," earlier in this chapter, for details.)

   You can add several URL icons to the Dock, but bear in mind that the Dock and its icons shrink to accommodate added icons, which makes them harder to see. Perhaps the best idea — if you want easy access to several URLs — is to create a folder full of URLs and put that folder on the Dock. Then you can just press and hold your cursor on the folder (or Control+click the folder) to pop up a menu with all your URLs.

Even though you can make the Dock smaller, you're still limited to one row of icons. The smaller you make the Dock, the larger the crowd of icons you can amass. You have to determine for yourself what's best for you: having lots of icons available in the Dock (even though they might be difficult to see because they're so tiny) or having less clutter but fewer icons in your Dock.

After you figure out which programs you use and don't use, it's a good idea to relieve overcrowding by removing the ones you never (or rarely) use.

Setting your Dock preferences

You can change a few things about the Dock to make it look and behave just the way you want it to. First, I look at global preferences that apply to the Dock itself. After that, I look at some preferences that apply only to folder and disk icons in the Dock.

Global Dock preferences

To change global Dock preferences, choose Dock Dock Preferences. The System Preferences application opens, showing an active Dock pane (see Figure 4-9).

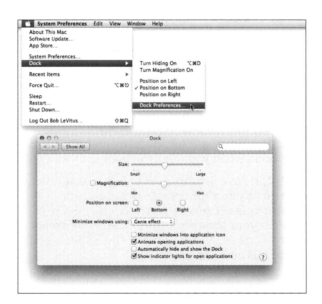

Figure 4-9: The Dock menu and the Dock System Preferences pane.

You can also open the Dock Preferences by right-clicking or Control+clicking the Dock Resizer and choosing Dock Preferences from the contextual menu.

Now you can adjust your Dock with the following preferences:

- **Size:** Note the slider bar here. Move this slider to the right (larger) or left (smaller) to adjust the size of the Dock in your Finder. As you move the slider, watch the Dock change size. (Now, *there's* a fun way to spend a Saturday afternoon!)

  As you add items to the Dock, the icons — and the Dock itself — shrink to accommodate the new ones.

- **Magnification:** This slider controls how big icons grow when you pass the arrow cursor over them. Or you can deselect this check box to turn off magnification entirely.

- **Position on Screen:** Choose one of these three radio buttons to attach the Dock to the left side, the right side, or the bottom of your screen (the default). Personally, I prefer it on the bottom, but you should probably try all three before you decide.

- **Minimize Windows Using:** From this handy pop-up menu (PC users would call it a *drop-down list,* but what the heck; there's no gravity in a computer screen anyway), choose the animation that you see when you click a window's Minimize button (the yellow gumdrop). The Genie Effect is the default, but the Scale Effect seems a bit faster to me.

  Want to amaze your friends? Surreptitiously hold down the Shift key when you click the Minimize button or the Dock icon of a minimized window to make the animation effect play in super slow motion.

- **Minimize Windows into Application Icon:** If you select this option, when you minimize a window by clicking its yellow gumdrop button, you won't see a Dock icon for that window.

  If this option isn't selected, each window you minimize gets its own personal icon on the right side of your Dock.

- **Animate Opening Applications:** Mac OS X animates *(bounces)* Dock icons when you click them to open an item. If you don't like the animation, deselect (that is, uncheck) this check box, and the bouncing ceases evermore.

- **Automatically Hide and Show the Dock:** Don't like the Dock? Maybe you want to free the screen real estate on your monitor? Then choose the Automatically Hide and Show the Dock check box; after that, the Dock displays itself only when you move the cursor to the bottom of the screen where the Dock would ordinarily appear. It's like magic! (Okay, it's like Windows that way, but I hate to admit it.)

If the Dock isn't visible, deselect the Automatically Hide and Show the Dock check box to bring back the Dock. The option remains turned off unless you change it by checking the Automatically Hide and Show the Dock check box. Choose ⌘⇨Dock⇨Turn Hiding On (or use its keyboard shortcut ⌘+Option+D).

The keyboard shortcut ⌘+Option+D is a toggle, so it reverses the state of this option each time you use it.

✓ **Show Indicator Lights for Open Applications:** Select this option if you want all open applications to display an indicator light below their Dock icons, like the Finder, Mail, Safari, iCal, and iTunes Dock icons in Figure 4-3. Those five programs are open, whereas the others — the ones without lights — are not. If you disable this option, though I can't imagine why you'd ever want to, none of your Dock icons will ever display an indicator light.

Folder and Disk Dock Icon Menu Preferences

If you click a folder or disk icon in the Dock, its contents are displayed in a Fan, Grid, or List menu, as shown in Figure 4-10.

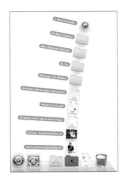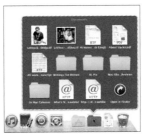

Figure 4-10: My Documents folder's Dock menu as Fan, Grid, and List.

If you right- or Control-click a folder or disk icon in the Dock, its Options menu is displayed, as shown in Figure 4-11.

Figure 4-11: The Options menu for my Documents folder.

Here are the choices on the Options menu:

- **Sort By,** which determines the order in which items in the folder or disk are displayed when you click its Dock icon.

- **Display As** determines what the Dock icon for a folder or disk looks like. If you choose Stack, as I have for the Documents folder icon in Figure 4-11, the icon takes on the appearance of an item in the folder or disk (a picture of me in Figure 4-11). If you choose Folder, the Dock icon looks like a folder, as does the Application folder icon to the left of the Documents icon in Figure 4-11.

- **View Contents As** lets you choose Fan, Grid, or List as the menu type for the folder or disk.

The default is Automatic, which is to say that the Dock tries to pick the menu for you. I much prefer picking the menu I consider most appropriate for a particular folder or disk. I like List menus best, especially for folders or disks with a lot of subfolders. As you can see in Figure 4-10, the List menu is the only one that lets you see and access folders inside folders (and subfolders inside other subfolders). For folders with images, I like the Grid menu because it displays easily discernible icons for the folder or disk's contents. The Fan menu is fantastic (ha!) when the folder or disk contains only a few items.

✓ **The Options submenu:**

  • **Remove from Dock** removes the icon from the Dock.

  • **Show in Finder** opens the window containing the item and selects the item. So, for example, in Figures 4-10 and 4-11, my Home folder would open, and the Documents folder inside it would be selected.

The Dock is your friend. Now that you know how it works, make it work the way you want it to. Put those programs and folders you use most in the Dock, and you'll save yourself a significant amount of time and effort.

5

The Finder and Its Desktop

In This Chapter

▶ Getting to know the Finder

▶ Using aliases: The greatest things since sliced bread

▶ View(ing) the Finder

▶ Navigating the Finder

▶ Customizing Finder windows

▶ Setting Finder preferences

▶ Getting info-mation on icons

*O*n your Mac, the Finder is your starting point — the centerpiece of your Mac experience, if you will — and it's always available. In Finder's windows or Desktop, you can double-click your way to your favorite application, your documents, or your folders. So in this chapter, I show you how to get the most from the Mac OS X Lion Finder and its Desktop.

Introducing the Finder and its Minions: The Desktop and Icons

The Finder is a special application unlike any other. It launches automatically as soon as you start your Mac and is always running in the background. The Desktop is a special part of the Finder unlike any other. Finally, icons and windows are the units of currency used by the Finder and Desktop.

Before I tackle any deep thoughts — such as what the Finder does or what the Desktop is — I start with a quick overview of some of the icons you're likely to encounter as you get to know the Finder and Desktop.

Figuring out what an icon is

What's an icon? Glad you asked. Each Finder icon represents an item or a container on your hard drive. Containers — hard disks, folders, CDs, DVDs, shared network volumes, and so on — can contain a virtually unlimited number of application files, document files, and folders.

Icons in the Dock and the Sidebar of Finder windows are not the same as the Finder icons I'll be discussing in this chapter — they're simply convenient pointers to actual Finder icons.

Technically, icons they are aliases. (If you don't yet know what an alias is, you're going to find out long before the thrilling conclusion of this chapter.)

Anyway, working with icons is easy:

- ✔ Single-click to select.
- ✔ Double-click to open.
- ✔ Click-and-drag to move.
- ✔ Release mouse button to drop.

But enough talk. It's time to see what these puppies actually look like.

Identifying your Finder icons in the wild

Although icons all work the same, they come in different kinds, shapes, and sizes. When you've been around the Macintosh for a while, you develop a sixth sense about what an icon contains and know just by looking at it.

The major icons types are

- ✔ **Application icons** are *programs* — the software you use to accomplish tasks on your Mac. Mail, Safari, and iCal are applications. So are Microsoft Word and Adobe Photoshop.

  Application icons come in a variety of shapes. For example, application icons are often square-ish, diamond-shaped, rectangular, or just oddly shaped. Figure 5-1 displays application icons of various shapes.

- ✔ **Document icons** are files created by applications. Letters created with TextEdit are documents. This chapter is a document created in Microsoft Word. And my spreadsheet, PDF, video, image, and song files are all documents.

Document icons are often reminiscent of a piece of paper, as shown in Figure 5-2.

✔ **Folder and Disk icons** are the Mac's organizational containers. You can put icons — and the applications or documents they stand for — in folders or disks. You can put folders in disks or in other folders, but you can't put a disk inside another disk.

Folders look like, well, manila folders (what a concept) and can contain just about any other icon. You use folders to organize your files and applications on your hard drive. You can have as many folders as you want, so don't be afraid to create new ones. The thought behind the whole folders thing is pretty obvious: If your hard drive is a filing cabinet, folders are its drawers and folders (duh!). Figure 5-3 shows some typical folder icons.

And while disks behave pretty much like folders, their icons often look like disks rather than folders, as shown in Figure 5-4.

Figure 5-1: Application icons come in many shapes.

Figure 5-2: Typical document icons.

Figure 5-3: The folders in my Home folder are pretty typical folders.

Figure 5-4: Disk icons generally look a lot like, well, disks.

If you're looking for details about how to organize your icons in folders, move them around, delete them, and so on, hang in there. The next chapter — Chapter 6 — is about organizing and managing files and folders.

There is actually one more type of icon you're going to need to know, and that's the alias icon. This little puppy is a wonderful — no, make that *fabulous* — organizational tool. I like aliases so much, in fact, that they get a whole entire section to themselves.

Aliases: Greatest Thing Since Sliced Bread

An *alias* is a tiny file that automatically opens the file, folder, disk, or network volume that it represents. Although an alias is technically an icon, it's different from other icons; it actually does nothing but open another icon automatically when you double-click it.

Put another way, aliases are organizational tools that let you have an icon appear in more than one place without having to create multiple copies of the file that icon represents.

An alias is very different from a duplicated file. For example, the iTunes application uses around 150 megabytes (MB) of hard-drive space. If I were to *duplicate* iTunes, I'd have two files on my hard disk, each requiring around 160MB of disk space.

An *alias* of iTunes, on the other hand, looks just like the duplicate and opens iTunes when you double-click it but requires less than 1MB of hard disk space.

So try placing aliases of programs and files you use most often in convenient places such as the Desktop or a folder in your Home folder.

In effect, Microsoft stole the alias feature from Apple. (If you've used Windows, you may know aliases as *shortcuts*.) But what else is new? And for what it's worth, the Mac's aliases usually don't break when you move or rename the original file; shortcuts sometimes do (or at least, they used to).

Why else do I think that aliases are so great? Well, they open any file or folder on any hard drive from anywhere else on any hard drive — which is a very good trick. But there are many other reasons why I think aliases rock:

To organize or not...

These days, there are users who prefer to have all of their files — every single one — in one folder, usually the Documents folder. There's nothing to prevent you from putting every file in one folder; Mac OS X Lion could care less.

That doesn't mean it's a good idea.

First, opening folders with thousands and thousands of files takes longer. And the more files there are, the longer it will be before you can use them. I don't know about you, but I don't like to wait, especially when I don't have to.

Second, folders with thousands of files become a nightmare in applications' Open dialogs.

The good news is that you'll learn how to tame the Open dialog, how to create and use subfolders, and suggestions for how to organize your own stuff.

For those who choose to ignore the good advice in this chapter and Chapter 6, Chapter 7 introduces Spotlight, which makes it simple to find and open almost any file quickly, even files in the same folder as tens of thousands of other files.

But I digress...

✓ **Convenience:** Aliases enable you to make items appear to be in more than one place, which on many occasions is exactly what you want to do. For example, keep an alias of your word processor on your Desktop and another in your Documents folder for quick access. Aliases enable you to open your word processor right away without having to navigate into the depths of your Applications folder every time you need it.

While you're at it, you might want to put an icon for your word processor in both the Dock and the Sidebar to make it even easier to open your word processor without a lot of clicking.

✓ **Flexibility and organization:** You can create aliases and store them anywhere on your hard drive to represent the same document in several different folders. This is a great help when you need to file a document that can logically be stored in any of several files. If you write a memo to Fred Smith about the Smythe Marketing Campaign to be executed in the fourth quarter, which folder does the document belong in? Smith? Smythe? Marketing? Memos? 4th Quarter? Correct answer: With aliases, it can go in every folder, if you like. Then you can find the memo wherever you look instead of guessing which folder you filed it in.

✓ **Integrity:** Some programs must remain in the same folder as their supporting files and folders. Many programs, for example, won't function properly unless they're in the same folder as their dictionaries, thesauruses, data files (for games), templates, and so on. Thus, you can't put the actual icon for such programs on the Desktop without impairing their functionality. An alias lets you access a program like that from anywhere on your hard drive.

I admit I'm somewhat old-school when it comes to organizing my files in the proper folders (see Chapter 6), but Lion's speedy Spotlight search mechanism, along with tools like Exposé, Launchpad, and Mission Control (all, not coincidentally, discussed in Chapter 7), let you find pretty much any file on your disk in seconds.

Creating aliases

When you create an alias, its icon looks the same as the icon that it represents, but the suffix *alias* is tacked onto its name, and a tiny arrow called a *badge* (as shown in the margin) appears in the bottom-left corner of its icon. Figure 5-5 shows an alias and its *parent* icon — the icon that opens if you double-click the alias.

To create an alias for an icon, do one of the following:

- Click the parent icon and choose File⇨Make Alias.
- Click the parent icon and press ⌘+L.
- Click the parent icon and use the Action menu's Make Alias command.
- Click an icon while holding down the Control key and then choose the Make Alias command from the contextual menu that appears. (You can explore contextual menus — which are very cool — in Chapter 2.)

  In all four of the previous techniques, the alias is created in the same folder as its parent. If that doesn't suit you, try this fourth way:

- Click any file or folder, press and hold down ⌘+Option, and then drag the file or folder while continuing to hold down ⌘+Option. Presto! An alias appears where you release the mouse button.

When I first create a file, I save it in its proper folder inside the Documents folder in my Home folder. If it's a document that I plan to work on for more than a day or two (such as a magazine article or book chapter), I make an alias of the document (or folder) and plop it on my Desktop. After I finish the article or chapter and submit it to an editor, I trash the alias, leaving the original file safe and sound in its proper folder.

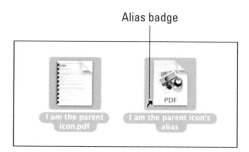

Figure 5-5: An alias (right) and its parent.

Deleting aliases

This is a short section because deleting an alias is such an easy chore. To delete an alias, simply drag it onto the Trash icon in the Dock. That's it! You can also Control+click it and choose Move to Trash from the contextual menu that appears, or select the icon and press ⌘+Delete.

Deleting an alias does *not* delete the parent item. (If you want to delete the parent item, you have to go hunt it down and kill it yourself.)

Hunting down an alias's parent

Suppose that you create an alias of a file, and later you want to delete both the alias and its parent file, but you can't find the parent file. What do you do? Well, you can use the Finder's Find function to find it (try saying that three times real fast), but here are three faster ways to find the parent icon of an alias:

- Select the alias icon and choose File⇨Show Original.
- Select the alias icon and press ⌘+R.
- Control+click the alias icon and choose Show Original from the contextual menu.

Any of these methods opens the window containing the parent document with its icon preselected for your convenience.

Introducing the Desktop

The Desktop is the backdrop for the Finder — everything you see behind the Dock and any open windows. The Desktop is always available and is where you can usually find your hard drive icon(s).

This will be a whole lot easier with a picture for reference, so take a gander at Figure 5-6, which is a glorious depiction of a typical Mac OS X Lion Finder.

If you're not familiar with the Finder's Desktop, here are a few tips that will come in handy as you become familiar with the icons that hang out there:

- **Icons on the Desktop behave the same as icons in a window.** You move them and copy them just as you would icons in a window. The only difference is that icons on the Desktop aren't in a window. Because they're on the Desktop, they're more convenient to use.

- **The first icon you should get to know is the icon for your hard drive (see Figure 5-7).** You can usually find it on the top-right side of the Desktop. Look for the name Macintosh HD or something like that, unless you've already renamed it. (I renamed my hard drive Lion HD in Figure 5-7; see the section on renaming icons in Chapter 6 if you'd like to rename your own hard drive.) You can see how selected and deselected hard-drive icons look in Figure 5-7, too.

- **Other disc or hard drive icons appear on the Desktop by default.** When you insert a CD or DVD, or connect an external hard drive, the disc or drive icon appears on the Desktop just below your startup hard-drive icon (space permitting).You can find details about working with discs and drives in Chapter 8.

If you don't see your hard drive icon on the Desktop, make sure the check box for hard drives is checked in Finder Preferences as described in the "Setting Finder preferences" section, later in this chapter.

✔ **You can move an item to the Desktop so you can find it right away.** Simply click its icon in any window and then, without releasing the mouse button, drag it out of the window and onto the Desktop. Then release the mouse button.

bobl folder (inside Users folder)   Desktop folder (inside bobl folder)

Users folder (inside Lion HD)   Sample file in the Desktop folder

Hard disk icons in a window   Sample folder in the Desktop folder

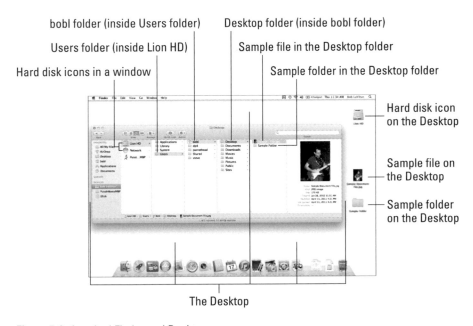

Hard disk icon on the Desktop

Sample file on the Desktop

Sample folder on the Desktop

The Desktop

Figure 5-6: A typical Finder and Desktop.

Figure 5-7: Selected and deselected hard-drive icons.

The true home of your Desktop icons

If you're curious about the inner workings of your Mac, you might find it interesting to check out the Desktop folder in your Home directory (that is, the Home folder). Just click the Home icon in any Finder window's Sidebar (or press ⇧+⌘+H to open a window displaying Home), and you see a folder named *Desktop,* which contains the same icons you place on the Desktop (but not the hard-drive icons). The reason for this folder is that each user has an individual Desktop. You find out much more about Home, users, and all that jazz in the upcoming chapters.

At the bottom of the Finder window in Figure 5-6 are two optional bars. The lower of the two is called the *status bar;* it tells you how many items are in each window and, if any are selected, how many you've selected out of the total, as well as how much space is available on the hard drive containing this window. And just above the status bar is the *path bar,* which shows the path from the top level of your hard drive to the selected folder (which is Desktop in Figure 5-6). You can show or hide the status bar by choosing View⇨Hide/Show Status Bar and show or hide the path bar by choosing View⇨Hide/Show Path Bar.

Bellying up to the toolbar

In addition to the Sidebar (mentioned in Chapter 2) and some good old-fashioned double-clicking, the Mac OS X Finder window offers navigation aids. Several of these are on the toolbar — namely, the Back and Forward buttons, as well as the extra-helpful view buttons. You can find other handy features on the Go menu, discussed a little later in this chapter.

The toolbar, in case you didn't know, is the thick gray band right below the title bar, as shown in Figure 5-8. On it are tools and buttons that let you navigate quickly and act on selected icons. To activate a toolbar button, click it once.

You say you don't want to see the toolbar at the top of the window? Okay! Just choose View⇨Hide Toolbar or use its keyboard shortcut (⌘+Option+T), and it's gone. (If only life were always so easy!) Want it back? Choose View⇨Show Toolbar or use the same keyboard shortcut: ⌘+Option+T.

Alas, hiding the toolbar also hides the useful Sidebar and status bar. If only you could choose to hide them independently. . . . I find this fact annoying because I use the Sidebar a lot but don't use the toolbar nearly as often. To make matters worse, Lion has a new menu item — View⇨Hide Sidebar (shortcut: ⌘+Option+S) — that lets you hide the Sidebar without hiding the toolbar. For some unfathomable reason, you can't do the opposite and hide the toolbar while keeping the Sidebar and status bar visible! No, instead, if you choose View➪Hide Toolbar (shortcut ⌘+Option+T) or click the gray jellybean, the Sidebar and status bar disappear along with the toolbar. Boo. Hiss.

When the toolbar is hidden, opening a folder opens a *new* Finder window rather than reusing the current one (which is what happens when the toolbar is showing unless you've changed this preference in Finder preferences or are using Column view).

So here's the lowdown on the toolbar's default buttons, from left to right in Figure 5-8:

Figure 5-8: A Finder window's default toolbar.

If you've customized your toolbar by choosing View➪Customize Toolbar, yours won't look exactly like Figure 5-8.

- ✔ **Forward and Back buttons:** Clicking the Forward and Back buttons displays the folders that you've viewed in this window in sequential order. If you've used a web browser, it's a lot like that.

  Here's an example of how the Back button works. Say you're in your Home folder; you click the Favorites button, and a split-second later, you realize that you actually need something in the Home folder. Just a quick click of the Back button and — *poof!* — you're back Home. As for the Forward button, well, it moves you in the opposite direction, through folders that you've visited in this window. Play around with them both; you'll find them invaluable.

  The keyboard shortcuts ⌘+[for Back and ⌘+] for Forward are even more useful (in my opinion) than the buttons.

- ✔ **View buttons:** The four view buttons change the way that the window displays its contents.

  You have four ways to view a window: Column, Icon, List, and Cover Flow. Some people like columns, some like icons, and others love lists or flows. To each her own. Play with the four Finder views to see which one works best for you. For what it's worth, I usually prefer Column view with a dash of List view thrown in when I need a folder's contents sorted by creation date or size. And the new Cover Flow view is great for folders with documents because you can see the contents of many document types right in the window, as I explain shortly.

Don't forget that each view also has a handy keyboard shortcut: ⌘+1 for Icon view, ⌘+2 for List view, ⌘+3 for Column view, and ⌘+4 for Cover Flow view.

Views are so useful you'll find an entire section devoted to them coming up in just a few pages.

✔ **Arrange:** Click this button to see a pop-up menu with options for displaying this window's contents, as shown in Figure 5-9.

Figure 5-9: The Arrange pop-up menu and my Documents folder arranged by Application.

Though available in the View menu of earlier versions of Mac OS X, it's new as a toolbar feature in Lion, and it's a winner. In Figure 5-9, I've selected Date Last Opened, and my Documents folder reflects that choice. While you can sort items by Date Last Opened in List view (more on that is coming up shortly), using the Arrange menu works for all four views and has keyboard shortcuts to boot. I use them often, and you should too!

✔ **Quick Look:** Clicking this button displays the contents of the currently selected file in a floating window without launching an application. It's so sweet, I devote an entire section to it in Chapter 6.

✔ **Action:** Click this button to see a pop-up menu of all the context-sensitive actions you can perform on selected icons, as shown in Figure 5-10.

✔ **Search:** The toolbar's Search box is a nifty way to search for files or folders. Just type a word (or even just a few letters), and after a few seconds, the window fills with a list of files that match.

You can also start a search by choosing File⇨Find (shortcut: ⌘+F).

You find out a lot more about searching in Chapter 7.

Figure 5-10: Use the Action pop-up menu to perform common actions on the selected item or items (the Movies and Pictures folders).

The View(s) from a Window

Views are part of what makes your Mac feel like *your* Mac. Lion offers four views so you can select the best one for any occasion. Some people like one view so much that they rarely (or never) use others. Other people, like me, memorize the keyboard shortcuts to switch views instantly without reaching for the mouse.

Try 'em all, and use the one(s) you prefer.

Moving through folders fast in Column view

Column view is a darn handy way to quickly look through a lot of folders at once, and it's especially useful when those folders are filled with graphics files. The Column view is my favorite way to display windows in the Finder.

To display a window in Column view, shown in Figure 5-11, click the Column view button on the toolbar (as shown in the margin) and then choose View➪As Columns from the Finder's menu bar or press ⌘+3.

Figure 5-11: A Finder window in Column view.

Here's how I clicked around in Column view to see the list of folders and files you see in Figure 5-11:

1. When I click the bobl icon in the Sidebar, its contents appear in the column to the right.

2. When I click the Pictures folder in this column, its contents appear in the second column.

3. When I click the iChat Icons folder in the second column, its contents appear in the third column.

4. When I click the Gems folder in the third column, its contents appear in the fourth column.

5. Finally, when I click the Emerald Square.gif icon in the fourth column, the contents of that file appear, along with some information about it: It's a Graphics Interchange Format (GIF) file, 2KB in size, created on 5/28/11, and so on. That's called the Preview column.

When you're poking around your Mac in Column view, the following tips are good to know:

 ✔ **You can have as many columns in a Column view window as your screen can handle.** Just drag any edge or corner of the window to enlarge it so new columns have room to open. Or click the green Zoom (also known as Maximize) gumdrop button to expand the window to "just big enough" to display all columns with content in them.

 ✔ **You can use the little grabber handles at the bottom of every column to resize the column widths.**

  They're pretty versatile:

   • If you drag a handle left or right, the column to its left resizes.

- If you hold down the Option key when you drag, *all* the columns resize at the same time.

- If you double-click one of these little handles, the column to its left expands to the width of the widest item it contains.

- If you Option+double-click any handle, all the columns expand at the same time to the width of the widest item each one contains.

✔ **The preview column displays information about the highlighted item to its left, but only if that item isn't a folder or disk.** (If it is a folder or disk, its contents would be in this column.) For many items, the picture you see in the preview column is an enlarged view of the file's icon. But if the item is a graphic file (even a PDF) saved in a format that QuickTime can interpret (most graphic file formats), a preview picture appears instead, as shown in Figure 5-11. If you don't like having the preview displayed, you can choose View➪Show View Options and turn off Show Preview Column.

Perusing in Icon view

Icon view is a free-form view that allows you to move your icons around within a window to your heart's content. Check out the Finder window shown in Figure 5-1, earlier in this chapter, to see what Icon view looks like.

Icon view: The ol'-stick-in-the-mud view

In all fairness, I must say that many perfectly happy Macintosh users love Icon view and refuse to even consider anything else. Fine. But as the number of files on your hard drive increases (as it does for every Mac user), screen real estate becomes more and more valuable. In my humble opinion, the only real advantages that Icon view has over Column or List view are the ability to arrange the icons anywhere you like within the window and to put a background picture or color behind your icons. Big deal.

I offer this solution as a compromise: If you still want to see your files and folders in Icon view, make them smaller so that more of them fit in the same space on-screen. This is what I do

with any icons I have on my Desktop (because the Desktop allows only Icon view).

To change the size of a window's icons, use the little slider in the bottom-right corner of the Finder window when the status bar is showing. (If it's not, choose View➪Status Bar (or press ⌘+/).

Bigger icons make me crazy, but if you like them that way, your Mac can accommodate you. You can also alter the space between icons by dragging the Grid Spacing slider left or right.

Note: If you like Icon view, consider purchasing a larger monitor; I hear that monitors now come in a 30-inch size.

To display a window in Icon view, click the Icon view button in the toolbar (shown in the margin), choose View⇨As Icons from the Finder's menu bar, or press ⌘+1.

Learn to love the Icon Size control in the lower-right corner of Icon view windows or in the top-right corner when the Sidebar and Toolbar are hidden.

The Finder's View menu also offers a few commands that might help you glance through your icons more easily:

✔ **Clean Up:** Choose this command to align icons to an invisible grid; you use it to keep your windows and Desktop neat and tidy. (If you like this invisible grid, don't forget that you can turn it on or off for the Desktop and individual windows by using View Options.) Clean Up is available only in Icon view or when no windows are active. If no windows are active, the command instead cleans up your Desktop. (To deactivate all open windows, just click anywhere on the Desktop.)

If you're like me, you've taken great pains to place icons carefully in specific places on your Desktop. Cleaning up your Desktop destroys all your beautiful work and moves all your perfectly arranged icons. And alas, cleaning up your Desktop is not something you can undo.

If any icons are selected (highlighted) when you pull down the View menu, you see Clean Up Selection rather than Clean Up. If you choose this command, it moves only the icons that are currently selected.

✔ **Arrange By:** This command rearranges the icons in the active window in your choice of nine ways, which happen to be the same nine options in the Arrange pop-up menu (which you've already seen in Figure 5-9).

Like Clean Up, Arrange By is available only for windows viewed as icons.

Listless? Try touring folders in List view

Now I come to my second-favorite view, List view (shown in Figure 5-12). The main reason why I like it so much is the little triangles to the left of each folder, known as *disclosure triangles,* which let you see the contents of a folder without actually opening it. This view also allows you to select items from multiple folders at once and move or copy items between folders in a single window.

To display a window in List view, click the List view button on the toolbar (shown in the margin), choose View⇨As List from the Finder's menu bar, or press ⌘+2.

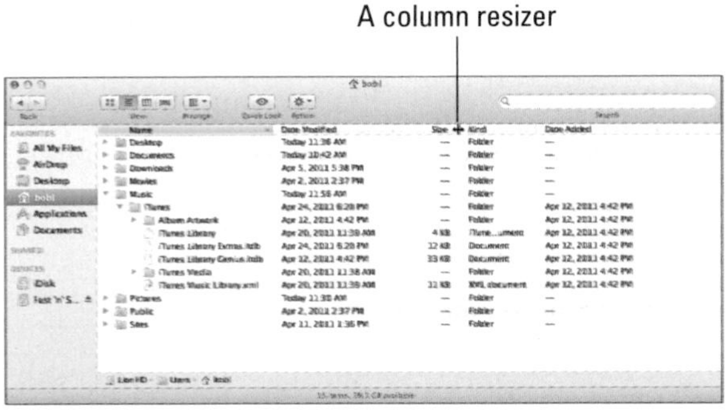

A column resizer

Figure 5-12: A window in List view.

When you're in List view, the following tips can help you breeze through your folders to find what you're looking for:

- ✏ **To disclose a folder's contents, click the triangle to its left or, if it's selected, press the right-arrow key.** Figure 5-12 shows the result of either clicking the triangle to the left of the iTunes folder or selecting (highlighting) the iTunes folder and pressing the right-arrow key.

  If you press Option+right arrow, all the folder's subfolders also expand. So if I had pressed the Option key before I pressed the right-arrow key in Figure 5-12, the Album Artwork and iTunes Media folders would have expanded. And if either of those folders contained any folders, it would have been expanded as well.

- ✏ **Click the column header to sort items in List view.** Notice the little triangle at the right edge of the selected column (the Name column in Figure 5-12). If this little arrow points up, the items in the corresponding column sort in descending order; if you click the header (Name) once, the arrow points down, and the items are listed in the opposite (ascending) order. This behavior is true for all columns in List view windows.

- ✏ **You can change the order in which columns appear in a window.** To do so, press and hold a column's name and then drag it to the left or right until it's where you want it. Release the mouse button, and the column moves.

  The exception (isn't there always an exception?) is that the Name column always appears first in List view windows; you can move all other columns about at will. In fact, you can even hide and show columns other than Name if you like using the View Options window.

You can fine-tune all four views and the Desktop by using the View Options window. Just choose View➪Show View Options or press ⌘+J. The options you see apply to the active window or the Desktop. Click the Use as Defaults button to apply these options to all windows in that view (that is, Icon, List, Column, or Cover Flow).

✔ **To widen or shrink a column, hover over the dividing line between that columns and drag left or right.** When your cursor is over the dividing line in the header, it changes to a double-headed resizer, as shown in the margin and in Figure 5-12 (where I'm enlarging the Size column by clicking between it and the Kind column).

You gotta go with the flow

If you're familiar with the Cover Flow feature in iTunes or if you own an iPhone, iPod touch, or iPad (which do a Cover Flow thing when you turn them sideways in their iPod music-player mode), you're already familiar with Cover Flow.

To display a window in Cover Flow view, click the Cover Flow view button on the toolbar (shown in the margin), choose View➪As Cover Flow from the Finder's menu bar, or press ⌘+4. Figure 5-13 shows Cover Flow view.

Figure 5-13: A window in Cover Flow mode.

Cover Flow view has two cool features:

✔ The item that's selected in the list (Me and Mini Me.jpg in Figure 5-13) appears in a preview in the top part of the window.

✔ You can flip through the previews by clicking the images to the left or right of the current preview image (me wearing a stethomouse in the figure) or by sliding the black scroll bar below the preview to the left or right.

Finder on the Menu

The Finder menu is packed with useful goodies, most of which are available in its menus. In this section, I look at those that pertain specifically to using the Finder, such as . . .

The actual Finder menu

Here are a few of the main items you can find on the Finder menu:

- **About Finder:** Choose this command to find out which version of the Finder is running on your Mac.

  Okay, so this menu item isn't particularly useful — or at least not for very long. But when a different application is running, the About Finder item becomes About *application name* and usually gives information about the program's version number, the developers (the company and the people), and any other tidbits that those developers decide to throw in. Sometimes these tidbits are useful, sometimes they're interesting, and sometimes they're both.

- **Preferences:** Use the choices here to control how the Finder looks and acts. Find out the details in "Setting Finder preferences," later in this chapter.

- **Services:** One of the really cool features of Mac OS X applications is the accessibility of Services. If nothing is selected in the Finder, the Services menu is empty, as shown in Figure 5-14 A. When an icon or icons are selected, there are two Services you can choose, as shown in Figure 5-14 B. Finally, if a word or words are selected, you have a myriad of options, as shown in Figure 5-14 C.

  In other words, the items you see in the Services menu are context-sensitive, so what you see in yours will depend on what you have selected. If you look in the Services menu and don't find anything interesting, try selecting something else and looking again; you might be pleasantly surprised.

  Choose the last item in the menu, Services Preferences, and you can enable dozens of useful Services that aren't available by default.

- **Hide Finder (⌘+H):** Use this command when you have Finder windows open and they're distracting you. Choosing it makes the Finder inactive (another program becomes active) and hides any open Finder windows. To make the Finder visible again, either choose Show All from the Application menu (which bears the name of the active application, such as TextEdit, System Preferences, and so on) or click the Finder icon, shown in the margin here, in the Dock.

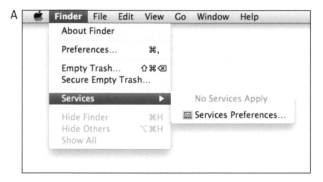

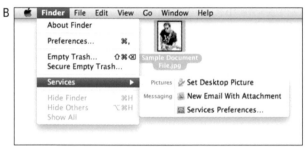

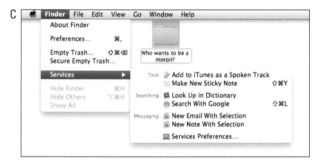

Figure 5-14: Services available with nothing selected (A), an icon selected (B), and a word selected (C).

The advantage to hiding the Finder — rather than closing or minimizing all your windows to get a clean screen — is that you don't have to open them all again when you're ready to get the windows back. Instead, just choose Show All (to see all windows in all apps) or click the Finder button in the Dock to see all Finder windows.

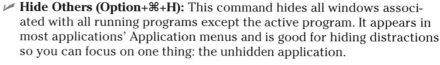

✔ **Hide Others (Option+⌘+H):** This command hides all windows associated with all running programs except the active program. It appears in most applications' Application menus and is good for hiding distractions so you can focus on one thing: the unhidden application.

Another easy way to hide all open applications and windows while activating the Finder is to hold down the ⌘ and Option keys and click the Finder icon in the Dock. This technique works with whatever application is active, not just the Finder. So if you're surfing the web and decide you want to see only Safari's windows on your screen, ⌘+Option+click the Safari button in the Dock, and it will happen instantly.

✔ **Show All:** Use this command as the antidote to both of the Hide commands. Choose this, and nothing is hidden anymore.

You can achieve much of the same effect as all this hide-and-show jazz by using Exposé and/or Spaces, both discussed in Chapter 7.

Finally, if you noticed that the Finder menu's Empty Trash command isn't mentioned here, that's because it's mentioned briefly in Chapter 4 and gets detailed coverage in Chapter 6.

Like a road map: The current folder's pop-up menu

In the center of the window's title bar is the name of the folder that you're viewing in this window: the highlighted folder. You know that already. What you might not know is that it offers a hidden road map to this folder from the top level. The following steps explain how it works:

1. **⌘+click and hold the folder's name (Desktop) in the title bar.**

   A pop-up menu appears, with the current folder (Desktop, in Figure 5-15) at the top.

2. **Select any folder in the menu, and it becomes the highlighted folder in the current window; release the mouse button, and that folder's contents are displayed.**

   As shown in Figure 5-15, the contents of the Desktop folder — a file and a folder — are displayed in the window. If I released the mouse button, the contents of the highlighted folder (bobl) would appear.

3. **After jumping to a new folder, you can click the Back button.**

   Hey, you're right back where you were before you touched that pop-up menu!

Figure 5-15: Traverse folders from this convenient pop-up menu.

Don't forget that you can display the path bar near the bottom of the window (it's showing in Figure 5-12) by choosing View➪Show Path Bar. Then you can double-click any folder displayed in the path bar to open it.

Going places with the Go menu

The Go menu is chock-full of shortcuts. The items on this menu take you to places on your Mac — many of the same places you can go with the Finder window toolbar — and a few other places.

The following list gives you a brief look at the items on the Go menu:

- **Back (⌘+[):** Use this menu option to return to the last Finder window that you had open. It's equivalent to the Back button on the Finder toolbar, in case you have the toolbar hidden.

- **Forward (⌘+]):** This command is the opposite of using the Back command, moving you forward through every folder you open. Remember that if you haven't gone back, you can't go forward.

- **Enclosing Folder (⌘+↑):** This command tells the Finder window to display the folder where the currently selected item is located.

- **All My Files (⇧+⌘+F):** This command shows you all of your document files at once.

This is a good time to use the Arrange pop-up menu to sort these files into some semblance of order.

✔ **Documents (⇧+⌘+O):** You'll probably use this command often, as the Documents folder is a great place to save documents you create.

✔ **Desktop (⇧+⌘+D):** Use this command to display the Desktop folder, which contains the same icons as the Desktop you see behind open windows.

✔ **Downloads (Option+⌘+L):** This opens your Downloads folder, which is where files you download in Safari, save as attachments in Mail, or receive via AirDrop (explained shortly) are saved by default.

✔ **Home (⇧+⌘+H):** Use this command to have the Finder window display your Home folder (which is named with your short name).

✔ **Computer (⇧+⌘+C):** This command tells the Finder window to display the Computer level, showing Network and all your disks.

✔ **AirDrop (⇧+⌘+R):** AirDrop lets you share files wirelessly with anyone around you. There's no setup required and no special settings. Just click the AirDrop icon in the Finder sidebar, use this menu item, or use the keyboard shortcut, and your Mac automatically discovers other people nearby who are using AirDrop.

It's great as long as the others are also running Mac OS X Lion. Fortunately, that's the case at my house. Pre-Lion, when files needed to be shuffled between family Macs, I would usually take care of it from my Mac in the office. AirDrop makes file sharing easy enough that my wife and kids now transfer files all the time with no spousal or fatherly intervention required.

✔ **Network (⇧+⌘+K):** This command displays whatever is accessible on your network in the Finder window.

✔ **iDisk (⇧+⌘+I):** Use this submenu to mount your iDisk, another user's iDisk, or another user's iDisk Public Folder.

✔ **Applications (⇧+⌘+A):** This command displays your Applications folder, the usual storehouse for all the programs that came with your Mac (and the most likely place to find the programs you install).

✔ **Utilities (⇧+⌘+U):** This command gets you to the Utilities folder inside the Applications folder in one fell swoop. The Utilities folder is the repository of such useful items as Disk Utility (which lets you erase, format, verify, and repair disks) and Disk Copy (which you use to create and mount disk-image files). You find out more about these useful tools in Chapter 18.

✔ **Recent Folders:** Use this submenu to quickly go back to a folder that you recently visited. Every time you open a folder, Mac OS X creates an alias to it and stores it in the Recent Folders folder. You can open any of these aliases from the Recent Folders command on the Go menu.

✔ **Go to Folder (⇧+⌘+G):** This command summons the Go to Folder dialog, shown in Figure 5-16. Look at your Desktop. Maybe it's cluttered with lots of windows, or maybe it's completely empty. Either way, suppose you're several clicks away from a folder that you want to open. If you know the path from your hard drive to that folder, you can type the path to the folder in the Go to the Folder text box (separating folder names with forward slashes [/]) and then click Go to move (relatively) quickly to the folder you need.

The first character you type must also be a forward slash, as shown in Figure 5-16, unless you're going to a subfolder of the current window (bobl in Figure 5-16).

This particular dialog is a tad clairvoyant; it tries to guess which folder you mean by the first letter or two that you type. For example, in Figure 5-16, I typed the letter **A** and paused, and the window guessed that I wanted *Applications.* Then I pressed the right-arrow key to accept the guess and typed **U**, and the window guessed the rest *(tilities)* and filled it in for me.

✔ **Connect to Server (⌘+K):** If your Mac is connected to a network or to the Internet, use this command to reach those remote resources.

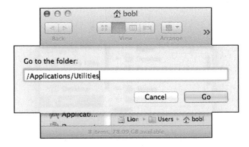

Figure 5-16: Go to a folder by typing its path.

Customizing Finder Windows

The Finder is outrageously handy. It not only gives you convenient access to multiple windows, but also offers ways to tweak what you see till you get what works best for you. So whereas earlier sections in this chapter explain what the Finder is and how it works, the following sections ask, "How would you like it to be?"

Adding folders to the Sidebar

Adding whatever folder you like to the Sidebar is easy. All you need to do is select the item you want to add and choose File⇨Add to Sidebar from the menu bar (or press ⌘+T). You can now reach the item by clicking it in any Finder window's Sidebar. And you can move files or folders into that folder by dragging them onto the Sidebar icon for the item.

To remove an item from the Sidebar, right- or Control-click the item and choose Remove from Sidebar. Or ⌘-click the item and drag it off the sidebar, as shown in Figure 5-17.

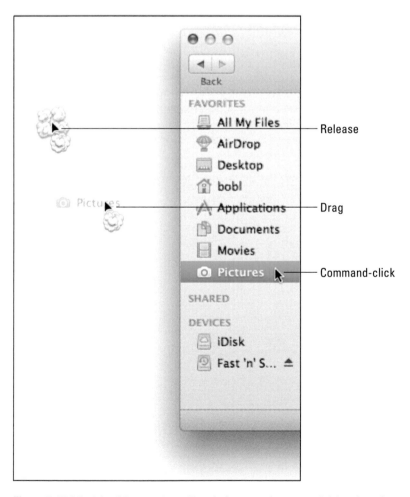

Figure 5-17: I find the "drag-and-poof" technique much more satisfying than the menu.

Setting Finder preferences

You can find Finder and Desktop preferences by choosing Finder➪Preferences. In the Finder Preferences window that appears, you find four panes: General, Labels, Sidebar, and Advanced, all of which are shown in Figure 5-18.

Figure 5-18: Set Finder preferences here.

In the General pane, you find the following options:

- ✔ **Show These Items on the Desktop check boxes:** Select or deselect these check boxes to choose whether icons for hard drives; external disks; CDs, DVDs, and iPods; and connected servers appear on the Desktop. Mac OS X Lion selects all four options by default (which mimics earlier versions of Mac OS). But if you don't want disk icons cluttering your beautiful Desktop, you have the option of deselecting (clearing) these check boxes. If they're deselected, you can still work with CDs, DVDs, and other types of disks. You just have to open a Finder window and select the one you want in the Sidebar.

✔ **New Finder Windows Open pop-up menu:** Here, you can choose whether opening a new Finder window displays All My Files (my favorite), your Home folder, the Documents folder, or other disk or folder. (All My Files is the default.)

✔ **Always Open Folders in a New Window check box:** Selecting this box spawns a new window each time you open a folder or disk. (Old-timers may recognize this behavior from Mac OS 9.)

Don't enable it and windows open "in place," which prevents window clutter. If you want a new window, press ⌘ before you double-click. This forces the folder to open in a new window. Between this feature and Column view, I rarely need more than two or three windows on-screen, and I get by most of the time with a single window in Column view.

✔ **Spring-loaded folders and windows:** This one's easier to do than to explain, so do this: Check the box to enable the feature and then drag any icon (except a disk icon) onto any folder or disk icon. When the folder or disk icon is highlighted, don't release the mouse button. After a delay (which you set via the Delay slider), the highlighted folder icon "springs" open. If you drag the item onto another folder now, that folder springs open. And so on. This continues until you release the mouse button, at which time the item you're dragging is dropped into whichever folder is open at the time. Notice that each time you drag the item onto a different folder the previous folder springs shut automatically. That's spring-loaded folders for you.

As long as the box is checked you can make folders spring open instantly by pressing the spacebar regardless of the delay you've specified with the Delay slider.

The Labels pane lets you rename the colored labels that appear in the File menu. The default names are the same as their color, but you can change them to anything you like by entering new labels in the text boxes. To demonstrate this, I changed the first item from its default name (Red) to *Urgent (Formerly Red)* in Figure 5-18.

To assign a label to any icon, select the icon, choose File⇨Label and then click one of the colored dots. The selected icon takes on that color. Why would you want to do that? Well, partly because colorized icons are festive, but mostly because you can then use the label as one of the criteria for searches, as described earlier in the chapter.

Here's an example: If you apply the red label to every file and folder associated with, say, Project X — all the folders, DOC files, PDF files, JPEG files, and so on — you can later search for items with the red label and see all these items at once, regardless of what folder they're stored in or what application created them.

That said, many users find labels useless and go years without ever applying a single label to a file or folder.

The Sidebar pane lets you choose which items are displayed in the Sidebar. Select the check box to display the item; deselect the check box to not display it.

The Advanced pane is just big enough to offer the following check boxes and a pop-up menu:

- ✔ The Show All Filename Extensions check box tells the Finder to display the little two-, three-, four-, or more-character filename suffixes (such as .doc in summary.doc) that make your Mac's file lists look more like those of a Windows or Linux user. The Finder hides those from you by default, but if you want to be able to see them in the Finder when you open or save files, you need to turn on this option.

- ✔ The Show Warning before Changing an Extension check box allows you to turn off the nagging dialog that appears if you attempt to change the two-, three-, four-, or more-character file extension.

- ✔ The Show Warning before Emptying the Trash check box (on by default) allows you to turn off the nagging dialog telling you how many items are in the Trash and asking whether you really want to delete them.

- ✔ The Empty Trash Securely check box makes Secure Empty Trash the default. The Secure Empty Trash feature overwrites deleted files with meaningless data so neither the files nor their contents can be recovered.

- ✔ The When Performing a Search pop-up menu lets you choose the default search location when you initiate a search as described earlier in this chapter. Your choices are Search This Mac, Search the Current Folder, and Use the Previous Search Scope (as shown in Figure 5-18).

Digging for Icon Data in the Info Window

Every icon has an Info window that gives you — big surprise! — information about that icon and enables you to choose which other users (if any) you want to have the privilege of using this icon. (I discuss sharing files and privileges in detail in Chapter 16.) The Info window is also where you lock an icon so that it can't be renamed or dragged to the Trash.

To see an icon's Info window, click the icon and choose File➪Get Info (or press ⌘+I). The Info window for that icon appears. Figure 5-19 shows the Info window for the QuickTime Player icon.

Figure 5-19: A typical Info window for an application (QuickTime Player, in this case).

Documents, folders, and disks each have slightly different Info windows. In this section, I give you highlights on the type of information and options that you can find.

The gray triangles reveal what information for an icon is available in this particular Info window. The sections that you see for most icons include the following:

- **Spotlight Comments:** Provides a field in which you can type your own comments about this icon for Spotlight to use in its searches. (I talk about this a little earlier in this chapter and discuss Spotlight searches in Chapter 7.)

- **General:** For information of the general kind, such as

  - *Kind:* What kind of file this is — an application, document, disk, folder, and so on

  - *Size:* How much hard drive space this file uses

  - *Where:* The path to the folder that contains this file

  - *Created:* The date and time that this file was created

  - *Modified:* The date and time that this file was last modified (that is, saved)

  - *Version:* Copyright information and the file's version number

  - *Label:* Choose or change the color label.

Five other check boxes may or may not appear in the General section of a particular Info window. Here's the scoop on this quintet of optional options:

- *Open in 32-bit mode* (check box): Most late-model Macs can take advantage of Lion's high-performance 64-bit processing mode. Some applications are designed to take advantage of Lion's faster 64-bit processing mode. But sometimes an application that should run in 64-bit mode doesn't work properly. If an application doesn't work properly — it often quits unexpectedly, freezes, or refuses to launch at all — try checking this box. It couldn't hurt.

- *Shared folder* (check box): Designates the folder as Shared, so other users are allowed to see and use its contents. You find out all about sharing in Chapter 16.

- *Stationery Pad* (check box): This one only appears in the Info window of document icons. If you select it, the file becomes a template. When you open a Stationery Pad document, a copy of its contents appear in a new Untitled document that you would typically save with a descriptive name.

- *Locked* (check box): If this box is checked, you receive a warning if you try to put the item in the Trash: "This item is locked. Do you want to move it to the Trash anyway?" Your options are Stop and Continue. If you continue, the item goes into the Trash as usual. Then, when you try to empty the Trash, you receive another warning: "There are some locked items in the Trash. Do you want to remove all the items, including the locked ones, or just the unlocked ones?" Your choices this time are Cancel, Remove Unlocked Items, and Remove All Items. If you choose to Remove All Items, the locked item(s) are deleted. If you choose Remove Unlocked Items, the locked item(s) remain in the Trash, and you receive the "There are some locked items" warning again the next time you try to empty it.

  To remove the locked item from the Trash, click the Trash icon in the Dock and then drag the locked item out of the Trash and into a folder or onto the Desktop.

✔ **More Info:** When the file was created, modified, and last opened (documents only).

✔ **Name & Extension:** Tells the full name, including the (possibly hidden) extension.

✔ **Preview:** When you select a document icon, the menu offers a Preview option that you use to see a glimpse of what's in that document. You can also see this preview when you select a document icon in Column view; it magically appears in the rightmost column. If you select a QuickTime movie or sound, you can play your selection right there in the preview pane without launching a separate application. Neat.

✔ **Sharing & Permissions:** Governs which users have access to this icon and how much access they are allowed. (See Chapter 16 for more about access privileges.)

If you press the Option key before you pull down the Finder's File menu, the Get Info command changes to Show Inspector (or ⌘+Option+I). The Inspector window looks and acts like a Get Info window for the most part, with one whopping exception: It displays info for the currently active window. Click a different window, and the inspector displays different info. Cool, eh?

And that's about it for icons, which are among the most fundamental parts of what makes your Mac a Mac (and not a toaster or an Xbox).

Part II
Lion Taming (Or "Organization for Smart People")

The 5th Wave   By Rich Tennant

AFTER INSTALLING OS X, NED AND LORETTA SELECT THE COMPUTER'S BACKGROUND

"Oh – I like this background much better than the basement."

In this part . . .

Peruse the chapters in this part to discover how to organize just about everything on your Lion. Don't get all worked up — this stuff is easy. In fact, I think of this part as "The Lazy Person's Guide to Getting and Staying Organized."

I start by showing you more about the all-important Finder, and then move on to the two most important skills of all: saving and opening files. You'll then spend a bit of time with Lion's impressive timesaving tools and discover the joys of dealing with disks (and discs) — a good thing to know indeed! Next is a short discourse on using your calendars to stay organized and other important information, all without tearing your hair out.

It might sound imposing, but I assure you this part is (mostly) painless.

6

The Care and Feeding of Files and Folders

In This Chapter

▷ Checking out the Mac OS X folder structure

▷ Getting (and staying) organized

▷ Opening icons

▷ Saving your document before it's too late

T his could be the most important chapter in this book. If you don't understand how to open and save files by using the Open dialog and Save sheets or how to use the file and folder system, you'll have a heck of a time getting the hang of your Mac. Ask any longtime Mac user; the old lament is pretty common: "Well, I saved the file, but now I don't know where it went." It happens all the time with new users; if they don't master these essential techniques, they often become confused about where files are located on their hard drives.

This chapter is a tonic for finding the file or folder you want. Knowing where your files are is something every Mac user should grok. Hang with me and pay attention; everything will soon become crystal-clear.

All My Files (in the Sidebar) is a fast and easy way to find a file or folder (although the sheer number of files it displays may overwhelm you, no matter how you sort or arrange them). And Chapter 7 is chock-full of tools and tips for finding files and folders when you misplace them. Furthermore, although you can often find files or folders by using Spotlight, you have to remember enough details about the file or its contents for Spotlight to find it.

At the end of the day, all the aforementioned techniques are useful and good to know, but take it from me: It's often faster and easier if you know exactly where a file or folder is than to hunt for it.

Later in the chapter, I look at using Open dialogs and Save sheets within applications to find files and folders. You see them only *after* you launch a program and use that program's File menu to open or save a file. (For more on launching applications, read the parts of Chapter 5 about icons; for more on creating and opening documents, see the documentation or help file for the program that you're using.)

Don't forget there's a Spotlight search field in Open dialogs and Save sheets.

Understanding the Mac OS X Folder Structure

Start by looking at the folder structure of a typical Mac OS X installation. Open a Finder window, and click the icon for your hard drive (which is typically called Macintosh HD) in the Sidebar. You should now see at least four folders: Applications, Library, System, and Users.

Within the User folder, each user with an account on this Mac has his own set of folders containing documents, preferences, and other information that belongs to that user and account.

If you're the sole person who accesses your Mac, you probably have only one user. Regardless, the folder structure that Mac OS X uses is the same whether you have one user or dozens.

Within the Users folder, you find your personal Home folder and a Shared folder, where you can put files you want to share with other users.

All these files are stored in a nested folder structure that's a bit tricky to understand at first. This structure makes more sense after you spend a little time with it and figure out some basic concepts.

If you display the path bar at the bottom of your windows by choosing View➪Show Path Bar, it'll start to make sense much sooner.

If you take a look at Figure 6-1, you can see how these main folders are related to one another. In the sections that follow, you take a look at each of these folders in more depth and find out more about what's nested inside each one.

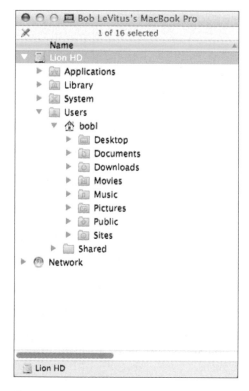

Figure 6-1: A bird's-eye view of key folders on your Mac and their structure.

Understanding nested folders

Folders within other folders are often called *nested folders*. To get a feel for the way nested folders work in Mac OS X, check out Figure 6-2. You can see the following from the figure:

- The Desktop is the top-level folder in this example; all the other folders and files you see reside within the Desktop folder.

- Folder 1 is inside the Desktop folder, which is one level deep.

- Folder 2 is inside Folder 1, which is one level deeper than Folder 1, or two levels deep.

- Folder 3 is inside Folder 2 and is three levels deep.

- The two files inside Folder 3 are four levels deep.

Folder two: Two levels deep

Folder on Desktop: One level deep | Folder three: Three levels deep

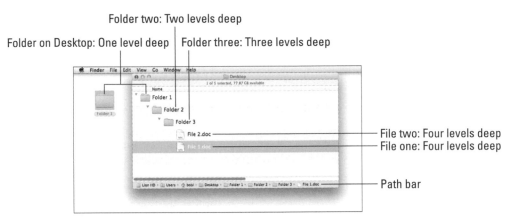

File two: Four levels deep
File one: Four levels deep

Path bar

Figure 6-2: Nested folders, going four levels deep.

If the preceding list makes sense to you, you're golden. What's important here is that you're able to visualize the path to Folder 3. That is, to get to files inside Folder 3, you open Folder 1 and then open Folder 2 to be able to open Folder 3. Understanding this concept is important to understanding the relationships between files and folders. Keep reviewing this section, and eventually, the concept will click. You'll slap yourself in the head and say, "Now I get it!"

From the top: The Computer folder

I start with the Computer folder, which is the top level of the folder hierarchy. The Computer folder shows all the storage devices (hard drives, CD- or DVD-ROM, USB flash drive, and so forth) that are currently connected to your Mac. The following steps show how you can start at the Computer folder and drill down through the folder structure:

1. **To find the Computer folder, choose Go⇨Computer or press ⇧⌘+C.**

   In Figure 6-1, the Computer folder is called Bob LeVitus's MacBook Pro, and it contains a hard-drive icon (Lion HD) and a Network icon, with which you can access servers or other computers on your local network. (If that seems mysterious, read Chapter 16 for the whole scoop on sharing files with other Macs and sharing your Mac with other users.)

   If you don't see a Computer icon in your Sidebar, choose Finder⇨ Preferences, click the Sidebar icon at the top, and then select the Computer check box. You can change the computer name (Bob LeVitus's MacBook Pro in Figure 6-1) in the Sharing System Preferences pane, which you can access by launching the System Preferences application (from the Applications folder, the Dock, or the menu) and then clicking the Sharing icon.

You might have more or fewer icons in your Computer folder than you see in Figure 6-1 (depending on how many disks you have mounted).

2. **Double-click the icon that holds your Mac OS X stuff.**

    (Technically, this drive is called your boot drive.) In Figure 6-1, that hard drive is called Lion HD. I have no idea what yours is called, of course; if you haven't changed it, it's probably called Macintosh HD.

3. **Check out the folders you find there.**

    You should see at least four folders (unless you've added some; if you installed the Xcode programming tools, for example, you have more). In the next few sections, I walk you through what you can find in each one.

Peeking into the Applications folder

The Applications folder, located at the root level of your boot drive (the one with OS X installed on it), is accessible by clicking the Applications icon in the Sidebar, by choosing it the Go menu, or by pressing ⇧+⌘+A. In this folder, you find applications and utilities that Apple includes with Mac OS X. Most users of a given Mac have access to all the items in the Applications folder, with the exception of managed accounts or accounts with Parental Controls, as discussed in Chapter 16.

Finding fonts (and more) in the public Library folder

The Library folder, at the root level of your Mac OS X hard drive, is like a public library; it stores items available to everyone who logs into an account on this Mac. You can find three Library folders on your hard drive: the one at the root level of your OS X disk, a second inside the root-level System folder, and a third in your Home folder.

What's that you say? You don't see a Library folder inside your Home folder? Well it's like this: In earlier versions of Mac OS X, you would have seen a folder named Library between the Downloads and Movies folders in your Home folder (or mine — bobl — in Figure 6-1).

But that was then, and this is now. In Mac OS X Lion, the Home Library folder is hidden from view to protect you from yourself. You'll discover the secret to making it visible if you need it in the "Your personal Library card" section of this chapter, which is coming up.

Leave the /System/Library **folder alone.** Don't move, remove, or rename it, or do anything within it. It's the nerve center of your Mac. In other words, you should never have to touch this third Library folder.

You find a bunch of folders inside the Library folder at root level (the public Library folder). Most of them contain files that you never need to open, move, or delete.

By and large, the public Library subfolder that gets the most use is the Fonts folder, which houses many of the fonts installed on the Mac. For the most part, fonts can be made available in one of two ways:

- ✓ **To everyone who uses the Mac:** If that's the case, they're stored here in the Fonts folder.

- ✓ **To a single user:** In this case, you place the fonts in the user's Library folder (the one in the user's Home folder).

I discuss fonts more in Chapter 14. Meanwhile, some other public Library subfolders that you might use or add to are the iMovie, iTunes, iPhoto, and iDVD folders (where you put plug-ins for those programs); the Scripts folder (which houses AppleScripts accessible to all users); and the Desktop Pictures folder (where you can place pictures to be used as Desktop backgrounds).

Leave the "public" Library folder pretty much alone unless you're using the Fonts folder or know what you're adding to one of the other folders. Don't remove, rename, or move any files or folders. Mac OS X uses these items and is very picky about where they're kept and how they're named. While I'm on the subject, it's also a good idea not to remove, rename, or move applications installed by Lion in the Applications folder.

Note: Under most circumstances, you won't actually add items to or remove items from folders in this Library yourself. Software installers usually do the heavy lifting for you by placing all their little pieces in the appropriate Library folders. You shouldn't need to touch this Library often, if ever. That said, knowing what these folders are — and who can access their contents — might come in handy down the road a piece.

The locations of the three libraries are illustrated in Figure 6-3.

If your Mac is set up for multiple users, only users with administrator (admin) privileges can put stuff in the public (root-level) Library folder. (For more information on admin privileges, check out Chapter 16.)

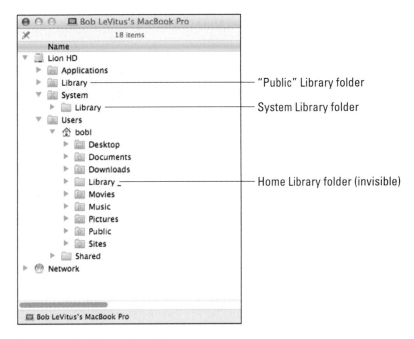

Figure 6-3: A guide to which Library is which.

Let it be: The System folder

The System folder contains the files that Mac OS X needs to start up and keep working.

Leave this folder alone. Don't move, remove, or rename it or anything within it. It's part of the nerve center of your Mac.

The usability of the Users folder

When you open the Users folder, you see a folder for each person who has a user account on the Mac, as well as the Shared folder.

The Shared folder that you see in the Users folder allows everyone who uses the Mac to use the files stored there. If you want other people who use your Mac to have access to a file or folder, the Shared folder is the proper place to stash it. You can see my Shared folder right below my Home folder (bobl) in Figure 6-1, earlier in this chapter.

I realize that a lot of people don't share their Macs with others, and if you're one of these folks, you may wonder why I keep mentioning sharing and multiple users and the like. Well, Mac OS X is based on the Unix operating system — a multiuser operating system used on high-end servers and workstations that are often shared by several people. Mac OS X has both the benefit of this arrangement and a bit of the confusion caused when a single user (could it be you?) fires up a computer that *could* be set up for several people. That's why Mac OS X folders are organized the way they are — with different hierarchies for each user and for the computer as a whole.

There's no place like Home

From the Users folder, you can drill down into the Home folder to see what's inside. When the user logs on to this Mac, his Home folder appears whenever he clicks the Home icon in the Sidebar, chooses Go⇨Home, or uses the keyboard shortcut ⇧+⌘+H.

Your Home folder is the most important folder to you as a user — or at least the one where you stash most of your files. I strongly recommend that you store all the files you create in subfolders within your Home folder — preferably, in subfolders in your Home/Documents folder. The advantage of doing so is that your Home/Documents folder is easy to find, and many programs use it as the default folder for opening or saving a file.

When you open your Home folder, you see a Finder window with a little house icon and your short username in the title bar. Seeing your short username in the title bar tells you that you're in *your* Home folder. Every user has a Home folder named after his or her short username (as specified in the Users & Groups System Preferences pane). Figure 6-4 shows that my Home folder is named bobl — the short name I used when I first set up my Mac.

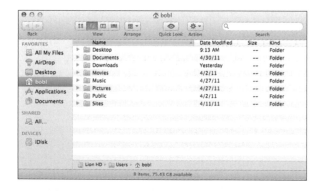

Figure 6-4: My Home folder.

If your Mac has more than one user, you can see the other users' Home folders in your Users folder, but Mac OS X prevents you from opening files from or saving files to them.

By default, your Home folder has several folders inside it created by Mac OS X. The following four are the most important:

- ✔ **Desktop:** If you put items (files, folders, applications, or aliases) on the Desktop, they're actually stored in the Desktop folder.

- ✔ **Documents:** This is the place to put all the documents (letters, spreadsheets, recipes, and novels) that you create.

- ✔ **Library:** Preferences (files containing the settings you create in System Preferences and other places) are stored in the Library folder, along with fonts that are available only to you (as described earlier in this chapter) and other stuff that you — and only you — expect to use. This folder is hidden, by default, in Lion, but I show you how to deal with that later in this chapter.

- ✔ **Public:** If others on your local area network use file sharing to connect with your Mac, they can't see or use the files or folders in your Home folder, but they can share files you've stored in your Home folder's Public folder. (Read more about file sharing and Public folders in Chapter 16.)

You can create more folders, if you like. In fact, every folder that you *ever* create (at least every one you create on this particular hard drive or volume) *should* be within your Home folder. I explain more about creating folders and subfolders and organizing your stuff inside them later in this chapter.

The following are a few more tidbits to keep in mind as you dig around your Home folder:

- ✔ If you decide that you don't want an item on the Desktop anymore, delete it by dragging its icon from the Desktop folder to the Trash or by dragging its icon from the Desktop itself to the Trash. Both techniques yield the same effect: The file is in the Trash, where it remains until you empty the Trash. Or if you don't want it on the Desktop anymore but don't want to get rid of it either, you can drag it from the Desktop into any other folder you like.

- ✔ The other five folders that you should see in your Home folder are Downloads, Movies, Music, Pictures, and Sites. All these folders except Sites are empty until you (or a program like iTunes, iPhoto, or iMovie that creates files inside these folders automatically the first time you launch them) put something in these folders. The Sites folder contains a few files that your Mac needs if you enable Web Sharing in the Sharing System Preferences pane, as I describe in Chapter 16.

Your personal Library card

The invisible Library subfolder of your Home folder is the repository of everything that Mac OS X needs to customize *your* Mac to *your* tastes. If you want to add something to a Library folder, it's usually best to add it to your Home/Library folder. You won't spend much time (if any) adding things to the Library folder or moving them around within it, and that's probably why it's now hidden from sight. Still, I think it's a good idea for you to know what's in your Home/Library.

In the "Finding fonts (and more) in the public Library folder" section, earlier in this chapter, I discuss the Library folder that's used to specify preferences for the Mac as a whole. But *this* Library folder is all about you and your stuff.

Be cautious with all Library folders. Mac OS X is very persnickety about how the folders and files within it are organized. As I discuss earlier in the chapter, you can add items to and remove items safely from most Public or Home Library folders, but *leave the folders themselves alone.* If you remove or rename the wrong folder, you could render OS X inoperable. It's like the old joke about the guy who said to the doctor, "It hurts when I do that," and the doctor replies, "Then don't do that."

To find your hidden Home/Library folder, do this:

1. **Hold down the Option key on your keyboard.**

2. **Click the Go menu.**

   The (formerly) invisible Library folder appears in the Go menu as long as the Option key is pressed, as shown in Figure 6-5.

3. **Select Library, and release the mouse button.**

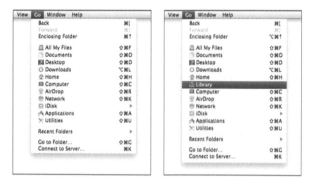

Figure 6-5: A normal Go menu (left) and a Go menu with the Option key pressed (right).

You should see several folders in the Home/Library folder; the exact number depends on the software that you install on your Mac. You probably have folders called Mail, Safari, Logs, and Preferences, for example.

Some of the most important standard folders in the Library folder include the following:

- ⌐ **Application Support:** Some applications store their support files here; others store theirs in the main (root-level) public Library folder.

- ⌐ **Fonts:** This folder is empty until you install your own fonts here. The fonts that come with Mac OS X aren't stored here, but in the Library folder at root level for everyone who uses this Mac. I discuss this topic earlier in this chapter. If you want to install fonts so that only you have access to them, put them in the Fonts folder in *your* Library folder.

  The easiest way to install a font is to double-click its icon and let Lion's Font Book utility handle it for you, as described in Chapter 14. But I'd be remiss if I didn't also mention how to install a font manually:

  - • *To install a font that only you can use:* Drag the font file's icon to the Fonts folder in your Home/Library. The font is available only to this user account (because other users can't use fonts stored in *your* Home/Library folder).

  - • *To install a font for all users of this Mac:* Drag the font file's icon into the Fonts folder in the public Library folder — the one at root level that you see when you open your hard drive's icon.

- ⌐ **Preferences:** The files here hold the information about whichever things you customize in Mac OS X or in the applications you run. Whenever you change a system or application preference, that info is saved to a file in the Preferences folder.

  Don't mess with the Preferences folder! You should never need to open or use this folder unless something bad happens — if, for example, you suspect that a particular preferences file has become *corrupted* (that is, damaged). My advice is to just forget that you know about this folder and let it do its job. In fact, let me take it a step further and say, "Don't mess with *any* of the folders inside your Home/Library folder unless you have a darn good reason." If you don't know why you're doing something to a folder (other than the Fonts folder) in your Home/Library, *don't do it.*

There must be some good reasons why Apple decided to hide the Home/Library folder in Mac OS X Lion, and I'm sure that one of them is to keep you from accidentally screwing something up.

Saving Your Document Before It's Too Late

If you have a feel for the Mac OS X folder structure, you can get down to the important stuff — namely, how to save documents and where to save them. You can create as many documents as you want, using one program or dozens of 'em, but all could be lost if you don't save the files (or versions of the files) to a storage device such as your hard drive or other disk.

When you *save* a file, you're committing a copy to a disk — whether it's a disk connected directly to your Mac, one available over a network, or a removable disk such as a USB flash drive or portable hard disk.

Lion introduces three new features — Resume, Auto Save, and Versions — to make your life easier.

In previous versions of Mac OS X, applications generally showed a blank page or nothing at all when you launched them. Lion's cool new Resume feature automatically reopens all windows on-screen when you Quit an app. Then, when you launch the app again, all the windows are reopened in the same position on-screen as when you Quit. Best of all, Resume seems to work with most third-party apps.

Programs have offered Auto Save before, but now it's baked into Mac OS X Lion. Auto Save automatically saves your work as you work, when you pause, and every 5 minutes whether you need it or not.

For as long as we've had Macs, we've saved unique versions of our files, creating and managing them with the Save As command or by duplicating and renaming them in the Finder. Now Lion takes care of version control for you by automatically saving versions as described in the preceding paragraphs.

That's the good news, but there's also bad news. . . .

Although Auto Save and Versions are baked right into Mac OS X, third-party apps require a software update before they can take advantage of these features. So please don't get too comfortable with Auto Save and Versions until you're sure that your applications take advantage of these features.

In these sections, I show you how to save your masterpieces. Prevent unnecessary pain in your life by developing good saving habits. I recommend that you save your work (or save a version in apps that support versions)

- Every few minutes
- Before you switch to another program

  ✓ Before you print a document

  ✓ Before you stand up

The keyboard shortcut for Save or Save a Version in almost every Mac program is ⌘+S. Memorize it. See it in your dreams. Train your finger muscles to do it unconsciously. Use it (the keyboard shortcut) or lose it (your unsaved work).

If you don't heed this advice — and the program that you're using crashes while switching programs, printing, or sitting idle (the three likeliest times for a crash) — you may lose everything you did since your last save or saved version. The fact that a program crash doesn't bring down the entire system or force a restart is small consolation when you've lost everything you've typed, drawn, copied, pasted, or whatever since the last time you saved or saved a version.

Stepping through a basic Save or Save a Version

This section walks you through the steps you'll use the first time you save a document. The process is the same whether your app supports Auto Save and Versions or not. It's only after the initial save that Auto Save and Versions come into play.

In a few sections of this book, I ask you not only to read the instructions while sitting in front of your Mac, but also to perform each step of the instructions as described. This section is one of them. If you read it and follow along, I can pretty much guarantee that it'll make sense. If you read it somewhere other than at your Mac, it could be a mite confusing.

Saving a file works pretty much the same way in any application you use to create documents. For this example, I use Mac OS X's word processing application, TextEdit, but the process would be very similar in Microsoft Word, Adobe Photoshop, Apple Keynote, or any other application.

If you're going to follow along as I recommend, please launch the TextEdit program now (it's in your Applications folder), and type a few words on the Untitled page that appears after you launch it.

Now that we're both on the same page, both literally and figuratively, here's how saving a file works:

When you choose to save a file for the first time (by choosing File➪Save or pressing ⌘+S), a Save sheet appears in front of the document that you're saving, as shown in Figure 6-6. I call this a *basic* Save sheet (as opposed to an *expanded* Save sheet, which I get to in a moment):

1. **In the Save As field, type a name for your file.**

   When a Save sheet appears for the first time, the Save As field is active and displays the name of the document. The document name (usually, Untitled) is selected; when you begin typing, the name disappears and is replaced by the name you type.

2. **If the Where pop-up menu lists the location where you want to save your file, choose that location, and proceed to Step 5; if not, click the disclosure button (the one with the little triangle to the right of the word *Untitled* in Figure 6-6).**

   You can choose any folder or volume listed in a Finder window's Sidebar by clicking a basic Save sheet's Where pop-up menu and taking your pick. Or if you click the disclosure button, the sheet expands so that you can navigate folders just as you would in the Finder: by opening them to see their contents.

Disclosure triangle

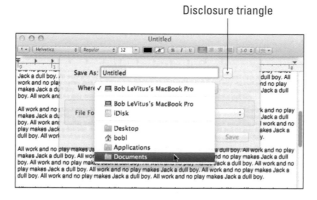

Figure 6-6: A basic Save sheet looks a lot like this.

In a basic Save sheet, the Where pop-up menu acts as a shortcut to the Documents, Desktop, Applications, Home (bobl), iDisk, and Computer (Bob LeVitus's MacBook Pro) folders, as shown in Figure 6-6.

If you switch to expanded view by clicking the disclosure button, the Where pop-up menu shows the path to the folder the file will be saved into (Documents in Figure 6-6 and Figure 6-7).

I think that the Where menu should be the same in both basic and expanded Save sheets, as it was before Mac OS X 10.5 Leopard. It seems more confusing to have the contents of this menu change based on whether the Save sheet is expanded or not.

Figure 6-7: An expanded Save sheet looks similar to these (list view top left, column view top right, icon view bottom left, and Cover Flow view bottom right).

Switch between the basic and expanded Save sheets a few times by clicking the disclosure button. Make sure that you see and understand the difference between what you see in the Where menu in a basic Save sheet and what you see in the Where menu in an expanded Save sheet.

3. **To begin navigating the expanded Save sheet to find the folder where you want to save your file, choose among views by clicking the Icon, List, Column, or Cover Flow view button.**

(The buttons look like their counterparts in Finder windows.)

Click and hold the Icon view button, and Icon Size and Label Position menus appear; use these menus to choose size and label position for icons in Save sheets using Icon view. Your choices remain in effect in icon view in the Save sheets of all applications until you click and hold the Icon view button to change them again.

In icon view, you double-click a folder to open it. List view offers disclosure triangles (as you see in list-view Finder windows), so single-click the disclosure triangles of folders to see their contents. In column view, you click an item on the left to see its contents on the right, just as you do in a column-view Finder window.

You can also use the Forward and Back buttons or the Sidebar, both available only in an expanded Save dialog, to conveniently navigate your disk. Many of these navigation aids work just like the ones in the Finder; flip back to Chapter 5 for more details.

You can enlarge the Save sheet to see more the same way you enlarge a Finder window: Drag an edge or corner of the sheet.

If you can't find the folder in which you want to save your document, type the folder's name in the Search box. It works just like the Search box in a Finder window, as shown in Chapter 5. You don't even have to press Enter or Return; the Save sheet updates itself to show you only items that match the characters as you've typed them.

4. **Select the folder where you want to save your file in the Where pop-up menu.**

5. **If you want to create a new subfolder of the selected folder to save your file in, click the New Folder button, give the new folder a name, and then save your file in it.**

In Figure 6-8, I've selected an existing folder named Novels. You can tell that it's selected because its name is displayed in the Where menu and highlighted below that in the first column.

The selected folder is where your file will be saved.

Figure 6-8: Saving a file in the Novels folder (which is in the Documents folder).

The keyboard shortcut for New Folder is ⇧+⌘+N regardless of whether you're in a Save sheet or the Finder. If I wanted to create a new folder inside the Novels folder in Figure 6-8, I could have clicked the New Folder button or pressed the shortcut.

6. **In the File Format pop-up menu, make sure the format selected is the one you want.**

7. **If you want to turn off the display of file extensions (such as** .rtf, .pdf, **and** .txt) **in Save sheets, select the Hide Extension check box.**

8. **Double-check the Where pop-up menu one last time to make sure that the correct folder is selected; then click the Save button to save the file to the active folder.**

    If you click Save, the file appears in the folder you selected. If you change your mind about saving this file, clicking Cancel dismisses the Save sheet without saving anything anywhere. In other words, the Cancel button returns things to the way they were before you displayed the Save sheet.

After you've saved a file for the first time, choosing File⇨Save, File⇨Save a Version, or pressing ⌘+S won't bring up a Save sheet. Instead, what happens next depends on whether the app supports Lion's Auto Save and Versions.

If the app doesn't, the command is called Save, without the words *a Version* appended. This command (or its shortcut, ⌘+S) resaves your document in the same location and with the same name without any further effort on your part. If you want to save a unique version, choose the Save As command, and save the file under a new name.

If the app does support Auto Save and Versions, the upcoming section "Versions could be the new Save As" shows those features in action.

When you use apps that don't support Auto Save and Versions, I beg you to get into the habit of pressing ⌘+S often. It can't hurt — and just might save your bacon someday.

One last thing: In Figures 6-6, 6-7, and 6-8, I used the Save sheet for TextEdit as an example. In programs other than TextEdit, the Save sheet might contain additional options, fewer options, or different options and therefore might look slightly different. The File Format menu, for example, is a feature specific to TextEdit; it might not appear in other applications' Save sheets. Don't worry. The Save sheet always *works* the same way, no matter what options it offers.

Versions could be the new Save As

Apps that support Auto Save and Versions have the Save a Version command on the File menu; programs that don't support Auto Save and Versions have the Save As command instead.

Save As resaves a file that has already been saved by giving it a different name. Before Lion's Auto Save and Versions, you used Save As if you needed to create a different version of a document. Why would you want to do that? Here's a good (albeit kind of rude) example:

Tabbing around the Save or Save As sheet

In the expanded view, if you press the Tab key while the Save As field is active, it becomes inactive, and the Search box becomes active. Press Tab again, and the Sidebar becomes active. Press the Tab key one more time, and the file list box (more accurately known as the *detail pane*—the part with Icon, List, Column, or Cover Flow view buttons in it) becomes active. That's because the file list box, the Search box, the Sidebar, and the Save As field are mutually exclusive. Only one can be active at any time.

You can always tell which item is active by the thin blue or gray border around it.

When you want to switch to a different folder to save a file, click the folder in the Sidebar or click anywhere in the file list box to make the file list active.

The following tricks help you get a hold on this whole active/inactive silliness:

- Look for the thin blue border around elements on the sheet or a blue highlighted Sidebar item. This border indicates which part of the Save sheet is active.

- If you type while the file list box is active, the list box selects the folder that most closely matches the letter(s) that you type.

It's a little strange because you won't see what you type: You'll be typing blind, so to speak. Go ahead and give it a try.

- When the file list is active, the letters that you type don't appear in the Save As field. If you want to type a filename, you have to activate the Save As field again (by clicking in it or using the Tab key) before you can type in it.

- If you type while the Sidebar is active, nothing happens. You can, however, use the up- and down-arrow keys to move around in the Sidebar.

- Regardless of which box or field is active at the time, when you press the Tab key, the next in sequence becomes active.

- Pressing Shift reverses the order of the sequence. If you press Shift+Tab, the active item moves from the Save As field to the file list box to the Sidebar to the Search box and back to the Save As field again.

If you don't feel like pressing the Tab key, you can achieve the same effect by clicking the file list box, the Sidebar, or the Save As field to make it active.

Suppose that you have two cousins, Kate and Nancy. You write Kate a long, chatty letter, and save this document with the name `Letter to Kate`. At some point afterward, you decide that you want to send almost the same letter to Nancy, but you want to change a few things. So you change the part about your date last night (Nancy isn't as liberated as Kate) and replace all references to Kate's husband, Kevin, with references to Nancy's husband, Norman. (Aren't computers grand?)

So you make all these changes in Letter to Kate, but you haven't saved this document yet, and although the document on your screen is actually a letter to Nancy, its filename is still Letter to Kate. Think of what would happen if you were to save it now without using the Save As feature: Letter to Kate reflects the changes that you just made. (The stuff in the letter meant for Kate is blown away, replaced by the stuff that you just wrote to Nancy.) Thus, the filename Letter to Kate is inaccurate. Even worse, you might no longer have a copy of the original letter you sent to Kate!

The solution? Just use Save As to rename this file Letter to Nancy by choosing File⇨Save As. A Save sheet appears, in which you can type a different filename in the Save As field. You can also navigate to another folder, if you like, and save the newly named version of the file there.

Now you have two distinct files: Letter to Kate and Letter to Nancy. Both contain the stuff they should, but both started life from the same file. *That's* what Save As is for.

Now that you understand what Save As is for, here's an easier way: Before you start, duplicate the document (choose File⇨Duplicate or ⌘+D). Rename the copy, and open it. This way, when you're done making changes, you don't have to remember to choose Save As; you can just perform your habitual Save. This approach also protects you from accidentally saving part of the letter to Nancy without changing the file's name first (which you're likely to do if you're following my advice about saving often). So when you decide that you're going to reuse a document, Save As *before* you begin working on it, just to be safe.

Versions give you the benefits of Save As without any action on your part, but only a handful of programs supported Auto Save and Versions at press time.

You'll probably be using the Save As technique for quite some time with many (if not most) apps, but I'd be remiss if I glossed over Lion's new way of doing things. In Lion, a snapshot called a Version is saved automatically as you work, when you pause, every 5 minutes, and when you choose File⇨Save a Version (⌘+S).

Click the triangle to the right of the title of a document to see various things you can do with Versions, as shown in Figure 6-9.

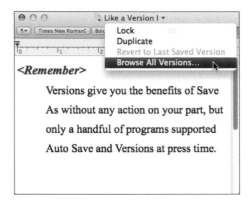

Figure 6-9: Click the triangle to the right of the document's title to see this menu of options for Versions.

Open Sez Me

You can open any icon in the Finder — whether it's a file or a folder — in at least six ways. (Okay, there are at least *seven* ways, but one of them belongs to aliases, which I discuss in great detail back in Chapter 5.) Anyway, here are the ways:

- ✔ Click the icon once to select it and then choose File➪Open.
- ✔ Click the icon twice in rapid succession.

   If the icon doesn't open, you double-clicked too slowly. You can test (and adjust) your mouse's sensitivity to double-click speed in the Mouse (or Trackpad) System Preferences pane, which you can access by launching the System Preferences application (from the Applications folder, the Dock, or the menu) and then clicking the Mouse (or Trackpad) icon.

- ✔ Select the icon and then press either ⌘+O or ⌘+↓.
- ✔ Right-click or Control-click it and then choose Open from the contextual menu.
- ✔ If the icon is a document, drag it onto the application icon (or the Dock icon of an application) that can open that type of document.
- ✔ If the icon is a document, right-click or Control-click it and then choose an application from the Open With submenu of the contextual menu.

You can also open any document icon from within an application, of course. Here's how that works:

1. **Just launch your favorite program, and choose File⇨Open (or press ⌘+O, which works in most Mac programs).**

   An Open dialog appears, like the one shown in Figure 6-10.

Figure 6-10: The Open dialog using column view.

When you use a program's Open dialog, only files that the program knows how to open appear enabled (in black rather than light gray) in the file list. In effect, the program filters out the files it can't open, so you barely see them in the Open dialog. This method of selectively displaying certain items in Open dialogs is a feature of most applications. Therefore, when you're using TextEdit, its Open dialog dims all your spreadsheet files (because TextEdit can open only text, Rich Text Format, Microsoft Word, and some picture files). Pretty neat, eh?

2. **In the dialog, simply navigate to the file you want to open (using the same techniques you use in a Save sheet).**

   Click All My Files in the Sidebar or use Spotlight if you can't remember where the file resides.

3. **Select your file, and click the Open button.**

For what it's worth, some applications allow you to select multiple files in their Open dialogs by holding down either Shift (for contiguous selections) or ⌘ (for noncontiguous selections). If you need to open several files, it's worth a try; the worst thing that could happen is that it won't work and you'll have to open the items one at a time.

Some programs, including Microsoft Word and Adobe Photoshop, have a Show or Format menu in their Open dialogs. This menu lets you specify the type(s) of files you want to see in the Open dialog. You can often open a file that appears dimmed by choosing All Documents from the Show or Format menu (in those applications with Open dialogs that offer such a menu).

Mac OS X also offers a few tricks that help you find files you want to open, as well as decide what application opens a file. Check out the following sections for more tips, tricks, and troubleshooting help.

With a Quick Look

The Quick Look command displays the contents of the selected file in a floating window without launching an application, as shown in Figure 6-11. This feature can be handy if you want to peek at the contents of a file before you open it to make sure that you have the right one. Simply select the file and then choose File⇨Quick Look, press ⌘+Y, or (easiest of all) merely press the spacebar.

The bad news is that while Quick Look works with many types of files — Microsoft Office, Apple iWork, plain-text, PDF, TIFF, GIF, JPEG, PNG, and most types of audio and video — it doesn't work with *all* files. You'll know it didn't work if Quick Look shows you a big document icon instead of the contents of that file.

Previous

Next

Grow (zoom) window | Slide show (index sheet)

Close Quick Look window

Open with default app (Preview)

Full Screen

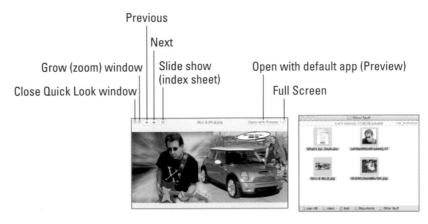

Figure 6-11: The Quick Look window showing the contents of the Mini & Me.jj.jpg file.

To get the window to occupy the entire screen (Slideshow mode), do any of the following:

✔ Hold down Option, and choose File➪Slideshow.

✔ Press ⌘+Option+Y.

✔ If your file is already open in the Quick Look window, click the double-diagonal-arrow button at the bottom of the window.

In Slideshow (full-screen) mode, press Esc to return to the Quick Look window.

If you select multiple items before you invoke Quick Look, as I've done in Figure 6-11, a pair of slideshow icons appears at the top of the Quick Look window (shown in the margin) so that you can view all the selected items at the same time as *index sheets,* as shown in Figure 6-12.

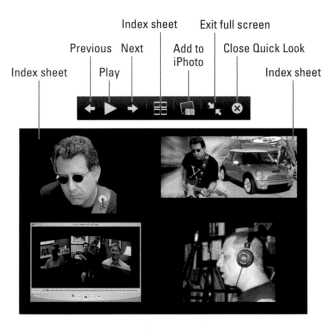

Figure 6-12: The slide show controls that appear in full screen mode (top) and four files in a Quick Look index sheet (bottom).

When you're finished with Quick Look window, click the X button in the top-left corner (refer to Figure 6-11); if you're in full screen mode, click the X button in the slide show control bar, as shown in Figure 6-12; or press ⌘+Y, which works in either mode.

With drag-and-drop

Macintosh drag-and-drop is usually all about dragging text and graphics from one place to another. But there's another angle to drag-and-drop — one that has to do with files and icons.

You can open a document by dragging its icon onto that of the proper application. You can open a document created with Microsoft Word, for example, by dragging the document icon onto the Microsoft Word application's icon. The Word icon highlights, and the document launches. Usually, of course, it's easier to double-click a document's icon to open it; the proper application opens automatically when you do — or at least, it does most of the time. Which reminds me . . .

When your Mac can't open a file

If you try to open a file, but Mac OS X can't find a program to open that file, Mac OS X prompts you with an alert window. I tried to open a very old (1993) Microsoft Word file — a file so old that most of you won't recognize the original file extension for Word documents (`.wrd`) — as shown in Figure 6-13.

There is no application set to open the document "PowerBooks For Dummies.wrd".

Search the App Store for an application that can open this document, or choose an existing application on your computer.

Choose Application...   Cancel   Search App Store

Figure 6-13: Oops! Mac OS X helps you find the correct application.

Click Cancel to abort the attempt to open the file, or click the Choose Application or Search App Store button to select another application to open this file.

If you click the Choose Application button, a dialog appears (conveniently opened to your Applications folder and shown in Figure 6-14). Applications that Mac OS X doesn't think can be used to open the file are dimmed. For a wider choice of applications, choose All Applications (instead of Recommended Applications) from the Enable pop-up menu.

Lion is the first version of Mac OS X that runs in 64-bit mode by default on Intel processors that support 64-bit processing. What that means is that your Mac can theoretically process data in bigger chunks than an older 32-bit processor. (The *actual* difference in performance between 64-bit and 32-bit processors is, for a variety of reasons, much less than two times.)

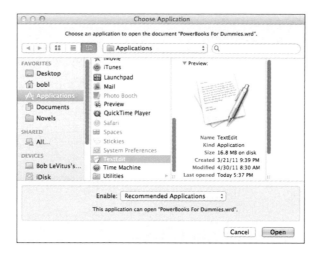

Figure 6-14: Choosing an application to open this document.

You can't open every file with every program. If you try to open an MP3 (audio) file with Microsoft Excel (a spreadsheet), for example, it just won't work; you get an error message or a screen full of gibberish. Sometimes, you just have to keep trying until you find the right program; at other times, you don't have a program that can open the file.

When in doubt, Google the file extension. You'll usually find out more than you need to know about what application(s) create files with that extension.

With the application of your choice

I don't know about you, but people send me files all the time that were created by applications I don't use . . . or at least that I don't use for that document type. Mac OS X lets you specify the application in which you want to open a document in the future when you double-click it. More than that, you can specify that you want all documents of that type to open with the specified application. "Where is this magic bullet hidden?" you ask. Right there in the file's Info window.

Assigning a file type to an application

Suppose that you want all `.tif` graphic files that usually open in Preview to open instead in Pixelmator, a more capable third-party program. Here's what to do:

1. **Click one of the files in the Finder.**

2. **Choose File⇨Get Info (⌘+I).**

3. **In the Info window, click the gray triangle to disclose the Open With pane.**

4. **From the pop-up menu, choose an application that Mac OS X believes will open this document type.**

   In Figure 6-15, I'm choosing Pixelmator. Now Pixelmator opens when I open this file (instead of Preview).

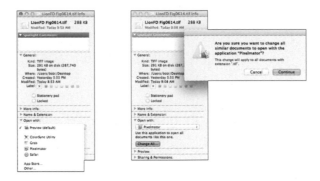

Figure 6-15: Before (left) and after (right) changing the application that opens this document.

5. **(Optional) If you click the Change All button at the bottom of the Open With pane, as shown on the right side of Figure 6-15, you make Pixelmator the new default application for all `.tif` files that would otherwise be opened in Preview.**

   Notice the handy alert that appears when you click the Change All button and how nicely it explains what will happen if you click Continue.

Opening a file with an application other than the default

Here's one more technique that works great when you want to open a document with a program other than its default. Just drag the file onto the application's icon or alias icon or Dock icon, and presto — the file opens in the application.

If I were to double-click an MP3 file, for example, the file usually would open in iTunes (and, by default, would be copied into my iTunes Library). But I frequently want to listen to MP3 files with QuickTime Player, so they're not added to my iTunes music library. Dragging the MP3 file onto QuickTime

Player's icon in the Applications folder or its Dock icon (if it's in the Dock) solves this conundrum quickly and easily.

If the icon doesn't highlight, and you release the mouse button anyway, the file ends up in the same folder as the application with the icon that didn't highlight. If that happens, just choose Edit⇨Undo (or press ⌘+Z), and the mislaid file magically returns to where it was before you dropped it. Just remember — don't do anything else after you drop the file, or Undo might not work. If Undo doesn't work, you must move the file back to its original location manually.

Only applications that *might* be able to open the file highlight when you drag the file on them. That doesn't mean the document will be usable — just that the application can *open* it. Suffice it to say that Mac OS X is smart enough to figure out which applications on your hard drive can open what documents — and to offer you a choice.

Organizing Your Stuff in Folders

I won't pretend to be able to organize your Mac for you. Organizing your files is as personal as your taste in music; you develop your own style with the Mac. But now that you know how to open and save documents when you're using applications, these sections provide food for thought — some ideas about how I organize things — and some suggestions that can make organization easier for you regardless of how you choose to do it yourself.

The upcoming sections look at the difference between a file and a folder; show you how to set up nested folders; and cover how some special folder features work. After you have a good handle on these things, you'll almost certainly be a savvier — and better organized — Mac OS X user.

Files versus folders

When I speak of a *file,* I'm talking about what's connected to any icon except a folder or disk icon. A file can be a document, an application, an alias of a file or an application, a dictionary, a font, or any other icon that *isn't* a folder or disk. The main distinction is that you can't put something *in* most file icons.

The exceptions are icons that represent Mac OS X packages. A *package* is an icon that acts like a file but isn't. Examples of icons that are really packages include many software installers and applications, as well as "documents" saved by some programs (such as Keynote, GarageBand, or TextEdit files saved in its `.rtfd` format). When you open an icon that represents a package in the usual way (double-click, choose File⇨Open, press ⌘+O, and so on), the program or document opens. If you want to see the contents of an icon that represents a package, you have to right- or Control-click the icon first and then choose Show Package Contents from the contextual menu. If you see an item by that name, you know that the icon is a package; if you don't see Show Package Contents on the contextual menu, the icon represents a file, not a package.

When I talk about *folders,* I'm talking about things that work like manila folders in the real world. Their icons look like folders, like the one in the margin to the left; they can contain files or other folders, called *subfolders.* You can put any icon — any file or folder — inside a folder.

Here's an exception: If you try to put a disk icon in a folder, all you get is an alias to the disk *unless* you hold down the Option key. Remember that you can't put a disk icon in a folder that exists on the disk itself. In other words, you can copy a disk icon only to a *different disk;* you can never copy a disk icon to a folder that resides on that disk. For more about aliases, flip to Chapter 5; for details on working with disks, see Chapter 8.

File icons can look like practically anything. If the icon doesn't look like a folder, package, or one of the numerous disk icons, you can be pretty sure that it's a file.

Organizing your stuff with subfolders

As I mention earlier in this chapter, you can put folders inside other folders to organize your icons. A folder "nested" inside another folder is called a *subfolder.*

You can create subfolders according to whatever system makes sense to you — but why reinvent the wheel? Here are some organizational topic ideas and naming examples for subfolders:

- **By type of document:** Word-Processing Documents, Spreadsheet Documents, Graphics Documents
- **By date:** Documents May–June, Documents Spring '03
- **By content:** Memos, Outgoing Letters, Expense Reports
- **By project:** Project X, Project Y, Project Z

When you notice your folders swelling and starting to get messy (that is, filling with tons of files), subdivide them again by using a combination of these methods that makes sense to you. Suppose that you start by subdividing your Documents folder into multiple subfolders. Later, when those folders begin to get full, you can subdivide them even further, as shown in Figure 6-16.

Figure 6-16: Before (left) and after (right) organizing the Novels and Finances folders with subfolders.

TECHNICAL STUFF

Creating subfolders . . . or not

How full is too full? When should you begin creating subfolders? That's impossible to say, at least in a one-size-fits-all way, but having too many items in a folder can be a nightmare — as can having too many subfolders with just one or two files in each one. My guideline is this: If you find more than 15 or 20 files in a single folder, begin thinking about ways to subdivide it.

On the other hand, some of my biggest subfolders contain things that I don't often access. My Bob's Correspondence 1992 folder, for example, contains more than 200 files. But because I want to keep this folder on my hard drive in case I do need to find something there — even though I don't use it very often — its overcrowded condition doesn't bother me. (Your mileage may vary.)

Here are some tips to help you decide whether to use subfolders or just leave well enough alone:

- ✔ **Don't create subfolders until you need them.** In other words, don't create a bunch of empty folders because you think you might need them someday. Wait to create new folders until you need them. That way, you avoid opening an empty folder when you're looking for something else — a complete waste of time.

- ✔ **Let your work style decide the file structure.** When you first start working with your Mac, you might want to save everything in your Documents folder for a week or two (or a month or two, depending on how many new documents you save each day). When a decent-size group of documents has accumulated in the Documents folder, consider taking a look at them and creating logical subfolders for them.

My point (yes, I do have one!): Allow your folder structure to be organic, growing as you need it to grow. Let it happen. Don't let any one folder get so full that it's a hassle to deal with. Create new subfolders when things start to get crowded. (I explain how to create folders in the next section.)

If you want to monkey around with some subfolders yourself, a good place to start is the Documents folder, which is inside your Home folder (that is, the Documents folder is a *subfolder* of your Home folder).

If you use a particular folder a great deal, put it in your Dock, or make an alias of it and move the alias from the Documents folder to your Home folder or to your Desktop (for more info on aliases, see Chapter 5) to make the folder easier to access. Or drag the folder (or its alias) to the Sidebar, where it's always available, even in Open dialogs and Save sheets. If you write a lot of letters, for example, you could keep an alias to your Correspondence folder in your Home folder, in the Dock, or on your Desktop for quick access. (By the way, there's no reason why you can't have a folder appear in all three places, if you like. That's what aliases are all about, right?)

If you create your own subfolders in the Documents folder, you can click that folder in the Dock to reveal them, as shown in Figure 6-17. I show you how to customize the Dock in Chapter 4.

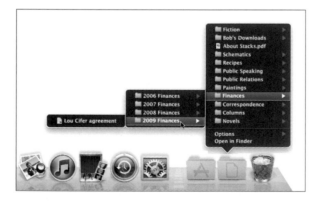

Figure 6-17: It's super-convenient to have your Documents folder in the Dock.

It's even more convenient if you choose to view the Documents folder as a list, as described in Chapter 4 and shown in Figure 6-17!

Creating new folders

So you think that Apple has already given you enough folders? Can't imagine why you'd need more? Think of creating new folders the same way you'd think of labeling a new folder at work for a specific project. New folders help you keep your files organized, enabling you to reorganize them just the way you want. Creating folders is really quite simple.

To create a new folder, just follow these steps:

1. **Decide which window you want the new folder to appear in — and then make sure that window is active.**

   If you want to create a new folder right on the Desktop, make sure that *no* window is active.

   You can make a window active by clicking it, and you can make the Desktop active if you have windows on-screen by clicking the Desktop itself.

2. **Choose File⇨New Folder (or press ⇧+⌘+N).**

   A new, untitled folder appears in the active window with its name box already highlighted, ready for you to type a new name for it.

3. **Type a name for your folder.**

   If you accidentally click anywhere before you type a name for the folder, the name box is no longer highlighted. To highlight it again, select the icon (single-click it) and then press Return (or Enter) once. Now you can type its new name.

   Give your folders relevant names. Folders with nebulous titles like sfdghb or Stuff — or, worst of all, Untitled — won't make it any easier to find something six months from now.

   For folders and files that you might share with users of non-Macintosh computers, here's the rule for maximum compatibility: Use no punctuation and no Option-key characters in the folder name. Periods, slashes, backslashes, and colons in particular can be reserved for use by other operating systems. When I say Option-key characters, I'm talking about special-purpose ones such as ™ (Option+2), ® (Option+R), ¢ (Option+4), and even © (Option+G).

Navigating with spring-loaded folders

A *spring-loaded folder* pops open when you drag something onto it without releasing the mouse button. Spring-loaded folders work with all folder or disk icons in all views and in the Sidebar. Because you just got the short course on folders, subfolders, and various ways to organize your stuff, you're ready for your introduction to one of my favorite ways to get around my disks, folders, and subfolders.

Here's how spring-loaded folders work:

1. **Select any icon except a disk icon.**

   The folder highlights to indicate that it's selected.

2. **Drag the selected icon onto any folder or disk icon — but don't release the mouse button.**

   I call this *hovering* because you're doing just that: hovering the cursor over a folder or disk icon without releasing the button.

   In a second or two, the highlighted folder or disk flashes twice and then springs open, right under the cursor.

   You can press the spacebar to make the folder spring open immediately.

3. **After the folder springs open, perform any of these handy operations:**

   • Continue to traverse your folder structure this way. Subfolders continue to pop open until you release the mouse button.

   • If you release the mouse button, the icon you've been dragging is dropped into the active folder at the time. That window remains open — but all the windows you traversed clean up after themselves by closing automatically, leaving your window clean and uncluttered.

   • If you want to cancel a spring-loaded folder, drag the cursor away from the folder icon or outside the boundaries of the sprung window. The folder pops shut.

After you get used to spring-loaded folders, you'll wonder how you ever got along without them. They work in all four window views, and they work with icons in the Sidebar or Dock. Give 'em a try, and you'll be hooked.

You can toggle spring-loaded folders on or off in the Finder's Preferences window. There's also a setting for how long the Finder waits before it springs the folders open. See Chapter 5 for more on Finder preferences.

Smart Folders

As Steve Jobs is fond of saying near the end of his annual keynote addresses, "There is one more thing." Those things are called Smart Folders.

Smart Folders let you save search criteria and then tell them to work in the background to reflect those criteria in real time. In other words, Smart Folders are updated continuously, so they display all the files on your computer that currently match the search criteria. So, for example, you can create a Smart Folder that contains all the Rich Text Format files on your computer that you've opened in the past two weeks, as shown in Figure 6-18. Or you can create a Smart Folder that displays graphics files, but only the ones bigger (or smaller) than a specified file size. Then all those files appear in one convenient Smart Folder.

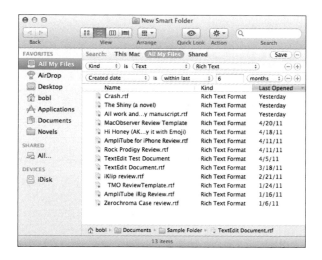

Figure 6-18: A Smart Folder that displays only Rich Text Format files created in the past six months.

The possibilities are endless. Because Smart Folders use aliaslike technology to display items, the actual files reside in only one location: the folder where you originally put them. True to their name, Smart Folders don't gather the files themselves in a separate place; rather, they gather *aliases* of files, leaving the originals right where you stashed them. Neat!

Also, because Spotlight (discussed in the final section of this chapter) is built deep into the bowels of the Mac OS X file system and kernel, Smart Folders are updated in real time and so are always current, even after you've added or deleted files on your hard drive since creating the Smart Folder.

Smart Folders are so useful that Apple provides five ways to create one. The following steps show you how:

1. **Start your Smart Folder by using any of the following methods:**

   - Choose File⇨New Smart Folder .

   - Press ⌘+Option+N.

   - Choose File⇨Find.

   - Press ⌘+F.

   - Type at least one character in the Search box of a Finder window.

   If you have All My Files selected in the Sidebar, you can't use the last method, because All My Files is a Smart Folder — one with a weird icon, but a Smart Folder nonetheless.

2. **Refine the criteria for your search by clicking the + button to add a criterion or the – button to delete one.**

3. **When you're satisfied and ready to turn your criteria into a Smart Folder, click the Save button below the Search box.**

   A sheet drops down.

4. **Choose where you want to save your folder.**

   While the Save sheet is displayed, you can add the Smart Folder to the Sidebar, if you like, by clicking the Add to Sidebar check box.

5. **When you're finished editing criteria, click the Save button to save the folder with its criteria.**

After you create your Smart Folder, you can save it anywhere on any hard drive and then use it like any other folder. There's also an option to display it in your Sidebar, if you want.

If you want to *change* the criteria for a Smart Folder you created earlier, open the folder, click the Action-menu button in its toolbar, and choose Show Search Criteria, as shown in Figure 6-19.

Figure 6-19: Open a Smart Folder you've created, and click the Action-menu button to change its search criteria.

Alternatively, you can right- or Control-click the Smart Folder (even one in the Sidebar) and choose Show Search Criteria from the contextual menu.

When you're finished changing the criteria, click the Save button to resave your folder. Don't worry — if you try to close a Smart Folder you've modified without saving your changes, Mac OS X politely asks if you want to save this Smart Folder and warns that if you don't save, the changes you made will be lost. You may be asked whether you want to replace the previous Smart Folder of the same name; usually, you do.

Smart Folders (with the exception of the Sidebar's All My Files, which has its own weird little icon) display a little gear in their center, as shown in Figure 6-19, making them easy to tell apart from regular folders.

Smart Folders can save you a lot of time and effort, so if you haven't played with them much (or at all) yet, be sure to give 'em a try.

Shuffling Around Files and Folders

Sometimes, keeping files and folders organized means moving them from one place to another. At other times, you want to copy them, rename them, or compress them to send to a friend. These sections explain all those things and more.

All the techniques that I discuss in the following sections work at least as well for windows that use list, column, or Cover Flow view as they do for windows that use icon view. I use icon view in the figures in this section only because it's the best view for pictures to show you what's going on. For what it's worth, I find moving and copying files much easier in windows that use list or column view.

Comprehending the Clipboard

Before you start moving your files around, let me introduce you to the Clipboard. The *Clipboard* is a holding area for the last thing that you cut or copied. That copied item can be text, a picture, a portion of a picture, an object in a drawing program, a column of numbers in a spreadsheet, any icon (except a disk), or just about anything else that can be selected. In other words, the Clipboard is the Mac's temporary storage area.

Most of the time, the Clipboard works quietly in the background, but you can ask the Clipboard to reveal itself by choosing Edit⇨Show Clipboard. This command summons the Clipboard window, which lists the type of item (such as text, picture, or sound) on the Clipboard — and a message letting you know whether the item on the Clipboard can be displayed.

As a storage area, the Clipboard's contents are temporary. *Very* temporary. When you cut or copy an item, that item remains on the Clipboard only until you cut or copy something else. When you do cut or copy something else, the new item replaces the Clipboard's contents, and the newcomer remains on the Clipboard until you cut or copy something else. And so it goes.

Whatever is on the Clipboard heads straight for oblivion if you crash, lose power, log out, or shut down your Mac, so don't count on it too heavily or for too long.

The Clipboard commands on the Edit menu are enabled only when they can actually be used. If the selected item can be cut or copied, the Cut and Copy commands in the Edit menu are enabled. If the selected item can't be cut or copied, the commands are unavailable and are dimmed (gray). If the Clipboard is empty or the current document can't accept what's on the Clipboard, the Paste command is dimmed. Finally, when nothing is selected, the Cut, Copy, and Clear commands are dimmed.

Icons can't be cut; they can only be copied or pasted. So when an icon is selected, the Cut command is always gray.

Copying files and folders

One way to copy icons from one place to another is to use the Clipboard.

When a file or folder icon is selected, choose Edit⇨Copy (or use its shortcut, ⌘+C) to copy the selected icon to the Clipboard. Note that this doesn't delete the selected item; it just makes a copy of it on the Clipboard. To paste the copied icon in another location, choose Edit⇨Paste (or use its shortcut, ⌘+V).

Other methods of copying icons from one place to another include these:

- ✔ **Drag an icon from one folder icon onto another folder icon while holding down the Option key.** Release the mouse button when the second folder is highlighted. This technique works regardless of whether the second folder's window is open. If you don't hold down the Option key, you move the icon to a new location rather than copy it, as I explain a little later in this section.

  When you copy something by dragging and dropping it with the Option key held down, the cursor changes to include a little plus sign (+) next to the arrow, as shown in the margin. Neat!

- ✔ **Drag an icon into an open window for another folder while holding down the Option key.** Drag the icon for the file or folder that you want to copy into the open window for a second folder (or other hard disk or removable media such as a USB flash drive).

✔ **Choose File⇨Duplicate (⌘+D) or right- or Control-click the file or folder that you want to duplicate and then choose Duplicate from the contextual menu that appears.** This makes a copy of the selected icon, adds the word *copy* to its name, and then places the copy in the same window as the original icon. You can use the Duplicate command on any icon except a disk icon.

You can't duplicate an entire disk onto itself. But you can copy an entire disk (call it Disk 1) to any other actual, physical, separate disk (call it Disk 2) as long as Disk 2 has enough space available. Just hold down Option, and drag Disk 1 onto Disk 2's icon. The contents of Disk 1 are copied to Disk 2 and appear on Disk 2 in a folder named Disk 1.

You can cut an icon's name, but you can't cut the icon itself; you may only copy an icon.

To achieve the effect of cutting an icon, select the icon, copy it to the Clipboard, paste it in its new location, and then move the original icon to the Trash.

If you're wondering why anyone would ever want to copy a file, trust me: Someday, you will. Suppose that you have a file called Long Letter to Mom in a folder called Old Correspondence. You figure that Mom has forgotten that letter by now, and you want to send it again. But before you do, you want to change the date and delete the reference to Clarence, her pit bull, who passed away last year. So now you need to put a copy of Long Letter to Mom in your Current Correspondence folder. This technique yields the same result as making a copy of a file by using Save As, which I describe earlier in this chapter.

When you copy a file, it's wise to change the name of the copied file. Having more than one file on your hard drive with exactly the same name isn't a good idea, even if the files are in different folders. Trust me that having 10 files called Expense Report or 15 files named Doctor Mac Consulting Invoice can be confusing, no matter how well organized your folder structure is. Add distinguishing words or dates to file and folder names so that they're named something more explicit, such as Expense Report Q3 2010 or Doctor Mac Consulting Invoice 4-4-2011.

You can have lots of files with the same name *on the same disk* (although, as I mention earlier, it's probably not a good idea). But your Mac won't let you have more than one file with the same name and extension (.txt, .jpg, .doc) *in the same folder.*

Pasting from the Clipboard

As I mention earlier in this chapter, to place the icon that's on the Clipboard someplace new, click where you want the item to go and then choose Edit⇨Paste or use the keyboard shortcut ⌘+V to paste what you've copied or cut.

Pasting doesn't purge the contents of the Clipboard. In fact, an item stays on the Clipboard until you cut, copy, restart, shut down, log out, or crash. This means that you can paste the same item over and over and over again, which can come in pretty handy at times.

Almost all programs have an Edit menu and use the Macintosh Clipboard, which means you can usually cut or copy something from a document in one program and paste it into a document in another program.

Usually.

Moving files and folders

You can move files and folders around within a window to your heart's content as long as that window is set to icon view. Just click and drag any icon to its new location in the window.

Some people spend hours arranging icons in a window until they're just so. But because using icon view wastes so much screen space, I avoid using icons in a window.

You can't move icons around in a window that is displayed in list, column, or Cover Flow view, which makes total sense when you think about it. (Well, you can move them to put them in a different folder in list, column, or Cover Flow view, but that's not moving them around, really.)

As you might expect from Apple by now, you have choices for how you move one file or folder into another folder. You can use these techniques to move any icon (folder, document, alias, or program icon) into folders or onto other disks.

 ✔ **Drag an icon onto a folder icon.** Drag the icon for one folder (or file) onto the icon for another folder (or disk) and then release when the second icon is highlighted (see Figure 6-20). The first folder is inside the second folder. Put another way, the first folder is a subfolder of the second folder.

  This technique works regardless of whether the second folder's window is open.

✔ **Drag an icon into an open folder's window.** Drag the icon for one folder (or file) into the open window for a second folder (or disk), as shown in Figure 6-20.

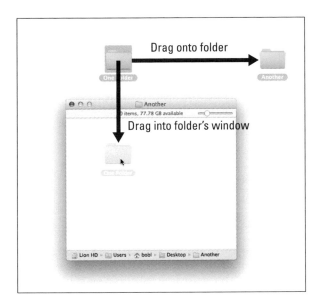

Figure 6-20: Two ways of putting one folder into another.

If you want to move an item from one *disk* to another disk, you can't use the preceding tricks. Your item is copied, not moved. If you want to *move* a file or folder from one disk to another, you have to hold down the ⌘ key when you drag an icon from one disk to another. The little Copying Files window even changes to read *Moving* Files. Nice touch, eh?

Selecting multiple icons

Sometimes you want to move or copy several items into a single folder. The process is pretty much the same as it is when you copy one file or folder (that is, you just drag the icon to where you want it and drop it there). But you need to select all the items you want before you can drag them en masse to their destination.

If you want to move all the files in a particular folder, simply choose Edit➪ Select All or press ⌘+A. This command selects all icons in the active window, regardless of whether you can see them on-screen. If no window is active, choosing Select All selects every icon on the Desktop.

But what if you want to select only some of the files in the active window or on the Desktop? Here's the most convenient method:

1. **To select more than one icon in a folder, do one of the following:**

   • *Click once within the folder window (don't click any one icon), and drag your mouse (or keypad) while continuing to hold down the mouse button.*

   You see an outline of a box around the icons while you drag, and all icons within or touching the box become highlighted (see Figure 6-21).

   • *Click one icon and then hold down the Shift key while you click others.*

   As long as you hold down the Shift key, each new icon that you click is added to the selection. To deselect an icon, click it a second time while still holding down the Shift key.

   • *Click one icon and then hold down the ⌘ key while you click others.*

   The difference between using the Shift and ⌘ keys is that the ⌘ key doesn't select everything between it and the first item selected when your window is in list or column view. In icon view, it really doesn't make much difference.

   To deselect an icon, click it while holding down the ⌘ key.

2. **After you select the icons, click one of them (clicking anywhere else deselects the icons) and drag them to the location where you want to move them (or Option+drag to copy them).**

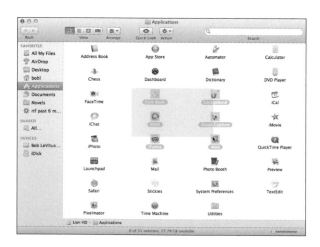

Figure 6-21: Select more than one icon by clicking and dragging your mouse.

Be careful with multiple selections, especially when you drag icons to the Trash. You can easily — and accidentally — select more than one icon, so watch out that you don't accidentally put the wrong icon in the Trash by not paying close attention. (I detail how the Trash icon works later in this chapter.)

Playing the icon name game: Renaming icons

Icon, icon, bo-bicon, banana-fanna fo-ficon. Betcha can change the name of any old icon! Well, that's not entirely true. . . .

If an icon is locked or busy (the application is currently open), or if you don't have the owner's permission to rename that icon (see Chapter 16 for details about permissions), you can't rename it. Similarly, you should never rename certain reserved icons (such as the Library, System, and Desktop folders).

To rename an icon, you can either click the icon's name directly (don't click the icon itself, because that selects the icon) or click the icon and then press Return (or Enter) once.

Either way, the icon's name is selected and surrounded with a box, and you can type a new name (as shown in Figure 6-22). In addition, the cursor changes from a pointer to a text-editing I-beam. An I-beam cursor is the Mac's way of telling you that you can type now. At this point, if you click the I-beam cursor anywhere in the name box, you can edit the icon's original name. If you don't click the I-beam cursor in the name box but just begin typing, the icon's original name is replaced by what you type.

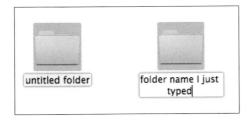

Figure 6-22: Change an icon's name by typing over the old one when it's highlighted.

If you've never changed an icon's name, give it a try. And don't forget: If you click the icon itself, the icon is selected, and you won't be able to change its name. If you do accidentally select the icon, just press Return (or Enter) once to edit the name of the icon.

Compressing files

If you're going to send files as an e-mail enclosure, creating a compressed archive of the files first and sending the archive instead of the originals usually saves you time sending the files and saves the recipient time downloading them. To create this compressed archive, simply select the file or files and then choose File➪Compress. This creates a compressed .zip file out of your selection. The compressed file is smaller than the original — sometimes by quite a bit.

Getting rid of icons

To get rid of an icon — any icon — merely drag it onto the Trash icon on your Dock.

Trashing an alias gets rid of only the alias, not the parent file. But trashing a document, folder, or application icon puts it in the Trash, where it *will* be deleted permanently the next time you empty the Trash. The Finder menu offers a couple of commands that help you manage the Trash:

- **Finder➪Empty Trash:** This command deletes all items in the Trash from your hard drive, period.

  I'll probably say this more than once: *Use this command with a modicum of caution.* After a file is dragged into the Trash and the Trash is emptied, the file is gone, gone, gone unless you have a Time Machine or other backup. (Okay, maybe ProSoft Engineering's Data Rescue II or some other third-party utility can bring it back, but I wouldn't bet the farm on it.)

- **Finder➪Secure Empty Trash:** Choosing this command makes the chance of recovery by even the most ardent hacker or expensive disk-recovery tool difficult to virtually impossible. Now the portion of the disk that held the files you're deleting will be overwritten with randomly generated gibberish. You're hosed unless you have a Time Machine or other backup.

If you put something in the Trash by accident, you can almost always return it whence it came: Just invoke the magical Undo command. Choose Edit➪Undo or press ⌘+Z. The accidentally trashed file returns to its original location. Usually.

Unfortunately, Undo doesn't work every time — and it remembers only the very last action that you performed when it does work — so don't rely on it too much.

Timesaving Tools

In This Chapter

▶ Finding your files and folders, fast

▶ Taking charge with Mission Control

▶ Learning to love Lion's Launchpad

*I*n this chapter, I show you the ins and outs of three terrific timesaving tools: Spotlight, Mission Control, and Launchpad. Each is designed to let you use your Mac better, faster, and more elegantly. Yes, you can use your mouse and click your way to any file or folder on any disk. But these features are built into Lion for your convenience.

At the risk of repeating myself, Apple frequently provides more than one way to accomplish a task in Mac OS X, so there's duplication and overlap among and between the tools in this chapter and tools you've read about elsewhere in this book. Don't worry. Take what you need, and leave the rest. Some people love Spotlight; others rarely use it. Mission Control can be amazingly helpful, especially on laptops with small screens, but many users don't care for it.

My advice: Try all the tools and techniques in this chapter at least a few times before you decide whether you want or need them.

Finding Files and Folders Faster

Even if you follow every single bit of advice provided in this chapter, a time will come when you won't be able to find a file or folder, although you know for certain that it's right there on your hard drive. Somewhere. Fortunately, Lion includes a fabulous technology called Spotlight that can help you find almost anything on any mounted disk in seconds. Spotlight can

- ✔ Search for files
- ✔ Search for folders
- ✔ Search for text inside documents
- ✔ Search for files and folders by their metadata (creation date, modification date, kind, size, and so on)

Spotlight finds what you're looking for and then organizes its results logically, all in the blink of an eye (on most Macs).

Spotlight is both a technology and a feature. The technology is pervasive throughout Lion — and is the underlying power behind the search boxes in many Apple applications and utilities such as Mail, Address Book, System Preferences, and Finder. You can also use it right from the Spotlight menu — the little magnifying glass at the right end of the menu bar. Also, you can reuse Spotlight searches in the future by turning them into Smart Folders (which I explain in Chapter 6).

Finding files and folders has never been faster or easier than it is in Lion. So in these sections, I look at the two separate but related ways that Spotlight helps you find files, folders, and even text inside document files: the Search box in Finder windows and the Spotlight menu.

Using the Search box in Finder windows

With its power provided by Spotlight, this definitely isn't your father's Search box.

Press ⌘+Option+F to move the cursor to the search box of the active window.

The following steps walk you through all the features:

1. **Type a single character in the Search box.**

   The window starts displaying the results, as shown in Figure 7-1.

   If you want to change the criteria for one or more of these items, it's the same as changing criteria for a Smart Folder: Click the item in the Sidebar and then click the Action-menu button and choose Show Search Criteria. When you're done changing the search criteria, click the Save button to resave your folder.

2. **If the folder or volume you want to search isn't This Mac or your Home folder, open the folder you want to search, and type your query in the Search box in that folder's window.**

Figure 7-1: As soon as you type the first character in the Search box, the results begin to appear.

The default is to search files' contents. To search for a file by its file name, choose Filename Contains (*a* in Figure 7-1) from the drop-down menu.

3. **When you find the file or folder, you can open any item in the list by double-clicking it.**

You can also start a search by choosing File➪Find (shortcut: ⌘+F).

Keep these points in mind when you perform a search:

✔ You have a choice of where to search. My Home folder (bobl) is selected in Figure 7-2.

✔ You can choose additional search criteria — such as the kind of file (PDF in Figure 7-2) and the last date the file was opened (within last 60 days in Figure 7-2) — as well as other attributes, including modification date, creation date, keywords, label, file contents, and file size.

✔ To add another criterion, simply click the + button on the right side of the window.

✔ To save a search for reuse in the future, click the Save button on the right side of the window.

Try choosing different options from the window's Arrange menu — Application, Date Last Opened, and so on — to see the search results presented in different ways.

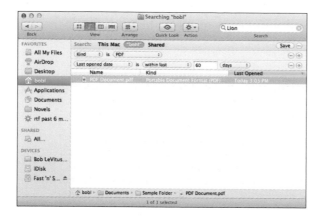

Figure 7-2: Search your whole Mac or a specific folder (and its subfolders) and then narrow your search using one or more criterion.

So there you have it — fast searches made easy in the Finder. But there are many ways to access the power of Spotlight, and the Search box in the toolbar of Finder windows is merely one of them.

Using the Spotlight menu and window

Another way to search for files and folders is to use the Spotlight menu itself — the magnifying-glass icon at the far right end of your menu bar. Click the icon to open the Spotlight Search box and then type a character, word, or series of words in the Search box to find an item, as shown in Figure 7-3.

Memorize and use the super-convenient and easy-to-remember keyboard shortcut for opening the Spotlight search box, which is ⌘+spacebar by default. If you don't find ⌘+spacebar appealing as a shortcut, you can change it to whatever you like in the Spotlight System Preferences pane.

If you highlight an item in Spotlight's results list, a preview pops up to its left, a là *What's Up, Dock.doc* in Figure 7-3. That's a nice feature, new in Lion.

Spotlight is more than just a menu and Search box; it also uses a technology that's pervasive throughout Mac OS X and apps including (but certainly not limited to) Mail, Address Book, and many, many more. The reason why it's so spectacularly speedy is that it "indexes" your files when your Mac is idle. The upshot is that Spotlight knows file locations and contents soon after a file is created or modified.

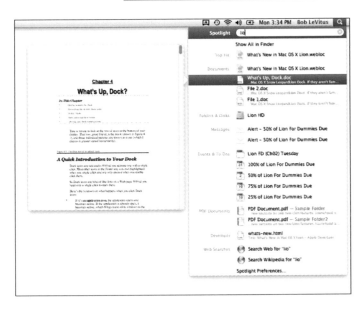

Figure 7-3: Click the magnifying glass to reveal the Search box (top);
type in the Search box, and your results appear instantly (bottom).

You can also use the Spotlight window to create and perform more sophisticated searches. You can access this window in two ways:

✔ Click the Show All in Finder item on the Spotlight menu or press
⌘+Option+spacebar.

You can change this shortcut to whatever you like in the Spotlight System Preferences pane.

✔ Use the criteria at the top of the window to narrow your search.

This is exactly the same process you use to create Smart Folders, as discussed in Chapter 6! If you want to make a Smart Folder from a search you perform, just click the Save button.

Regardless of which method you choose to invoke it — the Search box in a Finder window, the Spotlight Search box in the menu bar, or the Spotlight window — Spotlight saves you time and effort.

Finding files by other attributes

After you add a search attribute by clicking the + button, choose a search attribute from its pop-up menu: Kind, Last Opened Date, Last Modified Date, Created Date, Name, or Contents. Select an item, and its relevant pop-up menus and/or text entry fields appear, as shown in Figure 7-4.

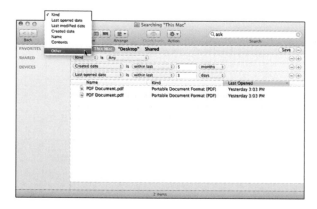

Figure 7-4: Narrowing a search using the Kind, Created Date, and Last Opened Date search attributes.

Choose Other, however, and a long list of additional search attributes appears, as shown in Figure 7-5.

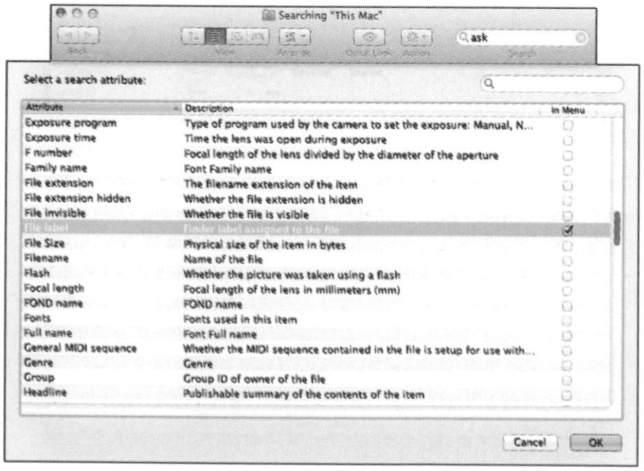

Figure 7-5: Just some of the search attributes that appear when you choose Other.

In Figure 7-5, I've selected the File Label search attribute in the list, and because I expect to use this search attribute often, I've also selected its In Menu check box. As a result, a File Label search attribute appears below the Last Opened Date attribute, and File Label appears in the pop-up menu for easy access, as shown in Figure 7-6.

File Label menu item

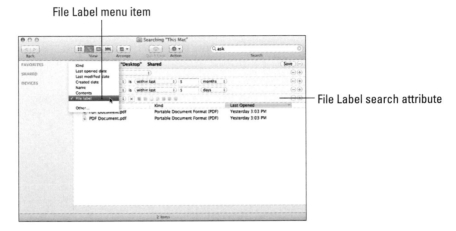

File Label search attribute

Figure 7-6: File Label is added to this search as an attribute and to the pop-up menu for future convenience.

It took a few steps to use File Label as a search attribute this first time, but the next time I need it, I'll just choose it from the pop-up menu and be on my way.

Exposé Yourself to Mission Control's Spaces

 Two of my favorite tools in Snow Leopard were Exposé and Spaces, a positively peachy pair of utilities that went together like peanut butter and chocolate. They went together so well, in fact, that Apple teamed them up in their very own System Preferences pane: the eponymous Exposé & Spaces System Preferences pane.

You won't find the Exposé & Spaces System Preferences pane in Lion, but rest assured that Exposé and Spaces are alive and well in Lion, having survived a name change to Mission Control.

Figure 7-7 shows the new Mission Control System Preferences pane (the pane formerly known as Exposé & Spaces) in all its glory.

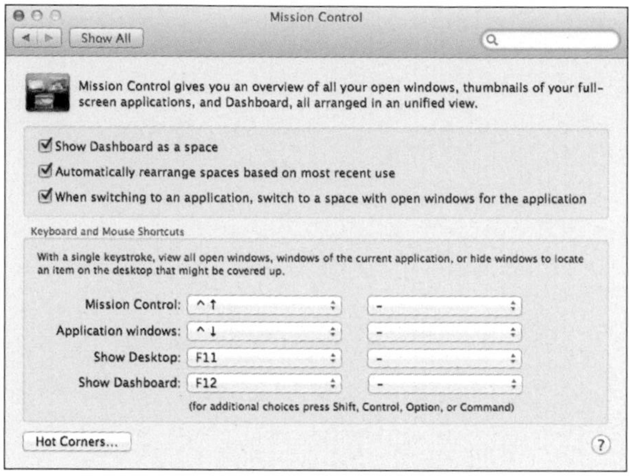

Figure 7-7: The Mission Control System Preferences pane.

The painless Mission Control pane

The top part of the pane contains three check boxes: Show Dashboard as a Space; Automatically Rearrange Spaces Based on Most Recent Use; and When Switching to an Application, Switch to a Space with Open Windows for the Application. You know what Dashboard is all about (from Chapter 3), but because I haven't introduced you to Spaces yet (but will shortly), these checkboxes will make sense to you only after you read the sections that follow. Suffice it to say that they do what you think they'll do. You should experiment with the settings, turning them on and off, to see which way you prefer them.

Moving right along, most of this pane handles keyboard and mouse shortcuts for Mission Control. These eight pop-up menus — four each for keyboard and mouse shortcuts — let you specify the trigger for each of the four features with a keystroke or mouse button. The default keyboard shortcuts appear below, but yours may differ; to change them, click the appropriate pop-up menu and make a new selection.

TIP

Hold down the ⌘, Option, Control, and/or Shift keys when you choose an item from the keyboard shortcut menu (the four pop-up menus on the left in Figure 7-7) to add modifier keys to the keyboard shortcuts you create. So, for example, if you held down ⌘+Shift when you selected F11 from a pop-up menu, the keyboard shortcut for that feature would be ⌘+Shift+F11.

A picture is worth a thousand words, so check out Figures 7-8, 7-9, and 7-10 as you read about each feature.

✔ To see Mission Control, which displays all open windows in all open applications, as shown in Figure 7-9, press Control+↑.

TIP

If you hover over a window on the Mission Control screen (shown in Figure 7-9) and press the spacebar, you see a preview of the window's contents, which is especially helpful when a window is partially obscured by another window.

✔ To see all open windows belonging to the current application (TextEdit in Figure 7-10), press Control+↓.

✔ To hide all open windows and display the Desktop, press F11 or fn+F11.

✔ To summon forth the Dashboard (which displays your widgets, as I explain in Chapter 3), press F12 (or fn+F12).

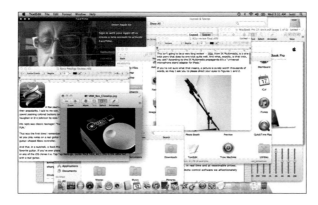

Figure 7-8: On most days, my screen looks something like this, with a myriad of open windows from numerous apps obscuring one another.

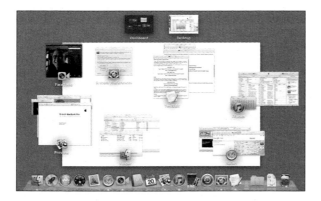

Figure 7-9: After invoking Mission Control (Control+↑).

Figure 7-10: After invoking Application Windows (Control+↓) when TextEdit was active.

Notice that when you're using Mission Control, windows appear at a reduced size. Identifying information — either the program or window name — appears below it, making it easier to discern what each item contains. When you click any of these small windows, Mission Control deactivates, and the window you clicked becomes the active window.

Check out the way that Mission Control's Application Windows screen (see Figure 7-10) includes a row of document icons near the bottom of the screen. They represent the TextEdit documents I created or modified most recently. Click the stack at the right end of the row to see more documents. You read more about TextEdit in Chapter 14, but trust me that this new feature makes it a cinch to reopen documents you've used recently.

Hot corners!

In the bottom-left corner of the Mission Control System Preferences pane is a Hot Corners button, which lets you designate any or all of the corners of your screen as hot spots to trigger Mission Control, Dashboard, Launchpad, Screen Saver, or Display Sleep. Click the menu for a corner, and select the feature you want associated with that corner. Then, whenever you move your cursor onto that corner and leave it there for a second or two, the feature executes.

Hot corners have been part of Mac OS since time immemorial and are still as useful as ever. I like to set the top-right corner to start my screen saver and the bottom-right corner to disable it, for example.

Mission Control is enabled by default, but you can disable any or all of its features by turning off its trigger: Just choose the minus sign from a pop-up menu instead of a keyboard or mouse-button shortcut. The four mouse triggers on the right side of Figure 7-7 are all disabled, for example.

Spaces from 30,000 feet (An overview)

If Mission Control lets you manage your windows in real time, Spaces lets you manage windows by organizing them in groups called *spaces* and then switching from space to space with a keystroke or gesture.

When you use spaces, only two kinds of windows are shown: windows from applications associated with the active space and windows from applications launched while that space is active.

If you find yourself spending too much time moving and resizing windows on-screen, consider setting up spaces for specific tasks. You might have one space dedicated to a specific project, another for web surfing, and a third for e-mail, each with all its windows arranged just the way you like them.

Think of a space as being a single screen, set up just the way you like it, with its windows arranged just the way you like them. Take, for example, the three spaces shown in Figures 7-11, 7-12, and 7-13. I have one for web surfing (Figure 7-11), one for mail (Figure 7-12), and one for working in the Finder (Figure 7-13), each one with its windows arranged exactly as I like 'em.

Figure 7-11: My web-surfing space, with three Safari windows (Consulting, Downloads, and Activity) right where I like 'em on my screen.

Figure 7-12: My Mail space, with three Mail windows (Apple Hot News, Addresses, and Activity) arranged just so.

Figure 7-13: My Finder space, with two windows in list view (All My Files and Trash), plus one each in column view (Dr. Mac 2011) and icon view (BL Pix).

Moving right along, you manage your spaces with Mission Control, a new feature in Lion that provides an overview of what's running on your Mac, including all your spaces, the Dashboard, and all open windows. In a nutshell, this dynamic duo makes it easier than ever to manage and maintain the mélange of Finder and application windows that conspire to clutter and eventually consume your screen.

To see it in action, press the Mission Control key (Control+up arrow by default). If you have a trackpad, you can also swipe upward using three fingers to see Mission Control, which will look something like Figure 7-14 based on the three spaces shown in Figures 7-11 through 7-13.

Figure 7-14: Mission Control showing off three spaces (Desktops 1, 2, and 3) and the Dashboard.

Note that you won't see the Dashboard in Mission Control if you've cleared the Show Dashboard as a Space check box in the Mission Control System Preferences pane.

In earlier versions of Mac OS X, spaces were called *spaces.* Mission Control, improbably, uses the words *spaces* and *Desktop* interchangeably, so as you see in Figure 7-14, my three spaces are named Desktop 1, Desktop 2, and Desktop 3. I think it's dumb, and I'm going to continue to call a space a space regardless of what Mission Control labels them.

To add a new pace, first enter Mission Control; then move the cursor to the top-right corner of the screen and click the Add (+) button.

You don't see a + button? It's hidden and appears only when your cursor is nearby. You can see it in the top-right corner of Figure 7-14; if you don't see a + button there on *your* screen, move the cursor to that general vicinity, and it magically appears.

You can use this technique to add as many spaces as you like. When you're finished using Mission Control, you can

> ✔ Click a space at the top of the screen to switch to it.
>
> *or*
>
> ✔ Press the Mission Control key or swipe with three fingers to return to the space you were using when you entered Mission Control.

These gestures require a Magic Mouse, Magic Trackpad, or laptop with buttonless trackpad.

Getting around in Space(s)

You just saw one way to move from one space to another — enter Mission Control and click the space you want to use. You can also navigate spaces in the following ways:

- ✔ Press the Control key and the left- or right-arrow key to move to the next or previous space.

- ✔ Swipe left or right with three fingers to move to the next or previous space.

- ✔ Press the Control key and the number key for the space you want to use. Pressing Control+2, for example, activates Desktop 2.

    You can disable keyboard commands by choosing the dash in the Keyboard Shortcuts tab of the Keyboard System Preferences pane.

There will be times when you want to move a window from one space to another. To do so:

- ✔ Drag a window to the left or right edge of the screen, and pause. After a short delay, the window pops into the space on the left or right of the current space.

- ✔ Press and hold down the mouse button on the window you want to move while pressing the Control key and the

    - • Left-arrow key to move the window to the space on the left of the current space

    - • Right-arrow key to move the window to the space on the right of the current space

    - • Number key of the space to move the window to that space

    or

- ✔ Start in the space that has the window you want to move. Enter Mission Control, drag the window from the middle part of the screen onto the space you want to move it to, and then release the mouse button.

It's often useful to assign a specific application to a specific space. To do so, first launch the application in question; then press and hold its Dock icon, and choose Options, as shown in Figure 7-15.

Here's the rundown on those options:

✏ **To have the application open in every space, choose All Desktops.**

When the application is running, it will appear in every space.

✏ **To have the application open only in the current space, choose This Desktop.**

The application opens in this space. If you're working in a different space and switch to this application, its assigned space scrolls into view.

✏ **To have the application open in whatever space you're using, choose None.**

Figure 7-15: Press and hold an application's Dock icon to assign the application to a specific space (Desktop).

Finally, should you want to delete one or more spaces, simply enter Mission Control, and move the cursor over the space. A Delete button — an X that should look familiar if you use an iPhone, iPad, or iPod touch, or the Dashboard — appears in the top-left corner, as shown in Figure 7-16. Click it to delete that space.

Figure 7-16: Hover the cursor over a space, and a Delete button (X) appears.

Deleting a space doesn't delete or quit any applications or close any documents. Applications and windows in a deleted space move to the space called Desktop (the one *without* a numeric suffix).

The bottom line is that Spaces can be particularly useful for those with a smaller display. This feature is an acquired taste, so even if you have a small screen, you may not care for it.

My advice: Try it for a while, and if you decide that you hate it, turn its triggers off (by selecting the minus sign) and be done with it.

Launchpad: The Place for Applications

Launchpad presents all of the applications in your Applications folder in a view that looks like the home screen of any iOS device (that is, iPhone, iPad, or iPod touch). In fact, if you use one of these devices, I suspect that you could skip everything that follows about Launchpad, because it works almost exactly like the home screen on an iPhone or other i-device.

Click Launchpad's Dock icon (shown in the margin). It fills your screen with big, beautiful application icons, as shown in Figure 7-17.

Figure 7-17: Launchpad, in all its glory.

I changed my Desktop picture from plain white to a photograph (of flamingos) for Figure 7-17. The photo is actually in focus; the nifty blur effect happens only when Launchpad is active. Sure, it's just eye candy, but at least it's *elegant* eye candy.

If your Launchpad has more than one page of apps, you see two or more white dots near the bottom of the screen (directly above the *W)*. To change pages, press the left- or right-arrow key.

To launch an app, just click its icon. In a heartbeat, Launchpad disappears, and the app replaces it on your screen.

Customizing Your Launchpad

Launchpad is configurable, just like home screens on i-devices. As you're about to see, you can rearrange app icons on a page, move them from one page to another, organize them in folders, and delete them. Say it all together now: "Just like on i-devices."

For those who are unfamiliar with iOS or devices that run it, here's how these things work on your Mac:

- **To rearrange icons:** Click and drag the app to its new location.
- **To move apps to the next or previous page:** Click and drag the app to the left or right edge of the screen. When the next page of apps appears, drag the app to its new location on that page.
- **To add an app to your Dock:** Click and drag the app onto the left side of the Dock.
- **To create a folder for apps:** Drag one app's icon on top of another app's icon to create a folder.
- **To add an app to a folder:** Drag the app onto that folder to add them.
- **To move an app out of a folder:** Click the folder to open it, and drag the app out of the folder.
- **To change a folder's name:** Click to open the folder, click the current name, and then type a new name.
- **To uninstall apps:** Click an app's icon, but don't release the mouse button until all the icons begin to wiggle. Apps that can be uninstalled display a Delete button (X); click to uninstall the app.

  Press Esc to stop the wiggling.

If an icon doesn't have a Delete button, it's part of Mac OS X Lion and can't be uninstalled.

Dealing with Disks

In This Chapter

▶ Initializing and erasing your disks
▶ Using PC-formatted disks
▶ Creating your own CDs and DVDs
▶ Ejecting disks

*I*n this chapter, I show you disk basics: how to format them for your Mac, how to format them so that your Windows-using brethren (and sisteren) can use them, how to eject them, how to copy or move files between disks, and much more. Onward!

This chapter offers lots of info that applies to every Mac user — including folder management and moving or copying files to and from disks other than your internal hard drive. I also show you how to work with optical media such as CD-R, CD-RW, DVD-R, DVD+R, DVD-RW, DVD+RW, and DVD+R DL (dual-layer) — types of discs that many Mac users deal with regularly. You almost certainly have an internal SuperDrive (CD and DVD player/burner). Or you might have added external storage devices such as a USB flash drive; a USB, FireWire, or Thunderbolt hard drive; or an optical disc player/ recorder.

? you sure you want to burn the c
.aby Burn – The CD " to a disc?

You can use this disc on any Mac or Windows
disc without burning it, click Eject.

Disc Name: Burn Baby Burn – The C

Burn Speed: 8x

n Folder To: Burn Baby Burn – The C

Is that a disk or a disc?

So how do you spell this critter, anyway? Sometimes, you see it spelled d-i-s-k; at other times, you see it spelled d-i-s-c. If you're wondering what's up with that, here's the skinny. In the good old days, the only kind of computer disk was a disk with a k: floppy disk, hard drive, Bernoulli disk, and so on. Then one day, the compact disc (you know, a CD) was invented. The people who invented it chose to spell it with a c instead of a k, probably because it's round like a discus (think track and field). From that time on, both spellings have been used more or less interchangeably.

Now, some people will tell you that magnetic media (floppy, hard, Zip, Jaz, and so on) are called disks (spelled with a k) and that optical media — that is, discs that are read with a laser, such as CD-ROMs, CD-RWs, audio CDs, and DVDs — are called discs (spelled with a c). Maybe that's true, but the two terms have been used pretty much interchangeably for so long that you can't depend on the last letter to tell you whether a disk is magnetic or optical.

The bottom line is that I'm going to compromise. When I'm speaking generally about something that could be either a disk or a disc, I stick with the term disk. But if I'm speaking strictly about optical media (CDs and DVDs), I use the term disc.

I hope that's clear. If not, my editors made me do it.

Comprehending Disks

You should think of the disk icons that appear on the Desktop (and/or in the sidebars of Finder windows) as though they were folders. That's because your Mac sees disks as nothing *but* giant folders. When you double-click one, its contents appear in a Finder window; to that extent, it works just like a folder. You can drag stuff in and out of a disk's window, and you can manipulate the disk's window in all the usual ways — again, just like a folder.

If you don't see your hard disk icon(s) on the Desktop or in the Sidebar, open Finder Preferences (choose Finder➪Preferences or ⌘+comma) and select the appropriate items in the General and Sidebar tabs, as described in Chapter 5.

Although (for all intents and purposes) disks *are* folders, disks do behave in unique ways sometimes. The following sections explain what you need to know.

Some disks need to be formatted first

Brand-new disks sometimes need to be *formatted* — prepared to receive Macintosh files — before you can use them.

When you connect an unformatted hard disk, your Mac usually pops up a dialog that asks what you want to do with the disk. One option is usually to *format* (or *initialize*) the disk — that is, get it ready to record data. If you choose to format the disk, the Disk Utility program launches itself so you can format the disk from the Erase tab.

If you ever need to format or initialize a blank disk and don't see the dialog, all you have to do is open Disk Utility manually (it's in your Applications/ Utilities folder) and use its Erase tab to format the disk.

Moving and copying disk icons

Moving a file icon from one on-screen disk to another works the same way as moving an icon from one folder to another, with one notable exception: When you move a file from one disk to another, you automatically make a copy of it, leaving the original untouched and unmoved. If you want to move a file or folder completely from one disk to another, you have to delete that leftover original by dragging it to the Trash or by holding down the ⌘ key when you drag it from one disk to the other.

You can't remove a file from a read-only disc (such as a CD-R or DVD-R) or from a folder to which you don't have write permission. But you should be able to move or delete files and folders from all other kinds of disks that you might encounter.

Copying the entire contents of any disk or volume (CD, DVD, or external hard drive, among others) to a new destination works a little differently:

1. **Click the disk's icon.**

2. **Hold down the Option key, and drag the disk icon onto any folder, any disk icon, or any open Finder window.**

   When the copy is completed, a folder bearing the same name as the copied disk appears in the destination folder or disk. The new folder contains each and every file that was on the disk of the same name.

Copying files in this way is handy when you want to grab all the files from a CD or DVD and put them on your hard drive.

If you don't hold down the Option key when you drag a disk icon to another destination, your Mac creates an *alias* of the disk (that is, a link back to the original) instead of a copy of its contents. As you might expect, the alias will be almost worthless after you eject the disk; if you open it, it will ask you to insert the original disk.

If you like using the Duplicate command, note that you can't use the Duplicate keyboard shortcut (⌘+D) on a disk, although you can use it on a folder.

For the full details of moving, copying, and pasting, flip to Chapter 6.

Surprise: Your PC Disks Work, Too!

One of the most excellent features of Mac OS X (if you have friends unfortunate enough not to own Macs, and you want to share files with them) is that it reads and writes CDs and DVDs that can be read by PCs.

Although your Mac can read disks formatted by a PC, the *files* on them might or might not work for you. If the files are documents, such as Microsoft Word .doc or Microsoft Excel .xls files, one of your Mac programs can probably open them. If the files are Windows programs (these often sport the .exe extension, which stands for *executable)*, your Mac can't do anything with 'em without additional software designed to run Windows programs.

So if you want to run Windows on your Mac, you need to use either Lion's built-in utility called Boot Camp or a third-party program such as Parallels Desktop from Parallels (www.parallels.com), Fusion from VMware (www.vmware.com), or the free VirtualBox (www.virtualbox.org). Boot Camp requires you to reboot your computer each time you want to use Windows; the third-party programs emulate PC hardware so that you can run genuine Microsoft Windows operating systems in Lion *without* rebooting your Mac.

So with a commercial app such as Parallels Desktop or VMware Fusion (both around $80), the free VirtualBox from Oracle, or Lion's included Boot Camp utility, your Mac *can* run those .exe files (which is to say most Windows programs).

None of these comes with a copy of Windows (required).

Parallels Desktop and VMware Fusion are almost as fast as a PC when running most Windows applications. Depending on which Intel-based Mac you have, they might even be speedy enough to play first-person shooters. Boot Camp is even faster but has the disadvantage of requiring you to leave the Lion environment and restart your Mac before you can use it. For most other stuff (including the Windows-bundled Solitaire), all three are capable of running Windows a heck of a lot faster than many PCs are.

Burning CDs and DVDs

With Mac OS X, you can play, create, and publish audio and video on optical media. Depending on which type of optical drive your Mac is equipped with, you can burn some or all of the following types of discs: CD -R, CD -RW, DVD -R, DVD +R, DVD -RW, DVD +RW, and DVD +R DL (dual layer).

These disc types are usually referred to as *plus* or *minus.* So when you see DVD -R, you pronounce it "DVD minus R," or when you see DVD +R DL, you pronounce it "DVD plus R dual layer" or "DVD plus R DL."

How can I tell what kind of discs my Mac can burn?

Great question. If you don't know what types of discs your Mac can burn, here's an easy way to find out:

1. In your Applications folder, open the Utilities folder and then open the System Information application.

2. In the Contents pane on the left, click Hardware and then Disc Burning, as shown in the following figure.

The right side of the window now reveals lots of information about the disc-burning capabilities of this Macintosh. The CD-Write and DVD-Write items tell you the types of discs your Mac is capable of burning.

The disc burner in the following figure can burn CD -R and -RW, and DVD -R, -R DL (dual layer), -RW, +R, +R DL (dual layer), and +RW optical discs.

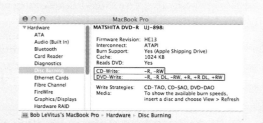

When you purchase blank discs, make sure that they're one of the types your burner supports.

In the sections that follow, I show you two ways to burn files on a CD or DVD. For the first way, you insert a disc and then select the files you want to burn. The second method, creating a burn folder, enables you to save the list of files you've burned.

Burning a music CD is a different process that's performed using iTunes. Don't worry — you find out all about that process in Chapter 12.

Burning on the fly

One way to burn files to a CD or DVD is to simply insert a blank disc and select the files you want to burn on the fly. Just follow these steps:

1. **Insert a blank disc.**

   You see an alert (as shown in Figure 8-1) that asks you what you want to do with the disc.

Figure 8-1: Insert a blank DVD into your optical media drive, and get ready to feel the burn.

In this case, the blank disc happened to be a DVD -R, but the same thing happens if you insert any supported recordable CD or DVD.

2. **Choose Open Finder from the Action pop-up menu.**

   Open Finder is the default choice unless you've changed that default in the CDs & DVDs System Preferences pane or as explained in the following tip.

   Your choices in the CDs & DVDs System Preferences pane for the default action when you insert a blank CD or DVD are

   - *Open Finder:* Mounts the blank disk in the Finder (as shown in the instructions that follow this tip)

   - *Open iTunes:* Opens iTunes automatically when you insert a blank CD

- *Open Disk Utility:* Opens the Disk Utility application automatically

- *Open iDVD* (for DVDs only, not CDs): Opens iDVD automatically

- *Open Other Application:* Lets you choose the application to use when you insert a blank CD or DVD disc

- *Run Script:* Runs a specified AppleScript when you insert a blank disc.

- *Ignore:* Leaves the disk in your drive but does nothing (that is, none of the above).

If you want to make any of these actions the default in the alert shown in Figure 8-1 and thus avoid a trip to the CDs & DVDs System Preferences pane, select the Make This Action the Default check box.

For the purposes of these steps, go with Open Finder for now.

3. Click OK.

Your blank CD *mounts* (appears as an icon) on the Desktop just like any other removable disc, but its distinctive icon tells you that it's a record-able CD (or DVD), as shown in Figure 8-2.

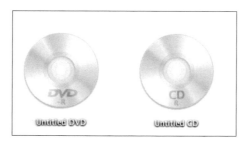

Figure 8-2: Recordable optical discs get a distinctive labeled icon.

4. Drag files or folders onto the disc icon on your Desktop until the disc contains all the files you want on it.

5. (Optional) If you like, you can change the disc's name from Untitled CD (or DVD) the same way that you change the name of any file or folder.

I've changed the name of the CD in Figure 8-3 to *Burn Baby Burn – the CD.*

6. When you're ready to finish (burn) your CD (or DVD), open its disc icon and click the Burn button in the top-right corner of the disc's window, or click the Burn icon (which looks like the warning symbol

for radioactivity) to the right of the disc in the Sidebar, both shown in Figure 8-3.

Notice that the amount of free space remaining on the disc (501.6MB in Figure 8-3) is displayed in the status bar at the bottom of the window. If you don't see the status bar, choose View⇨Status Bar.

Burn icon in sidebar   Burn button

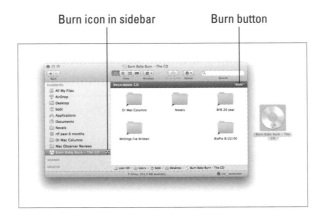

Figure 8-3: Click the Burn button in the window or the burn icon next to the disc's icon in the Sidebar to burn your disc.

Alternatively, you could

- Control-click or right-click the disc's icon and choose Burn *Your Disk's Name Here* from the contextual menu (that is, Burn "Burn Baby Burn – the CD" in Figure 8-4).

- Select the icon, and choose File⇨Burn *Disc Name* (left side of Figure 8-4). If you choose Eject, from either the contextual menu or the File menu, you're asked whether you want to burn the disc first.

- If you drag the disc icon to the Trash/Eject Disk icon in your Dock, the Trash/Eject Disk icon turns into the Burn Disc icon (which still looks like the warning symbol for radioactivity). Drop the disc icon on the radioactivity icon in the Dock, and the burning begins.

After you've chosen to burn a disc, you see the dialog shown in Figure 8-5.

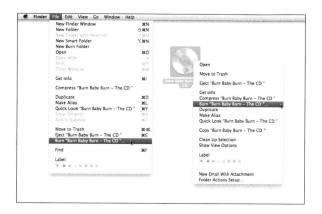

Figure 8-4: Two more ways to burn a disc.

Figure 8-5: The last step before the burning begins.

7. **Choose a speed from the Burn Speed pop-up menu, click the Burn button, and you're done.**

I usually use a slower but more reliable burn speed (8x in Figure 8-5) unless I'm in a huge hurry. I've had many discs fail when burned at the default highest speed possible. You can call those discs drink coasters unless they were rewritable (RW) discs. If that's the case, you can erase them with Disk Utility and try again.

I feel obliged to mention that CD-RW and DVD-RW discs rarely (if ever) work in devices other than your Mac, including CD (audio) players and DVD (video) players. When you burn a music CD or a video DVD and plan to watch it on a device other than your Mac, you shouldn't burn it on rewritable (RW) media.

Select the Save Burn Folder To check box if you think that you may want to burn another copy of this disc someday. (You find out more about burn folders in the next section of this chapter.)

Creating a burn folder

A burn folder lets you burn selected files to a CD or DVD many times. Perhaps the most useful thing you can do with a burn folder is to create one that contains your most important files and then regularly burn the current versions of those files to a CD or DVD as a backup.

Whenever you drag an item to a burn folder, the Finder creates an alias of that item in the burn folder. So when you burn a disc using a burn folder, the parent (original) files are burned to the disc, not the aliases.

Here's how to create and use a burn folder:

1. **Choose File⇨New Burn Folder.**

   A folder titled Burn Folder appears on the Desktop.

2. **Name the burn folder.**

3. **Drag some icons into the burn folder.**

4. **When you're ready to burn the folder's contents to a disc, double-click it, and click Burn.**

5. **Insert a disc, and follow the on-screen instructions.**

If the Finder can't find the parent file for an alias, it asks whether you want to cancel the burn or to continue without that item. If you cancel, the disc remains empty.

Here are a couple of other ways to burn the contents of a burn folder:

- ✔ If a burn folder is in the Sidebar of a Finder window, you can burn its contents to a disc quickly by clicking the burn icon to its right, as shown in Figure 8-3.

- ✔ Right-click or Control-click the burn folder and then choose Burn *Disc Name* (in Figure 8-4 it says, *"Burn Baby Burn – the CD"*) from the contextual menu.

Getting Disks out of Your Mac

The preceding sections tell you almost everything there is to know about disks except one important thing: how to eject a disk. Piece of cake, actually. Here are several ways, all simple to remember:

✔ Click the disk's icon to select it and then choose File➪Eject (or use the keyboard shortcut ⌘+E).

✔ Drag the disk's icon to the Trash. When you drag a disk's icon, the Trash icon in the Dock changes into an Eject icon, like the one shown in the left margin.

The preceding method of ejecting a disk is something that used to drive me (and many others) crazy before Mac OS X. In the olden days, the Trash icon didn't change into an Eject icon. This confused many new users, who then asked me the same question (over and over and over): "But doesn't dragging something to the Trash erase it from your disk?"

As I mention earlier in the chapter, this technique does something completely different if you've dragged any files onto the disc. In that case, the Trash icon turns into the radioactive symbol, and your Mac offers to burn the disc, as shown in Figure 8-5. Put another way, this ejection technique works only if the disc is blank, has already been burned, or is a store-bought prerecorded (read-only) CD or DVD.

✔ Click the little Eject icon to the right of the disc's name in the Sidebar.

✔ Press the Eject key on your keyboard if it has one. (If it has one, it probably has the Eject icon on it.)

If your keyboard doesn't have an Eject key, press the F12 key, and continue to hold it down for a second or two. On many keyboards that don't have an Eject key, this keyboard shortcut ejects a disc.

✔ Right-click or Control-click the disk icon and then choose Eject from the contextual menu.

There's one more way, if you like little menus on the right side of your menu bar. To install your own Eject menu on the menu bar, navigate to `System/Library/CoreServices/MenuExtras` and then open (double-click) the `Eject.menu` icon. Your Eject menu appears on the right side of your menu bar, as shown in Figure 8-6 (top). If you get tired of the icon on your menu bar, just drag it off, and it disappears with a satisfying poof, as shown in Figure 8-6 (bottom).

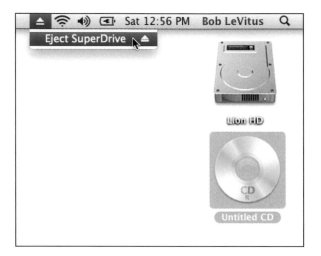

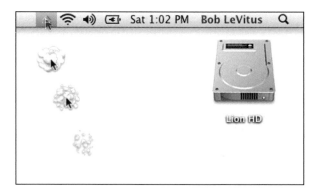

Figure 8-6: Using the Eject menu to eject a disc (top) and removing the Eject menu from the menu bar by ⌘+dragging it (bottom).

9

Organizing Your Life

In This Chapter

▶ Introducing iCal

▶ Creating and using iCal calendars

▶ Organizing events and to-do's with iCal

▶ Making sticky notes with Stickies

*W*hen you buy Mac OS X Lion, the folks at Apple generously include applications that can help simplify and organize your everyday affairs — namely, iCal and Stickies.

In fact, Mac OS X comes with a whole folder full of applications — software you can use to do everything from surfing the Internet to capturing an image of your Mac's screen to playing QuickTime movies to checking the time. Technically, most of these applications aren't even part of Mac OS X. Rather, the vast majority of them are what are known as *bundled* apps — programs that come with the operating system but are unrelated to its function. Readers (bless them) tend to complain when I skip bundled applications, so I mention almost all of them in this book.

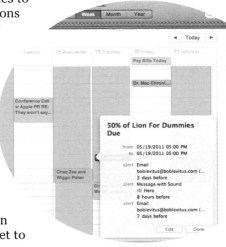

But in this chapter, you get a look at only the applications that help you organize your everyday life: your appointments, to-do items, notes to yourself, and all the various gadgets you may attach to and detach from your Mac.

The applications discussed in this chapter are stored in (where else?) the Applications folder, which you can get to in four ways:

▸ Click the Applications folder in the Sidebar of any Finder window.

▸ Choose Go➪Applications.

▸ Press ⌘+Shift+A.

The fourth way is new in Lion: Click the Launchpad icon in the Dock to see all the applications installed on this Mac (as you see in Chapter 7).

Other bundled apps you might be especially interested in include Safari (Chapter 10), Address Book and Mail (Chapter 11), iTunes (Chapter 12), a whole handful of multimedia applications that enable you to play video and more on your Mac (Chapter 13), and TextEdit (Chapter 14). For even more information on the Mac OS X bundled applications, check out *Macs For Dummies,* 10th Edition, by *USA Today* columnist Edward C. Baig or Mark Chambers' *OS X Lion All-in-One For Dummies,* both published by Wiley.

Keeping Track with iCal

iCal is a wonderful program that combines a comprehensive daily/weekly/ monthly appointment calendar and a to-do list. It offers multiple color-coded calendars, several types of reminder alerts, repeating event scheduling, and more. You can publish your calendar(s) on the web for others to view (which requires a MobileMe account or other WebDav server), and you can subscribe to calendars published by other iCal users.

It's a handy-dandy memory-enhancing tool, and if you make a habit of recording appointments and things to do in iCal, you'll almost never forget them.

I love iCal and keep it open at all times on my Macs. In the sections that follow, I share a handful of the features I find most useful.

Navigating iCal views

iCal lets you display the main iCal window just the way you like it:

- **You can view your calendar by the day, week, month, or year.** Figure 9-1 shows a weekly view. To select a view, click the Day, Week, Month, or Year button at the top of the window.

- **To move back or forward,** click the arrow buttons on either side of the Today button. You see the previous or next week in weekly view, you move back or forward by day in day view, and so on.

- **To go to today's date,** click the Go to Today button.

- **To add a new calendar,** click the New Calendar (+) button.

You can find all these items, most of which have handy keyboard shortcuts, in the iCal View menu, as shown in Figure 9-2. This menu offers almost total control of what you see and how you navigate.

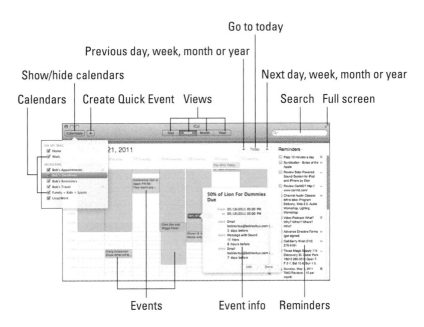

Figure 9-1: The iCal main window displaying the view I prefer: week view.

Figure 9-2: The iCal View menu.

If you want to master iCal, it would behoove you to spend some time experimenting with these views and with their navigation commands and options.

Creating calendars

If you refer to Figure 9-1, you see a list of my calendars in the top-left corner: Home, Work, Bob's Appointments, Bob's Deadlines, Bob's To Dos, and so on. The check boxes represent turn the visibility of a calendar on (checked) and off (unchecked).

My calendars appear in two sections — On My Mac and MobileMe — because I use Apple's MobileMe service to sync my calendars (and many other things you find out about in Chapter 10). If you're not a MobileMe subscriber, calendars that you create (such as the six calendars that appear in the MobileMe section in Figure 9-1) would appear in the On My Mac section instead.

To create a new calendar in iCal, follow these steps:

1. **Choose File➪New Calendar or press ⌘+Option+N.**

   A new calendar named Untitled is created and added to the calendar list.

2. **To give your calendar a name, select Untitled, and type a new name.**

3. **(Optional) To color-code the entries for this calendar, first select the calendar (by clicking it); choose Edit➪Get Info or press ⌘+I; and then select a color by clicking and holding the color swatch, as shown in Figure 9-3.**

   In my humble opinion, Other is the handy choice because it lets you select thousands of colors other than the seven colors available by default.

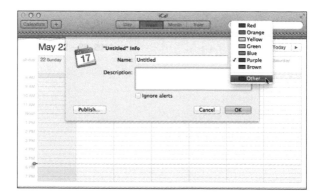

Figure 9-3: Change the color of a calendar by clicking and holding the color swatch.

TIP

Now any item you create while this calendar is selected (in the list that pops up from the Calendars button) appears on the selected calendar in the color you selected.

While you're in the Info sheet, you can also add a description of your calendar.

Grouping calendars

You can also organize calendars in groups that contain more than one calendar. To create a new calendar group in iCal, follow these steps:

1. **Choose File⊅New Calendar Group, press ⌘+Shift+N, or press Shift; then click the + button in the bottom-left corner of the main iCal window.**

   A new calendar group named Group is created and added to the calendar list.

2. **Give the new group a name by selecting Group and typing a new name.**

3. **To add calendars to the group, simply create a new calendar as described in the preceding section while the group is selected, or drag existing calendars below the group name in the list, as shown in Figure 9-4.**

   When you release the mouse button in Figure 9-4, the Personal calendar moves from between the Work and Untitled calendars to below the Family calendar in the Family + Personal group.

   Now you can show or hide all calendars in the group by selecting or deselecting a single check box. You can still show or hide individual calendars by selecting or deselecting their check boxes, of course.

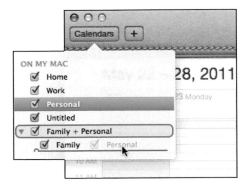

Figure 9-4: Add the Personal calendar to the Family + Personal group by dragging it below the group name, like this.

Here's how you might deploy this feature. You could create individual calendars for each member of your family and put all the individual family calendars in a group called Family. Then you could make all the family-member calendars visible or invisible with a single click of the group calendar's check box.

If you have a MobileMe account (as discussed in Chapter 10), you can publish your calendars and invite others to subscribe to them by choosing Calendar⇨Publish. The others receive an e-mail inviting them to subscribe to your calendar. This is what my family does. Each of us maintains and publishes his or her own calendar and subscribes to everyone else's. That way, we can all see at a glance who's doing what and when they're doing it. This is by far the slickest solution we've found.

Deleting a calendar or group

To delete a calendar or calendar group, select it in the list and choose Edit⇨ Delete. If the calendar has events on it or the group has calendars in it, you'll see an alert box asking if you're sure you want to delete that calendar or group; if not, the calendar or group will be deleted as soon as you choose Edit⇨Delete.

When you delete a calendar or group, all the events and reminder items in that calendar or group are also deleted. Although you *can* Undo a deleted calendar or group (choose Edit⇨Undo or press ⌘+Z), you must do so before you quit iCal. If you quit iCal without undoing a calendar or calendar-group deletion, everything on that calendar (or calendars) will be gone forever (unless, of course, you have Time Machine or another backup, as explained in Chapter 18).

Creating and managing events

The heart of iCal is the event. To create a new one, follow these steps:

1. **Choose File⇨New Event, press ⌘+N, double-click, or click and drag up or down anywhere on the calendar.**

   If you double-click or click and drag on the day of the event, you can skip Step 2, and you don't need to specify the date in Step 3.

   Alternatively, try Lion's new Create Quick Event (+) button. It's smart enough to interpret commands like "Family Movie at 7PM on Thursday" and create a new event on Thursday at 7 p.m., as shown in Figure 9-5.

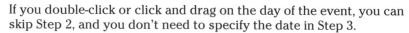

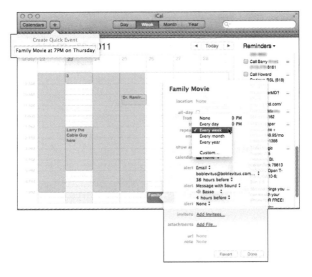

Figure 9-5: An event bubble for a one-hour event on my Home calendar.

2. **If the event doesn't appear in the proper place, just click it and drag it wherever you like.**

3. **To edit an event, select it and then choose Edit⇨Edit Event, press ⌘+E, or double-click it to open its event bubble, as shown in Figure 9-5.**

   All the items with little arrows on their right sides — *repeat, show as, calendar,* and *alerts* — are pop-up menus. The *repeat* menu is popped up in Figure 9-5.

4. **When you're satisfied with all of the event's items, click the Done button.**

If you prefer working in a little window rather than the event bubble, check out the Edit⇨Show Inspector command (⌘+Option+I), which displays the selected event in a window. Click a different event, and its info instantly fills the Inspector window. Try it; you might like it.

The difference is that the Inspector window changes contextually and displays information about the currently selected event. Get Info windows, on the other hand, display info for a specific event. Put another way, a Get Info window displays the info for a specific event, and you can have as many Get Info windows on the screen as you like. There's only one Inspector window; it displays info for whichever event is currently selected.

Inviting others to attend an event

To invite other people to your event, you can open Address Book or the iCal Address Panel (Window⇨Address Panel or ⌘+Option+A) and drag the contacts onto the event in iCal. Alternatively, you can type the first few letters of the name in the Invitees field, and names that match magically appear. In Figure 9-6, I typed the letters *st,* and iCal offered me a choice of my two contacts with names that start with *st* — namely, Stan LeVitus and Stan Lee. Sweet! (If you're unfamiliar with Address Book, flip to Chapter 11 for details.)

After you've added one or more invitees, click the Send button to invite them to the event. If the invitees have iCal, they can open the enclosure (which is included with your invitation e-mail), which adds the event to iCal with Accept, Decline, and Maybe buttons. All they have to do is click the appropriate button, and you receive an e-mail informing you of their decision along with an enclosure that adds their response to the event in iCal. Nice, eh?

If the invitee doesn't have iCal (or doesn't open the enclosure that was included with the e-mail invitation), he or she has to respond the old-fashioned way: by replying to your e-mail or calling you on the telephone.

Figure 9-6: Type the first few letters of a contact's name, and iCal provides a list of contact names that match.

Setting an alert

What's the point of putting an event on your calendar if you forget it? If you set an alert, iCal won't let you forget. To set an alert, click the word *None* with the double-headed arrow (just to the right of the word *alert)* in the Event info window. A menu appears. Choose the type of alert you want from the menu and then change its values to suit your needs. I find the Message with Sound and Email alerts so useful that I use both for almost every event I create.

You can have as many alerts as you like for each event. When you add an alert to an event, a new alert item appears below it. Just click the word *None* with the double-headed arrow just to the right of the word *alert* to create a second (or third or fifteenth) alert. To remove an alert, click the word *alert,* and choose *None* from the pop-up menu.

All the features mentioned so far are wonderful, but my very favorite iCal feature has to be alerts. I rarely miss an important event anymore; iCal reminds me of them with time to spare. Better still, I sync events and alerts between my Mac and my iPhone and iPad. I can create an event or alert on either device, and within a few minutes — through the magic of MobileMe — it magically appears on the other.

You don't have to have MobileMe to sync calendars on your Mac and iPhone, but without it, you'll be able to synchronize only when you connect your iPhone to your Mac with its included USB cable. With MobileMe, all syncing happens automatically — almost immediately, and wirelessly over Wi-Fi or cellular data networks.

To do or not to do: Setting reminders

iCal has one more trick up its sleeve to help you stay organized: the Reminder item. Unlike an event, a Reminder item isn't necessarily associated with a particular day or time and can be assigned a priority level: Low, Medium, High, or None.

If you don't see the Reminders list on the right side of the iCal window, but you'd like to, choose View➪Show Reminders, or use its shortcut, ⌘+Option+T.

To create a new Reminder, choose File➪New Reminder, press ⌘+K, or double-click anywhere on the Reminder list.

To sort or filter the Reminder list, click the small black triangle to the right of its name, as shown in Figure 9-7.

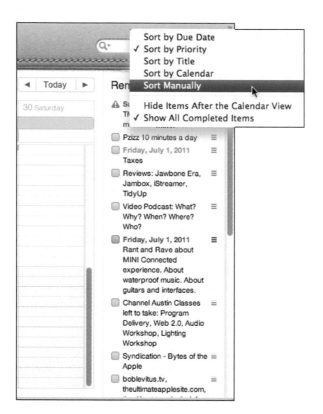

Figure 9-7: Sort the Reminder list by due date or other criterion, or sort manually to drag reminder events into any order you like.

Are you available?

A new iCal feature in Lion is the Availability panel (choose Window⇨ Availability Panel or press Shift+⌘+A). Most of you won't be able to take advantage of it because it requires you to have at least one calendar administered through a CalDAV server or Microsoft Exchange Server 2007 or later.

Unfortunately, this feature currently doesn't work if your calendars are hosted on Apple's MobileMe online service.

If you don't know what CalDAV or Exchange servers are, you can safely skip to the next section.

If your calendar is hosted on a CalDAV server, you may designate events as Free or Busy; if your calendar is hosted on an Exchange server, you may designate events as Free, Busy, Tentative, or Out of Office. The result is that workgroup members with access to this calendar can schedule events that don't conflict with other members' events.

Stickies

Stickies are electronic sticky notes for your Mac. They're convenient places to jot quick notes or phone numbers. Some Stickies are shown in Figure 9-8.

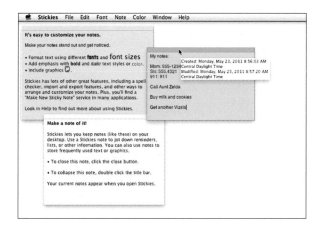

Figure 9-8: Create sticky notes for your Mac.

To create a new Sticky, choose File➪New Note.

Stickies are supremely flexible:

✔ Move them around on-screen (just drag 'em by their title bars).

✔ Change their text to any font and color you desire by using the Note menu.

✔ Make your Stickies any color you like by using the Color menu.

✔ Collapse a Sticky by double-clicking its title bar.

✔ Print a Sticky, and import or export text files from the Stickies application menu.

If you hover the cursor over a Sticky without clicking, the creation and modification dates and times pop up in a little tooltip-style window, as shown in Figure 9-8.

Anything that you type on a Sticky is automatically saved as long as you keep that note open. But when you close a note (by clicking its Close box, choosing File⇨Close, or pressing ⌘+W), you lose its contents forever. Fortunately, Stickies give you a warning and a second chance to save the note in a separate file on your hard drive. You can also export Stickies (choose File⇨Export Text) and save them as plain text, Rich Text Format (RTF) files, or as RTF with attachments (RTFD) files. The last two formats support fonts and other formatting that plain-text format does not.

Other Sticky goodies include a spell checker, spoken notes, text substitutions (such as Smart Quotes and Smart Dashes), and transformations (such as Make Upper or Lower case), all on the Edit menu. You'll also find a Make a New Sticky Note command on the Services menu of many programs.

Part III
Do Unto Lion: Getting Things Done

The 5th Wave — By Rich Tennant

©RICHTENNANT

"He seemed nice, but I could never connect with someone who had a screen saver like his."

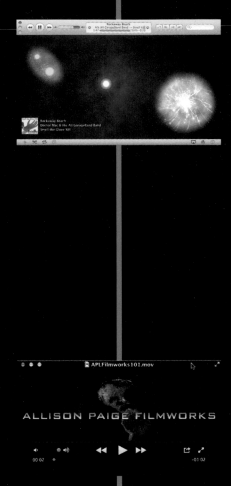

In this part . . .

Moving right along, Part III comprises how to do stuff with your Mac. In this section, it's off to the Internet first — how to get it working and what to do with it after that. Next you'll discover two of Apple's most imaginatively named programs: the excellent e-mail application called Mail and the wonderful address book called Address Book. That's followed by a pair of chapters devoted to working with media — music, movies, DVDs, and digital photos. Finally, you discover the basics of processing words and using fonts.

This is an excellent section, chock-full of useful information (if I do say so myself), and it's one you definitely don't want to miss.

10

Internet-Working

In This Chapter

▶ Getting an overview of the Internet

▶ Pre-surfing with the Network System Preferences pane

▶ Finding out about the MobileMe services

▶ Surfing the web with Safari

▶ Searching with Google

▶ Chatting with iChat

▶ Going face to face with FaceTime

*T*hese days, networking online is easier than finding a log to fall off: You simply use the Internet to connect your Mac to a wealth of information residing on computers around the world. Luckily for you, Mac OS X has the best and most comprehensive Internet tools ever shipped with a Mac operating system.

Mac OS X offers built-in Internet connectivity right out of the box. Mac OS X Lion comes with

- Apple's Safari web browser, which you use to navigate the web, download remote files, and more

- iChat, Apple's live online chatting client that works with other iChat users; people using AOL Instant Messaging (AIM) clients; and people using Jabber (an open-source chatting protocol), Google Talk, and Bonjour (which discovers other users on your local area network)

- The FaceTime app for video chats with other Mac or i-device users

- The Mail application (for e-mail)

In this chapter, I cover the top three things most people use the Internet for: the *World Wide Web* (that's the www. you see so often in Internet addresses), *video and audio chatting,* and *instant messaging.* You can find out all about Mail in Chapter 11.

But before I can talk about browsers, e-mail software, messaging, and chatting, I have to help you configure your Internet connection. When you're finished, you can play with your browsers, mail, and chat applications to your heart's content.

Getting Connected to the Internet

Before you can surf the Internet, you need to connect to it. If you're a typical home user, you need three things to surf the Internet:

- **A modem or other connection to the Internet,** such as a Digital Subscriber Line (DSL), a cable modem, or a satellite Internet service

  If you use technology other than DSL or cable modem to connect your computer to the Internet, your network administrator (the person you run to at work when something goes wrong with your computer) or ISP might have to help you set up your Mac because setting up those other configurations is (sigh) beyond the scope of this book.

- **An account with an ISP** (an Internet service provider such as AT&T, Comcast, or RoadRunner)

  The technical reviewer for this book reminds me that these days, that's not necessarily true. All you really need is free Wi-Fi, which is available everywhere — in stores, restaurants, parks, libraries, and other places — and a free e-mail account from Google or Yahoo.

- **A Mac (preferably one running Mac OS X 10.7 Lion)**

  You might need to tweak a few settings, as I explain in the upcoming section "Plugging in your Internet-connection settings."

After you set up each of these components, you can launch and use Safari, Mail, iChat, and any other Internet application you care to use.

Setting up your modem

If you have a cable modem, DSL, or other high-speed Internet connection — or are thinking about getting any of these — you can use them with your Mac. In most cases, you merely connect your Mac to the Internet via a cable plugged into the Ethernet port of your Mac and into an external box — which is connected to a coaxial or optical TV cable or plugged into a telephone outlet, depending on what kind of access you have to the Internet.

For a wireless connection, the setup is the same, but rather than plug the cable into the Ethernet port on your Mac, you plug it into a wireless router or AirPort base station. After this device is connected to the box supplied by your ISP, any Wi-Fi–equipped Mac (or PC) within range can connect to the Internet wirelessly on your network.

Your cable or DSL installer should have set everything up for you before he left your home or office. If you still cannot connect to the Internet, you should call that service provider and give them heck. Troubleshooting a high-speed connection is pretty abstruse (which puts it beyond the purview of this book).

Your Internet service provider and you

After you make sure that you have a working modem, you have to select a company to provide you access to the Internet. These companies are called *Internet service providers* (ISPs). The prices and services that ISPs offer vary, often from minute to minute. Keep the following in mind when choosing an ISP:

- ✔ **If your connection comes from a cable or telephone company, your ISP is probably that company.** In effect, the choice of ISP is pretty much made for you when you decide on cable or DSL service.

- ✔ **The going rate for unlimited broadband access to the Internet starts at around $25 or $30 per month.** If your service provider asks for considerably more than that, find out why. Higher-throughput packages for cable and DSL connections might run you twice that. For example, at this writing the highest-speed DSL package from AT&T is around $60 a month.

Because most Mac users like things to be easy, Mac OS X includes a cool feature in its Setup Assistant to help you find and configure an account with an ISP. When you installed OS X 10.7 (assuming that you did and that it didn't come preinstalled on your Mac), the Installer program might have asked you a bunch of questions about your Internet connection and then set everything up for you. This process is detailed in this book's Appendix. If you didn't have an Internet connection (an ISP) at that time, you need to configure the Network System Preferences pane yourself. Although I cover the Network System Preferences pane in depth in the next section, how to configure it so that your Mac works with your ISP is something you have to work out with that ISP. If you have questions or problems not answered by this book, your ISP should be able to assist you. And if your ISP can't help, it's probably time to try a different ISP.

Plugging in your Internet-connection settings

If you didn't set up your Internet connection when you installed OS X, you need to open System Preferences (from the Applications folder, the Dock, or the menu) and click the Network icon. The Network pane offers options for connecting your Mac to the Internet or to a network. The easiest way to use it is to click the Assist Me button at the bottom and let your Mac do the heavy lifting. Here are some tips and tricks to get you started.

If you're part of a large office network, check with your system administrator before you change anything in this pane. If you ignore this advice, you run the risk of losing your network connection completely.

Setting up your Internet connection manually in the Network System Preferences pane is beyond the purview of this book. That said, here's a very brief overview of the things you need to do should you feel inclined to configure your network connection manually.

Depending on the type of connection you have, you need to configure some or all of the items in the following list.

Once again, I highly recommend clicking the Assist Me button at the bottom of the Network System Preferences pane and letting your Mac set up your connection for you. If it asks you a question you can't answer, ask your ISP or network administrator for the answer. I can't possibly tell you how in this book because there are just too many possible configurations, and each depends on your particular ISP and service.

That said, here's a brief rundown on the most common things you might need to know to set up a network connection:

- ✓ **TCP/IP:** TCP/IP is the language of the Internet. You might be asked to specify things such as your IP address, domain name servers, and search domains.

- ✓ **PPP or PPPoE:** These acronyms stand for *Point-to-Point Protocol* and *Point-to-Point Protocol over Ethernet.* Which one you see depends on what service you're using to connect. All analog modems use PPP; some cable and DSL modems use PPPoE.

- ✓ **Proxies:** If you're on a large network or your Mac is behind a firewall, you might need to specify one or more proxy servers. If so, your network administrator or ISP can help you with configuration. If you're a home user, you'll probably never need to touch this tab. Finally, some ISPs require you to specify proxy servers; if you need to do this, ask your ISP what to do.

About MobileMe and iCloud

While this book was being written, Apple announced that the MobileMe subscription online service would be discontinued effective June 30, 2012.

By the time you read this book, it will be too late to purchase a subscription. A new service, iCloud, will be available this fall at no charge

to Lion and iOS 5 users. Further details may be available at `http://support.apple.com/kb/HT4597`.

If you have MobileMe, you already know what it is and how to use it; if you don't have it, you can't get it anymore. So that's all I'll say on the subject.

If you use your Mac in more than one place, you can set up a separate configuration for each location and then choose it from this menu. A *location*, in this context, consists of all settings in all items in the Network System Preferences pane. After you have this entire pane configured the way that you like, follow these steps to create separate locations:

1. **Pull down the Location menu, and choose Edit Locations.**

2. **Click the + button at the bottom of the Locations list.**

   A new, untitled Location appears in the list.

3. **Type a descriptive name for the new location, such as** AirPort at Starbucks **or** Ethernet at Joe's Office**.**

4. **Click Done and then click Apply.**

   From now on, you can change all your network settings at the same time by choosing the appropriate location from the Location pop-up menu.

If, on the other hand, your Mac has a single network or Internet connection (as most home users have), just leave the Location menu set to Automatic and be done with it.

Using the Network Setup Assistant (click the Assist Me button at the bottom of the Network System Preferences pane and then click the Assistant button) to create a network connection usually makes it unnecessary for you to have to deal with most of these items. Still, I thought you should at least know the basics.

Browsing the Web with Safari

With your Internet connection set up, you're ready to browse the web. In the following sections, I concentrate on browsing the web with Safari because it's the web browser installed with OS X Lion.

If you don't care for Safari, check out OmniWeb, Firefox, or Chrome, which are all free and have features you won't find in Safari.

To begin, just open your web browser. No problem. As usual, there's more than one way. You can launch Safari by any of these methods:

- ✔ Clicking the Safari icon in the Dock (look for the big blue compass that looks like a stopwatch, as shown in the margin)
- ✔ Double-clicking the Safari icon in your Applications folder
- ✔ Single-clicking a URL link in an e-mail or other document
- ✔ Double-clicking a URL link document in the Finder

When you first launch Safari, it automatically connects you to the Internet and displays the default Apple start page (see Figure 10-1). In the sections that follow, I cover the highlights of using Safari, starting at the top of the screen.

Figure 10-1: Safari displaying the Apple start page.

Navigating with the toolbar buttons

The buttons along the top of the window do pretty much what their names imply. From left to right, these buttons are

- **Back/Forward:** When you open a page and then move to a second page (or third or fourth), the Back button takes you to a previously visited page. Remember that you need to go back before the Forward button will work.

- **Add This Page (+):** When you find a page of interest or a page you know you'll want to remember, click this button to tell Safari to remember it for you in Lion's cool new Reading List or as a Bookmark — two topics I explore further a little later in this chapter.

To the right of the Add This Page button is the Address field. This is where you type web addresses, or *URLs* (Uniform Resource Locators), that you want to visit. Just type one and press Return to surf to that site.

But wait — there's more. To add other useful buttons to your toolbar, choose View⇨Customize Toolbar (or right-click anywhere in the toolbar and choose Customize Toolbar from the contextual menu). The Customize Toolbar sheet drops down, and you can drag items into or out of the toolbar to create your own custom set of buttons. In Figure 10-2, for example, I added (left to right) Home, AutoFill, Zoom In/Out, New Tab, Email (a link to this page), and Report Bug (to Apple) to my toolbar.

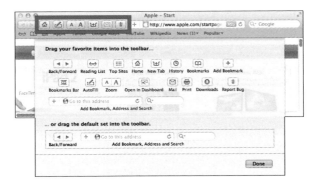

Figure 10-2: The Customize Toolbar sheet (bottom) and my customized toolbar (top, highlighted).

Web addresses almost always begin with `http://www`. But Safari has a cool trick: If you just type a name, you usually get to the appropriate web site that way without typing `http`, `//`, or `www`. If you type **apple** in the Address field and then press Return, for example, you go to www.apple.com. Or if you type **boblevitus**, you're taken to www.boblevitus.com. Try it — it's pretty slick.

Below the Address field is the Bookmark Bar, already populated with some buttons of web pages Apple thinks you might enjoy, including Apple, Yahoo!, Google Maps, YouTube, and Wikipedia.

The News and Popular buttons are actually *drop-down menus*. You can tell by the little black triangles after their names, as shown in Figure 10-3.

Figure 10-3: The News (and Popular) buttons are actually drop-down menus.

You can delete these bookmarks and/or add your own bookmarks to the Bookmark Bar, as described in the next section.

Bookmarking your favorite pages

When you find a web page you want to remember and return to, you bookmark it. Here's how it works:

1. **Click the Add (+) button in the Safari toolbar, choose Bookmarks➪Add Bookmark, or press ⌘+D.**

2. **Choose where to store the bookmark from the pop-up menu, as shown in Figure 10-4.**

3. **Rename the bookmark or use the name provided by Safari.**

4. **Click the Add button to save the bookmark.**

Figure 10-4: This page will appear in the Bookmarks Bar as "Consulting by Dr. Mac."

 To return to a bookmarked page, click it in the Bookmarks Bar, select it in the Bookmarks Menu, choose Bookmarks⇨Show All Bookmarks, press ⌘+Option+B, or click the Show All Bookmarks button (shown in margin) to see all your bookmarks in the Bookmarks window, as shown in Figure 10-5.

Figure 10-5: The Bookmarks window in all its glory.

Open bookmarked pages in the Bookmarks window by double-clicking them.

You can view the contents of any collection (that is, a folder full of bookmarks) by clicking its name in the Collections pane on the left side of the window. Figure 10-5 shows, in particular, the contents of the Bookmarks Bar folder with the contents of the News subfolder expanded.

To organize your Bookmarks window or place bookmarks on the toolbar or Bookmarks menu, move bookmarks by dragging them. You can place bookmarks and folders of bookmarks on the Safari Bookmarks Bar or Bookmarks menu by dragging them to the appropriate folder. If you drag a folder of bookmarks to the Bookmarks Bar folder (or directly onto the Bookmarks Bar itself), the result is a drop-down menu, as shown in Figure 10-3, earlier in this chapter.

To delete a bookmark, select it in the Bookmarks window and then press Delete key.

 If you enable Auto-Click for a folder of bookmarks, you don't get a drop-down menu when you click its button. Instead, all the pages in that folder open at once, each in its own separate tab. You can still use the drop-down menu, but you have to click and hold the button rather than just click. Conversely, if you want to open all the bookmarks in a folder that doesn't have Auto-Click enabled, you can ⌘+click it to open the pages in separate tabs.

 Bookmarks are favorites, and favorites are bookmarks. Both words refer to exactly the same thing: shortcuts to websites. In this chapter, I use *bookmarks* because that's what Safari calls them. Some other browsers call them *favorites*.

What's on your reading list?

 The Reading List serves as a repository for pages or links you want to read but don't want to read right now. It's a lot like a bookmark but easier to create on the fly, which makes the Reading List perfect for sites or links you don't need to keep forever (that's what bookmarks are for).

In the previous section, you saw one of the ways you can add a page to your Reading List: clicking the Add (+) button in the Toolbar.

 Another way to add a page to your Reading List is to open the page and then click the Reading List icon (the eyeglasses, as shown in the margin). The Reading List sidebar appears on the left side of the window, as shown in Figure 10-6. Click the Add Page button in the Reading List sidebar.

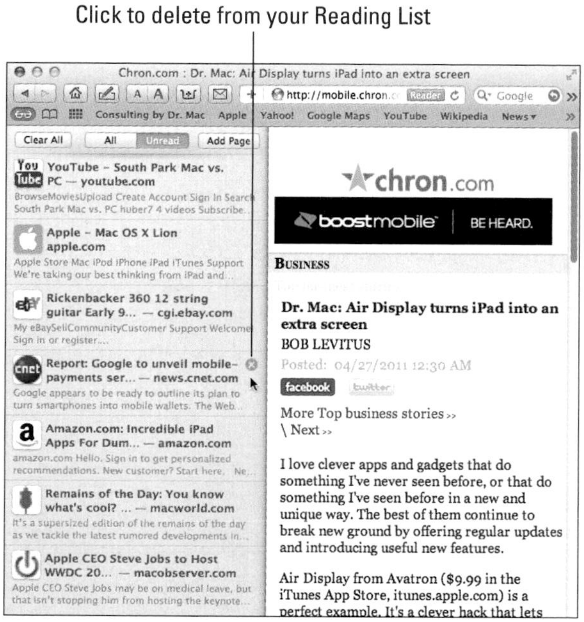

Click to delete from your Reading List

Figure 10-6: Use the Reading List for pages you want to visit soon.

To add a link to your Reading List without visiting the page, press the Shift key when you click. It's fast and works even when the Reading List sidebar is closed. Or right-click the link and choose Add To Reading List from the contextual menu.

Finally, to delete an item from your Reading List, click the X in its top-right corner, as shown in Figure 10-6. To delete them all at once, click the Clear All button.

If you don't see an X, move the cursor over the item you want to delete, and it magically appears.

Using the terrific Top Sites page

The Top Sites page has quickly become one of my favorite Safari features. It displays a selection of sites you visit frequently, as shown in Figure 10-7.

To see it, choose History➪Show Top Sites, press ⌘+Shift+1, or click the Top Sites button (shown in the margin), which you'll find to the right of the Show All Bookmarks button.

Figure 10-7: Top Sites displays your favorite sites.

As you surf the web, Safari learns your favorite sites and replaces the sites on the Top Sites page with the ones you visit most.

The little stars you see in the top-right corner of some sites in Figure 10-4 indicate that the page has changed since the last time you visited it (a very nice touch).

Click the Edit button in the bottom-left corner, and you can

- **Delete a site you don't want on your Top Sites page.** Click the little X in its top-left corner.

- **"Pin" a site to your Top Sites page to make it remain one of your Top Sites, even if you don't visit that page for a while.** Click the pushpin in its top-left corner. All the items in the top row of Figure 10-8 are marked as permanent Top Sites.

- **Change the number and size of the sites shown.** Choose Small (24 sites), Medium (12 sites, as shown in Figure 10-8), or Large (6, as shown in Figure 10-7).

Figure 10-8 shows all these actions.

Figure 10-8: This is what editing the Top Sites page looks like.

Simplifying surfing with RSS feeds

In the past few years, *blogs* (short for *web logs)* have cropped up all over the web — whether as online personal journals or corporate sources of business information. No wonder *RSS* — which adept bloggers translate as *Really Simple Syndication* — has emerged at the same time. You see synopses of what's available at the site on its *RSS feed* — what the special RSS links are called. In effect, you get an adjustable-length overview with a link to the full story. These steps give you a closer look at how RSS works:

1. **Look for an RSS icon.**

   When a web page is associated with an RSS feed, a little RSS icon appears at the right end of the address bar, as shown in Figure 10-9 and the margin.

2. **Click the RSS icon to see all the RSS synopses for the site, as shown in Figure 10-9.**

   The right side of the window gives you control over what you see and how it's displayed. You can search the articles by typing a word or phrase. You can drag the article-length slider to see more or less of each synopsis. Or you can click other items — Sort By, Recent Articles, Source, or Actions — to sort or filter the articles, display the page that this RSS feed represents (Apple Hot News in Figure 10-9), update the contents of this page, mail a link to this page to someone, or subscribe to this feed in Mail.

You can, of course, bookmark an RSS feed just as you would bookmark any web page. But if you really like a feed, you might want to subscribe to it in Mail, which shows you the updated contents of the feed in the Mail application (see Chapter 11).

3. Click it again, and the RSS synopses disappear.

They're replaced by the page contents, as shown earlier in Figure 10-1.

Figure 10-9: The RSS synopses for the Apple Hot News page, which were displayed when I clicked the RSS icon in Figure 10-1.

Searching with Google

Looking for something on the Internet? Check out Google, a fantastic search engine integrated with Safari to help you hunt down just about anything on the Internet in no time.

In this section, you discover how to use Google to search the Internet and find almost anything, as well as how to get help with Google when all else fails.

To search the Internet with Google, follow these steps:

1. **Type the beginning of a word or phrase in the Google field to the right of the address bar near the top of the Safari window.**

   As you type, Safari offers suggestions and recent searches, as shown in Figure 10-10.

2. **Click one of the list items, finish typing the word or phrase, or use the arrow keys to select a list item and then press Return or Enter to start the search.**

   Google almost immediately offers your search results, as shown in Figure 10-10.

Figure 10-10: A Google search for pictures of Vizsla dogs.

3. **Click one of the result links.**

   Links appear in blue and are underlined. You're taken instantly to that particular page.

4. **If a particular result isn't just what you're looking for, click the Back button, and try another result link.**

5. **If Google offers too many results that aren't just right, click the Advanced Search link near the top of the results page, and refine your search.**

   You can refine your search by using a multitude of options, as shown in Figure 10-11.

Figure 10-11: A Google advanced search for pictures of Vizsla dogs that are cute or puppies and not ugly, senior, or old.

6. Click the Advanced Search button.

A refined results page quickly appears. As before, click a result link to visit that page. If it's not just what you're looking for, click the Back button, and try a different result link.

 The little circle with an arrow in it on the right side of the Google field in Figure 10-11 and in the margin is the SnapBack to Last Search Results button. Click it to return to the Google results page for the last search you performed. Sweet!

That's pretty much all you need to know to have a great time surfing the web with Google.

 The little angle bracket icons on the right side of the toolbar and Bookmarks Bar in many of the preceding figures (shown in the margin) indicate that the window is too narrow to display all the tools or bookmarks. Click it, and a menu shows you the previously hidden choices, as shown in Figure 10-12.

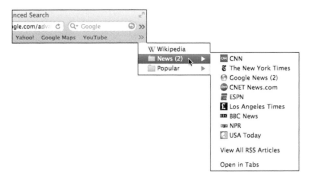

Figure 10-12: The Bookmarks Bar overflow menu shows the three hidden bookmarks.

One last thing: If you prefer to use Yahoo! or Bing instead of Google for searches, click the magnifying-glass icon in Safari's search field and choose it from the drop-down menu, which you can see in Figure 10-10.

Checking out Help Center

That's pretty much all you need to know to have a great time surfing the web. Actually, Safari has a lot more features, and I could write an entire chapter about using Safari, but one of the rules we *For Dummies* authors must follow is that our books can't run 1,000 pages long.

So I'm going to give you the next best thing: Open the Help Center (by choosing Help⇔Safari Help). A special Safari Help window appears; you can search for any Safari-related topic or solution to any Safari-related problem right there.

Communicating via iChat

Instant messaging and chat rooms provide for interactive communication among users all over the world. If you're into instant messaging, iChat gives you immediate access to all the other users of AIM, Jabber, Google Talk, and MobileMe. All you need are their screen names, and you're set to go. You can even join any AOL chat room just by choosing File⇔Go to Chat.

To get started, just launch iChat from either your Applications folder or your Dock.

Chit-chatting with iChat

Your text chats can be one to one, or they can be group bull sessions. iChat is integrated with the Address Book, so you don't have to enter your buddies' information twice. It also communicates directly with the Mail application. Here's all the essential info you need to get started:

- ✓ **To start a text chat,** open iChat, select a buddy in your buddy list, and choose Buddies⇨Invite to Chat.

  Each participant's picture (or icon) appears next to anything she says, which is displayed in a cartoonlike thought bubble, as shown in Figure 10-13. If you find the thought bubbles a little too childish, you can turn them off from the View menu.

- ✓ **To start a group text chat,** hold down the ⌘ key, click each person in your buddy list that you want to include, and then click the A button at the bottom of the buddy list. In a group text chat, everyone sees every message from every participant.

- ✓ **To attach a picture to a person in your Address Book** (as I have for myself with a photo on one Mac and a cartoon image on the other), copy a picture of that person to the Clipboard in your favorite graphics application (Preview, for example). Now open Address Book, and display the card for the person you want to add a picture to. Click the empty picture box at the top of the card, and paste the picture on the Clipboard. You should now see that picture on the Address Book card and also when you iChat with the person. Neat!

Figure 10-13: A chat with myself. (I have two Macs on the same network.)

✔ **To transfer files,** just drag the document's icon to the message box, as demonstrated in Figure 10-14, and press Return or Enter. The file zips across the ether. This is a very convenient way to share photos or documents without resorting to file sharing or e-mail.

When you drag an image file (LeVitusHead, in Figure 10-14) onto the iChat window's message box, as shown in Figure 10-14, you'll see an oversize semitransparent preview, so you're sure you're sending them the right image and not something totally embarrassing. Way to go, Mac OS X Lion.

✔ **To send an e-mail from iChat,** just select a buddy in iChat's buddy list and then choose Buddies⇨Send Email (or press ⌘+Option+E). Mail launches (if it's not already open) and addresses a new message to the selected buddy, ready for you to begin typing.

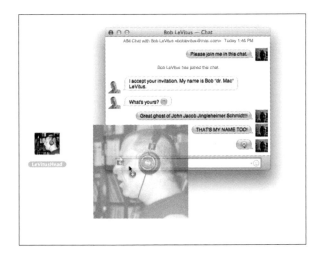

Figure 10-14: Transferring a file with iChat.

Chatting with audio and video

The greatest iChat feature is audio/video chatting, which is why it was once known as *iChat AV*. Apple dropped the *AV* part, but iChat still has fantastic audio and video features that are lots of fun — and ever-so-easy to set up and use.

With iChat, you can conference a video chat with up to three other people at the same time and audio chat with up to nine other folks at the same time.

To conduct a video or audio chat, follow these steps:

1. **Connect a FireWire camera and/or a supported microphone to your Mac.**

   Although many FireWire and USB camcorders and webcams will work fairly well for video chatting, Apple's iSight camera/microphone combination is designed just for this purpose (and works even better in most cases). It's built into all Mac notebooks and iMacs these days, so you likely won't have to buy a thing to video (and audio) chat.

   When you have appropriate hardware connected to your Mac, your buddies' names in the buddy lists display little green telephone or camera icons if they have the right hardware and an adequate Internet connection on their end.

2. **To start an audio- or videoconference, click the appropriate green icon(s).**

   Your buddies receive an invitation to begin an audio or video chat.

3. **If they accept the invitation, a Video Chat window appears, as shown in Figure 10-15.**

Figure 10-15: I'm iChatting with my buddy Dave Hamilton.

If your Mac has a built-in iSight camera or you have a compatible camcorder or webcam handy, why not give it a try? My chat handle is `boblevitus@ mac.com`; feel free to invite me to video chat if you see me online.

Sending files and messages with Bonjour and iChat

Mac OS X offers built-in support for Bonjour (Apple used to call it Rendezvous), which makes chatting even better. With Bonjour, Mac OS X can automatically recognize others on a local network who are available to chat. So you can send a quick message or files from one computer to another quickly and with minimum hassle. Just choose Window⇨Bonjour, and select the person with whom you want to chat from the Bonjour window. From there, you can send a message or file.

For Bonjour to connect to another computer, both users need to have Bonjour enabled and must either be connected to the same network or have AirPort for wireless networking built in. Beyond that, the connection is configuration-free; you don't have to do anything to be part of a Bonjour network because your Mac configures itself and joins up automatically.

If you're in the same Wi-Fi network and are both running Lion, however, Lion's new AirDrop (described in Chapter 16) is an even faster, easier way to transfer files between two Macs.

Remote Screen Sharing: Remarkable and superbly satisfying

I'd like to call your attention to one last iChat feature. It's called Remote Screen Sharing, was introduced in Mac OS X 10.5 Leopard, and is possibly the most useful iChat feature of all time. It lets you control another Mac anywhere in the world, or another Mac user can control your Mac from any location.

So now when Mom calls you and says, "I'm trying to get my mail, but the thing that I click disappeared," you don't have to try to decipher her description and explain how to replace the Mail icon in the Dock. Instead, you calmly say to her, "Mom, just open up iChat, and let me show you how to fix that." Here's how it works:

1. She launches iChat on her Mac. You launch iChat on yours.

2. She clicks your name in her buddy list and chooses Buddies⇨Share My Screen (or you click her name in your Buddy list and choose Buddies⇨Share Remote Screen).

3. A window pops up on Mom's screen, where she grants you permission to control her screen; when permission is granted, you can see her screen on *your* Mac and control her Mac with your mouse and keyboard.

   More specifically, after she grants you permission, you see a *proxy image* of her screen that says *Switch to Momofyours2011's Computer,* as shown in Figure 10-16.

Figure 10-16: If I click the little proxy image of *Momofyours2011's Computer* on the left, my whole screen is taken over by *Momofyours2011's* computer's screen.

4. You click anywhere in the little Computer window *(Momofyours2011's Computer)* shown on the left in Figure 10-16, your screen changes — and instead of your stuff, you see Mom's Desktop, as shown in Figure 10-17.

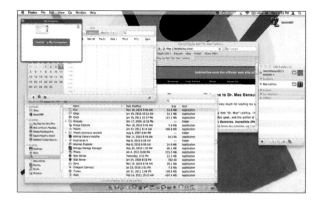

Figure 10-17: My computer is displaying my mom's computer screen.

At this juncture, your mouse and keyboard are controlling your mom's computer, which you see full-screen on your computer. Neat, huh?

5. To go back to your Mac screen, just click the Switch to My Computer window at top left in Figure 10-17. The remote computer screen disappears, and yours comes back.

This is the best way to help another Mac user accomplish anything. In fact, my consulting business has been using similar software to help Mac users for years. It's fantastic to be able to talk to folks on the phone while you're controlling their Macs. You can fix things in a fraction of the time it would take to explain how to do it over the phone alone.

Before you get too excited about having all that control, note these few provisos:

✔ You and the other user must both be running Mac OS X 10.5 Leopard, Mac OS X 10.6 Snow Leopard, or Mac OS X 10.7 Lion.

✔ You and the other user must both have iChat accounts (on iCloud, MobileMe, AIM, Jabber, or Google Talk).

✔ You and the other user both need high-speed Internet access.

You can combine this feature with the iChat file-sharing feature described earlier to collaborate with others on documents or projects.

When you share your screen, the person you share it with has the same degree of access to your files that you have. It follows that you should share your screen only with people you deeply trust. Furthermore, if you have files on your Mac that you would prefer that the other person didn't see, I suggest you hide them deep in a subfolder somewhere or delete them before you begin your screen-sharing session.

Video Calls with FaceTime

In the beginning, FaceTime brought video calling to the iPhone 4. It was iPhone 4-to-iPhone 4 only and required Wi-Fi (not 3G). Still, it was pretty cool and worked quite well. Not surprisingly, it soon spread to the iPad 2, the iPod touch, and the Mac.

What's that you say? I just told you all about iChat's video calling features? You're right, but whereas iChat does it for Mac or PC users, only FaceTime lets you do it with iPhone 4s, iPad 2s, and iPod touches.

In addition to its aforementioned video-with-i-devices prowess, FaceTime works very nicely for Mac-to-Mac video calls. And because it's a single-purpose application, many users find it easier and less intimidating to set up and use than iChat or Skype.

By the way, there's no Windows version of FaceTime at the moment, so you'll have to use iChat (or third-party software like Skype) to have cross-platform video chats.

To get started, just launch FaceTime from either your Applications folder or your Dock, and the main (only) FaceTime window appears, as shown in Figure 10-18.

Figure 10-18: The FaceTime window, ready to make a call.

The left side of the window shows what your Mac's camera is seeing (which happens to be me in Figure 10-18).

I clicked the iPhone entry to initiate a call from my Mac to my wife's iPhone. She was at the football game with my son Jacob, and I was soon talking to both of them, as shown in Figure 10-19.

Figure 10-19: What I saw on my Mac screen (left) and what they saw on their iPhone screen (right).

FaceTime uses Lion's Address Book (covered in Chapter 11), so if you have friends or family with iPhone 4s, iPad 2s, iPod touches, or Macs, just click their phone number or e-mail address to initiate a video call.

E-Mail Made Easy

In This Chapter

▶ Managing contacts with Address Book

▶ Mastering e-mail with Mail

In this chapter, you look at a pair of programs that work together and make managing your contacts and e-mail a breeze. You find out how both of these eponymous programs — Address Book and Mail — work, and how to use them individually and as a team.

I cover a lot of material in not a lot of space in this chapter, so if there's something you want to find out about Address Book or Mail that I don't cover, don't forget about the wonderful assistance you can find in Help➪Mail Help and Help➪Address Book Help.

Keeping Contacts Handy with Address Book

The Address Book is where you store contact information for your family, friends, and anyone else you want to keep track of. It works seamlessly with the Mail application, enabling you to quickly look up e-mail addresses when you're ready to send a message.

In fact, Address Book works with several applications, both on and beyond your Mac, including the following:

✔ Use it with iChat (covered in Chapter 10) to whip up a quick chat with your online friends.

✔ Use it with FaceTime (covered in Chapter 17) to video chat with friends and family.

✔ Use it with iCal (covered in Chapter 9) by choosing Window⇨Address Panel or pressing ⌘+Option+A. You can then drag any person in your Address Book from the Address Panel to any date and time on the calendar, and a special Meeting event is created automatically by iCal. The event even has a Send Invitation button; if you click it, it launches Mail and sends the person an invitation to this meeting. Very cool stuff.

✔ The Address Book application can also work with any other application whose programmers choose to make the connection or with any device that is compatible with Address Book. For example, FileMaker's Bento application ($49.99 in the Lion App Store) exchanges data with Address Book seamlessly, so changes made in Address Book appear in Bento (and vice versa) almost immediately.

You can find a list of such devices here: http://support.apple.com/kb/HT2824.

In the following sections, you find out the best ways to fill Address Book with contacts and keep those contacts organized.

Adding contacts

Follow these steps to create a new entry in the Address Book:

1. **Launch the Address Book application by double-clicking its icon in the Applications folder or clicking its Dock icon.**

   The Address Book appears. The first time that you open Address Book, you see two cards: Apple Computer and the one with the personal identification information you supplied when you created your account.

2. **To create a new entry, click the + button at the bottom of the Address Book's Name column.**

   An untitled address card appears. The First name text field is initially selected. (You can tell because it's highlighted, as shown in Figure 11-1.)

3. **Type the person's first name in the First text field.**

   Here, I type **Doctor**.

4. **Press Tab.**

   Your cursor should now be in the Last text field.

   You can always move from one field to the next by pressing Tab — in fact, this shortcut works in almost all Mac programs that have fields like these. (You can move to the previous field by pressing Shift+Tab.)

5. **Type the last name for the person you're adding to your Address Book.**

   Here, I type **Mac**.

   Continue this process, filling in the rest of the fields shown in Figure 11-2.

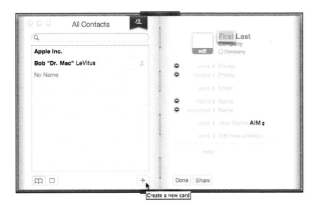

Figure 11-1: A new address card in Address Book.

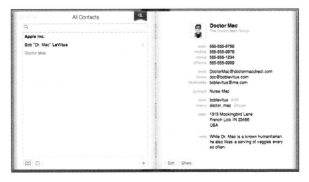

Figure 11-2: The address card displayed in the Address Book window.

6. **When you're done entering information, click the Done button to exit the editing mode.**

   The contact I created with this step appears in Figure 11-2.

   The little up and down arrows between the labels and their contents fields are for opening pop-up menus that offer alternative labels for the field. For example, if you were to click the arrows next to the word *Work,* you could choose Home, Mobile, Main, Home Fax, Work Fax, Pager, Other, or Custom to replace the label Work.

   The little contact card is called a *vCard* (virtual business card).

   To add more info about any Address Book entry, select the name in the Name column (Doctor Mac in Figure 11-2). You can tell when a name is selected because it is highlighted, as Doctor Mac is in Figure 11-2. Then click the Edit button at the bottom of the Address Book window, and make your changes.

Repeat this process for everyone you know and want to keep in touch with.

Importing contacts from other programs

If you already have contacts you created in another program, you might be able to import them into Address Book. Address Book can import contacts in vCard, LDIF, or Text file format.

The first thing you need to do is export the data from the other program in one of these formats. Then choose File⇨Import⇨vCard (or LDIF or Text file, as the case may be), choose the exported data file in the Open File dialog, and then click the Open button.

Creating a basic group

Now let me explain how to organize your contacts into groups. Why would you want to organize your contacts into groups? The main reason, at least for me, is practical: I can send e-mail to everyone in a group that I've defined with a single click. So when it's time to send out a press release, I can simply send it to my Press group, shooting the e-mail off to all 50 people I have in that group. And when I want to send an e-mail to all the parents of kids on my son's indoor football team, I merely address it to my Flag Football Parents group, and all 12 families in that group receive it.

Here's how to create a group and add contacts to it:

1. **Launch the Address Book application by double-clicking its icon in the Applications folder or clicking its Dock icon.**

2. **To create a new group, File⇨New Group or press ⌘+Shift+N.**

   An untitled Group appears in the Group column with "untitled group" highlighted.

3. **Type a descriptive name for this group and then press Enter or Return.**

   I named mine Family.

4. **Click All Contacts on the left side of the window to show all your contacts on the right side.**

5. **Click the contacts you want in the group on the right side.**

   Hold down the ⌘ key as you select contacts if you want to select more than one contact.

   TIP

   You can use the search field (magnifying-glass icon) at the top of the window to find a contact or contacts and then drag them onto the group to add them.

6. **Drag the selected contact names onto the group, as shown in Figure 11-3.**

Address Book considerately displays the number of contacts you're dragging, which happens to be seven in this instance.

Figure 11-3: Adding seven contacts to the Family group.

In summation, to add a contact to a group, drag the contact onto the group. And that's all there is to creating your own groups.

Setting up a Smart Group (based on contact criteria)

A second type of group — called a Smart Group — might be even more useful to you. A Smart Group gathers contacts in your Address Book based on criteria you specify. So, for example, you could create a group that automatically selects Apple staff members, as I demonstrate in a moment.

The big advantage of a Smart Group over a regular group is that when I add a new Apple contact, that contact automatically becomes a member of the Apple Smart Group with no further action on my part.

To create a Smart Group, follow these steps:

1. **Choose File⇪New Smart Group, press ⌘+Option+N, or click the + button at the bottom of the Group column and choose Smart Group from the pop-up menu.**

A Smart Group sheet appears in front of the Address Book window, as shown in Figure 11-4.

2. **Give the Smart Group a name.**

I named mine Apple.

Figure 11-4: Creating a new Smart Group.

3. **Select the appropriate items from the menus: Any, Company, Contains, Email, and so on.**

   In Figure 11-4, I've created a Smart Group that includes any contact that contains *Apple* in the Company field or *@apple.com* in any e-mail field.

4. **When you're happy with the criteria specified, click OK.**

You can tell if a group is set up as a Smart Group because its icon includes a gear.

To delete a group or Smart Group from your Address Book, click to select it and then choose Edit⇨Delete Group.

The Views are lovely

Notice the little red bookmark-looking thing, the one with the silhouette of a single person in Figure 11-3 (also shown on the left in the margin)? Now examine Figures 11-1 and 11-2, and notice that the little red bookmark-looking thing in those figures has *two* people in silhouette (also shown on the right in the margin). Those bookmarks are shortcuts to two of Address Book's three views.

Address Book's views are available in its View menu and by keyboard shortcut as well. Here's a visual guide:

- ✔ **If you see a bookmark-looking thing with two silhouettes:** You're in List and Card view (View⇨List and Card or ⌘+1), with the list of your contacts on the left and the details for the selected contact on the right, as shown in Figures 11-1 and 11-2.

- ✔ **If you see a bookmark-looking thing with one silhouette:** You're in Groups view (View⇨Groups or ⌘+3), with the list of your groups on the left and the list of your contacts on the right, as shown in Figure 11-3.

- ✔ **If all you see is a card for a single contact:** You're in Card Only view (View⇨Card Only or ⌘+2), as shown in Figure 11-5.

Figure 11-5: Choose View⇨Card Only or press ⌘+2 for the Card Only view.

Try it now: Open Address Book if it's not already open, and press ⌘+1, ⌘+2, and then ⌘+3. See how easy it is to find a view that works for you.

Sending e-mail to a contact or group

This section looks at how you can create and send an e-mail message to a contact or group in your Address Book.

You don't even have to open Address Book to send an e-mail to a contact or group contained in your Address Book. In the next section, you see how Mail finds contacts or groups for you without launching Address Book. But if you already have Address Book open, this technique for sending e-mail to a contact or group is probably most convenient.

To create a blank e-mail message to a contact, click and hold the label next to the e-mail address, and choose Send Email from the pop-up menu that appears, as shown in Figure 11-6.

Figure 11-6: Sending e-mail to someone in your Address Book is as easy as clicking here.

The Mail program becomes active, and a blank e-mail message addressed to the selected contact appears on your screen. Just type your e-mail as you normally would.

 There are two little icons in the bottom-left corner of the card window in Figure 11-6. The one on the left, which looks like a book, switches you to List and Card view; the one on the right, which looks like a little box, switches you to Card Only view.

Sending and Receiving E-Mail with Mail

Mail is a program for sending, receiving, and organizing your e-mail.

Mail is fast and easy to use, too. Click the Mail icon in the Dock or double-click the Mail icon in the Applications folder to launch Mail. The Mail icon looks like a canceled postage stamp, as shown in the margin.

You can use other applications to read e-mail. Mozilla (Thunderbird) and AOL, for example, have their own mail readers, as does Microsoft Office (Entourage or Outlook). But for Macs, the easiest and best mail reader around (meaning the best one on your hard drive by default) is almost certainly Mail. And of course, you can't beat the price; it's free!

 The following sections, in some cases, offer you starting points. Even so, you should find everything perfectly straightforward. If you run into a question that the following sections don't answer, remember that you can always call upon the assistance of Help (Help⇨Mail Help).

Setting up Mail

If this is your first time launching Mail, you need to set up your e-mail account(s) before you can proceed. A set of New Account screens appears automatically. Just fill in the blanks on each screen and click the Continue button until you're finished.

If you don't know what to type in one or more of these blank fields, contact your ISP (Internet service provider) or mail provider for assistance.

After you've set up one or more e-mail accounts, you see a Welcome message asking whether you'd like to see what's new in Mail. If you click Yes, Help Viewer launches and shows you the What's New in Mail page (while Mail's main window, which looks like Figure 11-7, appears in the background). Or if you click No, Mail's main window appears as the active window immediately.

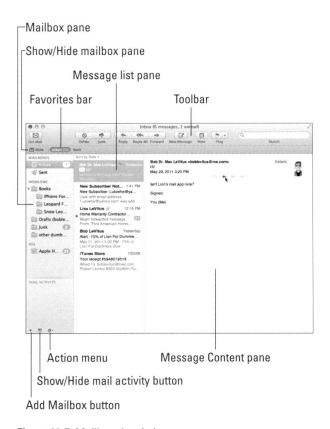

Mailbox pane

Show/Hide mailbox pane

Message list pane

Favorites bar

Toolbar

Action menu

Message Content pane

Show/Hide mail activity button

Add Mailbox button

Figure 11-7: Mail's main window.

Mail's main window is actually called a *viewer window* or *message viewer window*. You can have more than one of them on your screen, if you like; just choose File⇨New Viewer Window or press ⌘+Option+N.

Composing a new message

Here's how to create a new e-mail message:

1. **Choose File⇨New Message, click the New button on the toolbar, or press ⌘+N.**

   A new window appears. This is where you compose your e-mail message, as shown in Figure 11-8.

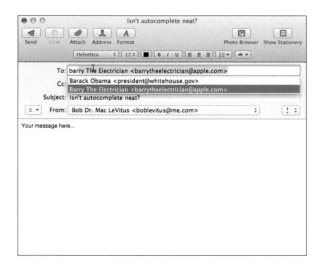

Figure 11-8: Composing an e-mail message.

2. **Place your cursor in the To field, and type someone's e-mail address.**

   Use my address (Lion4Dummies@boblevitus.com) if you don't know anyone else to send mail to.

    If the recipient is in your Address Book (as Barack Obama and Barry the Electrician are in mine), just type a few letters, and Mail's intelligent autocomplete function matches it up with Address Book. So, for example, I typed the letters *b-a-r,* and a list of people in my Address Book with *bar* in their names — namely, Barack Obama and Barry the Electrician in Figure 11-8 — appeared. I can select a name by clicking it, typing an additional letter or letters to narrow the search (typing an **r** would leave only Barry the Electrician; typing an **a** would leave only Barack Obama), or using the arrow keys and then pressing Return or Enter.

Isn't autocomplete neat?

3. **Press the Tab key twice to move your cursor to the Subject text field and then type a subject for this message.**

   I typed *Isn't Autocomplete neat?* in Figure 11-8.

4. **Click in the main message portion of the window, and type your message there.**

   I typed *Your message here…* in Figure 11-8.

5. **When you're finished writing your message, click the Send button to send the e-mail immediately, or close it to save it in the Drafts mailbox so you can work on it later.**

If you save your message to the Drafts mailbox (so you can write more later, perhaps), you can send it when you're ready by opening the Drafts mailbox, double-clicking the message, and then clicking the Send button.

Just for the record, here's what the buttons in the toolbar in Figure 11-8 are all about:

- *Send:* D'oh. Sends the message.

- *Chat:* Start a chat with one or more addressees.

- *Attach:* Opens a standard Open File sheet so you can pick a file or files to enclose with this message.

  To enclose multiple files, hold down the ⌘ key as you click each file you want to enclose.

  If the recipients of this message use Windows, you probably want to select the Send Windows-Friendly Attachments check box at the bottom of the Open File sheet.

- *Address:* Opens the Address Panel, a miniature representation of your Address Book. You can then drag contacts or groups from the Address Panel to the To or CC field of the message.

- *Format:* Shows or hides the Formatting toolbar, which is showing (between the toolbar and the To field) in Figure 11-8.

- *Photo Browser:* Opens the Photo Browser panel, which displays the photos in your iPhoto library and lets you drag and drop them into a mail message.

- *Show Stationery:* Opens a sheet with a selection of stationery you can use for your e-mail message. (You find out more about this feature in a few pages.)

- *The little arrow thingie to the left of the From pop-up menu:* This little doohickey is actually a pop-down menu that lets you add fields to your message header. What fields? Glad you asked. . . . You can choose CC Address Field, BCC Address Field, Reply-To Address Field, or Priority Field. Or if you choose Customize, you see all the available fields with check boxes next to them so you can turn them on or off at will.

Changes you make using this menu become defaults. In other words, if you add a BCC field to this message, *all* subsequent messages also have a BCC field.

A quick overview of the toolbar

Before you go any further, look at the nine handy buttons and a search field in the viewer window's toolbar by default:

- **Get Mail:** Checks for new e-mail.

- **Delete:** Deletes selected message or messages ("Hi" in Figure 11-7, shown earlier).

  To select more than one message in the list, hold down the ⌘ key when you click the second and subsequent messages.

- **Junk:** Marks the selected message or messages as junk mail. Mail has built-in junk-mail filtering that can be enabled or disabled in Mail Preferences. (Choose Mail➪Preferences and then click the Junk Mail icon on the toolbar.) If you receive a piece of *spam* (junk mail), select it and click this button to help train Mail's junk-mail filter.

  If a selected message has been marked as junk mail, the button changes to read Not Junk.

  For more info on junk-mail filtering, click the question-mark button in the Junk Mail pane of the Mail Preferences window.

- **Reply:** Creates a reply to the sender only.

- **Reply All:** Creates a reply to the sender and everyone who was sent the original message.

- **Forward:** Creates a copy of this message you can send to someone other than the sender or other recipients.

- **New Message:** Creates a new, blank e-mail message.

- **Note:** Creates a new, blank note. You can write yourself a note (or copy and paste information into a note) and save it for future reference. By default, it's placed in the Notes mailbox when you save it, but you can drag it into any mailbox you like.

✔ **Flag:** This drop-down menu lets you mark or unmark one or more messages with one of seven colored flags. The selected message in Figure 11-7, for example, is flagged in green.

Finally, on the toolbar is a Search field that finds a word or phrase in any item stored in Mail. When you begin typing, a drop-down menu appears, as shown in Figure 11-9, so you can narrow the search to people or subjects matching your search phrase. You can also click the buttons in the Favorites bar to limit your search to specific mailboxes or to search only specific parts of messages (All, Inbox, Sent, Drafts, and Flagged in Figure 11-9).

Figure 11-9: Searching for items with "bob" in them, in all of my mailboxes, reveals 265 items.

Searching in Mail should be familiar to you; it works the same way as searching in the Finder. So, for example, if you want to save a search as a Smart Mailbox (Mail's version of a Smart Folder in the Finder), you click the Save button, which is behind the drop-down menu in Figure 11-9.

I've mentioned the Favorites bar, a new feature in Lion, a couple of times now. Mail populates it with mailboxes you'll use often: Inbox, Sent, Drafts, and Flagged in Figure 11-9. Add your own mailboxes by dragging them from the Mailbox pane to the Favorites bar, as I've done with Lion For Dummies in Figure 11-9.

Working with stationery

Stationery for e-mail messages was new in Mac OS X 10.5 (Leopard), and although I personally find it dorky, you might think it's the greatest thing since kittens, so here are some tips for working with it. To use it, click the Show Stationery button in a New Message window.

I'm a Luddite when it comes to e-mail. When I started using e-mail a long, long time ago, it was considered bad form to add anything but text to an e-mail message. It was generally agreed that e-mail messages should include only what was necessary to convey the information and nothing more. That's why all these froufrou flowers and borders irritate me and why I find them a waste of bandwidth. So please do me a favor: If you decide to send me an e-mail message, please don't use goofy stationery.

Here are some tips to help you have more fun with stationery:

- **Adding favorites:** If you find you're using a particular stationery a lot, you can add it to the Favorites category to make it easier to use. To do so, merely click the appropriate category in the list on the left (Birthday, Announcements, Photos, Stationery, and Sentiments in Figure 11-10); then click the stationery you want to make a favorite and drag it onto the word *Favorites* in the list on the left. When *Favorites* highlights, drop the stationery, and presto — that piece of stationery will appear in the Favorites category evermore.

- **Greeking out:** You can change the Greek/pseudo-Latin text that appears in all the stationery by selecting it, deleting it, and typing whatever text you want to appear. You have to do it only once; the text you type in any stationery appears in all other stationeries.

- **Replacing pictures:** You can replace any picture in any stationery with a picture of your own. Just drag a picture — from the Photo Browser (Window➪Photo Browser) or the Finder — onto any picture in any piece of stationery. I've replaced the boilerplate text and all three of the dorky pictures in the Air Mail stationery, as shown in Figure 11-10.

- **Removing stationery:** If you decide you don't want to use stationery with a message after you've applied it, click the Stationery category and choose the Original stationery, which changes your message back to a clean, blank page.

Checking your mail

How do you check and open your mail? Easy. Just click the Get Mail button at the top of the main Mail window (refer to Figure 11-9) or press ⌘+Shift+N.

- **To read a new message,** select it. Its contents appear in the Message Content pane.

- **To delete a selected message,** click the Delete button on the toolbar.

- **To retrieve a message you accidentally deleted,** click Trash on the left and drag the message into the Inbox or other mailbox.

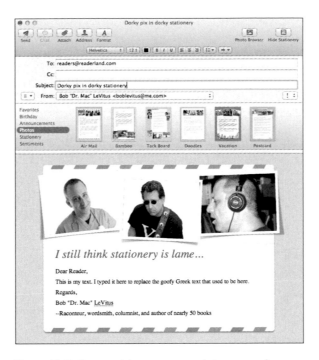

Figure 11-10: Drag and drop your own pictures anywhere you see a picture in a stationery.

✔ **To configure Mail to send and check for your mail every *X* minutes,** choose Mail⇨Preferences and then click the General icon at the top of the window. Pull down the Check for New Mail pop-up menu and make a selection — every 1, 5, 15, 30, or 60 minutes — or choose Manually if you don't want Mail to check for mail automatically at all. (The default setting is to check for mail every 5 minutes.)

✔ **To add a sender to Address Book,** when someone who isn't already in your Address Book sends you an e-mail message, simply choose Message⇨Add Sender to Address Book (shortcut: ⌘+Y).

Adding a sender to your Address Book has an additional benefit: It guards messages from that person against being mistaken for junk mail. In other words, your Address Book is a *white list* for the spam filter; if specific senders appear in your Address Book, their messages will never be mistakenly marked as junk mail.

Dealing with spam

Speaking of junk mail, although e-mail is a wonderful thing, some people out there try to spoil it. They're called *spammers,* and they're lowlifes who share their lists among themselves — and before you know it, your e-mail box is flooded with get-rich-quick schemes, advertisements for pornographic websites and chat rooms, and all the more traditional buy-me junk mail.

Fortunately, Mail comes with a pretty darn good Junk Mail filter that analyzes incoming message subjects, senders, and contents to determine which ones are likely to contain bulk or junk mail. When you open Mail for the first time, it's running in its training mode, which is how Mail learns to differentiate between what it considers junk mail and what you consider junk mail; all it needs is your input. Mail identifies messages it thinks are junk, but if you disagree with its decisions, here's what you do:

- Click the Not Junk button in the brown bar for any message that *isn't* junk mail.

- Conversely, if a piece of junk mail slips past Mail's filters and ends up in the Inbox, select the message and then click the Junk button in the Mail window's toolbar.

After a few days (or weeks, depending upon your mail volume), Mail should be getting it right almost all the time. When you reach that point, choose Move it to the Junk Mailbox on the Junk Mail tab of Mail's preferences window. Now Mail starts moving junk mail automatically out of your Inbox and into a Junk mailbox, where you can scan the items quickly and trash them when you're ready.

If (for some reason that escapes me) you prefer to receive and manually process your junk mail, you can turn off junk-mail processing by disabling it on the Junk Mail tab of Mail's preferences pane.

Changing your preferences

Actually, Mail's preferences (Mail⇨Preferences or ⌘+,) are more than you might expect from the name. This is the control center for Mail, where you can

- Create and delete e-mail accounts.

- Determine which fonts and colors are used for your messages.

- Decide whether to download and save attachments (such as pictures).

- Decide whether to send formatted mail or plain text.

- Decide whether to turn on the spell checker.

The default is to check spelling as you type, which many people (myself included) find annoying.

✔ Decide whether to have an automatic signature appended to your messages.

✔ Establish rules to process mail that you receive.

Mail rules rule

If you really want to tap the power of Mail, you need to set *rules*. With some cool rules, you can automatically tag messages with a color; file them in a specific mailbox; reply to/forward/redirect the messages automatically (handy when you're going to be away for a while); automatically reply to messages; and *kill-file* messages (just delete them without even bothering to look at them — what better fate for mail from people you hate?).

There's no way I can do rules justice in the few pages I have left for this chapter, but here's a quick look at how to create one:

1. **Choose Mail⇨Preferences.**

2. **Click the Rules icon on the toolbar of the Preferences window.**

3. **Click the Add Rule button.**

   The first condition should say From in its first pop-up menu and Contains in its second pop-up menu. Look at your options in these menus but return them to their original state — From and Contains — when you're done looking.

4. **In the field to the right of the Contains pop-up menu, type** LeVitus.

   Below the condition you just created, you should see an action under the words *Perform the Following Actions.* It should say Move Message in its first pop-up menu and No Mailbox Selected in its second pop-up menu.

5. **Look at the options on these menus, but this time, change the first one from Move Message to Play Sound and the second one from No Mailbox Selected to Blow.**

6. **Type a description of the rule, such as** Message from LeVitus, **in the Description field.**

   Your rule should look identical to Figure 11-11 now.

7. **Click OK.**

   Mail asks whether you want to apply your rule(s) to the selected mailboxes.

8. **Choose Apply if you want Mail to run this rule on the selected mailboxes, or choose Don't Apply if you don't.**

   And that's how you build a rule. From this point forward, every time you get a message from me, you hear the Blow sound.

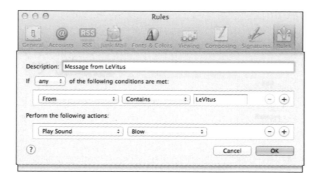

Figure 11-11: When you get a message from me, Mail plays the Blow sound.

Notice the little + (plus) and – (minus) buttons to the right of each condition and action. Use the + button to add more conditions or actions and the – button to delete a condition or action. If you have multiple conditions, you can choose Any or All from the pop-up menu above them, which executes this rule when either any of the conditions or all of the conditions are met. Either way, all the actions you create are always executed when this rule is triggered.

Mailboxes smart and plain

The following sections take a closer look at both types of mailboxes — plain and smart.

Plain old mailboxes

Plain mailboxes are just like folders in the Finder; you create them and name them, and they're empty until you put something in them. They even look like folders in Mail's mailbox pane. You use mailboxes to organize any messages you want to save.

Here are several ways to create a plain mailbox:

- Choose Mailbox➪New Mailbox.
- Click the little + sign at the bottom of the mailbox pane on the left side of the viewer window.
- Click the Action menu at the bottom of the mailbox pane (the one that looks like a gear), and choose New Mailbox.
- Right-click or Control-click in the mailbox pane, and choose New Mailbox from the contextual menu.

Whichever way you choose, the next thing that happens is that a sheet drops down with a Location pop-up menu and a field for you to type the name you want to give this mailbox. Choose On My Mac from the Location menu, and name the mailbox anything you like. Click OK, and the mailbox is created in the mailbox pane.

You can create *submailboxes* (mailboxes inside other mailboxes) to further subdivide your messages. To do so, click a mailbox to select it before you create a new mailbox.

In Figure 11-12, I've divided my Books mailbox into three submailboxes: iPhone For Dummies 3d Edition, Lion For Dummies, and Snow Leopard For Dummies.

Figure 11-12: My Books mailbox is divided into three submailboxes.

You can also drag and drop a mailbox from the top level of the list (such as Drafts, Junk, and Other Dumb Mail in Figure 11-12) onto another mailbox (such as Books or any of its three submailboxes) to make them submailboxes. If you drag a mailbox into a submailbox, it becomes a sub-submailbox. And so on.

To delete a mailbox, click it to select it and then

- Choose Mailbox⇨Delete Mailbox.
- Right-click or Control-click the mailbox, and choose Delete Mailbox.
- Click the Action menu at the bottom of the mailbox pane (the one that looks like a gear), and choose Delete Mailbox.

Intelligent smart mailboxes

A *smart mailbox* is Mail's version of the Finder's Smart Folder. In a nutshell, smart mailboxes are mailboxes that display the results of a search. The messages you see in a smart mailbox are *virtual;* they aren't really in the smart mailbox itself. Instead, the smart mailbox displays a list of messages stored in other mailboxes that match whatever criteria you've defined for that smart folder. As with Smart Folders in the Finder, smart mailboxes update automatically when new messages that meet the criteria are received.

Here are two ways to create a smart mailbox:

- Choose Mailbox⇨New Smart Mailbox.
- Press the + button at the bottom of the mailbox pane, and choose Smart Mailbox from the pop-up menu.

Whichever way you choose, the next thing that happens is that a sheet drops down with a field for the smart mailbox's name, plus some pop-up menus, buttons, and check boxes, as shown in Figure 11-13.

Figure 11-13: This smart mailbox gathers messages with the word *Lion* in the body or subject.

Name your smart mailbox; determine its criteria (by using the pop-up menus, plus and minus buttons, and check boxes), and then click OK. The smart folder appears in the mailbox pane with a little gear on it to denote that it's smart. You can see the Smart Lions smart mailbox in Figure 11-12. Notice that it has a gear, and plain mailboxes don't.

Sign here, please

If you're like me, you'd rather not type your whole signature every time you send an e-mail message, and you don't have to with Mail. If you create canned signatures, you can use them in outgoing messages without typing a single character.

Here's how it works:

1. **Choose Mail⇨Preferences or press ⌘+, (that's ⌘+comma).**

2. **Click the Signatures icon in the Preferences window's toolbar.**

3. **Click the name of the mail account you want to create this signature for in the left column (**boblevitus@me.com **in Figure 11-14).**

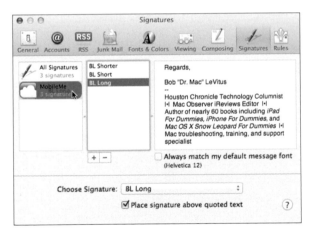

Figure 11-14: My newly created BL Long signature.

4. **Click the little + sign at the bottom of the middle column to create a new, blank signature.**

5. **Type a descriptive name for this signature to replace the default name Signature #1 (BL Long in Figure 11-14).**

6. **Type the signature exactly as you want it to appear in outgoing messages in the right column (Regards, Bob "Dr. Mac" LeVitus – * Houston Chronicle, and so on in Figure 11-14).**

7. **Drag the name you've assigned this signature (BL Long in Figure 11-14) onto the mail account you're using it with (**`boblevitus@ me.com`** in Figure 11-14).**

That's about it for signatures. If you have more than one signature, you can choose the one you want to use as the default for each account: Choose the account in the column on the left; then choose the appropriate signature from the Choose Signature pop-up menu.

TIP

If you have more than one signature, another cool thing happens: A Signature menu appears in new messages, as shown in Figure 11-15, so you can choose a signature other than the one you chose from the pop-up menu as the default (it's BL Short in Figure 11-15).

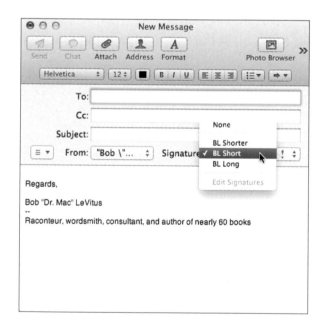

Figure 11-15: Choosing my BL Short signature from the Signature menu.

Take a (Quick) look and (Slide) show me some photos

One last cool feature, and you're finished with Mail. That cool feature is QuickLook, which includes a slick Slideshow option. Notice that there's a QuickLook button in the header of messages you receive that contain one or more pictures, as shown on the left in Figure 11-16. If you click the QuickLook button, a new window appears, displaying one of the enclosed pictures as shown on the right in Figure 11-16.

If you don't see a QuickLook button, click the blue Details button in the top-right corner (which says *Hide* in Figure 11-16 because the details are showing).

Figure 11-16: Click the QuickLook button in a message (left), and QuickLook displays one of the pictures in its own window (right).

Above my smiling face in the QuickLook window on the right in Figure 11-16 is a set of buttons. Here's the lowdown on what they do (from left to right):

- **Previous:** Click this button to see the previous picture.

- **Next:** Click this button to see the next picture.

- **Index Sheet:** Displays all the enclosed pictures at the same time, shrinking them to a smaller size if necessary to fit them all on the screen. Click a picture once to see its name; click a picture twice to display it full screen.

- **Open with Preview:** Opens the picture in the Preview application.

- **Full screen:** Adjusts the picture so it fills the screen, as shown in Figure 11-17.

Figure 11-17: QuickLook's full screen mode.

To close the QuickLook window, either click the little X in its top-left corner or click the QuickLook button in the message header again. Notice that when you're in full-screen mode, there are a couple of new buttons in addition to the ones I just mentioned in Figure 11-16. These new buttons are

 ✔ **Play/Pause:** Click this button to start or pause the slide show. It displays each of the enclosed pictures for around 5 seconds with a smooth dissolve transition between them.

 ✔ **Add to iPhoto:** Copies the picture into your iPhoto library.

To escape from full-screen mode, click the big X, shown in the bottom-right corner of Figure 11-17, or press the Esc key.

Shine On You Crazy Diamond (Parts I–V)
Pink Floyd — Wish You Were Here   8
3:27   –10:

Shine On You Crazy Di
Pink Floyd — Wish Y
3:27

12

The Musical Mac

In This Chapter

▶ Using iTunes

▶ Working with media

▶ Playing with playlists

▶ Backing up your iTunes media

A long time ago, before the iPod and the iTunes Store were born, iTunes was a program you used to store and manage your MP3 music files. Over the ensuing years, it has grown into much more. Today, iTunes not only manages your music collection, but manages your video collection as well. And if you use devices such as an iPod, Apple TV, iPad, or iPhone, you manage the music or video on *them* by using iTunes, too.

So the anachronistically named iTunes is the program you use to manage audio and video files on your hard drive and to manage syncing files with your iPod, Apple TV, iPhone, and iPad devices.

Although entire books have been dedicated to iTunes alone, I share the most important stuff — the handful of things you really need to know — in this chapter.

Introducing iTunes

iTunes is the Swiss Army knife of multimedia software. After all, what other program lets you play audio CDs; create (burn) your own audio or MP3 CDs; listen to MP3, AIFF, AAC, WAV, Audible.com, and several other types of files; view album cover art; enjoy pretty visual displays in time to the music; view and manage

TV shows, movies, and other video files; manage iPods (or other MP3 players), Apple TVs, iPads, and/or iPhones; listen to Internet radio stations; and more? On top of all that, it's your interface to the iTunes Store, the world's leading (legitimate) source of downloadable music and video content. (Whew!)

 To open iTunes, click its icon in the Dock or double-click its icon in the Applications folder. The iTunes window opens (see Figure 12-1).

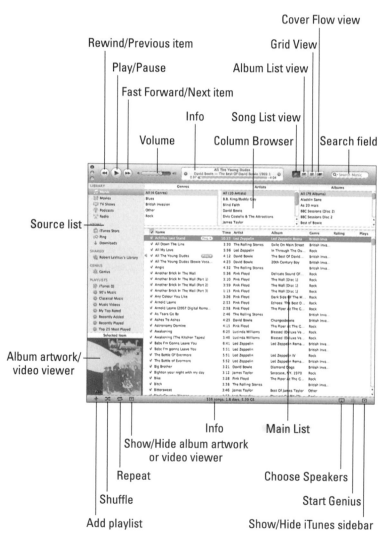

Figure 12-1: Dissecting the iTunes interface.

In a nutshell, whatever you select in the Source List on the left is reflected in the main list on the right. In Figure 12-1, the Music library is selected. At the bottom of the window, you can see that there are 536 songs in my Music library, which would take 1.8 days to listen to from start to finish and uses 5.39GB of space on my hard drive.

Rather than try to explain what every item shown in Figure 12-1 does, I encourage you to click anything and everything you see in the main iTunes window. Experiment with the views, show and hide the iTunes browser and album art, click different items in the Source List, and see what happens.

I'd like you to take note of a few other items:

- ✔ The iTunes main window shrinks to a much more manageable size when you click its green gumdrop button, as shown in the top part of Figure 12-2. Click the green gumdrop again to expand it back to its normal size.

  To switch between the small (top left) and ultra-small (top right) windows, click the bottom-right corner of the little window and drag left to shrink it or drag right to expand it.

- ✔ iTunes offers a ten-band graphic equalizer that can make your music (or video) sound significantly better. Just choose Window➪Equalizer to invoke it on-screen. You can see the equalizer in the lower part of Figure 12-2.

- ✔ Don't miss the iTunes Visualizer, which offers a groovy light show that dances in time to the music, as shown in Figure 12-3. You turn it on by choosing View➪Show Visualizer or pressing ⌘+T. If you like the default Visualizer, check out some of iTunes' other built-in Visualizers like Lathe, Jelly, or Stix, which are available in the Visualizer submenu. Search the web for *"iTunes Visualizer"* to find even more.

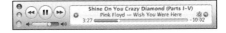

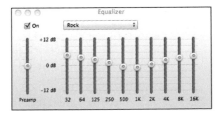

Figure 12-2: The iTunes equalizer (bottom) and minimized main window (top).

When you get sick of the Visualizer (as you surely will), just choose View⇨Hide Visualizer or press ⌘+T again to make it disappear.

Try this: Choose View⇨Full Screen or press ⌘+F while the Visualizer is running, and the Visualizer takes over your entire screen. Click anywhere on the screen to bring the iTunes window back.

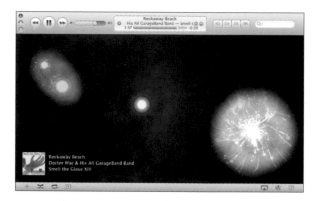

Figure 12-3: The iTunes psychedelic light show is known as the iTunes Visualizer.

Working with Media

iTunes is, first and foremost, a media manager and player, so the next thing I examine is how to get your favorite media *into* iTunes. Of course, there are a number of ways, depending upon the type of media and where the files reside. For example, you can add song or video files you've downloaded from websites or received as enclosures in e-mail messages. Or you can add songs by ripping audio CDs. You can buy music, movies, TV shows, audiobooks, and apps for your iPhone/iPod/iPad at the iTunes Store. You can subscribe to free podcasts at the iTunes Store as well. And you can listen to all sorts of music on the Internet radio stations included with iTunes.

The iTunes Store and Internet radio require that you be connected to the Internet before you can use them. And although both work over a dial-up Internet connection (more or less), both features work much better when used over a broadband connection.

In the following sections, you discover the various ways to add media — songs, movies, videos, and podcasts — to your iTunes library, followed by a quick course in listening to iTunes Internet radio stations.

Adding songs

You can add songs from pretty much any source, and the way you add a song to iTunes depends on where that song comes from. Here are the most common ways people add their songs:

- **Add a song file such as an MP3 or AAC file from your hard drive.** Either drag the document into the iTunes window, as shown in Figure 12-4, or choose File⟹Add to Library (shortcut: ⌘+O) and choose the file in the Open File dialog. In either case, the file is added to your iTunes Music library.

- **Add songs from a store-bought or homemade audio CD.** Launch iTunes and insert the CD. A dialog appears, asking whether you would like to import the CD into your iTunes library. Click the Yes button, and the songs on that CD are added to your iTunes Music library. If you don't see a dialog when you insert an audio CD, you can import the songs on that CD anyway. Just select the CD in the Source List on the left, and click the Import button near the bottom-right corner of the iTunes window.

TIP

If your computer is connected to the Internet, iTunes magically looks up the song title, artist name, album name, song length, and genre for every song on the CD. Note that this works only for store-bought CDs containing somewhat popular music — and that iTunes might not be able to find information about a very obscure CD by an even more obscure band, even if the disc is store-bought. And in most cases, it can't look up information for homemade (home-burned) audio CDs. Finally, it sometimes gets things wrong.

Figure 12-4: Drag and drop songs to the iTunes window to add them to your Music library.

✔ **Buy your songs from the iTunes Store.** Click the iTunes Store option in the Source List on the left. From the iTunes Store's home screen, you can either click a link or type a song title, album title, artist name, or keyword or phrase in the Search field and then press Return or Enter to start the search. When you've found an item that interests you, you can double-click any song to listen to a 30-second preview of it or click the Buy Song or Buy Album button to purchase the song or album, as shown in Figure 12-5.

✔ **Buy your songs from other online vendors such as Amazon.** Amazon (www.amazon.com) has a huge downloadable music store on the Web. Its MP3 Downloads section has more than a million songs, with more being added every day. The prices at Amazon are often lower than the prices for the same music at the iTunes Store.

Buy Album button   Sign in button

Click here to shop   Search field

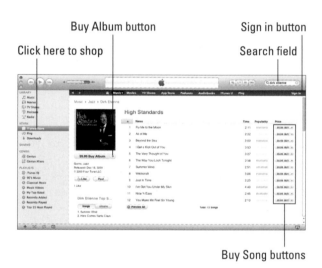

Buy Song buttons

Figure 12-5: At the iTunes Store, buying music is as easy as clicking the Buy Song or Buy Album button.

The first time you make a purchase from the iTunes Store, you have to create an Apple account, if you don't already have one. To do so, just click the Sign In button and then click the Create New Account button in the Sign In dialog. After your account is established, future purchases require just one or two clicks.

Adding movies and videos

To add a video file such as an MOV or MPEG document from your hard drive, either drag the document to the iTunes window, as shown in Figure 12-4, earlier in this chapter, or choose File⇨Add to Library (shortcut: ⌘+O) and choose the file in the Open File dialog. In either case, the file is added to your iTunes Movie library.

You can also buy movies, TV shows, and other video content from the iTunes Store. Shopping for video is almost the same as shopping for music. Here are the steps:

1. **Click the iTunes Store in the Source List on the left.**

2. **Either click a link or type a movie title, music-video name, actor or director name, or other keyword or phrase in the Search field, and press Return or Enter to start the search.**

3. **When you find a video item that interests you, double-click it to see a preview, or click the Buy Episode or Buy Video button to purchase the episode or video.**

Adding podcasts

Podcasts are like radio or television shows, except that when you subscribe to them, you can listen to or watch them (using iTunes or your iPod, iPad, or iPhone) at any time you like. Thousands of podcasts are available, and many (or most) are free. To find podcasts, follow these steps:

1. **Click the iTunes Store in the Source List on the left.**

2. **Click the Podcasts link on the store's home screen.**

3. **Click a link on the Podcasts screen, or type a keyword or phrase in the Search field.**

4. **When you find a podcast that appeals to you, double-click it to listen to a preview, click the Get Episode button to download the current episode of that podcast, or click the Subscribe button to receive all future episodes of that podcast automatically.**

   Figure 12-6 shows all these things for the Mac Geek Gab audio podcast from The Mac Observer.

For more information on most podcasts, just point at the little *i* button on the right side of the description field, as shown in Figure 12-6. You don't even have to click (though you can if you want to).

Subscribe button

Get Episode button

Get info button

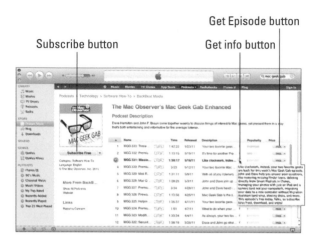

Figure 12-6: The Mac Geek Gab podcast from The Mac Observer.

Subscribing to a podcast is a cool deal. You can configure how often iTunes checks for new episodes — hourly, daily, weekly, or manually — and what to do when new episodes become available — download the most recent one, download all episodes, or do nothing — and how many episodes to keep in your iTunes Library — all, all unplayed, or a specific number between 2 and 10. To specify these settings, choose Podcasts in the Source List, click the name of the podcast you want to configure, and then click the Settings button near the bottom of the window.

Learning from iTunes U

Want to learn something for free? Click the iTunes U tab in the iTunes Store and you can choose from tens of thousands of free audio and video courses, including a good number produced by colleges and universities that include Harvard, Oxford, Stanford, and hundreds more.

You download or subscribe to a course the same way you download or subscribe to a podcast. Check it out the next time you're in the iTunes Store. It's a great way to learn something new for free.

Listening to Internet radio

Streaming audio is delivered over the Internet in real time. Think of streaming audio as being "just like radio" but using the Internet rather than the airwaves as its delivery medium.

There are two ways to listen to streaming Internet radio stations with iTunes: the easy way and the less-easy way. The easy way is to listen to one of the hundreds of Internet radio stations included with iTunes. They're even organized into convenient categories such as Alt/Modern Rock, Blues, Country, Jazz, Public, Top 40/Pop, Urban, and many more.

To listen to one of iTunes' included Internet radio stations, click the Radio item in the Source List on the left and then click a disclosure triangle to the left of each category name to reveal the stations in that category, as shown in Figure 12-7.

Figure 12-7: Listening to All Classic Hits (181.FM), one of 248 streams in the Classic Rock category.

The less-easy way is to find an Internet radio station on your own by surfing or searching the Web using Safari (or another Web browser). When you find an Internet radio station you'd like to listen to using iTunes, here's how to get it into iTunes:

1. **Copy its address (its URL) by highlighting it and choosing Edit⇨Copy (shortcut: ⌘+C).**

2. **Switch to (or launch) iTunes.**

3. **Choose Advanced⇨Open Stream (shortcut: ⌘+U).**

4. **Choose Edit⇨Paste (shortcut: ⌘+V).**

5. **Click OK.**

   The station appears in your iTunes library.

Strangely, there's no way to make an Internet radio station you've added yourself appear in iTunes' Radio category. Apparently, only Apple is allowed to decide what is and is not "radio." Harrumph.

All About Playlists

Playlists are a big deal in iTunes. Playlists let you manage otherwise-unmanageable amounts of media, such as the 5,000+ songs I have in my iTunes library. Playlists let you create subsets of a large collection, so it's easier to enjoy exactly the kind of music you want in iTunes or on your iPod. Two types of playlists exist:

- ✔ **Regular playlists** contain the songs (or videos, podcasts, or radio stations) that you specify by dragging them to the playlist.

- ✔ **Smart playlists,** on the other hand, select songs from your library based on criteria you specify. Furthermore, smart playlists are updated automatically if you add new items to your library that meet the criteria.

All playlists appear in the Source List on the left side of the iTunes window.

Creating a regular playlist

To create a regular playlist, follow these steps:

1. **Either click the + button in the bottom-left corner of the iTunes window or choose File⇨New Playlist (shortcut: ⌘+N).**

   A new playlist named "untitled playlist" appears in the Source List.

2. **(Optional) As long as the playlist's name, "untitled playlist," is selected and ready to be edited, you probably want to rename it something meaningful by typing a new name for it.**

   If you decide not to name it now, you can double-click it and type a new name anytime.

3. **To add a song to a playlist, click the song in your library and drag it to the playlist's name, and when the playlist's name becomes highlighted, release the mouse button.**

   The song is added to that playlist. Note that adding a song to a playlist doesn't remove it from the library. Conversely, if you delete a song from a playlist, the song isn't deleted from your library. And if you delete a playlist from the Source List, the songs it contains aren't deleted from your library. In other words, think of songs in playlists as being aliases of songs in your library.

4. **Select the playlist in your Source List, and click Play to listen to the songs it contains.**

If you don't want to drag songs to your playlist one by one, there's an easier way. To create a regular playlist that includes songs you've selected from your library, ⌘-click the songs you want to include in the playlist and choose File⇨New Playlist from Selection (shortcut: ⌘+Shift+N), as shown in Figure 12-8.

Figure 12-8: How to create a playlist from songs you've selected in your Music library.

You can also use that ⌘-click multiple songs technique to add a batch of songs to an existing playlist.

Working with smart playlists

To create a smart playlist that builds a list based on criteria and updates itself automatically, follow these steps:

1. **Either Option+click the + button in the bottom-left corner of the iTunes window or choose File⇨New Smart Playlist (shortcut: ⌘+Option+N).**

   The Smart Playlist window appears, as shown in Figure 12-9.

2. **Use the pop-up menus to select the criteria that will build your smart playlist, and click the + button to add more criteria.**

Figure 12-9: The Smart Playlist window lets you specify the criteria for your smart playlist.

3. Click OK when you're done.

The playlist appears alongside your other playlists in the Source List. You can tell it's a smart playlist by the gear on its icon. To modify the criteria of a smart playlist after it's been created, hold down the Option key, and double-click the smart playlist to reopen the Smart Playlist window and change the smart playlist's criteria.

Burning a playlist to CD

Another use for playlists is for burning audio CDs you can listen to on almost any audio CD player. The only trick is to make sure the total playing time of the songs in the playlist is less than the capacity of the blank CD you're using, which is usually 74 to 80 minutes. When you have all the songs you want on your CD on the playlist, choose File⇨Burn Playlist to Disc or click the Burn Disk button in the bottom-right corner of the main iTunes window. In a few minutes, you have an audio CD that contains all the songs on the playlist — and plays the songs in the order in which they appeared on the playlist.

Note that although the default type of disc iTunes burns is an audio CD, it can also burn two other types — MP3 CDs or data CDs (and DVDs):

- MP3 CD is a special format that can be played in many CD audio players and set-top DVD players. The cool thing about an MP3 CD is that rather than holding a mere 74 to 80 minutes of music, it can hold more than 100 songs! The uncool thing about MP3 CDs is that many older audio CD players won't play them.

- A data CD or DVD is nothing more than a disc formatted to be read and mounted by any computer, Mac or Windows.

To determine which format iTunes burns from your playlist, choose iTunes⇨ Preferences (shortcut: ⌘+,). Click the Advanced icon on the toolbar and then click the Burning tab. Radio buttons let you choose Audio CD, MP3 CD, or Data CD or DVD. Click the one you want, and you're golden.

Looking at two specific playlists

There are a couple more relatively new playlists I'd like to draw your attention to: The Genius and the iTunes DJ (that's the feature formerly known as *Party Shuffle*).

Who is the Genius?

The Genius is actually more of a "what": an iTunes feature that lets you find new music — in your iTunes library or the iTunes Store — that's related to a song of your choosing. Or, as the Genius splash screen you see when you turn the Genius on puts it, "Genius makes playlists and mixes from songs in your library that go great together. And the Genius sidebar recommends music from the iTunes Store that you don't already have." To get started, choose Store⇨Turn On Genius, if you haven't done so already. When you've finished reading, the Genius splash screen appears; click the Turn On Genius button in the bottom-right corner.

Turning Genius on sends information about your iTunes library to Apple. There's a Learn More button on the What Is Genius screen if you want to (d'oh!) learn more about it.

To use Genius, you must (for some unknown reason) have an iTunes Store account, even though the information the Genius sends to Apple about your iTunes library is stored anonymously. And even though no purchase is required, I think it's a dumb requirement — but that's the way it works, take it or leave it.

Assuming you take it, sign into your iTunes Store account if you have one or create one if you don't. After agreeing to the Genius Terms of Service the Genius gathers info about your iTunes library, sends the info to Apple, and then (finally) delivers your results. When all this is done, you can create Genius playlists and use the Genius sidebar.

How? Glad you asked! Click a song in your Library and then click the Start Genius button in the bottom-right corner of iTunes main window (that's it over there in the margin). After a bit of cogitation, iTunes presents you with its Genius selections based on the song you clicked. As shown in Figure 12-10, the song was *Wild Horses* by The Rolling Stones, and the Genius suggested *What Is and What Shall Never Be* by Led Zeppelin, *Keep Talking* by Pink Floyd, and twenty-two other songs.

Figure 12-10: The Genius suggests songs in the playlist that go nicely with the song the suggestions are based on.

If you're not a fan of British Invasion rock music, let me assure you that most of the songs in the Genius playlist pretty much do "go great together." If you don't have issues with all the legal mumbo jumbo, the iTunes Store account, or sending information about your iTunes library to Apple, give the Genius a try.

What do you say to iTunes DJ?

iTunes DJ is the new and improved version of the iTunes feature formerly known as Party Shuffle.

The big news here is that iTunes DJ is now actually *fun* at parties. Any guest who has the free Remote application lurking on an iPhone, iPad, or iPod touch can request any song in your iTunes library — and cast votes for songs in the current list. Figure 12-11 shows the iTunes DJ Settings window and the iTunes DJ voting screen on my iPhone.

To start the festivities, first click the iTunes DJ icon in the Playlists section of the Source List. iTunes selects some songs to get you started. Click the Settings button at the bottom right of the window to configure iTunes DJ, as shown in Figure 12-11. Click the Refresh button next to the Settings button to have the iTunes DJ select a fresh batch of songs.

Songs that have votes or songs that have been requested are not replaced when you click the Refresh button, so vote for all the songs you want to keep *before* you click the Refresh button.

Figure 12-11: The iTunes DJ Settings window in iTunes on your Mac (left) and the iTunes DJ screen on my iPhone (right).

Backing Up Your iTunes Media

After spending a bunch of time and money ripping and buying songs to populate your iTunes library, you might want to protect your investment by backing up your music.

Actually, you should back up *all* your data files, as Chapter 18 describes. But if you're tempted not to back up all your data, consider this: Apple won't replace music you've bought at the iTunes Store if you lose it.

Fortunately, iTunes makes it easy to back up your Music library with its built-in back-up-your-music command. To back up *your* music, here's the sequence:

1. **In iTunes, choose File⇨Library⇨Back Up to Disc.**

   The iTunes Backup dialog appears, as shown in Figure 12-12.

   You have two options for backing up your iTunes library: You can back up the entire iTunes library and playlists, or back up only items you've purchased at the iTunes Store. Regardless of which you choose, you have the option of backing up only items that have been added or modified since your last iTunes Backup. You can also choose a speed for burning the CD or DVD from the Preferred Speed pop-up menu.

   If you have a lot of stuff in your library, this could require a lot of discs. For example, my editor's backup took either 32 CDs or 5 DVDs. And my backup is so big (more than 100 gigabytes of music and video) that my only viable option is to back it up to a big external hard disk. The point is, before you begin, you should make sure you have enough blank discs to complete the backup.

Figure 12-12: The iTunes Backup dialog offers you these choices.

Typically, a CD can hold up to 700 megabytes of data; a DVD up to 4.7 gigabytes; and a dual-layer DVD up to 8.5 gigabytes. When you click on your iTunes library in the Source List, the number of items and size in megabytes (MB) or gigabytes (GB) appears at the bottom of the window.

2. **Make your choices and then click the Back Up button to start.**

I recommend you choose a speed one or two "notches" lower than the maximum. It'll take a little bit longer, but this way fewer discs fail to burn properly. In the long run, I think choosing a slower burn speed saves you time and money.

3. **Insert a blank CD or DVD, and the process begins.**

If your backup requires more than one disc, iTunes ejects the current disc, and you have to insert another.

It's a good idea to label these discs — iTunes Backup Disc 1, iTunes Backup Disc 2, and so on. That way, if you ever have to *use* your backup discs, you can insert the correct one when iTunes asks.

The cool part about using the iTunes built-in backup feature is that it performs *incremental* backups — backing up only the items added or changed since the last backup — which reduces the number of discs you need.

By the way, discs you create using the iTunes backup feature can be used only to restore your songs, playlists, and purchases; they can't be played in an audio CD or video DVD player. To restore your music from an iTunes backup, merely launch iTunes and insert the disc (or the first disc, if the backup required more than one disc).

One last thing: If you're new to iTunes, may I suggest exploring the excellent iTunes Tutorials, which you'll find in the Window menu, as shown in Figure 12-13.

Figure 12-13: You can learn a lot about iTunes from its most excellent tutorials.

The Multimedia Mac

In This Chapter

▶ Watching DVD movies on your Mac with DVD Player

▶ Watching movies with QuickTime Player

▶ Opening, viewing, printing, and converting file formats with Preview

▶ Importing media — photos and videos — to your Mac

"**M**edia content" is more than just music (the topic of Chapter 12), and your Mac is ready, willing, and able to handle almost any type of media (with any type of content) you can throw at it. Which is why, in addition to the aforementioned iTunes, Mac OS X Lion includes applications for viewing and working with media such as DVD movie discs, QuickTime movie files, as well as graphics in a variety of file formats such as PDF, TIFF, and JPEG.

In this chapter, you look at some bundled applications you can use to work with such media — namely, DVD Player, QuickTime Player, Preview, Front Row, and Image Capture — followed by a brief section about importing your own media (photos and videos) into your Mac.

Watching Movies with DVD Player

The DVD Player application includes snazzy little on-screen controllers, as shown in Figure 13-1. They enable you to watch your movies on your Mac in pretty much the same way you'd watch them on your TV with your DVD player.

Figure 13-1: DVD Player's on-screen controller gadgets.

If you've changed your preferences, DVD Player might not start automatically. See the upcoming sidebar for details.

Follow these steps to watch a DVD:

1. **Insert a video DVD into your Mac.**

   This step automatically launches the DVD Player application; if it doesn't, you can double-click the DVD Player icon in the Applications folder or single-click it in LaunchPad to start it.

   If you don't see the little controller gadgets, you can choose Window⇨Show Controller (shortcut: ⌘+Option+C) to display the gray remote control–looking gadget shown at the top of Figure 13-1, or you can move your cursor to the very bottom of the screen to see the transparent overlay controls shown at the bottom of Figure 13-1.

   The transparent overlay works only in Full Screen mode.

2. **Use the controls to play, stop, or pause your DVD and more.**

   The controls themselves should be self-explanatory to anyone who has ever used a set-top DVD player. If they're not familiar to you, hover the cursor over any control to reveal a tooltip. This works for buttons on either type of controller.

3. **Use the Controller drawer if you like to give DVD Player less commonly used, but still useful, commands.**

   To open (top right, Figure 13-1) or close (top left, Figure 13-1) the little Controller drawer, choose Controls⇨Open/Close Control Drawer, press ⌘+], or click the little pull tab (where you see the arrow cursors in Figure 13-1) and drag.

   The controller might disappear after a few seconds. To make it reappear, jiggle the mouse or choose Window⇨Show Controller (shortcut ⌘+Option+C).

If you're in Full Screen mode, the menu bar won't appear unless you move the cursor to the *top* of the screen. Doing so also makes the chapters/bookmarks/video clips overlay — which you use to choose a chapter, bookmark, or clip — appear just below the menu bar.

And the transparent controller shown at the bottom of Figure 13-1 won't appear unless you move the cursor to the *bottom* of the screen.

So move the cursor to the top of the screen to see the menu bar and chapters/bookmarks/video clips overlay, and move it to the bottom of the screen to see the transparent controller.

4. **Sit back and enjoy the inserted DVD movie on your Mac screen.**

There really isn't much more to it than that, but here are a few other useful tips and hints for using DVD Player:

✔ The View menu lets you choose viewing sizes for your movie, including Full Screen, which usually looks best.

✔ The Go menu lets you navigate to the DVD menu, beginning of the disc, previous or next chapter, or forward or back 5 seconds, with convenient keyboard shortcuts for each of these commands. It also includes several convenient submenus including Title, Chapter, and (my personal favorite) Bookmarks.

✔ To create a bookmark so you can jump directly to this exact moment in the movie, choose Go⇨Bookmarks. The Bookmarks window opens. Click the little plus button at the bottom and then type a name for this bookmark (or accept the name DVD Player offers — Bookmark 1, Bookmark 2, and so). Click the Add button and you're done. Now you can skip right to this frame of the movie from the Bookmarks submenu (in the Go menu) by double-clicking it in the Bookmarks window, or by selecting it in the bookmarks panel of the chapters/bookmarks/video clips overlay.

Move your cursor to the top of the screen in Full Screen mode to see the movie's chapters and bookmarks.

✔ Many user-configurable options are available in the Preferences window: DVD Player⇨Preferences (keyboard shortcut: ⌘+,).

✔ For more information about almost any DVD Player feature, choose Help⇨DVD Player Help.

Troubleshooting DVD Player settings

DVD Player is a pretty-easy-to-use application. However, you might find it's not working as expected for a couple of reasons:

- **You've changed the default setting:** The default setting, Open DVD Player When You Insert a Video DVD — is in the CDs & DVDs System Preferences pane, which you find in the System Preferences application.

- **Certain external DVD drives won't be recognized by DVD Player:** If that's the case, you need to use either the viewing software that came with the drive or a program such as VLC (VideoLAN Client).

- **Your Mac might not have a DVD player (although unless you have a MacBook Air, it's unlikely):** If you choose ⌘⇨About This Mac in the Finder, the About This Mac window has a More Info button. Click it to launch an application called System Information. Or you can launch System Information (which you find in the Utilities folder) the old-fashioned way — by double-clicking its icon. Either way, it can tell you whether you have a DVD drive in your Mac. Just click the Disc Burning item in the contents column on the left; the details appear on the right.

Playing Movies and Music in QuickTime Player

QuickTime is Apple's technology for digital media creation, delivery, and playback. It's used in a myriad of ways by programs such as Apple's iMovie, by websites such as YouTube (www.youtube.com), and in training videos delivered on CD or DVD.

 QuickTime Player is the Mac OS X application that lets you view QuickTime movies as well as streaming audio and video, QuickTime VR (Virtual Reality), and many types of audio files as well. The quickest way to launch it is by clicking its icon in the Dock. It also opens automatically when you open any QuickTime movie document file.

To play a QuickTime movie, merely double-click its icon — and QuickTime Player launches itself.

Using QuickTime Player couldn't be easier. All its important controls are available right in the player window, as shown in Figure 13-2.

Here are a few more QuickTime Player features you might find useful:

- **The Movie Inspector window** (Window⇨Show/Hide Movie Inspector or ⌘+I) provides a lot of useful information about the current movie, such as its location on your hard drive, file format, frames per second, file size, and duration.

- **The Trim control** (Edit⇨Trim or ⌘+T) lets you delete frames from the beginning and/or end of a movie.

✓ **The Share Menu** lets you email your movies; publish them to iTunes so
you can watch them on your iPods, iPhones, and AppleTVs; or upload
them to YouTube, Vimeo, Flickr, Facebook, or a MobileMe gallery.

Figure 13-2: QuickTime Player is simple to use.

Viewing and Converting Images and PDFs in Preview

You use Preview to open, view, and print PDFs as well as most graphics files
(TIFF, JPEG, PICT, and so on). *PDF files* are formatted documents that can
include text and images. User manuals, books, and the like are often distrib-
uted as PDF files. You can't edit the existing text in a PDF file with Preview,
but you can leaf through its pages, annotate and mark it up, and print it. You
can often select text and graphics in a PDF file, copy them to the Clipboard
(⌘+C), and paste (⌘+V) them into documents in other applications. It's also
the application that pops open when you click the Preview button in the
Print dialog, as described in Chapter 15.

Actually, that's not entirely true. You can edit one certain type of PDF file: a
form that has blank fields. Preview allows you to fill in the blanks and then
resave the document. And although it's technically not editing, you can annotate a PDF document by using the Annotate tools on the toolbar.

One of the most useful things Preview can do is change a graphic file in one
file format into one with a different file format. For example, you're signing up
for a web site and want to add a picture to your profile. The web site requires
pictures in the JPEG file format, but the picture file on your hard drive that
you'd like to use is in the TIFF file format. Preview can handle the conversion
for you:

1. **Open the TIFF file with Preview by double-clicking the file.**

   If another program (such as Adobe Photoshop) opens instead of
   Preview, drag the TIFF document onto the Preview icon or launch
   Preview and choose File➪Open (shortcut: ⌘+O) to open the TIFF file.

2. **Choose File⇨Export (⌘+Shift+S).**

3. **Choose the appropriate file format — such as JPEG — from the pop-up Format menu, as shown in Figure 13-3.**

Figure 13-3: Preview makes it easy to convert a TIFF graphic file into a JPEG graphic file.

4. **If you want to make sure you don't confuse your original image with the one in the new format, change the name of your file in the Save As box, too.**

5. **Click Save.**

As you can see in Figure 13-3, Preview lets you convert any file it can open to any of the following file formats: JPEG, JPEG-2000, OpenEXR, PDF, PNG, and TIFF.

Chances are good that you'll never need to convert a file to most of these formats, but it's nice to know that you could if you needed to.

 Almost every OS X program with a Print command lets you save your document as a PDF file. Just click and hold the PDF button (found in all Print dialogs) and choose Save As PDF. Then, should you ever need to convert that PDF file to a different file format, you can do so by using the preceding steps.

Importing Media

Chances are good that you'll want to import pictures or video from your digital camera or DV camcorder someday. It's a piece of cake. So in the following sections, I show you how easy it is to get your digital photos into your Mac and help you get started with digital video (which is a bit more complex).

In the sections that follow, I focus on applications that are a part of Mac OS X. Technically, that doesn't include the iLife applications. What I mean is that if you bought a Mac OS X Lion upgrade in a box at a store, it doesn't include iLife applications, such as iMovie and iPhoto. Your Mac almost certainly came with the iLife suite preinstalled, but depending upon how old your Mac is, you might not have the current versions, and the various versions all work differently. See the nearby sidebar for more details about iLife.

Downloading photos from a camera

This is the Mac I'm talking about, so of course, getting pictures from your digital camera onto your hard drive is a pretty simple task. Here's how to do it step by step using Image Capture:

1. **Turn on the camera, and set it to review or playback mode.**

   This step might not be necessary for some cameras. It was for my old Olympus, but isn't for my Nikon Coolpix P1.

2. **Connect the camera to your Mac with its USB cable.**

   At this point, Image Capture may launch automatically, or, if you have iPhoto, it may launch instead.

If you have both programs on your hard drive and the wrong one opens when you connect your camera, you can change that behavior in Image Capture's Device Settings pane. Launch Image Capture (it's in your Applications folder) if it didn't launch when you connected your camera. Now choose the appropriate application (Image Capture in Figure 13-4) from the Connecting This Camera Opens pop-up menu.

Figure 13-4: I've told my Mac to open Image Capture when I connect this camera.

3. **From the Image Capture window, you can either click Download All to download all the photos in your camera or click Download to select which photos to download, as shown in Figure 13-4.**

   • *To choose contiguous photos,* click the first photo you want to download, press Shift, and then click the last photo you want to download.

   • *To choose noncontiguous photos,* press ⌘ and click each photo you want to download. Either way, an orange highlight shows you which photos are going to be downloaded when you click the Download button (such as the first, third, fourth, and sixth photos in Figure 13-4).

In Figure 13-4, the Download To pop-up menu is set to the Pictures folder, which is the default setting. If you were to click the Download or Download All button now, Image Capture would download the photos in your camera to the Pictures folder inside your Home folder.

If you want to delete the photos from your camera after they're downloaded to your hard drive, select the photos you want to delete, and click the Delete button.

If a disk icon, often named No Name, appeared on your Desktop when you plugged in your camera, you have to eject that disk — by clicking the Eject Disk icon next to its name in the Image Capture window or by ejecting it in the Finder — before you disconnect your camera, or you could lose or damage files in your camera. So try to remember. If you don't, Image Capture scolds you with the scary warning dialog shown in Figure 13-5.

Figure 13-5: This warning means you forgot to eject your camera's disk.

Downloading DV video from a camcorder

Getting video from a DV camcorder to your hard drive is almost as easy as importing photos from your digital camera. Although it's beyond the scope of this book to explain how you download video, the following tips can help you get started.

iMovie works well for downloading video from miniDV and HD camcorders that include output via FireWire or USB 2.

If you do plan to use iMovie, don't forget about the built-in Help system (⌘+Shift+?). Here, you find extensive assistance, as shown in Figure 13-6, which is the main Help page for iMovie.

Never insert a mini-DVD into a slot-loading optical drive like the ones in all Macs (except the Mac Pro). If your camcorder records on mini-DVDs, you'll need to spring for a tray-loading optical drive.

Figure 13-6: Don't forget that help is just a click (or a keystroke) away.

Living the iLife

In previous editions of this book, I called iLife "one of the fantastic bargains in software" and said, "if you had to buy all these programs from other vendors (or for a Windows PC), you'd pay a whole lot more." And that was when the only way to get iLife was on a DVD for $79.

You can still get iLife '11 (latest version as of this writing) on DVD for $79, or iMovie, iPhoto, and GarageBand are available a la carte in the Mac App Store for $14.99 each. At present, you can't buy iWeb or iDVD a la carte, but both are included if you buy the suite on disc.

So if you don't have the latest version of iLife on your hard drive, take a look at the features and programs it includes (`www.apple.com/ilife`) and consider whether you'd benefit from all the new goodies you don't currently have.

 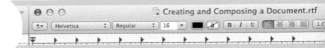

Words and Letters

In This Chapter

▶ Processing words with TextEdit

▶ Finding out all about Lion's fonts

▶ Managing fonts with Font Book

A s I discuss in previous chapters, your Mac is well equipped for creating and managing media — music, movies, DVDs, and photos. But your Mac is also ready to handle more common tasks, such as typing a letter or writing an essay.

I think it's fair to say that Lion's TextEdit application is all that many users will ever need for writing letters or essays.

If you need more control over your pages, try Pages from Apple (available in the Mac App Store for $19.99).

Furthermore, your Lion comes with a wide variety of fonts (sometimes called *typefaces*), plus a handy little app called Font Book for managing those fonts. Fonts allow you to change the way text looks on the screen and the printed page.

In this chapter, you look at the Mac OS X Lion text-composition program, called TextEdit, and explore fonts and how to manage them.

**ABCDEFGHIJK
NOPQRSTUVW
abcdefghijkl
nopqrstuvwx
23456789**

Processing Words with TextEdit

TextEdit is a word processor/text editor that you can use to write letters, scribble notes, or open Read Me files. It's not as sophisticated as Microsoft Word (or Apple's Pages, Quark Xpress, or Adobe InDesign, for that matter), but you can definitely use it for light word-processing and text editing. It's capable of doing a reasonable amount of text formatting, and can even check your spelling and read text to you in a natural-sounding and somewhat creepy voice.

TextEdit supports images, too. Just copy an image from another program and paste it into a TextEdit document. Or you can drag-and-drop an image into a TextEdit document from many applications.

TextEdit can even open Microsoft Word documents (.doc and .docx files). This is fabulous if you don't happen to have a copy of Microsoft Word on your hard drive.

So why would I need Microsoft Word?

You heard me. The free word processor included with Mac OS X Lion can not only open Microsoft Word files — even ones in the latest file format, .docx — but it can modify and save them again, too.

Why does this make me rave and marvel? Because now, even if you don't own a copy of Microsoft Word, you can open documents created by others using Word, edit, and resave them — all *without* having to buy your own copy of Word.

Don't get me wrong: If you need Microsoft Word, you need Microsoft Word. I use it as much as any other program, and there's nothing else like it. Yes, it's a bit bloated and may be overkill for some, but since TextEdit doesn't support many of Word's features — including but not limited to styled text, Word's style sheets, revision tracking, and display of graphics — it's really not a replacement for Word.

For example, here is a Word document in TextEdit (left) and Microsoft Word (right).

 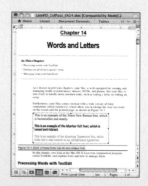

All the words and letters are in the TextEdit version, but as you can see, its formatting, styles, and graphics have all been stripped.

Still, TextEdit lets you open, edit, and save Word documents, which may be all you need. If you think you can get by without a full-featured, professional-quality writing tool like Word, this freebie (TextEdit) may very well be all the word processor you'll ever need.

If you like Microsoft Word, you may enjoy my *Office 2011 For Mac For Dummies,* also from Wiley.

Like all apps included with Lion, you find TextEdit in the Applications folder at root level on your hard disk.

The Dock doesn't have a TextEdit icon but if you like it, use it regularly, or would just like to have it in your Dock, either drag its icon from the Applications folder to the left side of the Dock or launch it, right-click (or Control-click) its Dock icon, and then choose Keep in Dock.

Creating and composing a document

When you launch TextEdit, a blank, untitled document appears on your screen. If one doesn't, choose File⇨New or press ⌘+N. Before you begin work on any document, save it to your hard drive by choosing File⇨Save or pressing ⌘+S. (If you're new to Mac OS Lion Save sheets, flip to Chapter 6 for details.)

As you work with the document, it's a good idea to save it every few minutes, just in case. After you've named a file, all you need to do to save its current state is choose File⇨Save a Version or press ⌘+S.

TextEdit uses Lion's version support and autosave features, so your work is saved on the fly. Don't be lulled into a false sense of security. Apple's apps do autosave and versioning, but most other apps don't. At least not yet. (Chapter 6 has the lowdown on versions and saving.)

Now begin typing your text. When you type text in a word processor, you should know a few handy things:

- ✔ **Press the Return (or Enter) key only when you reach the end of a paragraph.** You don't need to press Return at the end of a line of text; the program automatically wraps your text to the next line, keeping things neat and tidy.

- ✔ **Type a single space after the punctuation mark at the end of a sentence, regardless of what your typing teacher might have told you.** Word processors and typewriters aren't the same. With a typewriter, you want two spaces at the end of a sentence; with a word processor, you don't. (Typewriters use *fixed-width* fonts; computers mostly use fonts with variable widths. If you put two spaces at the end of a sentence in a computer-generated document, the gap looks too wide.) Trust me on this one.

- ✔ **Limit most documents to a maximum of two different fonts.** Mac OS X offers you a wide selection of fonts — but that doesn't mean you have to use them all in one document.

TIP

To put certain characters in your TextEdit document, choose Edit⇨Special Characters (shortcut: ⌘+Option+T). This command opens the Character Palette, where you can choose special characters such as mathematical symbols, arrows, ornaments, stars, accented Latin characters, and so on. To insert a character into your document at the insertion point, simply click it and then click the Insert button.

Working with text

TextEdit operates on the "select, then operate" principle, as do most Macintosh programs, including the Finder. Before you can affect text in your document — change its font face, style, size, margins, and so on — you need to select the text you want to operate on.

You can use several methods to select text in a document:

- ✔ If you double-click a word, the word is selected.

- ✔ If you triple-click a word, the entire paragraph that contains the word is selected.

- ✔ You can click anywhere in the document, hold down the Shift key, and then click again somewhere else in the document, and everything between the two clicks will be selected.

- ✔ You can click anywhere in the document, hold down the Shift key, and use the keyboard arrow keys to extend the selection. Figure 14-1 shows some text that is selected.

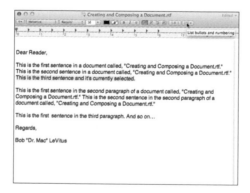

Figure 14-1: The last sentence in the first paragraph is highlighted, showing that it's currently selected.

Give all these methods of selecting text a try, decide which ones feel most comfortable and then memorize them for future use.

Rather than bore you with a rundown of what the buttons on TextEdit's toolbar do, just hover the cursor over any item to display its tooltip, as I've done for the Line and Paragraph Spacing drop-down menu in Figure 14-1.

When text is selected, you can operate on it. For example, you can use the Format menu's Font submenu to make text Bold, Italic, Outlined or Underlined, as shown in Figure 14-2.

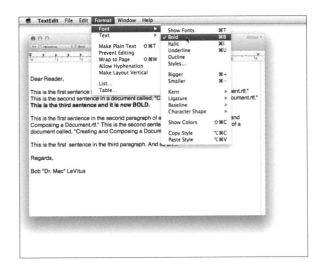

Figure 14-2: The selected sentence is the only part of the document affected by these formatting commands.

Another way I could have applied the Bold style to the text in Figure 14-2 is by clicking the B (for Bold) button on the toolbar. Note that the toolbar is only visible when working on a Rich Text document; if you were to choose Format⇨Make Plain Text (⌘+Shift+T), the toolbar would disappear.

The same idea applies to tabs and margins. In Figure 14-3, I've dragged the left-margin markers from 0 inches to half an inch. Notice that the selected text is now indented by half an inch.

Select some text in your document, and try all the items in the Format menu's Font and Text submenus. As you see, you have a great deal of control over the way your words appear on the screen. And because TextEdit, like most

Macintosh software, is WYSIWYG (What You See Is What You Get), when you print the document (by choosing File⇨Print), the printed version should look exactly like the version you see on the screen. For help with printing, see Chapter 15.

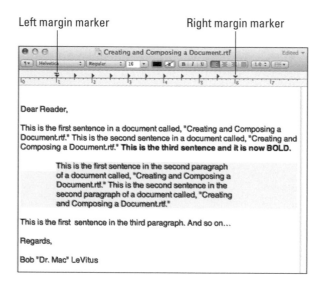

Left margin marker   Right margin marker

Figure 14-3: The selected paragraph is now indented.

Before you print your masterpiece, however, you might want to check your spelling and grammar — something that TextEdit makes extremely simple. Merely choose Edit⇨Spelling and Grammar⇨Check Document Now or press ⌘+; (semicolon). TextEdit highlights and underlines what it perceives to be mistakes in your document. Right-click (or Control-click) to correct the error, as shown in Figure 14-4.

Don't put too much faith in Lion's spelling and grammar checker. It's good but not perfect and no substitute for a good proofreading.

Adding graphics to documents

Last but not least, you have a couple of ways to add pictures to a TextEdit document. The first works as follows:

1. **Copy a picture in another program — Preview, Safari, or whatever.**

2. **Put the cursor where you want the picture to appear in your TextEdit document.**

3. Choose Edit⇨Paste.

The picture magically appears on the page.

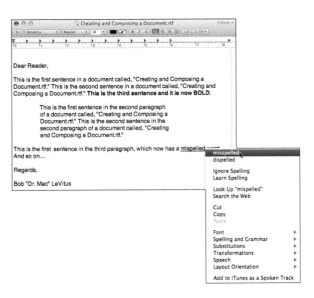

Figure 14-4: Right-click (or Control-click) to correct a spelling or grammar error.

Or you can drag a picture from the Finder or some application (such as Safari or Mail) to a TextEdit document, as I did in Figure 14-5.

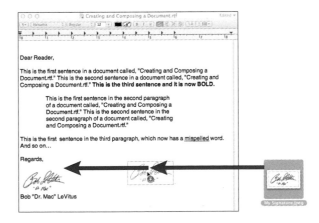

Figure 14-5: Dragging a picture into a TextEdit document.

Font Mania

You can jazz up your documents — or make them a little more serious — with different fonts. To a computer user, *font* means *typeface* — what the characters look like. Although professional typographers will scream at my generalization, I'll go with that definition for now.

Tens of thousands of different fonts are available for the Macintosh. You don't want to use the same font for both a garage-sale flyer and a résumé, right? Luckily for you, Mac OS X comes with hundreds of fonts. Some are pretty predictable, such as Times New Roman (the font of this paragraph), but OS X gives you some artsy ones, too, such as Brush Script. If you *really* get into fonts, you can buy single fonts and font collections anywhere you can buy software. Plenty of shareware and public-domain fonts are also available from online services and user groups. Some people have thousands of fonts. (Maybe they need to get out more.)

The preinstalled fonts live in two different folders, both called Fonts. One is in the Library folder at root level on your hard drive; the other is in the Library subfolder within the System folder.

Mac OS X actually has four Font folders. A third one, also called Fonts, is in the (hidden) Library folder in your home directory. The upcoming section explains the subtle distinctions among those three locations. The fourth one is in the Network/Library folder, and you see it only when you're connected to a NetBoot network server.

Types of fonts

You can find many font formats with names like OpenType, Mac TrueType, Windows TrueType, PostScript Type 1, bitmap, and dfont. No problem — Mac OS X supports them all. In fact, the only font format I know that Lion *doesn't* support is PostScript Type 3.

That said, the three most common formats for Macs are TrueType, PostScript Type 1, and OpenType.

- **TrueType fonts:** These standard-issue Apple fonts come with Mac OS X. They're in common use on Macs as well as on Windows machines. That's partly because these fonts are *scalable:* They use only a single outline per font, and your Mac can make their characters bigger or smaller when you choose a font size in a program.

- **Type 1 fonts:** These fonts are often referred to as *PostScript Type 1* fonts, and they're the standard for desktop publishing on the Mac (as well as Windows and Unix). Tens of thousands of Type 1 fonts are available. (Not nearly as many high-quality TrueType fonts exist.)

Type 1 fonts come in two pieces:

- A *suitcase* file to hold the bitmap that tells the computer how to draw the font on your screen.

- A *printer font* that tells the printer how to print the font on a page.

Some Type 1 fonts come with two, three, or four printer fonts, which usually have related names. Just keep all the parts together, and they should just work.

 OpenType fonts: OpenType fonts are really TrueType fonts in which PostScript information is embedded. This gives you the greater typographic control that high-end typesetters require while keeping the one-file convenience of TrueType.

Managing your fonts with Font Book

 Font Book lets you view your installed fonts, install new fonts, group your fonts into collections, and enable and disable installed fonts. As usual, you find the Font Book application in the Applications folder at root level on your hard disk.

The easiest way to install a new font is to double-click it in the Finder. Font Book opens and displays the font. Click the Install Font button to install the font.

Other ways you can install new fonts are to choose File⇨Add Fonts or press ⌘+O. A standard Open dialog allows you to select a font or fonts to be installed.

Note that by default, new fonts are installed in your Home folder's Fonts folder (Users/Home/Library/Fonts). You can change the default installation location in the Font Book preferences pane (Font Book⇨Preferences or ⌘+,).

To view a font, click its name in the Font list. To change the size of the viewed font, click the triangle in the top-right corner of the Font Book window (where it says *Fit* in Figure 14-6) and choose a new size from the drop-down list that appears, or type a number where the word Fit appears in Figure 14-6, or move the blue slider dot on the right side of the window up or down.

To *disable* a font so it no longer appears on any applications' Font menus, choose Edit⇨Disable or click the Disable button (the check mark in a square button) at the bottom of the window.

To enable a previously disabled font, choose Edit⇨Enable or click the Enable button (same as the Disable button).

Figure 14-6: Click a font in the Font list in the center to display its characters in the pane on the right.

Lion's Font Book looks out for your best interests; it won't allow you to disable or delete any fonts required by Lion — including (but not limited to) Lucida Grande, Helvetica, and Helvetica Neue.

Installing fonts manually

To install any new font manually, drag its icon into one of the two Fonts folders that you have access to. Why might you want to install them manually? If you install a font via the double-click-and-use-Font Book method, the font will be installed in your Home/Library/Fonts folder, and available only to you.

If you want other users to be able to access the new font, drag the font's icon to the Fonts subfolder inside the Library folder, which is at the root level of your hard drive. This Fonts folder has universal access. Or, if you usually want to install fonts for everyone, change the Default Install Location in Font Book Preferences (Font Book–>Preferences or ⌘+,).

The Fonts folder in the Library inside the System folder is reserved for Mac OS X and can't be modified easily. If you try to remove a font from it — or add one, for that matter — you first have to authenticate yourself as an administrator. Do yourself a favor, and *never* remove fonts from /System/Library/Fonts. You can really screw up your Lion operating system if you remove the wrong font. So don't go messing with the fonts in folders unless you know what you're doing. Otherwise, just use Font Book, which prevents you from doing anything bad to fonts.

Part IV
Making This Lion Your Very Own

The 5th Wave   By Rich Tennant

"No, that's not the icon for iCal, it's the icon for iCan't, the database of reasons you forgot an appointment."

In this part . . .

start this part by helping you decipher the myriad Print options so you can become a modern-day Gutenberg. Then you get a look at all the different ways you can share data with others and access data other users have shared. Finally, you look at a bunch of other cool technologies included with Mac OS X Lion to help you make your big cat look, feel, and act just the way you want her to.

There is something in this part for everyone, so don't touch that dial.

Publish or Perish: The Fail-Safe Guide to Printing

···

In This Chapter

▶ Connecting a printer

▶ Using Page Setup to prepare your document for printing

▶ Printing to most printers

▶ Mastering the printing process

···

When you want to get what's on your screen onto paper, printing under Mac OS X should be as simple as pressing the keyboard shortcut ⌘+P and then pressing Return or Enter. Happily, that's usually just how easy printing something is; when it isn't, printing can turn into a raging nightmare. If you configure your printer and printing software properly, however, printing is as easy as can be. And that's pretty darn simple.

In this chapter, I scare away the bogeymen to help you avoid any printing nightmares. I walk you through the entire process as though you just unpacked a new printer and plugged it in.

Before Diving In . . .

Before I even start talking about hooking up printers, you should know a few essential things. So here's a little list that tells you just what those things are:

> ✔ **Read the documentation that came with your printer.** Hundreds of different printer makes and models are available for the Mac, so if I contradict something in your printer manual, follow your manual's instructions first. If that effort doesn't work, try it my way; use the techniques in the rest of this chapter.

✔ **The Print and Page Setup sheets differ slightly (or even greatly) from program to program and from printer to printer.** Although the examples I show you in this chapter are representative of what you'll probably encounter, you might come across sheets that look a bit different. For example, the Print and Page Setup sheets for Microsoft Word include choices that I don't cover in this chapter (such as Even or Odd Pages Only, Print Hidden Text, and Print Selection Only). If you see commands in your Print or Page Setup sheet that I don't explain here, they're specific to that application; look within its documentation for an explanation. Similarly, many graphics apps — such as Apple's iPhoto, Adobe Illustrator CS5, and Photoshop CS5 — have added numerous gadgets, list boxes, radio buttons, and so forth to their Print dialogs, to the point where you might not even recognize them as Print dialogs.

✔ **Don't forget about the Help.** Of course it's built into Lion and better than ever, but many third-party programs support this excellent Apple technology, which can be the fastest way to figure out a feature that has you stumped. So don't forget to check out the Help menu before you panic. (I cover the Help menu in Chapter 1.)

Ready: Connecting and Adding Your Printer

Before you can even think about printing something, you have to connect a printer to your Mac and then tell OS X that the printer exists.

If you have a printer and are able to print documents already you can skip ahead to the "Set: Setting Up Your Document with Page Setup" section. The info between here and there pertains only to setting up a *brand-new* printer — one that still has its manual. (That's a hint.)

Connecting your printer

Once again, I must remind you that you *could* connect your Mac to thousands of printer models, and each one is a little different from the next. In other words, if what you're about to read doesn't work with the printer you're trying to connect, again I implore you to RTFM (that's *Read the Fine Manual,* in case you're wondering). It should tell you how to load your ink or toner cartridges.

That said, here are some very general steps to connect a printer to your Mac:

1. **Connect the printer to your Mac with the cable snugly attached at both ends (printer and Mac).**

   For your printer to work, you have to somehow connect it to a data source. (Think of your phone — you can't receive calls without some sort of connector between the caller and the callee.)

What about wireless printing?

For those who wish to print wirelessly over Wi-Fi (assuming your printer supports it), I'm afraid you're on your own.

Here's why: The procedure for setting up a Wi-Fi printer is different for each manufacturer; hence, I can't provide such instructions in the allotted number of pages.

Here's some good news, though: I have set up a number of Epson, Canon, and Kodak Wi-Fi printers and have never had a problem. Every one of them was easy to set for wireless printing by following the instructions that came with the printer.

If you don't have the instructions or can't find them, visit the manufacturer's website and search for your printer model's manual.

2. **Plug the printer's AC power cord into a power outlet.**

   Yup, I mean the regular kind of outlet in the wall; on a power strip; or, best of all, on a UPS (Uninterruptible Power Supply).

   Some printers require you to plug one end of the AC power cord into the printer; others have the AC power cord attached permanently. The point is that your printer won't work if it's not connected to a power source.

3. **Turn on your printer.**

   Look in the manual if you can't find the power switch; look at the sidebar titled "What about wireless printing?" if you have misplaced your manual.

4. **If your printer came with software, install it on your Mac, following the instructions that came with the printer.**

5. **(Optional) Restart your Mac.**

   You need to do this only if you had to install software and the Installer told you to restart.

Setting up a printer for the first time

After you connect your computer and printer with a compatible cable, provide a power source for your printer, and install the software for your printer, you're ready . . . to configure your Mac. You have to do that so your Mac and your printer can talk to each other.

Many, if not all, of the steps involving the Print & Scan System Preferences pane require that your printer be turned on and warmed up (that is, already run through its diagnostics and startup cycle) beforehand. So before doing anything else, make sure your printer is turned on, warmed up, and connected to your Mac.

Any port on a Mac

Before you can print, you need to plug the printer cable into the appropriate port on the back (or side) of your Mac.

Therein lies the rub. Mac technology has changed dramatically since the previous editions of this book, when I used to say, "Begin by connecting the printer to the Printer port on the back of your Mac (with both the Mac and the printer turned off, of course — but you knew that, didn't you?)." Ah, nostalgia. Now I tell you, "You need to plug the printer cable into the appropriate port. . . ." Why am I being so vague? Because I have to be. You see, these days, printers don't always connect to the same port:

✓ Many (if not most) connect through a Universal Serial Bus (USB) port. If you're going to use your printer wirelessly with an Apple AirPort Extreme base station or Time Capsule device, you'll connect your printer to that device's USB port rather than your Mac's USB port.

✓ Other printers connect to the Ethernet port or to an Ethernet hub (which is in turn connected to the back of your Mac).

✓ A (very) few connect via a FireWire port.

✓ And more and more printers now connect wirelessly via Wi-Fi or Bluetooth.

So read the printer's instructions, and plug your printer into the appropriate hole (port) for your Mac or set it up for wireless printing.

Typically, though, your printer connects to your machine via USB. Don't confuse the USB cable with your printer's AC power cord (the kind you find on everyday appliances). If your printer didn't come with a cable that fits into one of the ports on your Mac, contact your printer manufacturer and ask for one; it's cheesy not to provide the proper cable with a printer.

The first time you connect your printer, you may see an alert asking whether you want to download and install software for your printer. My printer happens to be an Epson Workforce 630, as shown in Figure 15-1.

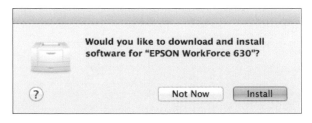

Figure 15-1: Connecting a printer to your Mac; Lion offers to look for software.

You do, so click the Install button. At this point you may see a License Agreement window. If so, click the Agree button to proceed. (You may click Disagree if you wish, but that halts the installation process.)

After clicking the Install and Agree buttons, a Software Update window may appear and tell you it's finding software. If it does, just leave it alone; it disappears after a minute or two. Don't click the Stop button unless you want to abort the installation.

If you've connected a new printer and *didn't* see an alert like the one shown in Figure 15-1, don't panic. You can still set up your printer by following the instructions below.

So regardless of whether you saw an alert window, agreement window, and/or Software Update window, here are the steps to set up that printer for the first time:

1. **Launch System Preferences, click the Print & Scan icon, and then click your printer's name in the Printers list on the left side of the window.**

   You can open System Preferences from the menu, or launch it from the Applications folder, Dock, or Launchpad.

   Lion is a pretty smart cat; it should have already recognized your printer at this point. If so, your printer's name appears in the Printers list of the Print & Scan System Preferences pane, as shown in Figure 15-2. My printer's name, as you can see in Figure 15-2, is Epson WorkForce 630.

Figure 15-2: Printers Lion recognizes appear in the Printers list; click the plus sign (+) button to add other printers.

If your printer *isn't* in the list at this point, click the + button at the bottom of the Printers list and either select it from the list of nearby printers or choose Add Other Printer or Scanner.

If you still can't "see" your printer, you probably need to install (or reinstall) its driver software manually, either from the CD or DVD that came with the printer or by downloading the latest driver software from your printer manufacturer's website. See the nearby sidebar for more on drivers.

2. **Select the printer you want selected by default when you print documents from the Default Printer pop-up menu (Last Used is selected in Figure 15-2).**

3. **Select the default paper size you want to use with this printer from the Default Paper Size menu (usually US Letter if you live in the United States, as shown in Figure 15-2).**

That's all there is to it. Close System Preferences, and you're ready to print your first document! Before you do, however, make sure you have the document set up to look just the way you want it to look printed. Read through "Set: Setting Up Your Document with Page Setup" for more info.

One last thing: Printer sharing

To share a printer with others on your local area wired or wireless network, select it in the Printers list on the left side of the Print & Scan System Preferences pane and then click the Share This Printer on the Network check box.

If the lock in the bottom-left corner of the Print & Scan pane is locked, you may have to click it and provide your administrator password before you can click the check box.

If Printer Sharing is not enabled, an alert that says Printer Sharing Is Turned Off appears below the check box, as shown in Figure 15-2. Click the Sharing Preferences button on the right and the Sharing System Preferences pane (which I discuss in much detail in Chapter 16) replaces the Print & Scan pane. Just click the check box next to Printer Sharing to turn it on.

Go for a driver

Many printer manufacturers introduce new drivers with enhanced functionality periodically. So the driver software on the CD in the box with your printer could be six months or even a year old when you buy that printer. It's always a good idea to determine whether the CD contains the latest version of the printer driver, so visit the printer manufacturer's website, check it out, and download a more recent version of the printer driver if necessary.

Apple includes a library of printer drivers with Lion, which should cover most popular printer brands and models. These drivers are installed by default. Lion also checks to see whether a newer driver is available — for every driver in its library — and if it finds one, offers to download and install the new driver, as shown in Figure 15-1, earlier in this chapter.

If you chose *not* to install some or all of them when you installed Mac OS X Lion, you almost certainly need to install the appropriate printer drivers manually before your printer appears in the Print & Scan System Preferences pane's Printers list.

Set: Setting Up Your Document with Page Setup

After you set up your printer, the hard part is over. You should be able to print a document quickly and easily — right? Not so fast, bucko. Read here how the features in the Page Setup sheet can help you solve most basic printing problems.

Become familiar with Page Setup. You might not need to use it right this second, but it's a good friend to know.

Many programs have a Page Setup command on their File menu. Note that some programs use the name *Page Setup,* and others use *Print Setup.* (Print Setup is the quaint, old-fashioned term, more popular in the System 6 era and in Windows than on today's Macs.) Either way, this is the sheet where you can choose your target printer, paper size, page orientation, and scale (as shown in Figure 15-3).

Users of network printers or PostScript printers might see slightly different versions of the Print and Page Setup sheets. The differences should be minor enough not to matter.

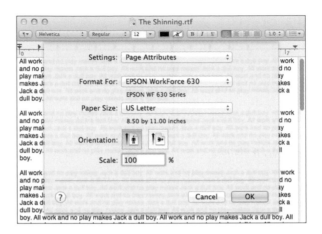

Figure 15-3: The Page Setup sheet in the TextEdit application.

Click the little question mark in the bottom-left corner of the Page Setup sheet at any time for additional help. If you do, Page Setup help opens immediately in the Help Center. (Okay, maybe not *immediately,* but Help Center in Lion is much, much faster than the Help Viewer in previous OS X incarnations.)

The options within the Page Setup sheet are as follows:

- ✔ **Settings:** When you have everything else in the Page Setup sheet configured just the way you want it for most documents, choose Save As Default to save this configuration as the default Page Setup for this application.

- ✔ **Format For:** In this pop-up menu, you find the name of the active printer. If you have several printers configured, you can choose any of them from this menu.

This menu usually defaults to Any Printer, which is the least effective setting. Unless the printer you want to use appears here, you might not get the full functionality that the printer offers.

- ✔ **Paper Size:** Use options in this pop-up menu to choose the type of paper currently in the paper tray of your printer or to choose the size of the paper that you want to feed manually. The dimensions of the paper that you can choose appear below its name.

Page Setup sheet settings (including Paper Size) remain in effect until you change them. For example, when you print an envelope, don't forget to change back to Letter before trying to print on letter-size paper again.

✔ **Orientation:** Choose among options here to tell your printer whether the page you want to print should be *portrait-oriented* (like a letter, longer than it is wide) or *landscape-oriented* (sideways, wider than it is long).

Some programs offer additional Page Setup choices. If your program offers them, they usually appear in the Settings pop-up menu in the Page Setup sheet. (Adobe Photoshop and Microsoft Word have them; TextEdit doesn't.)

✔ **Scale:** To print your page at a larger or smaller size, change this option to a larger or smaller percentage.

Print: Printing with the Print Sheet

After you connect and configure your printer and then set up how you want your document to print, you come to the final steps before that joyous moment when your printed page pops out of the printer. Navigating the Print sheet is the last thing standing between you and your output.

Although most Print sheets that you see look like the figures I show in this chapter, others might differ slightly. The features in the Print sheet are strictly a function of the program with which you're printing. Many programs choose to use the standard-issue Apple sheet shown in this chapter, but not all do. If I don't explain a certain feature in this chapter, chances are good that the feature is specific to the application or printer you're using (in which case the documentation for that program or printer should offer an explanation).

Printing a document

If everything has gone well so far, the actual act of printing a document is pretty simple. Just follow the steps here, and in a few minutes, pages should start popping out of your printer like magic. (In the sections that follow, I talk about some print options that you'll probably need someday.)

1. **Open a document that you want to print.**

2. **Choose File⇨Print (or press ⌘+P).**

   You see the basic Print sheet, as shown in Figure 15-4.

Figure 15-4: Your basic Print sheet.

3. Click Print.

Wait a few minutes for the network to tell the printer what to do, and then walk over to your printer to get your document.

Choosing File⇨Print (⌘+P) *won't* work for you if any one of the following is true for the software you're using:

- ✔ The Print command is on a different menu.
- ✔ There *is* no Print command. (Hey, it could happen.)
- ✔ The Print keyboard shortcut is anything but ⌘+P.

If any of the preceding is true for a program you're using, you just have to wing it. Look in all the menus and check out the product's documentation to try to get a handle on the Print command for that pesky program.

Choosing among different printers

Just as you can in the Page Setup sheet, you can choose which printer you want to use from the Printer pop-up menu of the Print sheet.

You can choose only among the printers you've added via the Print & Scan System Preferences pane, as I describe earlier in this chapter (in the section I lovingly refer to as "Setting up a printer for the first time").

This includes printers connected to wireless base stations and routers. After they're set up, Macs (and PCs) within wireless range can print to these printers wirelessly.

Choosing custom settings

If you've created a custom group of settings previously, you can choose them from the Presets pop-up menu of the Print sheet. I touch more on this feature in the "Saving custom settings" section later in this chapter.

By default, the Print sheet is displayed with its details hidden. As such, just three menus are available: Printer, Pages, and PDF, as shown in Figure 15-4. To reveal the rest of the Print options, click the Show Details button near the bottom of the Print sheet. An expanded Print sheet with all the details you're likely to need, as shown in Figure 15-5, replaces the more streamlined version shown in Figure 15-4.

Figure 15-5: Your expanded Print sheet.

Click in any of the fields and then press the Tab key. Your cursor jumps to the next text field in the sheet; likewise, press Shift+Tab to make the cursor jump to the previous field. By the way, this shortcut works in almost any program, window, dialog, or web page that has text fields.

✔ **Copies:** In this text field, set how many copies you want to print. The Print sheet defaults to one copy (1) in most applications, so you probably see the numeral 1 in the Copies field when the Print sheet appears. Assuming that's the case, don't do anything if you want to print only one copy. If you want to print more than one copy of your document, highlight the 1 that appears in the Copies field and replace it, typing the number of copies you want.

✔ **Pages:** Here, you find two radio buttons: All and From. The default behavior is to print your entire document, so the All option is preselected. But if you want to print only a specific page or range of pages, mark the From radio button and then type the desired page numbers in the From and To text-entry boxes.

Suppose that you print a 10-page document — and then notice a typo on Page 2. After you correct your error, you don't have to reprint the whole document — only the page with the correction. Reprint only Page 2 by typing **2** in both the From and To fields. You can type any valid range of pages (um, you can't print page 20 if your document is only 15 pages long) in the From and To fields.

✔ **Paper Size:** Use options in this pop-up menu to choose the type of paper currently in your printer's paper tray — or to choose the size of the paper that you want to feed manually. The dimensions of the paper appear below its name.

You've already seen this setting in Page Setup. The difference is that the settings here (in the Print sheet) apply only to this document, whereas the settings in Page Setup are the default for all documents and remain in effect until you change them in Page Setup. This can be very handy when, for example, you print an envelope. If you change the paper-size setting for the envelope document, you don't have to remember to change it back to Letter in Page Setup.

✔ **Orientation:** Once again, you've seen this setting in Page Setup. And once again, the choice you make in Page Setup is the default for all pages you print. Keep in mind that the setting you choose here (in the Print sheet) applies only to this document.

Choose among options here to tell your printer whether the page you want to print should be portrait-oriented or landscape-oriented.

The following list describes the features you can find in the unlabeled menu found in the expanded Print sheet (the one that says *TextEdit* in Figure 15-5). In addition to the TextEdit, Layout, and other options I cover in a moment, your pop-up menu might offer options such as Quality & Media, Color Options, Special Effects, Borderless Printing, and so on. (Whether you have these options depends on your printer model and its driver.) Check out these options if you have 'em; they usually offer useful features:

- ✔ **TextEdit:** The only TextEdit–specific options, as shown in Figure 15-5, are two check boxes. One governs whether to print a header and footer for this document; the other lets you choose to rewrap the contents of the document to fit the page.

  You can see the results of clicking these check boxes in the proxy image of your document on the left half of the sheet.

- ✔ **Layout:** Choose Layout to set the number of pages per printed sheet, the layout direction, and whether you prefer a border. Here are your options for Layout:

  - *Pages per Sheet:* Choose preset numbers from this pop-up menu to set the number of pages that you want to print on each sheet.

    Pages appear on-screen smaller than full size if you use this option.

  - *Layout Direction:* Choose one of the four buttons that govern the way the small pages are laid out on the printed page.

  - *Border:* Your choices from this pop-up menu are None, Single Hairline, Single Thin Line, Double Hairline, and Double Thin Line.

  - *Two-Sided:* If your printer supports two-sided (known as *duplex*) printing, the three radio buttons allow you to specify whether you're going to use two-sided printing and, if so, whether you'll be binding (or stapling) along the long or short edge of the paper.

  There are also two check boxes — Reverse Page Orientation and Flip Horizontally — that do just what they say if you enable them.

- ✔ **Color Matching:** Choose Color Matching to choose a color-conversion method (usually, either Apple's ColorSync or Vendor Matching technology). The idea here is to get the printed page to look as much like what's on your screen as possible.

✔ **Paper Handling:** Choose Paper Handling if you want to reverse the order in which your pages print or to print only the odd- or even-numbered pages. You can also specify whether the document's paper size is to be used (in which case you might have lines that break across pages) or whether the output should be scaled to fit the chosen paper size.

✔ **Cover Page:** Choose Cover Page to add a cover page.

✔ **Print Settings:** Choose Print Settings to choose paper type and print quality.

Saving custom settings

After you finalize printer settings, you can save them for future use. Just click the Presets pop-up menu and choose Save Current Settings as Preset, and provide a name for this preset. From then on, the preset name appears as an option in the Presets pop-up menu. Just choose your saved set before you print any document, and all the individual settings associated with that preset are restored.

To manage your custom settings, known in Lion-speak as *presets,* choose Show Presets from the Presets pop-up menu. This new Lion feature displays a list of your presets and their settings, and allows you to delete, duplicate, or rename (by double-clicking their current name) presets.

Preview and PDF Options

To see a preview of what your printed page will look like, choose Open PDF in Preview from the PDF pop-up menu in the bottom-left corner of the expanded Print sheet. When you do so, you see the page or pages that you're about to print displayed by the Preview application, as shown in Figure 15-6.

If you have any doubt about the way a document will look when you print it, check out Preview first. When you're happy with the document preview, just choose File➪Print, press ⌘+P, or click the Print button at the bottom of the Preview window. Or click the Cancel button to return to your application and make changes to the document.

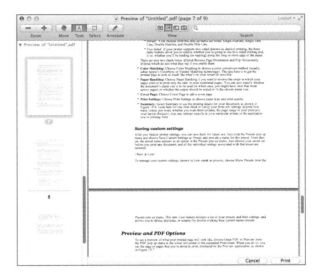

Figure 15-6: A preview of a TextEdit document.

Preview works with the Preview application that Apple includes with Mac OS X. With the Preview feature, you can do cool things like these:

✔ See all the pages in your document the way they will be printed, one by one.

✔ Zoom in or out to get a different perspective on what you're about to send to the printer (pretty cool!).

✔ Rotate the picture 90 degrees to the left or right.

✔ Spot errors before you commit to printing something. A little up-front inspection can save you a lot of paper, ink (or toner), and frustration.

Check out the Preview program's View menu, where you'll find (among other things), four useful views: Content Only, Thumbnails (shown in Figure 15-6), Table of Contents, and Contact Sheet, as well as the zoom commands and more.

While you're checking out menus, you won't want to miss the Tools menu, which lets you rotate pages, move forward or backward (through multipage documents); select the Move, Text, or Select tool (for which the useful keyboard shortcuts are ⌘+1, 2, and 3, respectively); and invoke the awesome new (in Lion) Magnifier, shown in Figure 15-7.

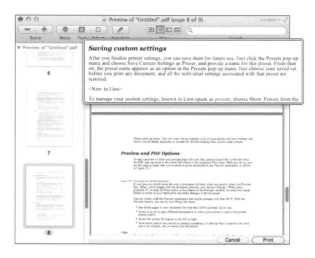

Figure 15-7: Preview app now includes a terrific Magnifier tool.

The Magnifier tool is so very darn cool that it has a rare single-key keyboard shortcut. That key is the ` (the accent, which shares a key with the tilde); press it to show or hide the Magnifier.

One last thing: Many of the tools and commands mentioned above are also available in the toolbar.

Add or delete buttons from the toolbar by choosing View➪Customize Toolbar.

Just the Fax . . .

Mac OS X includes the capability to fax a document right from the Print sheet. But before you can take advantage of it, you have to connect and add a fax modem. Fortunately, doing so is as easy as connecting and adding a printer (as described in the "Ready: Connecting and Adding Your Printer" section, earlier in this chapter): Just follow the same steps, replacing the word *printer* with the words *fax modem,* and you're good to go.

After your fax modem is connected and added, all you have to do to fax a document is choose Fax PDF from the PDF pop-up menu at the bottom of every Print sheet. When you do, the sheet becomes a Fax sheet, as shown in Figure 15-8.

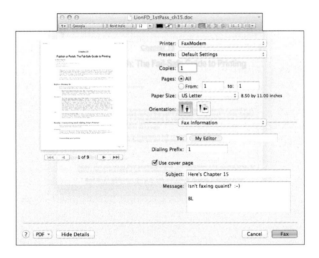

Figure 15-8: In Lion, faxing is just as easy as printing.

To fax a document, follow these steps:

1. **Choose Fax PDF from the menu that appears when you press and hold the PDF pop-up menu on the Print sheet.**

2. **Type the fax phone number of the recipient in the To field.**

   If you click the button with the silhouette on the right of the To field, you can select a recipient from the Mac OS X Address Book.

3. **Add a dialing prefix if your phone requires one (such as 1, which most U.S. phones require to dial a 10-digit, long-distance phone number).**

4. **Click the Use Cover page check box if you want a cover page, and if you do, you can type a subject in the Subject field and a brief message in the Message field.**

5. **Select your fax modem from the Printer pop-up menu, if it isn't already selected (as mine, named FaxModem, is in Figure 15-8).**

   Everything else in the Fax sheet is just the same as in the Print sheet, which you can read all about in the previous sections.

6. **Click the Fax button.**

   Your fax is sent.

Before you try to fax something out into the world, make sure you have a functioning fax modem — and that it's configured, set up properly, connected to a phone line, and turned on. If you don't get all those ducks in a row, this whole faxing process will (of course) fail. Note that no Mac that can run Lion includes an analog modem, so those machines don't have built-in hardware that supports faxing; you would need to purchase a modem or other hardware to use this feature (for example, a multifunction printer with fax capability).

Lion supports a new Bluetooth feature known as Dial-Up Networking (DUN) Profile, which allows a Bluetooth-enabled mobile phone to act as a modem and connect to an Internet service provider (ISP) and the Internet. Unfortunately, after repeated experimentation, I was unable to get any of my mobile phones to act as a fax modem. I mention it only because it's entirely possible that it *will* work with *your* mobile phone. (If it does, please drop me a note at Lion4Dummies@boblevitus.com, and let me know how you did it, what kind of phone you have, and what wireless carrier [for example, AT&T] you use. Thanks!)

16

Sharing Your Mac and Liking It

In This Chapter

▶ Comprehending sharing

▶ Knowing what's up with networks

▶ Setting up file sharing

▶ Finding out about users

▶ Understanding access and permissions

▶ Sharing files, folders, and disks with other users

▶ Sharing remotely

*H*ave you ever wanted to grab a file from your Mac while you were halfway around the world or even around the corner? If so, I have good news for you: It's not difficult with Mac OS X (believe it or not), even though computer networking in general has a well-deserved reputation for being complicated and nerve-wracking. The truth is that you won't encounter anything scary or complicated about sharing files, folders, and disks (and printers, for that matter) among computers as long as the computers are Macintoshes. And if some of the computers are running Windows, Mac OS X Lion even makes that (almost) painless. Your Macintosh includes everything that you need to share files and printers — everything, that is, except the printers and the cables (and maybe a hub). So here's the deal: You supply the hardware, and this chapter supplies the rest. And when you're done hooking it all up, you can take a rest.

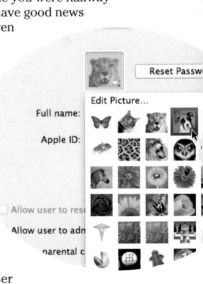

The first sections of this chapter provide an overview and tell you everything that you need to know to set up new user accounts and share files successfully. I don't show you how to actually share a file, folder, or disk until the "Connecting to a Shared Disk or Folder on a Remote Mac" section, later in this chapter. Trust me, there's a method to my madness. If you try to share files without doing all the required prep work, the whole mess becomes confusing and complicated pretty fast — kind of like networking Windows PCs.

One last thing: If you're the only one who uses your Mac, you don't intend to share it or its files with anyone else, and you never intend to access your Mac from another computer in a different location, you can safely skip this whole chapter if you like.

Introducing Networks and File Sharing

Macintosh file sharing enables you to use files, folders, and disks from other Macs on a network — any network, including the Internet — as easily as though they were on your own local hard drive. If you have more than one computer, file sharing is a blessing.

Before diving in and actually sharing, allow me to introduce a few necessary terms:

- ✔ **Network:** For the purposes of this chapter, a *network* is two or more Macs connected by Ethernet cables, wireless networking (Apple refers to this as AirPort or Wi-Fi), or FireWire cables (which are by far the least common type of network connection).

- ✔ **Ethernet:** A network protocol and cabling scheme that lets you connect two or more computers so they can share files, disks, printers, or whatever.

- ✔ **Ethernet ports:** Where you plug an Ethernet cable into your Mac.

   Be careful to match the cable to its specific jack. On your Mac and printer, the Ethernet ports look a lot like phone jacks, and the connectors on each end of an Ethernet cable look a lot like phone cable connectors. But they aren't the same. Ethernet cables are typically thicker, and the connectors (RJ-45 connectors) are a bit larger than the RJ-11 connectors that you use with telephones. (See examples of both types of ports in the margin.) Standard phone cables fit (very loosely) into Ethernet ports, but you shouldn't try that, either; they'll probably fall out with the slightest vibration. It's unlikely that such a mistake will cause any permanent damage, but it won't work and will be frustrating.

- ✔ **Local devices:** Devices connected directly to your computers, such as hard or optical drives. Your internal hard drive, for example, is a local device.

- ✔ **Remote devices:** Devices you access (share) over the network. The hard drive of a computer in the next room, for example, is a remote device.

✔ **Protocols:** Kinds of languages that networks speak. When you read or hear about networks, you're likely to hear the words *AppleTalk, EtherTalk* (or *Ethernet*), *SMB,* and *TCP/IP* bandied about with great regularity. These are all protocols. Macs can speak several different protocols, but every device (Mac or printer) on a network needs to speak the same protocol at the same time to communicate.

Support for the TCP/IP protocol is built into every Mac. Your Mac includes all the software you need to set up a TCP/IP network; the hardware you provide consists of Ethernet cables and a hub (if you have more than two computers) or an AirPort or other Wi-Fi Base Station. Here, I'm using *hub* generically; its more powerful networking cousins, switches and routers, also work for this purpose.

By the way, in addition to providing wireless networking, the AirPort Extreme wireless Base Stations — as well as the Time Capsule device — are all members of the router class of devices.

The Time Capsule is a pretty cool deal; it combines a wireless Base Station, three-port Ethernet router, and a big hard disk that can be shared by all computers on the network and also used as a Time Machine backup disk. I talk more about Time Capsule in Chapter 18.

Portrait of home-office networking

A typical Mac home-office network consists of two Macintoshes, an AirPort Extreme wireless Base Station (or other type of Ethernet hub or router), and a network printer. Check out Figure 16-1 to see the configuration of a simple network. In the figure, the black lines between the devices are Ethernet cables; the rectangular device with those cables going into it is an Ethernet hub, router, AirPort Extreme Base Station, or Time Capsule. (I tell you more about cables and such devices in the section "Three ways to build a network," later in this chapter.) You need enough Ethernet cable to run among all your devices.

With the setup shown in Figure 16-1, either Mac can use the other Mac's files, and both Macs can print to the same printer.

If you have a broadband Internet connection, you can also connect the cable or DSL modem to the hub/switch/router so all Mac users on the network can share the Internet connection.

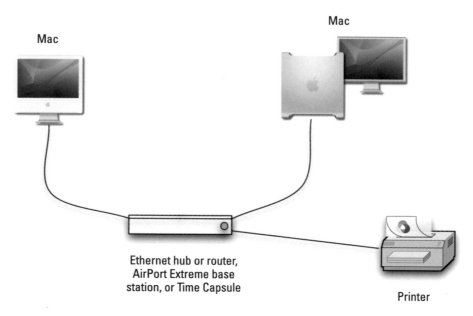

Figure 16-1: Two Macs and a printer make up a simple Mac network.

A network can — and often does — have dozens or hundreds of users. Regardless of whether your network has 2 nodes (machines) or 2,000, the principles and techniques in this chapter apply.

Three ways to build a network

In this chapter, I assume you're working on a small network, the kind typically found in a home or small business. If you're part of a megamonstrous corporate network, and you have questions about your particular network, talk to the PIC (*person in charge,* also known as your *network administrator*). In other words, if you're trying to build a meganetwork, you're going to need a book a lot thicker and harder to understand than this one.

File sharing made easy with Bonjour

Perhaps all you want to do is share an occasional file (not necessarily a printer or a home Internet connection or a folder of music files or pictures). In that case, check out *Bonjour,* previously known as Rendezvous. It's a zero-configuration network protocol that makes Mac networking simple. If two devices (and this includes all Macs running Mac OS X Jaguar or later) speak Bonjour, you don't have to do *any* configuration other than, possibly, turning on the sharing capability, as I explain in "Setting Up File Sharing," later in this chapter. Bonjour queries the other available networked devices to see what services they support, and then configures the connections for you automatically. Sweet!

Lion introduces a new (Wi-Fi only) sharing feature called *AirDrop* that appears in your Finder window Sidebar and locates all other AirDrop-capable Macs on your local wireless network. For AirDrop to work you don't need to turn on File Sharing or do anything else. Just click AirDrop in the Finder Sidebar, and you see AirDrop in the Finder window, as shown here:

The key here is that both Macs must

1. Be on the same Wi-Fi network

   and

2. Have an open Finder window with AirDrop selected.

To send a file (or multiple files and or folders) to the other Mac, just drag them onto the other Mac's icon. AirDrop displays a dialog on the other Mac asking whether they want to accept delivery; if they do, the items are transferred immediately to their Downloads folder.

When you close the AirDrop window, you are no longer visible to other AirDrop users. Thus, if you want to transfer files to other Bonjour Macs, use iChat as described in Chapter 10, selecting the other Bonjour Mac, establishing a chat, and dragging the item(s) into the message box. While AirDrop is front-and-center in a Finder window and incredibly simple to use, its limitations are that it is both Lion-only and Wi-Fi only; whereas iChat works with both Bonjour and your Buddy List to exchange files with anyone with whom you can chat, including PC users. But using iChat involves a few more steps (and isn't as pretty, if aesthetics matter to you).

The following list gives you three common ways to build a modern small home or office network:

- **AirPort:** If all your Macs are equipped with AirPort wireless cards, and you have an (AirPort or) AirPort Extreme Base Station, you don't need cables at all. Just plug in the Base Station, and Macs with AirPort cards can communicate with one another. If you use an Ethernet printer (connected to your Mac by Ethernet cable), you have to connect it to the Base Station before you can print from your wireless Macs. Both the Base Station and printer have Ethernet ports, so you can use a crossover cable (more about that in a minute) to make the connection.

  Recent vintage AirPort Extreme and Time Capsule devices from Apple include a USB port so you can connect any printer via USB and share it wirelessly (rather than having to use a more expensive Ethernet-equipped "networkable" printer).

  Although this setup is more expensive than connecting everything with Ethernet cables and a cheap hub or router, it's also more flexible because you can move your devices anywhere. (Well, almost anywhere; you're limited to a maximum of 150–200 feet from each Base Station, and that's assuming that there's absolutely nothing in the way to block your signal. Your mileage may — and probably will — vary.)

- **Traditional Ethernet:** All modern Macs have an Ethernet port, with the exception of the MacBook Air. To connect your Mac to a network, you need Ethernet cables for each Mac and a little device called a *hub, switch,* or *router.* This device is like the center of a wagon wheel; the wires coming out of it are the "spokes."

  A typical Ethernet hub includes two to eight Ethernet ports. You plug the hub into an electrical outlet and then connect Ethernet cables from each of your Macs and printers (from their Ethernet ports) to the hub. Voilà — instant network. These gadgets are pretty cheap, starting at around $10; cables start at a few bucks, increasing in price as the length and quality of the cable increase.

- **Small Ethernet:** If you have only two devices to network (two Macs or a Mac and an Ethernet printer, in most cases), you can use an Ethernet cable to connect them directly to each other via the Ethernet ports. You can purchase an Ethernet cable at your local electronics store.

  Plug one end of the Ethernet cable into one device and the other end into the other device.

For each of these setups, if you have a cable modem or Digital Subscriber Line (DSL) as your Internet connection, you might need a router or switch instead of a (cheaper) hub. Routers and switches are similar to hubs but cost a tiny bit more and have additional features that you might or might not need. Your ISP can tell you whether you're going to need one. For what it's worth, I have a cable modem, but it works fine with a cheap hub.

If you use an Apple AirPort Extreme Base Station or Time Capsule, you may not need a hub or router at all because all these devices incorporate small routers (each with three Ethernet ports). So they're all you need for up to three Ethernet devices. If, on the other hand, you have more than three Ethernet devices, you'll need to add a hub, switch, or router with some additional Ethernet ports to accommodate them all.

Setting Up File Sharing

Before you get into the nitty-gritty of sharing files, you must complete a few housekeeping tasks, such as enabling the appropriate type of file sharing. Follow these steps to do so:

1. **Choose ⚫⟶System Preferences and then click the Sharing icon.**

   The Sharing System Preferences pane appears. The first word of the long username of the first Admin account created on this computer appears in the Computer Name field by default, followed by the type of Mac (for example, Bob LeVitus's MacBook Pro).

2. **If you want to change the name of your computer from whatever Lion decided to call it to something more personal, do that now in the Computer Name text field at the top of the Sharing pane.**

   In Figure 16-2, you can see that I named mine Bob LeVitus's MacBook Pro. You can name yours anything you like.

3. **Select the File Sharing check box, as shown in Figure 16-2.**

   Now other users on your network can access files and folders on your computer, as you see later in this chapter.

   By default, only one folder in your Home folder is shared, and that folder is your Public Folder.

   If you want to access files or folders on this computer while you're using another computer on the network, you can so long as you first provide your username and password. Everyone else on the network can only see your Public folder.

   These are the safest settings. Unless you have good reason to tinker with them, you should probably not change anything here. That said, if you feel you must change these settings, you find out how to do so in the next section of this chapter.

Figure 16-2: Turning file sharing on and off.

4. **(Optional) If you want remote users to upload and download files to and from this computer, click the Options button and then select either or both of the Share Files and Folders Using AFP or SMB check boxes.**

    • Doing so gives users on the Internet but not on your local area network some alternatives to file sharing: an Apple File Protocol (AFP) or a client program that uses Server Message Block (Samba or SMB).

    • If you want to enable Windows or Linux users — or users of other operating systems — to share files with you, the SMB check box must be selected.

5. **Select the On check box (the leftmost column) for each account you want to enable to use these protocols to access your Mac, providing the password when prompted.**

6. **Click the Done button when you're done and then proceed to the following section to continue setting up your network.**

Access and Permissions: Who Can Do What

After you set up file sharing (as I explain in the preceding section), your next step on the path to sharing files on a network is telling your Mac who is allowed to see and access specific folders. Luckily for you, this just happens to be what I cover in the following sections.

Users and groups and guests

Macintosh file sharing (and indeed, Mac OS X as well) is based on the concept of users. You can share items — such as drives or folders — with no users, one user, or many users, depending on your needs.

- ✔ **Users:** People who share folders and drives (or your Mac) are *users*. A user's access to items on your local hard drive is entirely at your discretion. You can configure your Mac so only you can access its folders and drives, or so only one other person or group — or everyone — can share its folders and drives.

  When you first set up your Mac, you created your first user. This user automatically has administrative powers, such as adding more users, changing preferences, and having the clearance to see all folders on the hard drive.

  For the purposes of this book, I assume that some users for whom you create identities won't be folks who actually sit at your Mac, but those who connect to it only from remote locations when they need to give or get files. But you could allow such a user to use the same name and password to log in while sitting at your desk.

  For most intents and purposes, a remote user and a local user are the same. Here's why: After you create an account for a user, that user can log in to this Mac while sitting in your chair in your office; from anywhere on your local area network via Ethernet; or anywhere in the world via the Internet if you give him or her an Administrator, Standard, or Managed account.

- ✔ **Administrative users:** Although a complete discussion of the special permissions that a user with administrator permissions has on a Mac running Mac OS X is far beyond the scope of this book, note two important things:

  - The first user created (usually when you install OS X for the first time) is automatically granted administrator (Admin) powers.

  - Only an administrator account can create new users, delete some (but not all) files from folders that aren't in his or her Home folder, lock and unlock System Preferences panes, and a bunch of other stuff. If you try something and it doesn't work, make sure you're logged in as an Administrator or can provide an Administrator username and password when prompted.

  You can give any user administrator permissions by selecting that user's account in the Users & Groups System Preferences pane and then selecting the Allow User to Administer This Computer check box. You can set this check box when you're creating the user account or subsequently, if that works for you.

- **Groups:** *Groups* are Unix-level designations for privilege consolidation. For example, there are groups named staff and wheel (as well as a bunch of others). A user can be a member of multiple groups. For example, your main account is in the wheel and Admin groups (and others, too). Don't worry — you find out more about groups shortly.

- **Guests:** Two kinds of guests exist. The first kind lets your friends log into your Mac while sitting at your desk without user accounts or passwords. When they log out, all information and files in the guest account's Home folder are deleted automatically.

If you want this kind of guest account, you need to enable the Guest Account in the Users & Groups System Preferences pane. To do so, click the Guest Account in the list of accounts on the left and then select the Allow Guests to Log In to This Computer check box.

The second kind of guest is people who access Public folders on your Mac via file sharing over your local area network or the Internet. They don't need usernames or passwords. If they're on your local network, they can see and use your Public folder(s), unless you or the Public folder's owner has altered the permissions on one or more Public folders. If they're on the Internet and know your IP address, they can see and use your Public folder(s) if you don't have a firewall blocking such access. Public folders are all that guests can access, luckily.

You don't have to do anything to enable this type of guest account.

Creating users

Before users can share folders and drives (or have their own accounts on your computer, for that matter), they must have an account on your Mac. You can create two different kinds of accounts for them — a User Account or a Sharing Account.

- **When you create a User Account** for a person (I call that person and account *User 1*), the account has its own Home folder (called — what else? — User 1), which is filled with User 1's files. Nobody but User 1 can access files in this Home folder unless, of course, User 1 has provided someone the account name and password.

- **When you create a Sharing Account** for a person (I call that person and account *Sharing 1*), the person using that account doesn't have a Home folder and can't access other users' Home folders. Sharing 1 can access only the Public folders inside all the Home folders on that Mac.

You can create a new User Account only in the Users & Groups System Preferences pane. You can create a Sharing Account in the Users & Groups or Sharing System Preferences panes.

When you click the + button under the Users list in the Sharing System Preferences pane and choose a contact in your Address Book (as opposed to choosing an existing user account), you create a Sharing Account for that person.

Anyone can remotely access files or folders in your Public folder(s) over a LAN (local area network) or the Internet. But if you want them to be able to access folders or files other than those in the Public folder(s) on your Mac, they need either a User Account or a Sharing Account.

When you add (create) a user, you need to tell your Mac who this person is. This is also the time to set passwords and administrative powers for this new user. Here's the drill:

1. **Choose System Preferences (or click the System Preferences icon in the Dock), click the Users & Groups icon, and then make sure that the Password tab is selected.**

   The Users & Groups System Preferences pane appears. In this pane (shown in Figure 16-3), you can see the name of the first user (Bob LeVitus) and the administrative control that this user is allowed. (Note that the Allow User to Administer This Computer check box is selected.)

Figure 16-3: The Users & Groups System Preferences pane is where you manage user accounts on this Mac.

As I mention previously, the first user created (usually at the same time you installed OS X) always has administrator permissions.

2. **Click the + button beneath the list of users.**

A sheet appears in which you enter the new user's information.

If the + button is dimmed, here's how you get it functioning: First click the lock (at bottom left), supply an administrator name and password in the resulting dialog, and then click OK.

3. **Choose Standard from the New Account menu at the top of the sheet.**

4. **In the Name text box, type the full name of a user you want to add.**

In the Account Name text box, your Mac inserts a suggested abbreviated name (formerly known as the *short name*). Check out Figure 16-4 to see both.

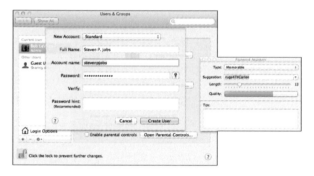

Figure 16-4: Name the new user and your Mac suggests a short name and password.

In Figure 16-4, I added Steven P. Jobs as a user, typing the full name in the Full Name field. You don't really need to type the user's full name, but I do so in this example to show you the difference between a Full Name and an Account Name.

5. **Press the Tab key to move to the next field.**

Mac OS X suggests an abbreviated version of the name in the Account Name field (as shown in Figure 16-4).

Because he's the only Steve who matters around here, I change the suggested Account Name from `stevenpjobs` to just plain `steve`, which is shorter than the short name recommended by Mac OS X. (In other words, I type **steve** in the Account Name field, replacing the suggested `stevenpjobs`.)

The name of each user's folder (in the Users folder) is taken from the short name that you enter when you create a user.

Users can connect to your Mac (or log in to their own Macs, for that matter) by using the short name, rather than having to type their full names. The short name is also used in environments in which user-names can't have spaces and are limited to eight or fewer characters. Although OS X Lion allows longer usernames (but no spaces), you might be better off keeping your short name shorter than eight characters, just in case.

6. **Tab to the Password field, and enter an initial password for this user.**

   The small, square button with the key to the right of the Password field, when clicked, displays the Password Assistant. You can use the Password Assistant, as shown on the right in Figure 16-4, to help generate a password that should be fairly easy for the user to remember (choose Memorable from the Password Assistant's Type pop-up menu) but hard for a cracking program to guess (or meet other requirements).

   To make your password even harder to guess or crack, choose Random or FIPS-181-compliant from the Password Assistant's Type pop-up menu.

7. **Press the Tab key to move your cursor to the Verify text field.**

8. **In the Verify text box, type the password again to verify it.**

9. **(Optional) To help remember a password, type something in the Password Hint text box to jog the user's memory.**

   If a user forgets her password and asks for a hint, the text that you type in the Password Hint field pops up, ideally causing the user to exclaim, "Oh, yeah . . . *now* I remember!" A password hint should be something simple enough to jog the user's memory, but not so simple that an unauthorized person can guess. Perhaps something like "Your first teddy bear's name backward" would be a good hint.

10. **Click the Create Account button to create the account.**

    The sheet disappears, and the new user now appears in the Users & Groups System Preferences pane's Users list.

11. **(Optional) Click the account picture above the Full Name field, and choose a different one.**

    Mac OS X suggests a picture from its default collection for each account, but you can select a different one from the pop-up mini-window shown in Figure 16-5, drag one in from the Finder (or iPhoto), or take a photo with an attached or built-in camera (such as an iSight) by choosing Edit Picture.

12. **(Optional) Click the Set button next to Apple ID to enter (or create) the user's Apple ID.**

Figure 16-5: Choosing a different picture for the selected user (here, it's Steven P. Jobs).

Changing a user

Circumstances might dictate that you need to change a user's identity, password, or accessibility, or perhaps delete a user. Follow these steps to change a user's name, password, or administration permissions:

1. **Choose ⌘⇨System Preferences (or click the System Preferences icon in the Dock or Launchpad).**

   The System Preferences window appears.

2. **In the System Preferences window, click the Users & Groups icon.**

   The Users & Groups System Preferences pane appears.

   If the lock icon at the bottom of the window is locked, you have to click it and provide an administrator password before you can proceed.

3. **Select the user's name in the accounts list.**

   The information for that person appears.

4. **Make your changes by selecting the existing username and then replacing the old with new text or a different setting.**

   • If you want to change the password, click the Reset Password button and make your changes in the sheet that appears.

- To change the picture or other capabilities, click the Picture, Login Options, Allow User to Administer This Computer (to make this user an administrator on this Mac), or Enable Parental Control check box (more on this in a moment) and make the appropriate changes.

    To change a user, you must be logged in using an account that has administrator powers.

5. **Quit the System Preferences application or choose a different System Preferences pane.**

    Your changes are saved when you leave the Users & Groups pane.

Removing a user

To delete a user — in effect, to deny that user access to your Mac — select the user you want to delete in the list of accounts and then click the – button. A sheet appears, offering three choices:

- **Save the Home folder in a disk image** saves a disk image of the user's Home folder in a folder named Deleted Users (which it creates inside the Users folder).

- **Don't change the Home folder** removes the user from the Users & Groups System Preferences pane and login screen but leaves that user's Home folder in the Users folder. *(Deleted)* is appended to the folder's name, so if I had selected this option in the previous example, Steven P. Jobs' Home folder would be renamed *steve (Deleted)*.

- **Delete the Home folder** does what it says. You have the option of a secure erase (the contents get overwritten multiple times) if you select this option.

To remove a user from your Mac, you must be logged in using an account that has administrator permissions.

Limiting a user's capabilities

Sometimes — especially with younger children, computerphobic family members, or employees in a small business — you want to limit what users can access. For example, you might want to make certain programs off limits. You do this by clicking the Parental Controls button in the Users & Groups System Preferences pane.

1. **Choose ⇨System Preferences (or click the System Preferences icon in the Dock).**

    The System Preferences window appears.

2. **In the System Preferences window, click the Users & Groups icon.**

   The Users & Groups System Preferences pane appears.

3. **Click the user's name to select it, click the Enable Parental Controls check box, and then click the Open Parental Controls button.**

   Note that clicking the Open Parental Controls button without first selecting the Enable Parental Controls check box puts you in the Parental Controls preference pane with a button front and center for you to click to turn Parental Controls on. So either select the check box as instructed or click the Enable Parental Controls button here.

   To change any of these items, you must be logged in using an account that has administrator powers, and the account you're modifying can't have administrator powers.

   The Parental Controls System Preferences pane for that person appears with five tabs: Apps (shown in Figure 16-6), Web, People, Time Limits, and Other.

Figure 16-6: You can control an account's access in five categories.

4. **Set the controls in each of the five tabs.**

   - *Apps:* Determine which applications the user may access. Set whether she can modify the Dock. Also determine whether she's restricted to a very limited and simplified Finder interface.

   - *Web:* Control access to websites.

- *People:* Determine whether Mail or iChat (or both) communicants will be limited to a specified list. This option also lets you notify someone (usually yourself) when the user tries to exchange e-mail with a contact not in the approved list. You can also maintain a log of all iChat text conversations.

- *Time Limits:* Set time limits for weekdays and weekends, and prevent access to this computer during specified hours on school nights and weekends. Notice that the definition of *school night* doesn't take vacations or holidays into consideration.

- *Other:* Determine whether profanity is hidden during Dictionary access, control whether the user can add or remove printers or modify printer settings, prevent (or allow) burning CDs and DVDs in the Finder, and control whether the user is allowed to change their password.

5. **Quit the System Preferences application or choose a different System Preferences pane.**

   Your changes are saved when you leave the Parental Controls pane.

A quicker way to set or change Parental Controls for an already existing account is to click the Parental Controls icon in the System Preferences application (instead of Users & Groups).

Last but not least, you can apply Parental Controls to the Guest Account, but you can't apply them to any account that has administrator permissions.

To turn off Parental Controls for a Managed account, navigate to the Parental Controls System Preferences pane, select the account in the list on the left, click the Action menu at the bottom of the list (the one that looks like a gear), and choose Turn off Parental Controls for *<username>*.

If you want to apply the same Parental Controls settings to more than one user, set them as described above for the first user and then select that account in the Accounts list in Parental Controls, click the Action menu, and choose Copy Settings. Then select the user you wish to have the same settings, click the Action menu, and choose Paste Settings.

Mac OS X knows best: Folders shared by default

When you add users in the Users & Groups System Preferences pane as I describe earlier, Mac OS X automatically does two things behind the scenes to facilitate file sharing: It creates a set of folders, and it makes some of them available for sharing.

Each time you add a Managed, Standard, or Administrator user, Mac OS X creates a Home folder hierarchy for that user on the Mac. The user can create more folders (if necessary) and also add, remove, or move anything inside these folders. Even if you create a user account solely to allow him or her to exchange files with you, your Mac automatically creates a Home folder for that user. Unless you, as the owner of your Mac, give permission, the user can't see inside or use folders outside the Home folder (which has the user's name), with only three exceptions: the Shared folder in the Users folder, the top level of other user account folders, and the Public folders in every other user's folder, as well as the Shared folder within the Users folder. A description of the latter follows:

- **Public:** A Public folder is located inside each user's folder. That folder is set up to be accessible (shared) by any user who can log in to the Mac. Furthermore, any user can log in (as a guest) and copy things out of this folder as long as he knows your Mac's IP address, even if he doesn't have an account on this Mac at all. Files put into the Public folder can be opened or copied freely.

  It's not hard for someone to obtain your IP address. For example, when you visit most web pages, your IP address is saved to that site's log file. So be careful what you put in your Public folder. This is also an excellent reason to employ a firewall. Lion has an excellent software implementation available via the Firewall tab in Security & Privacy System Preferences (see Chapter 18), and most routers (for example, AirPort Extreme) include a hardware firewall.

  Inside each user's Public folder is a Drop Box folder. As the name implies, this folder is where others can drop a file or folder for you. Only the owner can open the Drop Box to see what's inside — or to move or copy the files that are in it. Imagine a street-corner mailbox; after you drop your letter in, it's gone, and you can't get it back out.

- **Shared:** In addition to a Public folder for each user, Mac OS X creates one Shared folder on every Mac for all users of this Mac. The Shared folder *isn't* available to guests, but it's available to all users who have an account on this machine. You find the Shared folder within the Users folder (the same folder where you find folders for each user). The Shared folder is the right place to put stuff that everyone with an account on this Mac might want to use. (If you haven't already, check out my introduction to the Mac OS Lion folder structure in Chapter 6.)

Sharing a folder or disk by setting permissions

As you might expect, permissions control who can use a given folder or any disk (or partition) other than the startup disk.

Why can't you share the startup disk? Because Mac OS X won't let you. Why not? Because the startup disk contains the operating system and other stuff that nobody else should have access to.

Throughout the rest of this chapter, whenever I talk about *sharing a folder,* I also mean *sharing disks and disk partitions other than your startup disk* (which, when you think of it, are nothing more than big folders anyway). Why am I telling you this? Because it's awkward to keep typing *a folder or any disk (or partition) other than your startup disk.* So anything that I say about sharing a folder also applies to sharing any disk (or partition) other than your startup disk. Got it?

You can set permissions for

- ✔ The folder's owner
- ✔ A subset of all the people who have accounts on the Mac (a group)
- ✔ Everyone who has the Mac's address, whether they have an account or not (guests)

To help you get a better handle on these relationships, a closer look at permissions, owners, and groups is coming right up.

Contemplating permissions

When you consider who can use which folders, three distinct kinds of users exist on the network. I describe each of them in this section. Then, in the "Useful settings for permissions" section, later in this chapter, I show you how to share folders with each type of user. Here's a quick introduction to the different user types:

- ✔ **Owner:** The *owner* of a folder or disk can change the permissions to that folder or disk at any time. The name you enter when you log in to your Mac — or the name of your Home folder — is the default owner of Shared folders and drives on that machine. Ownership can be given away (more on that in the "Useful settings for permissions" section, later in this chapter). Even if you own the Mac, you can't change permissions for a folder on it that belongs to another user (unless you get Unix-y and do so as root). The owner must be logged in to change permissions on his folders.

   Mac OS X is the owner of many folders outside the Users folder. If OS X owns it, you can see that system is its owner if you select the folder and choose File➪Get Info (or press ⌘+I).

   Folders that aren't in the User directories generally belong to system; it's almost always a bad idea to change the permissions on any folder owned by system.

If you *must* change permissions on a file or folder, select its icon and choose File⟹Get Info (shortcut: ⌘+I), and then change the settings in the Sharing & Permissions section at the bottom of the resulting Get Info window. I urge you not to change permission settings if you're not absolutely sure of what you're doing and why.

✔ **Group:** In Unix systems, all users belong to one or more *groups*. The group that includes everyone who has an account with administrator permissions on your Mac is called Admin. Everyone in the Admin group has access to Shared and Public folders over the network, as well as to any folder that the Admin group has been granted access to by the folder's owner.

For the purposes of assigning permissions, you can create your own groups the same way you create a user account: Open the Users & Groups System Preferences pane, click the little plus sign, choose Group from the New Account pop-up menu, type the name of the group, and then click the Create Group button.

The group appears in the list of users on the left, and eligible accounts appear with check boxes on the right, as shown in Figure 16-7.

✔ **Everyone:** This category is an easy way to set permissions for everyone with an account on your Mac at the same time. Unlike the Admin group, which includes only users with administrative permissions, this one includes, well, everyone (everyone with an account on this Mac, that is).

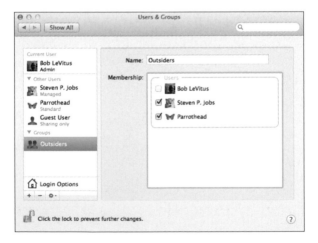

Figure 16-7: This group, Outsiders, contains my Parrothead and Steven P. Jobs accounts.

If you want people without an account on this Mac to have access to a file or folder, that file or folder needs to go in your Public folder, where the people you want to see it can log in as guests.

Sharing a folder

Suppose you have a folder you want to share, but it has slightly different rules than those set up for the Public folder, for the Drop Box folder within the Public folder, or for your personal folders. These rules are *permissions,* and they tell you how much access someone has to your stuff.

Actually, the rules governing Shared and Public folders are permissions, too, but they're set up for you when Mac OS X is installed.

I suggest that you share only folders located in your Home folder (or a folder within it). Because of the way Unix works, the Unix permissions of the enclosing folder can prevent access to a folder for which you *do* have permissions. Trust me, if you share only the folders in your Home folder, you'll never go wrong. If you don't take this advice, you could wind up having folders that other users can't access, even though you gave them the appropriate permissions.

By the way, you can set permissions for folders within your Public folder (like the Drop Box folder) that are different from those for the rest of the folder.

I said this before, but it bears repeating: Whenever I talk about *sharing a folder,* I also mean sharing disks — and disk partitions other than your startup disk (which you just can't share, period). So don't forget that anything I say about sharing a folder also applies to sharing any disk (or partition) other than your startup disk. Though you can't explicitly share your startup disk, anyone with administrator access can mount it for sharing from across the network (or Internet).

To share a folder with another user, follow these steps:

1. **Choose ⇒System Preferences (or click the System Preferences icon in the Dock).**

   The System Preferences window appears.

2. **In the System Preferences window, click the Sharing icon.**

   The Sharing System Preferences pane appears.

3. **Click File Sharing in the list of services on the left.**

   The lists of shared folders and their users appear on the right, as shown in Figure 16-8.

Figure 16-8: Changing the privileges of the Recipes folder for the group Everyone.

If an entry in, for example, the Shared Folders list is too long for you to make out the folder name, hover your pointer over it, and a tooltip will appear, giving you the full name.

4. **Click the + (plus) button under the Shared Folders column to add the folder you wish to share (Recipes in Figure 16-8).**

   If you select the Shared Folder check box in a folder's Get Info window, that folder already appears in the list of Shared Folders, so you won't have to bother with Step 4.

Alas, while checking the Shared Folder check box in a folder's Get Info window causes it to appear in the Sharing System Preferences pane's Shared Folders list, you still have to complete the steps that follow to assign that folder's users and privileges.

5. **Click the + (plus) button under the Users column to add a user or group if the user or group you desire isn't already showing in the Users column.**

6. **Click the double-headed arrow to the right of a user or group name, and change its privileges.**

   I'm changing the permission for Everyone to No Access in Figure 16-8.

   You can choose among three types of access for each user or group, as shown in Table 16-1.

   If you're the folder's owner (or have administrator access), you can click the padlock icon and change the owner and/or group for the file or folder.

Table 16-1	Privileges
Permission	*What It Allows*
Read & Write	A user with Read & Write access can see, add, delete, move, and edit files just as though they were stored on her own computer.
Read Only	A Read Only user can see and use files that are stored in a Shared folder but can't add, delete, move, or edit them.
Write Only (Drop Box)	Users can add files to this folder but can't see what's in it. The user must have read access to the folder containing a Write Only folder.
No Access	With no permissions, a user can neither see nor use your Shared folders or drives.

Useful settings for permissions

The following sections show you just some of the most common ways that you can combine permissions for a folder. You'll probably find one option that fits the way you work and the people you want to share with.

Owner permissions — in this case, single silhouette; Bob LeVitus (Me) in Figure 16-9 — must be at least as expansive as Group permissions (double silhouette; Staff in Figure 16-9) and Group permissions must be at least as expansive as Everyone's permissions (triple silhouette; Everyone in Figure 16-9). So to set the Everyone privilege to Read & Write, the Group and Owner privileges must also be set to Read & Write.

In the following examples, I show how to set permissions in the Sharing System Preferences pane. Another way to set permissions is by selecting an icon in the Finder and choosing File⇨Get Info (shortcut: ⌘+I), and then changing the settings in the Sharing & Permissions section at the bottom of the resulting Get Info window. The two methods are pretty much interchangeable, so you can use whichever is more convenient.

Allow everyone access

In Figure 16-9, I configure settings that allow everyone on a network to access the Bob's Downloads folder. Everyone can open, read, and change the contents of this Shared folder. Do this by choosing Read & Write for Others from the pop-up menu to the right of the user's name in the Sharing System Preferences pane or the folder's Get Info window.

Figure 16-9: Allow everyone access, if you want.

Allow nobody but yourself access

The settings shown in Figure 16-10 reflect appropriate settings that allow owner-only access to the Bob's Downloads folder. No one but me can see or use the contents of this folder. Members of the Staff group can drop files and folders into this folder (see Drop Box section). Use the pop-up menus to choose Write Only (Drop Box) as the Staff privilege and No Access as the Everyone privilege.

Figure 16-10: Allow access for no one but the folder's owner.

Allow all administrative users of this Mac access

Check out Figure 16-11 to see settings that allow the group Staff (in addition to the owner, `Bob LeVitus`) access to see, use, or change the contents of the Bob's Downloads folder. Use the pop-up menu to choose Read & Write for the Staff privilege.

Figure 16-11: Allow access for the Staff group and the folder's owner.

Allow others to deposit files and folders without giving them access: A drop box

The settings in Figure 16-12 enable everyone to drop their own files or folders in the Bob's Downloads folder without being able to see or use the contents of the Shared folder. After a file or folder is deposited in a drop folder, the dropper can't retrieve it because he doesn't have permission to see the items in the drop folder.

Figure 16-12: Everyone can drop files and folders into this folder.

Read-only bulletin boards

If you want everyone to be able to open and read the files and folders in this Shared folder — but not to modify them — choose Read Only from the pop-up menus for Group and Others. If you do this, however, only the owner can make changes to files in this folder.

One more privilege

The Apply to Enclosed Items button, at the bottom of the Sharing and Permissions section of Get Info windows in the Finder, does exactly what its name implies. This feature (which is only available in Get Info windows and doesn't appear in the Sharing System Preferences pane) is a fast way to assign the same permissions to many subfolders at the same time. After you set permissions for the enclosing folder the way you like them, click this button to give these same permissions to all folders inside it.

What is true of Get Info windows is also true of their Inspector window variant. Show Inspector replaces Get Info on the File menu when the Option key is pressed (also Option+⌘+I).

Be careful — there is no Undo for this action.

Unsharing a folder

To unshare a folder that you own, change the permissions for every other user and/or group to No Access. When you do, nobody but you has access to that folder.

If you're not sure how to do this, see the "Sharing a folder" and "Useful settings for permissions" sections, earlier in this chapter.

Connecting to a Shared Disk or Folder on a Remote Mac

After you set up sharing and assign permissions, you can access folders remotely from another computer. (Just make sure first that you have the correct administrative permissions to it.)

File sharing must be activated on the Mac where the shared files/folders reside; it doesn't have to be activated on the Mac that's accessing the files/folders. When file sharing is turned off, you can still use that Mac to access a remote Shared folder on another machine as long as its owner has granted you enough permissions and has file sharing enabled.

If file sharing is turned off on your Mac, others won't be able to access your folders, even if you've assigned permissions to them previously.

If you're going to share files, and you leave your Mac on and unattended for a long time, logging out before you leave it is a very good idea. This prevents anyone who just walks up to your Mac from seeing your files, e-mail, applications, or anything else that's yours — unless you've given that person a user account that has permissions for your files. If you don't want to log out, at least consider requiring that your password be entered when waking from sleep or dismissing the screen saver (General tab of Security & Privacy System Preferences).

On to how to access your Home folder from a remote Mac — a supercool feature that's only bound to get more popular as the Internet continues to mature.

The following steps assume that you have an account on the remote Mac, which means you have your own Home folder on that Mac.

To connect to a Shared folder on a Mac other than the one you're currently on, follow these steps:

1. **Make sure that you're already set up as a user on the computer that you want to log in to (Lisa & Jacob's Eye Mac, in this example).**

   If you need to know how to create a new user, see the "Creating users" section, earlier in the chapter.

2. **On the computer that you're logging in from (my MacBook Pro in this example), click the Show button to show the Shared section in the Sidebar if it's not already showing.**

   (The button says Hide in Figure 6-13 because the shared section is showing.)

   All available servers appear. (There are eight in Figure 16-13.)

3. **Click the name of the remote Mac (Lisa & Jacob's Eye Mac) you want to access in the Sidebar.**

   At this point, you're connected to the remote Mac as a guest, as shown in Figure 16-13.

Figure 16-13: Connected to Lisa & Jacob's Eye Mac as a guest.

4. Click the Connect As button.

The Connect dialog appears. The name of the person logged in on Bob LeVitus's MacBook Pro automatically appears in the Name field (my account name, bobl, in Figure 16-14).

If that's not your user name on the Mac you're trying to access, type that username in the Name field.

Figure 16-14: The Connect dialog needs my password.

If you select the Remember This Password in My Keychain check box in the Connect dialog, Mac OS X remembers your password for you the next time you connect to this server. Sweet!

5. Select the Guest radio button if you don't have an account on the remote computer and then click Connect; if you're logging in as a user, skip to Step 6.

Pressing ⌘+G is the same as marking the Guest radio button, and pressing ⌘+R is the same as marking the Registered User radio button.

As a guest user, you see Public Folders for users who have accounts on Lisa & Jacob's Eye Mac (Lisa LeVitus, Bob LeVitus, and Jacob in Figure 16-13) but nothing else.

6. Type your password, and click the Connect button.

After I've connected as a registered user, I see my Home folder (bobl in Figure 16-15), everyone else's Public folders, and hard disks connected to that Mac (BiggestBoy in Figure 16-15).

Figure 16-15: Connecting to Lisa & Jacob's Eye Mac as Bob LeVitus (bobl).

File sharing must be active on Lisa & Jacob's Eye Mac (the Mac I'm accessing remotely in the example). If file sharing weren't active on Lisa & Jacob's Eye Mac, its name wouldn't appear in the Shared section of the Sidebar, and I wouldn't be able to connect to it. But file sharing doesn't have to be active on the computer *you're* using (Bob LeVitus's MacBook Pro in this example) to give you access to the remote computer and make this trick work.

When you access your Home folder on a remote Mac as I've done in this example, you see an icon with the short name of your Home folder on that Mac (bobl in Figure 16-16) on the Desktop of the Mac you're using (unless you've deselected Connected Servers in Finder's General Preferences pane, under Show These Items on the Desktop).

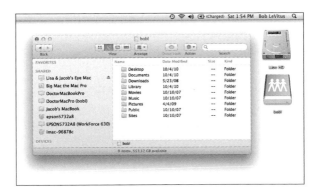

Figure 16-16: Accessing my Home folder on Lisa & Jacob's Eye Mac remotely: A disk icon with its short name (bobl) appears on my Desktop.

7. **When you finish using the remote Mac, disconnect by using one of these methods:**

   • Drag the shared-volume icon (bob1 in Figure 16-16) to the Eject icon in the Dock.

     When a disk or volume is selected (highlighted), the Trash icon turns into a little arrow, which represents *eject*. Nice touch, eh?

   • Right-click or Control-click the shared volume icon and then choose Eject from the contextual menu that appears.

   • Select the shared-volume icon and choose File⇨Eject.

   • Select the shared-volume icon and press ⌘+E.

   • In a Finder window Sidebar, click the little Eject symbol to the right of the remote computer's name (Lisa & Jacob's Eye Mac in Figure 16-16).

   • If you've finished working for the day, and you don't leave your Mac on 24/7 (as most folks do), choose ⌘⇨Shut Down or Log Out. Shutting down or logging out automatically disconnects you from shared disks or folders. (Shut Down also turns off your Mac.)

Changing Your Password

You can change your password at any time. Changing your password is a good idea if you're concerned about security — for example, if there's a chance your password has been discovered by someone else.

You can change the password for your account on your own Mac, or you can change the password you use to connect to your account on a remote Mac. I show you how to do both in the following sections.

Changing your account password on your Mac

To change the password on your own Mac, just follow these steps:

1. **Choose ⌘⇨System Preferences, or double-click its icon in your Applications folder and then click the Users & Groups icon.**

   The Users & Groups System Preferences pane appears.

2. **Select your account in the list on the left.**

   Your account information appears in the area on the right.

3. **Click the Change Password button.**

   A sheet drops down.

4. **Type your current password in the Old Password field.**

   This demonstrates that you are who you're supposed to be, not some-one who just walked up to your unattended Mac.

5. **Type your new password in the New Password field.**

6. **Retype your new password in the Verify field.**

7. **(Optional but recommended) Type a hint in the Password hint field.**

8. **Click the Change Password button.**

   Assuming that you entered your old password correctly, the sheet disappears.

9. **Close the System Preferences window.**

Changing the password of any account but your own on your Mac

To change a password on your own Mac, just follow these steps:

1. **Choose System Preferences, or double-click its icon in your Applications folder and then click the Users & Groups icon.**

   The Users & Groups System Preferences pane appears.

   You may have to click the lock (at bottom left), supply an administrator name and password in the resulting dialog, and then click OK before you can proceed.

2. **Select the account you want to change the password for in the list on the left.**

   The account information appears in the area on the right.

3. **Click the Reset Password button.**

   A sheet drops down.

4. **Type the new password in the New Password field.**

5. **Retype the new password in the Verify field.**

6. **(Optional but recommended) Type a hint in the Password Hint field.**

7. **Click the Reset Password button.**

8. **Close the System Preferences window.**

Changing the password for your account on someone else's Mac

When you log in to a remote Mac, you can change your own password if you like. Follow these steps to do so:

1. **Log in to the remote computer on which you want to change your password.**

   See the "Connecting to a Shared Disk or Folder on a Remote Mac" section, earlier in this chapter, if you don't know how to log in to a remote computer.

   The Connect dialog appears.

2. **Type your username in the Connect dialog, if it's not already there.**

3. **Click the Change Password button in the bottom-left corner of the dialog.**

   A sheet for changing your password appears.

4. **Type your current password in the Old Password field.**

5. **Type your new password in the New Password and Verify fields.**

   You can use the Password Assistant (the little key to the right of the New Password text box) to help you generate a secure password.

6. **Click the Change Password button.**

   Your password is changed, and you return to the Connect dialog.

7. **(Optional) Type your new password and then click Connect to log in to the other Mac.**

   You can skip this step by clicking the Cancel button in the Connect dialog if you don't need to use anything on the remote Mac at this time. Your password is still changed, and you need to use the new password the next time you log in to this Mac.

   Select the Add Password to Keychain check box in the Connect dialog to store your passwords in a single place on the Mac; this way you don't have to retype them each time you access a Mac or other remote resource. (Read more about the Keychain in Chapter 19.)

Five More Types of Sharing

Several more types of sharing exist, and I'd like to at least mention a few in passing. All are found in (where else?) the Sharing System Preferences pane, which you can find by launching the System Preferences application (from the Applications folder, ☀ menu, or Dock) and clicking the Sharing icon.

DVD or CD Sharing

When you select this one, remote users can access CDs and DVDs in your Mac's optical drive(s). You can select to have Lion notify you and request permission when a remote user makes such a request.

Screen Sharing

Here's the sharing that I consider the coolest . . . . Screen Sharing lets you control another Mac on your network from your Mac. In essence, you see the other Mac's screen on *your* Mac — and control it using *your* mouse and keyboard.

To set up Screen Sharing on the Mac you want to control remotely, follow these steps:

1. **Open the Sharing System Preferences pane by launching the System Preferences application (from the Applications folder,** 🍎**, Launchpad, or Dock) and clicking the Sharing icon.**

2. **Select the check box for Screen Sharing in the list of services on the left.**

3. **Click either the All Users or Only These Users radio button.**

   If you clicked Only These Users, click the + button and add the user or users you want to allow to control this Mac remotely. Notice that the Staff group is included by default.

To take control of your Mac from another Mac, follow these steps:

1. **Click the now-you-see-it-now-you-don't Show tag to the right of Shared to open the Shared section in the Sidebar, if it's not already open.**

   All available servers appear.

2. **Click the name of the remote Mac you want to control.**

3. **Click the Share Screen button.**

   Depending on whether you clicked the All Users or Only These Users radio button, you may have to enter your name and password and then click the Connect button.

   A window with the name of the remote Mac in its title bar appears. In it you see the screen of the Mac you're looking to control remotely.

4. **Go ahead and click something.**

   Pull down a menu or open a folder. Isn't that cool? You're controlling a Mac across the room or in another room with your mouse and keyboard!

Printer Sharing

This one's a snap. If you turn on Printer Sharing in the Sharing System Preferences pane, other people on your local network can use any printer connected to your computer.

Scanner Sharing

Analogous to Printer Sharing, Scanner Sharing allows others on your local network to use scanners connected to your Mac.

Web Sharing

Web Sharing enables others to share documents on your computer through the web. You can set up a website just by adding Hypertext Markup Language (HTML) pages and images to the Sites folder in your Home folder and then activating Web Sharing in the Sharing pane of System Preferences.

Web Sharing works only while your Mac is connected to the Internet or an internal network, and it requires the speed of a direct connection. If you use a modem and connect to the Internet by dialing up, this capability won't be a lot of use to you.

Furthermore, even if you keep your Mac connected to the Internet 24 hours a day with a Digital Subscriber Line (DSL) or cable-modem connection, using this feature could violate your agreement with your Internet service provider (ISP), because some ISPs prohibit you from hosting a website. Also, most cable and DSL connections use dynamic IP address assignment through Dynamic Host Configuration Protocol (DHCP), which means your IP address will change from time to time.

On the other hand, some ISPs don't care whether you run a website. Check with yours if you're concerned. I do turn on this feature occasionally, but (because I don't use it 24/7) I never bothered to check with my ISP. Do me a favor, and don't rat me out.

Internet Sharing

If your Mac has an Internet connection and another Mac nearby doesn't, you can enable Internet Sharing, and that Mac can share your Internet connection. The following steps show you how:

1. **Open the Sharing System Preferences pane by launching the System Preferences application (from the Applications folder, menu, Launchpad, or Dock) and clicking the Sharing icon.**

2. **Select the check box for Internet Sharing in the list of services on the left.**

3. **Choose the connection you want to share — AirPort, FireWire, or Ethernet — from the Share Your Connection From pop-up menu.**

4. **Select the check boxes next to connections other computers will use — Wi-Fi, Ethernet, or Built-In FireWire.**

   Figure 16-17 shows Internet Sharing configured to share my Ethernet Internet connection with another Mac by using Wi-Fi.

Figure 16-17: Sharing my Ethernet Internet connection with another Mac using Wi-Fi.

5. **(Optional) Click the Wi-Fi Options button to name, select a wireless channel for, enable encryption for, and/or set a password for your shared network.**

   That's all there is to it.

Bluetooth Sharing

If you have a Bluetooth mobile phone or PDA, and your Mac has Bluetooth, you can configure many of the default behaviors for transferring files to and from your Mac. A picture is worth a thousand words, so Figure 16-18 shows all the things Bluetooth Sharing lets you configure.

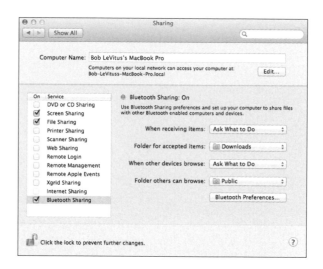

Figure 16-18: You can configure items for Bluetooth file transfers between your Bluetooth phone or PDA and your Bluetooth-equipped Mac.

VoiceOver:
○ On ● Off
Turn VoiceOver on or off: ⌘fn F5

17

Open VoiceOver Utility...

VoiceOver:
○ On ● Of

Features for the Way You Work

In This Chapter

▶ Talking to your Mac

▶ Listening to your Mac

▶ Enhancing productivity by using automation

▶ Trying out more useful technologies and techniques

▶ Running Microsoft Windows on your Mac (really!)

This chapter delves into some Mac OS X Lion features that might very well improve the ways you interact with your computer. Unlike the more mainstream applications and utilities I discuss in Part I — Desktop, Finder, Screen Saver, Appearance, Keyboard, Trackpad, Mouse, and such — the items in this chapter are a little more esoteric. In other words, you don't *have* to use any of the technologies I'm about to show you. That said, many of these items can make you more productive and can make using your Mac even better. So I'd like to believe that at least some of you will *want* to use the cool features I'm about to introduce.

Talking and Listening to Your Mac

Your primary methods for interacting with your Mac are typing and reading text. But there's another way you can commune with your faithful computer: voice.

Whether you know it or not, your Mac has a lot of speech savvy up its sleeve (er . . . up its processors?), and can talk to you as well as listen and obey. In the following sections, you discover how to make your Mac do both.

Talking to your Mac

Speech Recognition enables your Mac to recognize and respond to human speech. The only thing you need to use it is a microphone, and all laptops and iMacs have a built-in mic these days, as does the Apple LED Cinema Display that you can (optionally) purchase for use with any (Lion-capable) Mac.

Speech Recognition lets you issue verbal commands such as "Get my mail!" to your Mac and have it actually get your e-mail. You can also create AppleScripts and then trigger them by voice.

An *AppleScript* is a series of commands, using the AppleScript language, that tells the computer (and some applications) what to do. You find out more about AppleScript later in this chapter.

Setting up for Speech Recognition

To start using Speech Recognition, launch System Preferences and follow these steps:

1. **Open the Speech System Preferences pane.**

2. **Click the Speech Recognition tab, and click the Settings subtab.**

3. **Click the On button for Speakable Items, as shown in Figure 17-1.**

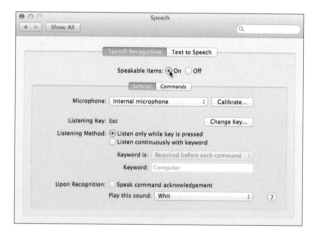

Figure 17-1: Turn Speech Recognition on and off in the Settings subtab on the Speech System Preferences pane's Speech Recognition tab.

4. **Choose the microphone you want to use from the Microphone pop-up menu.**

   If you have a laptop or an iMac, you can get better results from just about any third-party microphone. The one that's built into your Mac works, but it isn't the greatest microphone on the planet.

5. **To test that microphone, click the Calibrate button, and follow the on-screen instructions.**

   There are two ways — called *listening methods* — you can use with Speech Recognition. The first listening method is to press a listening key — Esc by default — when you want to talk to your Mac. The second listening method is to have your Mac listen continuously for you to say a special keyword — "Computer," by default — when you want to talk to your Mac.

6. **(Optional) To change the listening key from Esc to a different key, click the Change Key button and then press the key you want to use as your listening key.**

7. **(Optional) To change the listening method from Listening Key to Listening Continuously with Keyword, click the appropriate radio button.**

   If you select Listening Continuously, you have two more options:

   a. To change the way your Mac listens for the keyword — Optional before commands, Required before each command, or Required 15 or 30 seconds after last command — make your selection from the Keyword Is pop-up menu.

   b. To change the keyword from Computer to something else, type the word you want to use in the Keyword field.

   I call mine OK MacBook Pro, so when people are watching, I can casually say things like "OK, MacBook Pro, get my mail" or "OK, MacBook Pro, log me out," and watch their jaws drop when they realize that I'm talking to my laptop and it's actually doing what I ask.

8. **(Optional) You can have your commands acknowledged by your Mac, if you like, by selecting the Speak Command Acknowledgement check box.**

9. **(Optional) You can choose a sound other than Whit from the Play This Sound pop-up menu.**

10. **Click the Commands subtab on the Speech System Preferences pane's Speech Recognition tab, and select the check box for each command set you want to enable.**

I can't see any reason not to enable them all unless you don't use Apple's Address Book, in which case you don't need to enable it.

11. **Click the Helpful Tips button, and read the tips.**

12. **Click each command-set name, and if the Configure button is enabled, click it and then follow the on-screen instructions.**

13. **If you create an AppleScript you want to be speakable, click the Open Speakable Items Folder.**

    The Speakable Items folder is opened for you.

14. **Place the script in the folder.**

    When you speak its name, the script is executed.

    If the Speech System Preferences pane isn't open, and you want to open the Speakable Items folder, you can find it in your Home/Library/Speech folder.

15. **Close the Speech System Preferences pane when you're done.**

Using Speech Recognition

Here's how Speech Recognition works. For the sake of this discussion, I use the "Press Esc" listening method.

When Speech Recognition is turned on, a round feedback window appears on-screen, as shown in Figure 17-2.

Figure 17-2: The round Speech Recognition feedback window.

I'm not pressing the Esc key in Figure 17-2, so the word *Esc* appears in the middle of the window to remind me which key to press before I speak a command.

Now, here's how to actually use Speech Recognition:

1. **To see what commands are available, click the little triangle at the bottom of the feedback window, and select Open Speech Commands Window, as shown in Figure 17-2.**

   As you might expect, selecting Speech Preferences from this menu opens the Speech System Preferences pane for you.

   The Speech Commands window appears on-screen, as shown in Figure 17-3.

Figure 17-3: The Speech Commands window.

2. **Peruse the Speech Commands window, and find a command you'd like to execute by speaking its name.**

3. **Speak that command exactly as written.**

   In this example, I press the Esc key and say to my Mac, "Tell me a joke."

   At this point, several things happen:

   • In the feedback window, Esc disappears, and the microphone lights up to subtly indicate that my Mac is waiting for speech input.

   • The command and my Mac's response appear in little boxes above and below the Feedback window.

   • The Speech Commands window changes to reflect the command I've spoken.

   My Mac then says, "Knock, knock," and the bottom part of the Speech Commands window displays the commands I can speak in response.

   You can see all this in Figure 17-4. And that's pretty much it for Speech Recognition.

Figure 17-4: Here's what happened when I pressed Esc and said, "Tell me a joke."

This technology is clever and kind of fun, but it can also be somewhat frustrating when it doesn't recognize what you say. And it requires a decent microphone — although the mic built into most Macs sometimes works okay. The bottom line is that I've never been able to get Speech Recognition to work well enough to continue using it beyond a few hours at best. Still, it's kind of cool (and it's a freebie), and I've heard more than one user profess love for it. Which is why it's included here.

Listening to your Mac read for you

The camera pans back — a voice tells you what you've just seen, and suddenly it all makes sense. Return with me now to those thrilling days of the off-camera narrator. . . . Wouldn't it be nice if your Mac had a narrator to provide a blow-by-blow account of what's happening on your screen?

Or . . .

Your eyes are tired from a long day staring at the monitor, but you still have a lengthy document to read. Wouldn't it be sweet if you could sit back, close your eyes, and let your Mac read the document to you in a (somewhat) natural voice? The good news is that both are possible with Mac OS X Lion — the former with VoiceOver and the latter with Text to Speech.

VoiceOver

Lion's VoiceOver technology is designed primarily for the visually impaired, but you might find it useful even if your vision is 20/20. VoiceOver not only reads what's on the screen to you, but also integrates with your keyboard so you can navigate around the screen until you *hear* the item you're looking for. When you're there, you can use Keyboard Access to select list items, select check boxes and radio buttons, move scroll bars and sliders, resize windows, and so on — with a simple key press or two.

 To check it out, launch the System Preferences application (from Launchpad, the Applications folder,  menu, or Dock), click the Universal Access icon, and then click the Seeing tab or press ⌘+F5 (⌘+Fn+F5 on notebook/laptop models and some newer Apple keyboards).

After VoiceOver is enabled, you can turn it on and off in the Seeing tab of the Universal Access System Preferences pane or by pressing ⌘+F5 or (⌘+Fn+F5 on notebook/laptop models).

While it's on, your Mac talks to you about what is on your screen. For example, if you clicked the Desktop, your Mac might say something along the lines of "Application, Finder; Column View; selected folder, Desktop, contains 8 items." It's quite slick. Here's another example: When you click a menu or item on a menu, you hear its name spoken at once, and when you close a menu, you hear the words "Closing menu." You even hear the spoken feedback in the Print, Open, and Save (and other) dialogs.

VoiceOver is kind of cool (talking alerts are fun), but having dialogs actually produce spoken text becomes annoying really fast for most folks. Still, I urge you to check it out. You might like it and find times when you want your Mac to narrate the action for you.

The VoiceOver Utility

The VoiceOver Utility lets you specify almost every possible option the VoiceOver technology uses. You can adjust its verbosity; specify how it deals with your mouse and keyboard; change its voice, rate, pitch, and/or volume; and more.

You can open the VoiceOver Utility by clicking the Open VoiceOver Utility button on the Seeing tab of the Universal Access System Preferences pane or the usual way: by double-clicking its icon (which you find in your Applications/Utilities folder).

Of course, you might get the machines-are-taking-over willies when your Mac starts to talk to you or make sounds — but if you give it a try, it could change your mind.

I wish I had the space to explain further, but I don't. That's the bad news. The good news is that VoiceOver Help is extensive and clear, and it helps you harness all the power of VoiceOver and the VoiceOver Utility.

Text to Speech

The second way your Mac can speak to you is using Text to Speech, which converts on-screen text to spoken words. If you've used Text to Speech in earlier versions of Mac OS X, you'll find that it's pretty much unchanged.

Why might you need Text to Speech? Because sometimes hearing is better than reading. For example, I sometimes use Text to Speech to read a column or page to me before I submit it. If something doesn't sound quite right, I give it another polish before sending it off to my editor.

You can configure this feature in the Speech System Preferences pane:

1. **Open the System Preferences (from Launchpad, the Applications folder, Dock, or menu), click the Speech icon, and then click the Text to Speech tab.**

2. **Choose one of the voices in the System Voice pop-up menu to set the voice your Mac uses when it reads to you.**

3. **Click the Play button to hear a sample of the voice you selected.**

4. **Use the Speaking Rate slider to speed up or slow down the voice.**

5. **Click the Play button to hear the voice at its new speed.**

   I really like Alex, who says, "Most people recognize me by my voice." My second favorite is Fred, who says, "I sure like being inside this fancy computer."

6. **Select the Announce When Alerts Are Displayed check box if you want to make your Mac speak the text in alert boxes and dialogs.**

   You might hear such alerts as "The application Microsoft Word has quit unexpectedly" or "Paper out or not loaded correctly."

7. **Click the Set Alert Options button to choose a different voice to announce your alerts — the phrase your Mac speaks ("Alert," "Attention," "Yo, dude," and the like) when alerting you.**

   You can also set the delay between the time the alert appears and when it's spoken to you.

8. **(Optional) If you like, select either of these two check boxes: Announce When an Application Requires Your Attention or Speak Selected Text When the Key Is Pressed.**

   They both do what they say they'll do. In the case of the latter, you assign the key you want to press by clicking the Set Key button.

9. **(Optional) If you want to have the clock announce the time, click the Open Date & Time Preferences button, and you're whisked to that System Preferences pane; then click the Clock tab and select the Announce the Time check box.**

   That's it for your preferences.

Now, to use Text to Speech to read text to you, copy the text to the Clipboard, launch TextEdit, paste the text into the empty untitled document, click where you want your Mac to begin reading to you, and then choose Edit➪Speech➪Start Speaking. To make it stop, choose Edit➪Speech➪Stop Speaking.

Automatic Automation

Mac OS X Lion offers a pair of technologies — AppleScript and Automator — that make it easy to automate repetitive actions on your Mac.

AppleScript is "programming for the rest of us." It can record and play back things that you do (if the application was written to allow the recording — Finder, for example, was), such as opening an application or clicking a button. You can use it to record a script for tasks that you often perform and then have your Mac perform those tasks for you later. You can write your own AppleScripts, use those that come with your Mac, or download still others from the web.

Automator is "programming without writing code." With Automator, you string together prefabricated activities (known as *actions*) to automate repetitive or scheduled tasks. How cool is that?

Automation isn't for everyone. Some users can't live without it; others could go their whole lives without ever automating anything. So the following sections are designed to help you figure out how much — or how little — you care about AppleScript and Automator.

AppleScript

Describing AppleScript to a Mac beginner is a bit like three blind men describing an elephant. One man might describe it as the Macintosh's built-in automation tool. Another might describe it as an interesting but often-overlooked piece of enabling technology. The third might liken it to a cassette recorder, recording and playing back your actions at the keyboard. A fourth (if there were a fourth in the story) would assure you that it looked like computer code written in a high-level language.

They would all be correct. AppleScript, a built-in Mac automation tool, is a little-known (at least until recently) enabling technology that works like a cassette recorder for programs that support AppleScript recording. And scripts do look like computer programs. (Could that be because they *are* computer programs? Hmm . . .)

If you're the kind of person who likes to automate as many things as possible, you might just love AppleScript because it's a simple programming language you can use to create programs that give instructions to your Mac and the applications running on your Mac. For example, you can create an AppleScript that launches Mail, checks for new messages, and then quits Mail. The script could even transfer your mail to a folder of your choice. Of course, Mac OS X 10.4 Tiger also introduced Automator, which includes a whole lot of preprogrammed actions that makes a task like the one just described even easier.

I call AppleScript a time-and-effort enhancer. If you just spend the time and effort it takes to understand it, using AppleScript can save you oodles of time and effort down the road.

Therein lies the rub. This stuff is far from simple; entire books have been written on the subject. So it's far beyond the purview of *Mac OS X Lion For*

Dummies. Still, it's worth finding out about if you'd like to script repetitive actions for future use. To get you started, here are a few quick tips:

- **You can put frequently used AppleScripts in the Dock or on your Desktop for easy access.**

- **Apple provides a script menu extra that you can install on your menu bar in AppleScript Utility's Preferences window** — along with a number of free scripts to automate common tasks, many of which are in the Example Scripts folder. (An alias to that folder is present in the AppleScript folder.) Furthermore, you can always download additional scripts from `www.apple.com/applescript`.

- **Many AppleScripts are designed for use in the toolbar of Finder windows,** where you can drag and drop items onto them quickly and easily.

- **Other scripts can enhance your use of iTunes, iPhoto, and iDVD.**

- **AppleScript Editor (in the Utilities folder inside the Applications folder) is the application you use to view and edit AppleScripts.** Although more information on AppleScript Editor is beyond the scope of this book, it's a lot of fun. And the cool thing is that you can create many AppleScripts without knowing a thing about programming. Just record a series of actions you want to repeat, and use AppleScript Editor to save them as a script. If you save your script as an application (by choosing Format⇨Application in the Save sheet), you can run that script by just double-clicking its icon.

- **If the concept of scripting intrigues you, I suggest that you open the Scripts (in the root-level Library) folder.** Rummage through this folder to check out the scripts available at `www.macosxautomation.com/applescript/`. Furthermore, you can always download additional scripts from `www.apple.com/applescript`. When you find a script that looks interesting, double-click it to launch the AppleScript Editor program, where you can examine it more closely.

Automator

Automator does just what you'd expect: It enables you to automate many common tasks on your Mac. If it sounds a little like AppleScript to you (which I discuss in the preceding section), you're not mistaken; the two have a common goal. But this relatively new tool (introduced in Mac OS X Tiger) is a lot simpler to use, albeit somewhat less flexible, than AppleScript.

For example, in AppleScript, you can have *conditionals* ("if *this* is true, do *that*; otherwise do something else"), but Automator is purely *sequential* ("take *this,* do *that,* then do the next thing, and then . . .").

The big difference is that conditionals allow AppleScripts to take actions involving *decision-making* and *iteration* ("while *this* is true, do *these* things"); Automator workflows can't make decisions or iterate.

The upsides to Automator are that you don't have to know anything about programming, and you don't have to type any archaic code. Instead, if you understand the process you want to automate, you can just drag and drop Automator's prefab Actions into place and build a *workflow* (Automator's name for a series of Actions).

You do need to know one thing about programming (or computers), though: Computers are stupid! You heard me right — even my top-of-the-line MacBook Pro is dumb as a post. Computers do only what you tell them to do, although they can do it faster and more precisely than you can. But all computers run on the GIGO principle — garbage in/garbage out — so if your instructions are flawed, you're almost certain to get flawed results.

Another similarity between Automator and AppleScript is that it's up to the developers of the applications you want to automate to provide you the Actions or scripting support. Not all developers do so. For example, in Apple's wonderful iLife suite of multimedia applications, iTunes, iPhoto, and iDVD are all AppleScript-able — and they've supplied Actions for Automator users. iMovie and versions of GarageBand prior to GarageBand '09 don't support AppleScript. Furthermore, iMovie, GarageBand, and iWeb don't include any Automator actions at this time.

When you launch the Automator application, you see the window and sheet shown in Figure 17-5. Choose one of the starting points if you want Automator to assist you in constructing a new workflow, or choose Workflow to start building a workflow from scratch.

I choose Service for the sake of this demonstration (you see why in a second). When I do, I see the window shown in Figure 17-6.

The Library window on the left contains all the applications Automator knows about that have actions defined for them. Select an application in the top part of the Library window, and its related actions appear below it. When you select an action, the pane at the bottom of the Library window (Text to Audio File in Figure 17-6) explains what that Action does, what input it expects, and what result it produces. Just drag Actions from the Action list into the window on the right to build your workflow.

Figure 17-5: Choose a starting point, and Automator will assist you; choose Workflow to start a workflow from scratch.

Figure 17-6: I'm building a Service to convert any text I select to an audio file I can listen to at my leisure.

This particular Service, which took me less than 5 minutes of trial and error to perfect, is quite useful. First, I select text from any source — a web page, Microsoft Word document, e-mail message, or whatever. Then I right-click or Control-click and select my newly created Text-to-Audio Service from the Services menu. Mac OS X then converts the selected text into an audio file, which I can have read to me in iTunes at home, or on my iPhone or iPad in the car, on a plane, or just about anywhere. Sweet!

Automator is a very useful addition to Mac OS X; it's deep, powerful, and expandable, yet relatively easy to use and master. Do yourself a favor, and spend some time experimenting with ways Automator can save you time and keystrokes. You won't regret it.

A Few More Useful Goodies

Even more neat and useful technologies are built into Lion, but I'm running out of space. So here are, at least in my humble opinion, the best of the rest.

App Store

The App Store app is the Mac OS X software version of the iTunes Store for media. Here, you'll find applications of all types — Business, Finance, Entertainment, Graphics, Productivity, Social Networking, and many more — at prices that start at zero (free).

Just about everything I tell you in Chapter 12 about the iTunes Store could be said for the App Store. It looks the same; it works the same; it uses the same credit card you have on file at the iTunes Store.

If you see a little number on the App Store icon in your Dock, it means that number of your apps have updates available. Launch the App Store app and click the Updates tab to see the apps with updates awaiting them. Even if you don't see a little number in the App Store's Dock icon, it wouldn't hurt to launch the App Store every once in a while to check for updates manually, as the little number sometimes fails to appear in the App Store Dock icon.

Universal Access

Universal Access is mostly designed for users with disabilities or who have difficulty handling the keyboard or mouse. The Universal Access System Preferences pane has a check box and four tabs.

Select the Enable Access for Assistive Devices check box at the bottom of the window to use special equipment to control your computer.

The Seeing tab

On the Seeing tab, you can turn on a terrific feature called *hardware zoom,* which lets you make things on your screen bigger by zooming in on them. Toggle it on and off with the shortcut ⌘+Option+8. Zoom in and out using the shortcuts ⌘+Option+= (the equals key) and ⌘+Option+– (the minus key), respectively. Try this feature even if you're not disabled or challenged in any way; it's actually a great feature for everyone.

You can also display the screen as white on black (like a photographic negative), as shown in Figure 17-7. The shortcut is ⌘+Option+Control+8; use the same keyboard shortcut to toggle back to normal. If you're in the normal black-on-white mode, you can desaturate your screen into a *grayscale display* (so it works like a black-and-white TV).

Figure 17-7: The White on Black option reverses what you see on-screen, like this.

Finally, the Options button lets you specify minimum and maximum zoom levels, display a preview rectangle when zoomed out, and toggle image smoothing on or off.

The Hearing tab

The Hearing tab lets you choose to flash the screen whenever an alert sound occurs.

This feature, created for those with impaired hearing, is quite useful if you have a MacBook Pro or MacBook and want to use it where ambient noise levels are high or if you don't want your Mac to disturb those around you.

There's also a Play Stereo Audio as Mono check box. Not sure why you'd need it, and I couldn't hear any difference when I tried it with a variety of stereo audio sources. The only thing I can think of is that it might be helpful for those who listen to audio using a monaural (that is, one ear only) Bluetooth headset or those with hearing impairment in only one ear.

The Keyboard tab

The Keyboard tab offers two types of assistance:

✔ The **Sticky Keys** application treats a *sequence* of modifier keys as a key combination. In other words, you don't have to simultaneously hold down ⌘ while pressing another key. For example, with Sticky Keys enabled, you can do a standard keyboard shortcut by pressing ⌘, releasing it, and then pressing the other key. You can select check boxes to tell you (with a beep and/or an on-screen display) what modifier keys have been pressed.

As useful as Sticky Keys can be, they're really awkward in applications like Adobe Photoshop, Adobe Illustrator, and other applications that toggle a tool's state when you press a modifier key. So if you're a big Photoshop user, you probably don't want Sticky Keys enabled.

✔ **Slow Keys** lets you adjust the delay between when a key is pressed and when that key press is accepted.

The Mouse & Trackpad tab

The Mouse & Trackpad tab offers options for those who have difficulties using a mouse or trackpad by using keys on the keyboard to navigate rather than a mouse or trackpad.

Figure 17-8 shows the specific shortcut keys for turning Mouse Keys on or off; moving the cursor on-screen; and clicking, dragging, and releasing the mouse button.

Notice that you have to press Fn while pressing the letter or number in parentheses on a laptop and other keyboards that don't have a numeric keypad.

You can also increase the cursor size from the normal setting (16x16) to about 64x64.

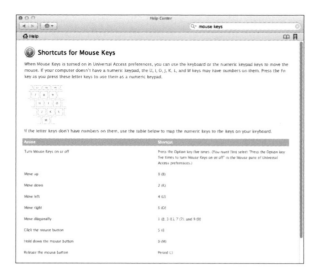

Figure 17-8: The keyboard commands for Mouse Keys.

Energy Saver

All Macs are Energy Star–compliant (and have been for years), allowing you to preset your machine to turn itself off at a specific time or after a specified idle period. To manage your Mac's energy-saving features, open the Energy Saver System Preferences pane by choosing ⌘⇨System Preferences and then clicking the Energy Saver icon.

If you have a notebook computer, you have two mostly identical tabs — Battery and Power Adapter — in your Energy Saver System Preferences pane. The battery tab controls your MacBook, MacBook Air, or MacBook Pro's behavior when it's running on battery power (not plugged in); the Power Adapter tab controls its behavior when it *is* plugged in.

If you have a desktop Mac, you won't have tabs, but you do have most of the same controls, including a pair of sliders that control sleep times for your computer and display. To enable Computer or Display sleep, move the appropriate slider to the desired amount of time. You can choose any number between 1 minute and 3 hours, or turn off either type of sleep entirely by moving its slider all the way to the right, to Never.

Setting the display to sleep is handy if you want your Mac to keep doing what it's doing, but you don't need to use the monitor. And if you're a notebook user, display sleep will save you some battery power.

To wake up your Mac from its sleep, merely move your mouse or press any key.

Below the Sleep sliders are some check boxes for other useful energy settings, such as

- **Put the Hard Disk(s) to Sleep When Possible:** Enabling this option forces your hard drive to sleep after a few minutes of inactivity. It's not a particularly useful feature on a desktop Mac, but if you have a laptop, letting your hard drive sleep when it's idle will save you some battery power.

- **Wake for Network Access:** Enable this option if you want your Mac to wake up automatically for Ethernet network access (handy in a corporate setting where an IT person maintains system configurations).

- **Restart Automatically if the Computer Freezes:** Enabling this option tells your Mac you want it to restart automatically if it becomes totally hosed.

- **Allow Power Button to Put the Computer to Sleep:** Does just what it says: Enable it, and tapping your Mac's power (on/off) button puts your computer to sleep immediately.

  To turn your Mac off, use the menu's Shut Down command or its keyboard shortcut (Control+power key).

- **Automatically Reduce Brightness Before Display Goes to Sleep:** Another one that does what it says.

If you have a laptop, you'll have some additional options, including

- **Slightly Dim the Display When Using This Power Source (Battery tab only):** Enable this, and the display dims slightly and uses slightly less power when you're running off the battery.

- **Show Battery Status in the Menu Bar:** This option adds a little battery-status indicator icon and menu, as shown in Figure 17-9.

Finally, to start up, shut down, or put your Mac to sleep at a predetermined time, click the Schedule button and then select the appropriate check box and choose the appropriate options from the pop-up menus.

Figure 17-9: The Battery Status indicator and its menu.

Bluetooth

Bluetooth is wireless networking for low-bandwidth peripherals, including mice, keyboards, and mobile phones. If your Mac has Bluetooth built in or is equipped with a USB Bluetooth adapter, you can synchronize wirelessly with phones and Palm devices, print wirelessly to Bluetooth printers, and use Bluetooth mice and keyboards.

To manage your Mac's Bluetooth features, open the Bluetooth System Preference pane by choosing ⇨System Preferences and then clicking the Bluetooth icon.

Ink

Ink is the Mac OS X built-in handwriting-recognition engine. If you have a stylus and tablet connected to your Mac, just turn it on in this pane, and you can write anywhere you can type with the keyboard.

To manage your Mac's Ink features, open the Ink System Preferences pane by choosing ⇨System Preferences and then clicking the Ink icon.

The Ink pane is one you see only if you have one of the pen-input tablets that Ink supports connected to your Mac.

Most of the currently supported tablets come from Wacom (www.wacom.com), with prices starting under $100 for a small wireless stylus and tablet.

Automatic Login (Users & Groups System Preferences pane)

Some users don't care for the fact that Mac OS X Lion is a multiuser operating system — and dislike having to log in when they start up their Mac. For those users, here's a way to disable the login screen:

1. **Open the Users & Groups System Preferences pane, select yourself in the list of users, and click the Login Options button below the list.**

2. **Choose the account you want to be logged in automatically from the Automatic Login pop-up menu.**

   To disable the logging-in requirement, you have to be an administrator, and you might need to unlock the Users & Groups System Preferences.

When you disable logging in, you also affect all the preferences set by anyone else who uses your Mac unless they log out of your account and log into theirs. (Yikes.) So if your Desktop pattern, keyboard settings, and so forth are different from those of someone else who uses your machine, those preferences won't be properly reflected unless each of you has a separate, individual login account. Even if you're not worried about security, consider keeping logging in enabled if any other users have accounts on your machine or you don't want just anyone to be able to turn on your Mac and see your personal stuff.

Note that only one account is allowed to use autologin. If another user wants to use this Mac, you need to choose ⌘⇨Log Out, press ⌘+Shift+Q, or have Fast User Switching enabled. And if you've disabled automatic login in the Security System Preferences pane, you can't enable it here.

Boot Camp

Boot Camp is Lion's built-in technology that allows you to run Microsoft Windows XP, Vista, or 7 on any Intel-based Mac. If your Mac meets the following requirements, you can run Windows on your Mac (if you so desire):

- ✓ An Intel-based Mac (of course)
- ✓ At least 10GB of free hard drive space (though you'll almost certainly need more)
- ✓ A hard drive that isn't partitioned
- ✓ A blank recordable CD
- ✓ A printer (for printing the instructions, which you'll want to do)
- ✓ A full install copy of Microsoft Windows XP, Vista, or Windows 7 Home Premium, Professional, or Ultimate

You really do need a *full retail* copy of Windows, one that was purchased in a retail box. If your copy of Windows came with your Dell or HP, you probably won't be able to install it under Boot Camp.

To install Windows on your Mac, here are the basic steps you need to follow:

1. **Launch the Boot Camp Assistant application, which is in your Applications/Utilities folder.**

   This step creates a partition on your hard drive for Windows and then burns a special CD with all the drivers you'll need to use Windows on your Mac.

2. **Install Windows on the new partition.**

3. **Install the drivers from the CD you just burned.**

   From now on, you can hold down Option during startup and choose to start up from either the Mac OS X Lion disk partition or the Windows partition.

   It's that simple. However, if these installation steps seem beyond your comfort level, just ask your favorite Mac geek for help.

If running Windows on your Mac appeals to you, you might want to check out Parallels Desktop or VMWare Fusion (around $80 each) or VirtualBox (free). All three programs not only allow you to run Windows on your Mac, but also let you do so without partitioning your hard drive or restarting every time you want to use Windows. In fact, you can run Mac and Windows programs simultaneously with all three of the above. For more information, read the section on PC disks in Chapter 8.

Part V
The Care and Feeding of Your Lion

The 5th Wave — By Rich Tennant

"The odd thing is he always insists on using the latest version of MAC OS."

In this part . . .

Here I get into the nitty-gritty underbelly of handling trouble in Mac OS X. In this part, I cover topics like protecting your valuable data by backing it up, and I discuss everything you need to know about Macintosh security (which, thankfully, isn't all that much). Next you look at some utilities that might or might not be useful but that you should know about anyway. Finally, you find out what to do when things go wonky (which also, thankfully, doesn't happen very much) and experience a quick run-through of Dr. Mac's (okay, Dr. Bob's) top troubleshooting tips for those infrequent times when a good Lion goes bad.

This material is a little geekier than the first four parts, but it could very well be the most important information in the book. Don't miss out!

18

Safety First: Backups and Other Security Issues

In This Chapter

▶ Backing up . . . it's easy

▶ Discovering why you should back up

▶ Finding out what happens to you if you don't back up

▶ Keeping your Mac safe from rogue viruses and malicious attacks

▶ Protecting your data from prying eyes

*A*lthough Macs are generally reliable beasts (especially Macs running Mac OS X), someday your hard drive (or SSD) will die. I promise. They *all* do. And if you don't back up your drive (or at least back up any files that you can't afford to lose) before that day comes, chances are good that you'll never see those files again. And if you do see them again, my friend, it will be only after paying someone like my buddy Scott Gaidano, the founder of DriveSavers Data Recovery Service. And even if you pay, there's no guarantee of success.

DriveSavers is the premier recoverer of lost data on hard drives. The people there understand Mac hard drives quite well, do excellent work, and can often recover stuff that nobody else could. (Ask the producers of *The Simpsons* about the almost-lost episodes.) Understandably, DriveSavers charges accordingly. Here are some phone numbers for DriveSavers: 800-440-1904 toll free and 415-382-2000.

In other words, you absolutely, positively, without question *must back up* your files if you don't want to risk losing them. Just as you adopt the Shut Down command and make it a habit before turning off your machine, you must remember to back up important files on your hard drive to another disk or device — and back them up often.

How often is often? That depends on you. How much work can you afford to lose? If your answer is that losing everything you did yesterday would put you out of business, you need to back up daily or possibly twice a day. If you would lose only a few unimportant documents, you can back up less frequently.

Following the comprehensive coverage of backup options, I look at the possible threat to your data from viruses and other icky things, as well as how you can protect against them.

Finally, I look at what you can do to keep other people from looking at your stuff.

Backing Up 1s (Not) Hard to Do

You can back up your hard drive in basically three ways: the super-painless way with Lion's excellent Time Machine, the ugly way using the brute-force method, or the comprehensive way with specialized third-party backup software. Read on and find out more about all three. . . .

Backing up with Lion's excellent Time Machine

Time Machine is a most excellent backup system that was introduced with Mac OS X Leopard — and it's only gotten better. I say it's a system because it consists of two parts: the Time Machine System Preferences pane, shown in Figure 18-1, and the Time Machine application, shown in Figure 18-2.

To use Time Machine to back up your data automatically, the first thing you need is another hard drive that's the same size as or larger than your startup disk. It can be a FireWire hard drive, a USB 2 hard drive, a Thunderbolt hard drive, an SSD (if you can afford to use a Solid State Drive for backups), or even another internal hard drive, if your Mac is a Mac Pro like one of mine.

Another option is an Apple Time Capsule, a device that combines an AirPort Extreme wireless base station with a large hard drive so you can automatically back up one or more Macs over a wired or wireless network.

Figure 18-1: The Time Machine System Preferences pane.

Figure 18-2: The Time Machine application is ready to restore a file in the Finder.

The first time a new disk suitable for use with Time Machine is connected to your Mac, a dialog asks if you want to use that disk to back up with Time Machine. If you say yes, the Time Machine System Preferences pane opens automatically, showing the new disk already chosen as the backup disk.

 If that doesn't happen, or you want to use an already-connected hard drive with Time Machine, open the Time Machine System Preferences pane, and click the big On/Off switch to On. Now click the Select Disk button, and select the hard drive you want to use for your backups. Mine is called enihcaMemiT T2 (that's *Time Machine* spelled backward and T2 for 2 terabytes) in Figure 18-1.

The only other consideration is this: If you have other hard disks connected to your Mac, you should click the Options button to reveal the Do Not Back Up list, which tells Time Machine which volumes (disks) *not* to back up. To add a volume to this list, click the little + button; to remove a volume from the list, select the volume and then click the − button.

The Options sheet also has a check box for warning you when old backups are deleted; check it if you want to be warned. And if your Mac is a laptop, a second check box governs whether Time Machine backs up your Mac when it's on battery power.

A third check box asks if you want to lock your documents a day, week, month, or year after their last edit. (For more info on locking documents, look back at Chapter 6.)

For the record, Time Machine stores your backups for the following lengths of time:

- ✓ Hourly backups for the past 24 hours
- ✓ Daily backups for the past month
- ✓ Weekly backups until your backup disk is full

When your backup disk gets full, the oldest backups on it are deleted and replaced by the newest.

When does it run? Glad you asked — it runs approximately once per hour.

If you enable and set up Time Machine as I've just described, you'll never forget to back up your stuff, so just do it.

What does Time Machine back up?

Time Machine backs up your whole hard disk the first time it runs and then backs up files and folders that have been modified since your last backup. That's what backup systems do. But Time Machine does more — it also backs up things like contacts in your Address Book, pictures in your iPhoto Library, and events in your iCal calendars, not to mention its support of versions and locking. Those features — sweet ones indeed — make Time Machine unlike any other backup system.

How do I restore a file (or a contact, a photo, an event, and so on)?

To restore a file or any other information, follow these steps:

1. **Launch the appropriate program — the one that contains the information you want to restore.**

   If what you want to restore happens to be a file, that program is the Finder, which, as you know, is always running. So to restore an individual file, you don't actually need to launch anything. But to restore a contact, a photo, an e-mail message, or an event, for example, you need to launch Address Book, iPhoto, Mail, or iCal, respectively.

2. **With the appropriate application running (or the appropriate Finder window open), launch the Time Machine application, as shown in Figure 18-2.**

   It will be easier to restore a file in the Finder if the folder the file is in (or was in) is the *active* folder (that is, open and frontmost) when you launch the Time Machine application. If not, you have to navigate to the appropriate folder before you can perform Step 3.

3. **Click one of the bars on the right side of the screen *or* click the big "forward" and "back" arrows next to them to choose the backup you want to restore from (Sunday, May 22, 2011 at 6:12PM in Figure 18-2).**

   While the current backup is Sunday, May 22, 2011 at 6:12PM, note that my cursor is hovering over the bar for Sunday, April 24, 2011. If I were to click that bar, I'd see the contents of the Documents folder as they were on April 24.

4. **Select the file, folder, Address Book contact, iPhoto photo, e-mail message or iCal event you wish to restore.**

5. **Click the big Restore button below the big forward and back arrows.**

If the file, folder, Address Book contact, iPhoto photo, e-mail message, or iCal event exists in the same location today, Time Machine politely inquires as to your wishes, as shown in Figure 18-3.

Figure 18-3: Time Machine politely asks what you want it to do with the file you're restoring.

Backing up by using the manual, brute-force method

If you're too cheap to buy a second hard drive, the most rudimentary way to back up is to do it manually. You would accomplish this by dragging said files a few at a time to another volume — a CD-R, CD-RW, DVD-R, or DVD-RW. (If you use an optical disc, don't forget to actually *burn the disc;* merely dragging those files onto the optical-disc icon won't do the trick.)

By doing this, you're making a copy of each file that you want to protect. (See Chapter 8 for more info on removable storage.)

Yuck! If doing a manual backup sounds pretty awful, trust me — it is. This method can take a long, long time; you can't really tell whether you've copied every file that needs to be backed up; and you can't really copy only the files that have been modified since your last backup. Almost nobody in his right mind sticks with this method for long.

Of course, if you're careful to save files only in your Documents folder, as I suggest several times in this book, you can probably get away with backing up only that. Or if you save files in other folders within your Home folder or have any files in your Movies, Music, Pictures, or Sites folders (which often contain files you didn't specifically save in those folders, like your iPhoto photos and iTunes songs), you should probably consider backing up your entire Home folder.

As you read in the following section, that's even easier if you use special backup software.

Backing up by using commercial backup software

Another way to back up your files is with a third-party backup program. Backup software automates the task of backing up, remembering what's on each backup disc (if your backup uses more than one disc), and backing up only files that have been modified since your last backup.

Furthermore, you can instruct your backup software to back up only a certain folder (Home or Documents) and to ignore the hundreds of megabytes of stuff that make up Mac OS X, all of which you can easily reinstall from the Mac OS X Install DVD.

Your first backup with commercial software might take anywhere from a few minutes to several hours and use one or more optical discs — CD-R, CD-RW, DVD-R, DVD-RW, magneto-optical disc — or nonoptical media, such as another hard drive or any kind of tape backup. Subsequent backups, called *incremental backups* in backup-software parlance, should take only a few minutes.

 If you do incremental backups, be sure to label all the discs you use during that operation; if you use multiple discs, number them. Your backup software may prompt you with a message such as `Please insert backup disk 7`. If you haven't labeled your media clearly, you could have a problem figuring out which disc *is* disc 7 or which disc 7 belongs to that particular backup set.

One of the best things about good backup software is that you can set it up to automate your backups and perform them even if you forget. And although Time Machine is a step in the right direction and might be sufficient for your needs, it's not good enough for me. I use a total of nine hard drives for backups.

Why You Need Two Sets of Backups

You're a good soldier. You back up regularly. You think you're immune to file loss or damage.

Now picture yourself in the following scenario:

1. You leave the office one day for lunch.

2. When you return, you discover that your office has been burglarized, struck by lightning, flooded, burned to the ground, or buried in earthquake rubble — take your pick.

3. Alas, while you did have a backup, the disk it was on was in the same room as your Mac, which means it was either stolen or destroyed along with your Mac.

This scenario is totally unlikely — but it *could* happen, and it does demonstrate why you need multiple backups. If you have several sets of backup disks, and don't keep them all in the same room as your Mac, chances are pretty good that one of the sets will work even if the others are lost, stolen, or destroyed.

My backup recommendations

I am continually testing new backup solutions, so the software I use can change from month to month. I've tried most of the popular backup solutions and many of the more obscure ones, but before I say anything about my current setup, here is what I'm trying to accomplish (at a minimum):

I want at least three (reasonably) current backup "sets" with copies of all of my files. I want to update two of them every day and keep the third somewhere offsite (in my safe deposit box at the bank). Every week or two, I swap whichever backup is at the bank for a fresh one — one of the two I update daily.

This scheme ensures that no matter what happens — even if my office burns; floods; is destroyed by tornado, hurricane, or an earthquake; or robbed — I won't lose more than a week or two of work. I can live with that.

Note that once I set them up, all four programs run automatically in the background with no further action on my part, a feature I think of as "set and forget."

My first line of defense, of course, is Lion's excellent Time Machine. There's no excuse not to use it. But although Time Machine maintains multiple copies of files, they're all stored on the same disk. And I always say, if something's worth backing up to one place, it's worth backing up to three.

And so, in addition to Time Machine, I use the excellent CrashPlan (`www.crashplan.com`; from $1.50/month), which backs up my Documents folder four times a day to two different hard drives. It also backs up my Home folder continuously to yet another hard drive, so every time I make a change to a document, the backup copy is updated in real time. Finally, it backs up my Home folder over the Internet to the CrashPlan cloud-based servers.

Every night at midnight, SuperDuper (`www.shirtpocket.com/`; $27.95) clones (duplicates) my startup disk to another hard drive, which provides me a bootable backup I can use with almost any other Mac.

Finally, I use the excellent and free Dropbox (`www.dropbox.com`) service to synchronize my current project folders among several Macs and my iPhone and iPad, giving me even more backup copies of my most important files.

There is one last thing: I test the integrity of each backup regularly, and so should you. For one thing, it confirms that the files I think are there are actually there, and it reassures me that the files in that backup set aren't corrupted or damaged and are capable of being restored successfully.

Non-Backup Security Concerns

As you've probably surmised by now, backing up your files is critical unless you won't mind losing all your data someday. And although backing up is by far your most important security concern, several other things could imperil your data — things like viruses or other types of malware, including worms, spyware, and intruder attacks. That's the bad news. The good news is that all those things are far more likely to affect Windows users than Mac users. In fact, I'd venture to say that viruses, worms, malware, spyware, and intruder attacks are rarer than hens' teeth for Mac users.

That said, here are a few precautions Mac users should consider, just in case.

About viruses and other malware

A computer *virus,* in case you missed it in *Time* magazine, is a nasty little piece of computer code that replicates and spreads from disk to disk. A virus could cause your Mac to misbehave; some viruses can destroy files or erase disks with no warning.

Malware (short for *malicious software)* is software that's hostile, intrusive, annoying, or disruptive. Malware is often designed to gain unauthorized access to your computer and/or collect personal data including passwords without your knowledge.

The difference between a virus and other types of malware is that malware doesn't spread by itself. It relies upon trickery, mimicry, and social engineering to induce unsuspecting users to open a malicious file or install a malicious program. So a virus is a type of malware, but not all malware are viral.

You don't hear much about viruses on the Mac because there have been few (if any) since the dawn of the modern OS X era (so many big cats ago). Almost all viruses are specific to an operating system — Mac viruses won't affect Windows users, Windows viruses won't affect Mac users, and so forth, and the vast majority of known viruses affect only (you guessed it) Windows.

The one real exception here is a "gift" from the wonderful world of Microsoft Office (Word and Excel, for example) users: the dreaded *macro viruses* that are spread with Word and Excel documents containing macros written in Microsoft's VBA (Visual Basic for Applications) language. But you're safe even from those if you practice safe computing as I describe (although you can unknowingly pass them along to a Windows users).

As it happens, so far, almost all the viral activity affecting Mac OS X involved various Windows macro viruses. In fact, at the time of this writing, I know of no OS X–specific viruses, nor of any that attacks Mac OS X exclusively — and (at least so far) none that causes damage. Still, the advice in this chapter is sound; one never knows when the little boys out there will decide to attack the Mac. OS X viruses aren't impossible or nonexistent; they just don't exist in known examples at this moment in time. But they could someday; better safe than sorry.

So there's no virus threat at present. But sadly, there is a very real malware threat that was discovered in early 2011. Here's how it works: While browsing the web (using any web browser), an alert informing you that your Mac is infected may appear on the screen. It graciously offers to perform a free virus scan, offering you three buttons: OK, Cancel, or Close. And that's the first bit of social engineering: The nasty file is downloaded to your hard disk regardless of which button you click.

Then, if your web browser's Open Safe Files After Downloading preference is enabled, the file automatically decompresses and launches the (quite real) Mac OS X Installer. Then, if you provide your administrator password when prompted, the malware — known as Mac Defender, Mac Security, and Mac Protector, among other names — is installed on your system. And recent reports seem to imply that a new variant doesn't even require your administrator password!

Once installed, the malicious program looks and acts just like real Mac software, with a convincing user interface and genuine-looking toolbar. At some point the program "discovers" a virus infection on your Mac, and that's when the real trouble begins. It offers you an upgrade, but only if you'll supply your credit-card number. . . . I don't know what happens to your card number at that point, but I'm certain it's not good.

So while there is at least one piece of malicious software going around, it is spread mostly via social engineering. Here's how to protect yourself:

- Disable Open Safe Files After Downloading in Safari Preferences.

- If a suspicious alert or window appears on your screen, Force Quit your web browser (⌘⇨Force Quit or ⌘+Option+Esc) immediately.

- If the Mac OS X Installer launches for no apparent reason, *do not click Continue!* Don't install the software, and for heaven's sake, don't type your administrator password.

- Don't run *any* installer — the one built into Mac OS X or a third-party kind — unless you're absolutely certain that it came from a trusted source.

- Don't use credit or debit cards with unfamiliar vendors and/or insecure web sites.

If you've already installed it, Apple has an article called "How to avoid or remove Mac Defender malware," which you'll find at `http://support.apple.com/kb/HT4650`. If you've installed it and also provided a credit-card number, contact your credit-card company immediately.

If you use disks that have been inserted into other computers, you need some form of virus-detection software. If you download and use files from web and File Transfer Protocol (FTP) sites on the Internet, you need some form of virus detection as well.

You don't have too much to worry about if

✔ You download files only from commercial online services, such as AOL, CNET, or MacUpdate, which are all very conscientious about malware.

✔ You use only commercial software and never download files from web sites with strange names.

You should definitely worry about malicious infection if

✔ An unsavory friend told you about a web site called `Dan'sDenOfPirated IllegalStolenBootlegSoftware.com`, and you actually visited it.

✔ You swap disks with friends regularly.

✔ You shuttle disks back and forth to other Macs.

✔ You use your disks at public computers or printing shops.

✔ You download files from various and sundry places on the Internet, even ones that don't sound as slimy as `Dan'sDenOfPiratedIllegal StolenBootlegSoftware.com`.

✔ You receive e-mail with attachments (and open them).

If you're at risk, do yourself a favor, and buy a commercial antivirus program. I'm not quite ready to install antivirus software myself; I find that it's obtrusive and slows my Mac. If you think you need protection, consider VirusBarrier X6 ($49.95; `www.intego.com`), MacScan ($29.99; `www.mac scan.securemac.com`), or ClamXAV (free; `www.clamxav.com`).

If you decide to do as I do and not as I just suggested, I urge you to visit some or all of the web sites in Chapter 23 regularly. If nothing else, you'll get advance warning the next time a particularly heinous piece of Mac malware is on the loose. I don't know about you, but I'll wait until then to reassess my position on this antivirus conundrum.

Firewall: Yea or nay?

According to the Mac OS X built-in Oxford American Dictionary, a firewall is

> *Part of a computer system or network that is designed to block unauthorized access while permitting outward communication.*

Using a firewall protects your computer from malicious users on other networks or the Internet and keeps them from gaining access to your Mac.

Unlike older versions of Windows, Mac OS X is quite difficult to crack. There have been few (if any) reports of outsiders gaining access to Macintosh computers running Mac OS X. One reason might be that Mac OS X has a built-in firewall. That's the good news. The bad news is that said firewall is disabled by default. You'll need to activate it if you want to be protected against unauthorized access to your computer.

If you use a router with its own firewall (and the router's firewall is enabled), do not activate the Lion firewall. Running multiple firewalls can cause issues.

To activate your firewall, follow these steps:

1. **Open the System Preferences application (from the Applications folder,  menu, Launchpad, or Dock).**

2. **Click the Security & Privacy icon and then click the Firewall tab.**

   The default setting is Allow All Incoming Connections, which is the least secure option.

3. **Click the Start button to turn the firewall on, if it's not already running.**

   (Optional) If the lock in the bottom-left corner of the Security & Privacy pane is locked, click it, and provide your administrator password.

4. **Click the Advanced button to configure your firewall's settings.**

5. **For the highest level of protection, select the Block All Incoming Connections check box.**

6. **Click OK.**

Alas, you probably won't want to keep this setting for long, as you won't be able to use awesome OS X features including iChat and file, screen, printer, and music sharing, to name a few. If (or when) it becomes desirable to allow certain incoming connections from outside computers, here's a short list of common scenarios and how to set up your firewall and sharing services for each:

- ✓ **Problem: You want to host a web site on your Mac, using the Mac OS X built-in Web Sharing feature.** If you've selected the firewall's Block All Incoming Connections setting, nobody can access your web site; access is blocked by the firewall.

Solution:

1. **Deselect the Block All Incoming Connections check box.**

2. **Click the Show All button at the top of the System Preferences window.**

3. **Click the Sharing icon.**

   Three sharing services are enabled by default, as shown in Figure 18-4.

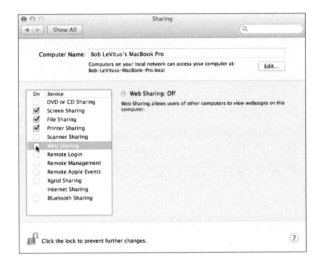

Figure 18-4: Lion turns on these three sharing services by default.

Here comes the cool part: Any additional services you enable here in the Sharing System Preferences pane are automatically enabled by the firewall.

4. **Check the box to enable Web Sharing.**

   To confirm that the firewall was smart enough to add Web Sharing when you enabled it in the Sharing System Preferences pane:

1. **Click the Show All button at the top of the System Preferences window.**

2. **Click the Security & Privacy icon.**

   If the lock in the bottom-left corner is locked, you'll have to click it and provide your administrator password to proceed.

3. Click the Advanced button.

I enabled Web Sharing in the Sharing System Preferences pane manually, and the firewall added Web Sharing automatically, as shown in Figure 18-5.

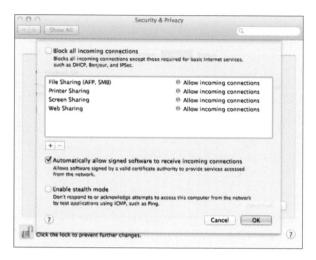

Figure 18-5: My firewall enabled Web Sharing automatically when I enabled Web Sharing in the Sharing System Preferences pane.

✔ **Problem: An application needs you to allow outside connections to it in order to function.** How would you know? Check the user manual, Read Me file, or application Help. Or you might see an error message that the program can't connect to the Internet. Don't worry — if a program requires you to open your firewall, you can almost certainly find some information in one (or more) of these places.

Solution: Click the little + button on the left near the bottom of the window. A standard Open File sheet drops down over the window; select the appropriate program, and click the Add button.

Your firewall will then allow incoming connections to that particular application.

Install recommended software updates

By default, your Mac checks with the mothership (Apple) once a week to see if there's any new or updated software for your Mac. If there is, your Mac informs you that a new Software Update is available and asks whether you'd like to install it. In almost all cases, you do. Apple issues Software Updates to fix newly discovered security concerns, fix serious bugs in Mac OS X, or to fix bugs in or add functionality to Apple applications.

You can perform this check manually by clicking the Software Update icon in the System Preferences window and then clicking the Check Now button. You also use the Software Update System Preferences pane to change the frequency of these checks, disable automatic checking completely, and/or instruct your Mac to automatically download any updates it finds.

Every so often, one of these Software Updates has an unintended side effect; while fixing one problem, it introduces a different problem. Apple is generally pretty careful, and this doesn't happen very often, but if you want to be safe, don't install a Software Update until you've visited MacFixIt (www. macfixit.com), Macworld (www.macworld.com), or MacInTouch (www. macintouch.com) and looked at their reports on the update you have in mind. If there are widespread issues with a particular Software Update, these two sites will have the most comprehensive coverage (and possible work-arounds).

Apps need updates too. So make a habit of launching the Mac App Store application now and then, clicking the Updates tab, and then updating any apps that require it.

One last thing: If you see a little number on the App Store's icon in the Dock, you have that many updates waiting. Launch the Mac App Store, and click the Updates tab.

Protecting Your Data from Prying Eyes

The last kind of security I look at in this chapter is protecting your files from other users on your local area network and users with physical access to your Mac. If you don't want anyone messing with your files, check out the security measures I describe in the following sections.

Blocking or limiting connections

The first thing you might want to do is open the Sharing System Preferences pane by launching the System Preferences application (from the Applications folder, 🍎 menu, or Dock) and clicking the Sharing icon. Nobody can access your Mac over the network if all the services in the Sharing pane are disabled and your firewall is set to either Block All Incoming Connections. See the section "Firewall: Yea or nay?" earlier in this chapter for details on these settings.

Locking down files with FileVault

If you absolutely, positively don't ever want anyone to be able to access the files in your Home folder, FileVault allows you to encrypt your entire Home folder and its contents. It protects your data with the latest government-approved encryption standard: Advanced Encryption Standard with 128-bit keys (AES-128).

When you turn on FileVault, you're asked to set a *master password* for the computer. After you do, you or any other administrator can use that master password if you forget your regular account login password.

If you turn on FileVault and then forget both your login password and your master password, you can't log in to your account — and your data is lost forever. Really. Not even DriveSavers has a hope of recovering it. So don't forget both passwords, okay?

FileVault is useful primarily if you store sensitive information on your Mac. If you're logged out of your user account and someone gets access to your Mac, there is no way they can access your data. Period.

Because FileVault encrypts your Home folder, some tasks that normally access your Home folder might be prevented. For one thing, some backup programs choke if FileVault is enabled. Also, if you're not logged in to your user account, other users can't access your Shared folder(s).

And because FileVault is always encrypting and decrypting files, it often slows your Mac when you add or save new files, and it takes extra time before it lets you log out, restart, or shut down.

To turn on FileVault, follow these steps:

1. **Open the Security & Privacy System Preferences pane.**
2. **Click the FileVault tab.**
3. **Click the Turn on FileVault button to enable FileVault.**

To turn off FileVault, click the Turn off FileVault button. At least that's how it's supposed to work, *but . . .*

The last time I tested this feature, when I tried to turn off FileVault, I got an error message and was unable to disable FileVault. I tried every trick I know (and I know a lot) and contacted Apple's support group, too. The issue was never resolved. I ended up having to erase the hard drive and restore files from backups (yet another reason multiple backups are a good thing).

Setting other options for security

The General tab of the Security & Privacy System Preferences pane offers several more options that can help keep your data safe. They are

- **Require Password after Sleep or Screen Saver Begins:** Enable this option if you want your Mac to lock itself up and require a password after the screen saver kicks in or it goes to sleep. It can become a pain in the butt, having to type your password all the time. But if you have nosy co-workers, family members, or other individuals you'd like to keep from rooting around in your stuff, you should probably enable this option.

  When enabled, this option offers a pop-up menu that lets you specify how long after sleep or screen saver this password protection should kick in. The options range from immediately to four hours.

- **Disable Automatic Login:** One of the login options in the Users & Groups System Preferences pane is automatic login. With automatic login enabled, you don't have to choose an account or type a password when you start up this Mac. Instead, it bypasses all that login stuff and goes directly to the Desktop of the designated account. If you want to disable this feature for all accounts — so that every user of this Mac sees the login screen and is required to choose an account and type a password — you should enable this option.

- **Require an Administrator Password to Access System Preferences with Lock Icons:** If you prefer that nonadministrator users be prevented from changing the settings in any System Preferences pane, enable this option.

- **Log Out after X Minutes of Inactivity:** This feature does what it says: It logs out the current user after a specified length of idle time.

- **Automatically Update Safe Downloads List:** When you attempt to open a downloaded application, Mac OS X reminds you where it came from before you open it for the first time. This option updates its list of applications it considers safe to launch.

- **Show a Message When the Screen is Locked:** Type the message you want on your screen when it's locked in this text entry box.

- **Disable Remote Control Infrared Receiver:** There was a time not too long ago that many Macs included a little Apple Remote control device (though none do anymore). To disable it for all users, enable this option.

Finally, the two items in the Privacy tab of the Security & Privacy System Preferences pane are

  ✓ **Send Diagnostic & Usage Data to Apple:** Anonymously sends details of system crashes, apps that quit unexpectedly, freezes, kernel panics to the mothership in Cupertino, Apple's world HQ. Engineers then pore over the data and issue software updates to eliminate the bugs. At least that's the theory . . .

  ✓ **Enable Location Services:** Select this option to allow applications and web sites to use your computer's current location to provide information, services, and features appropriate to where you are.

And that's all you really need to know about security and privacy (or at least enough to make you dangerous).

19

Utility Chest

In This Chapter

▶ Crunching numbers with the Calculator

▶ Setting up lots of stuff, including AirPort Base Stations and Bluetooth devices

▶ Plumbing your Lion's innards

▶ And much, much more . . .

$\mathcal{M}$ ac OS X Lion comes with a plethora of useful utilities that make using your computer more pleasant and/or make you more productive when you use your computer. In this chapter, I give you a glimpse of the ones that aren't covered elsewhere in this book.

The first item, Calculator, is in your Applications folder; all the other items in this chapter are in your Utilities folder, *inside* your Applications folder (or you can use the Utilities folder's keyboard shortcut, ⌘+Shift+U).

Calculator

Need to do some quick math? The Calculator application gives you a simple calculator with all the basic number-crunching functions that your pocket calculator has. To use it, you can either click the keys with the mouse or type numbers and operators (math symbols such as +, –, and =) using the number keys on your keyboard (or numeric keypad, if you have one). Calculator also offers a paper tape (Window⇨Show Paper Tape) to track your computations — and, if you want, provide a printed record. It can even speak numbers aloud (Speech⇨Speak Button Pressed and Speech⇨Speak).

Check out the Calculator in Figure 19-1.

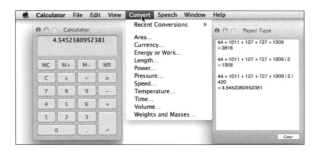

Figure 19-1: The Calculator (left), Convert menu (middle), and Paper Tape (right).

In my humble opinion, the most useful feature in the Calculator (after the paper tape) is the Convert menu — more specifically, the currency-conversion feature. It actually checks the Internet for the exchange rate before calculating the conversion for you. That's very cool.

Beyond that, Calculator has three modes: Basic, Scientific, and Programmer. Basic is the default, and you access the other two modes as follows:

- Pressing ⌘+2 (View⇨Scientific) turns the formerly anemic calculator into a powerful scientific calculator.

- Choosing View⇨Programmer (⌘+3) turns it into the programmer's friend, letting you display your data in binary, octal, hexadecimal, ASCII, and Unicode. It also performs programming operations such as shifts and byte swaps. (If you're a programmer, you know what all that means; if you aren't, it really doesn't matter.)

Activity Monitor

In Unix, the underlying operating system that powers Mac OS X, applications and other things going on behind the scenes are called *processes*. Each application and the operating system itself can run a number of processes at the same time.

In Figure 19-2, you see 78 different processes running, most of them behind the scenes. Note that when this picture was taken, I had half a dozen or more programs running, including the Finder, FaceTime, the Mac App Store, and Activity Monitor itself.

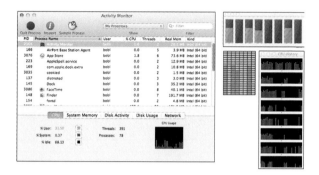

Figure 19-2: The Activity Monitor window (left) and the three little CPU Monitor windows (right).

To display the three CPU Monitor windows on the right side of the Activity Monitor window as shown in Figure 19-2, choose Window➪CPU Usage (keyboard shortcut ⌘+2), CPU History (keyboard shortcut ⌘+3), and/or Floating CPU Window (no keyboard shortcut).

You also select what appears in the Activity Monitor's Dock icon — CPU Usage, CPU History, Network Usage, Disk Activity, Memory Usage, or the Activity Monitor icon — by choosing View➪Dock Icon. All but the Activity Monitor icon appear *live,* meaning that they update every few seconds to reflect the current state of affairs.

To choose how often these updates occur, choose View➪Update Frequency.

But be careful — shorter durations cause Activity Monitor itself to use more CPU cycles, which can decrease overall performance.

Finally, the bottom portion of the Activity Monitor window can display one of five monitors. Just click the appropriate tab — CPU, System Memory, Disk Activity, Disk Usage, or Network — to see that particular monitor.

Geeks and troubleshooters (and even you) can use Activity Monitor to identify what processes are running, which user owns the process, and how
much CPU capacity and memory the process is using. You can even use this
feature to quit or force-quit a process that you think might be causing problems for you.

Messing around in Activity Monitor isn't a good idea for most users. If you're
having problems with an application or with Mac OS X, try quitting open
applications; force-quitting applications (press ⌘+Option+Esc — the Mac
"three-finger salute"); or logging out and then logging back in again before
you start mucking around with processes.

AirPort Utility

You use AirPort Utility to set up an AirPort Base Station and configure its
individual settings, such as base-station and wireless-network passwords,
network name, Internet connection type, and so on.

When you first open AirPort Utility, select the AirPort Base Station you want
to work with by clicking its icon on the left side of the window.

If you want assistance with setting up your base station, just click the
Continue button in the bottom-right corner of the AirPort Utility window.
You're asked a series of questions, and your base station is configured
accordingly. If you know what you're doing and want to change your base station's settings manually, choose Base Station⇨Manual Setup (⌘+L) instead.

Audio MIDI Setup

This program is the control center for any MIDI devices built into or connected to your Mac.

ColorSync Utility

ColorSync helps ensure color consistency when you're scanning, printing,
and working with color images. This package includes ColorSync software as
well as premade ColorSync profiles for a variety of monitors, scanners, and
printers. And the ColorSync Utility has a bunch of tools designed to make
working with ColorSync profiles and devices easier. You'll probably never
need it, but I wanted to let you know it's there, just in case.

To calibrate or not to calibrate?

One thing you might want to try, even if you never plan to use ColorSync, is calibrating your monitor. This process adjusts the red, green, blue, and white levels, and could make what you see on your screen look better than it does now.

To calibrate your monitor, follow these steps:

1. **Open the Displays System Preferences pane.**

2. **Click the Color tab and then write down the Display Profile that your Mac is currently using (it's highlighted in the Display Profile list).**

3. **Click the Calibrate button.**

   The Display Calibrator Assistant appears.

4. **Enable the Expert Mode check box.**

Trust me, you don't have to be an expert. This enables several additional calibration tests that make the process more effective.

5. **Follow the simple on-screen instructions to calibrate your monitor and create a custom display profile.**

   Yes, the instructions are simple. You may find that squinting helps on the first few tests, but anyone can do it.

6. **Give your profile a name; then click the Continue button.**

If you decide that you don't like the results of your calibration, just select the Display Profile that you wrote down in Step 2 from the Display Profile list in the Displays System Preferences pane. Your monitor goes back the way it was before you calibrated it.

A *ColorSync profile* is a set of instructions for a monitor, scanner, or printer, which tells the device how to deal with colors and white so the device's output is consistent with that of other devices, as determined by the ColorSync profiles of the other devices. In theory, if two devices have ColorSync profiles, their output (on-screen, on a printed page, or in a scanned image) should match perfectly. Put another way, the color that you see on-screen should be exactly the same shade of color that you see on a printed page or in a scanned image.

If you're not a graphic artist working with color files and calibrating monitors and printers to achieve accurate color matching, you probably don't need the ColorSync Utility (unless you've gotten hooked on iPhoto and want your printed inkjet color pictures to match up correctly).

If you're compelled to do whatever it takes to get accurate color on your monitor and printer, check out *Color Management For Digital Photographers For Dummies,* by Ted Padova and Don Mason (John Wiley & Sons, Inc.).

DigitalColor Meter

 The DigitalColor Meter program displays what's on your screen as numerical color values, according to two different systems: RGB (red-green-blue) or CIE (the abbreviation for a chromaticity coordinate system developed by the Commission Internationale de l'Eclairage, the international commission on illumination). If you're not a graphic artist or otherwise involved in the production of high-end color documents, or working in HTML, you'll probably never need it.

Disk Utility

 If you're having problems with your hard drive or need to make changes to it, Disk Utility is a good place to start.

Start by clicking a disk or volume in the column on the left and then click one of these five tabs.

First Aid tab

If you suspect that something's not quite right with your Mac, the First Aid portion of Disk Utility should be among your first stops. Use First Aid to verify and (if necessary) repair an ailing drive. To use it, click the First Aid button on the left side of the Disk Utility window. Click a volume's icon and then click Verify. You get information about any problems that the software finds. If First Aid doesn't find any problems, you can go on your merry way, secure in the knowledge that your Mac is A-okay. If verification turns up trouble, click Repair to have the problem fixed. You can also use First Aid to fix disk-permission problems.

 You won't be able to use the copy of Disk Utility in your Applications/Utilities folder to repair your Mac OS X boot disk. To do that, you must reboot from Lion's Recovery Disk or another bootable disk.

You can't use Disk Utility First Aid to fix a CD or DVD; neither can you use it to fix most disk image files. These disks are read-only and can't be altered.

Erase tab

Use Erase to format (completely erase) any disk except the current startup disk.

Of partitions and volumes

Partitioning a drive lets you create multiple volumes. A *volume* is a storage space that (from the Mac's point of view) looks and acts just like a hard drive; a *partition* is simply a designated volume on a drive, completely separate from all other partitions (volumes). You can create any number of partitions, but it's a good idea to limit yourself to no more than a small handful.

You can create drive partitions only on a newly formatted drive. So to partition a drive, first format it in Drive Setup and then create partitions. Before you do that, give some thought to

how large a partition you want to create. You won't be able to change your mind about it later.

By the same token, it's absolutely not necessary to use partitions unless you are running Boot Camp. Many users never partition a hard drive and get along just fine. If you do choose to partition, you should probably limit the number of partitions you create. An iMac with a 320GB drive will do just fine with one or two (or maybe three) partitions; there's no need to create more.

When you format a disk, you erase all information on it permanently. Formatting can't be undone — so unless you're *absolutely sure* this is what you want to do, don't do it. Unless you have no use for whatever's currently on the disk, make a complete backup of the disk before you format it. If the data is critical, you should have at least two (or even three) known-to-be-valid backup copies of that disk before you reformat.

Partition tab

Use this tab to create disk partitions (multiple volumes on a single disk). Mac OS X treats each partition as a separate disk.

When you select an item in the column on the left, you'll see only a partition tab when you select a disk such as the 500.11GB Hitachi and Seagate or 16.01GB Verbatim drives in Figure 19-3.

Be careful here. While some adjustments can be made to partitions without loss of data, not all adjustments can. You'll be warned if what you're about to do will permanently erase your data, but I thought I'd give you fair warning first.

By the way, you won't see a Partition tab if you select a volume or partition — PussInBootsMBP, Lion HD, Fast 'n' Small, and Tuff 'n' Tiny in Figure 19-3, instead of a disk (500.11GB Hitachi, 500GB Seagate, and 16.01GB Verbatim in Figure 19-3). Makes sense when you think about it.

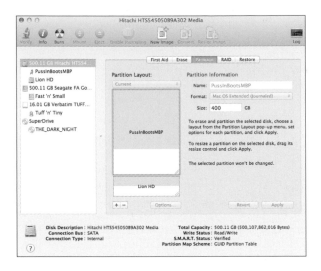

Figure 19-3: Select a disk (500.11GB Hitachi, 500GB Seagate, or 16.01GB Verbatim), and the Partition tab makes itself available.

RAID tab

By using Redundant Array of Individual (or Independent) Disks (RAID), you can treat multiple disks as a single volume, which is sort of the opposite of partitioning.

Restore tab

Use the Restore tab to restore your Mac to factory-fresh condition from a CD-ROM or disk-image file.

In most cases, you install new software on your Mac from a CD-ROM or DVD-ROM or from the Internet. Software vendors typically use an installer program that decompresses and copies files to their proper places on your hard drive. After you've installed the software, you're back in business.

Apple's variation on this theme is a humongous file called the *disk image* — everything you'd normally find on a disk, without the disk. These days, more developers are adopting the disk-image format for their downloadable installers and updaters. When mounted on your Desktop (more on what *mounting* means in a minute), a disk image looks and acts just like a real disk. You can open it and see its contents in a Finder window, copy files from its window to another disk, drag it to the Eject button to remove it from your Desktop — go wild. To make a disk image appear on your Desktop, you double-click the image file. At that point, the Disk Utility application takes over and puts an icon (which for all intents and purposes looks like a disk) on your Desktop.

Disk Utility not only mounts images when you double-click them, but also lets you create your own disk-image files and burn them onto CD-ROMs and DVD-ROMs.

Because you can transfer disk images via the Internet — and because they act just like disks — they're great substitutes for CD-ROMs and other disk-based software installers. A software maker can create both a CD version of an installer and a disk image that can be downloaded.

By the way, you find out more about Disk Utility (mostly how to use it for troubleshooting) in Chapter 20.

Grab

Want to take a picture of your screen? You can use Grab to take a picture of all or part of the screen and then save that file for printing or sending around (say, to all your screaming fans who want to see your Desktop pattern or how you've organized your windows).

For the first edition of this book, I used Grab to create the screen shots, but I've used the superb Snapz Pro X utility (Ambrosia Software; www.ambrosia sw.com) for the figures in subsequent editions. In addition to taking much more flexible screen shots, it does full-motion screen recording.

Grab's best feature is its capability to do a timed screen capture. Like those cameras that let you start the timer and then run to get into the shot, Grab gives you 10 seconds to bring the window you want to the front, pull down a menu, and get the cursor out of the way or whatever you need to do to get the screen just right.

Grab's default behavior is to display no cursor. If you want to show a cursor in your screen shots, choose Grab⇨Preferences and then select a pointer from the ten choices in the Preference dialog. To have no cursor, click the topmost, leftmost item, which is an empty box that indicates *no cursor*.

Grapher

 Grapher is a venerable piece of eye candy that shows off your CPU's computational power. A quick, visual math instructor, Grapher can graph equations in two or three dimensions and speaks hexadecimal, octal, base ten, and binary to boot. You can even graph curves, surfaces, inequalities, differential equations, discrete series, and vector, and scalar fields . . . whatever that means. (I found all that information in Apple Help.)

Keychain Access

 A *keychain* is a way to consolidate your passwords — the one you use to log into your Mac, your e-mail password, and passwords required by any Web sites. Here's how it works: You use a single password to unlock your keychain (which holds your various passwords) and then you don't have to remember all your other passwords. Rest assured that your passwords are secure because only a user who has your keychain password can reach the other password-protected applications.

 The Keychain Access utility is particularly cool if you have multiple e-mail accounts, and each one has a different password. Just add them all to your keychain, and you can get all your mail at the same time with one password.

 A special "master" keychain called the Login Keychain is created automatically for every Mac OS X Lion user.

Here's how to add passwords to your login keychain:

✔ **To add passwords for applications,** just open Mail or another application that supports the keychain. When the program asks for your password, supply it and choose Yes to add the password to the keychain.

How do you know which programs support the Keychain Access utility? You don't until you're prompted to save your password in a keychain in that Open dialog, connect window, or so forth. If a program supports Keychain Access, it offers a check box for it in the user ID/password dialog or window.

✔ **To add a web site password to a keychain,** open the Keychain Access application, and click the Password button. In the New Password Item window that opens, type the URL of the page (or copy and paste it) in the Keychain Item Name text field; type your username in the Account Name field; and then type your password in the Password text field, as shown in Figure 19-4.

Keychain Item Name:

http://www.macworld.com

Enter a name for this keychain item. If you are adding an Internet password item, enter its URL (for example: http://www.apple.com)

Account Name:

DoctorMac

Enter the account name associated with this keychain item.

Password:

••••••••••

Enter the password to be stored in the keychain.

Password Strength: Weak

☐ Show Typing

Cancel   Add

Figure 19-4: Add a URL to the keychain manually by using Keychain Access.

To use the new URL password, use Safari to open the URL. If the account name and password aren't filled in for you automatically, choose Edit⇨ AutoFill Form (⌘+Shift+A), and they will be. Now just click the appropriate button on the web page to log in.

If you select the User Names and Passwords check box on the AutoFill tab of Safari's Preferences window (Safari⇨Preferences or ⌘+,), you don't have to add sites, accounts, or passwords manually. Instead, the first time you visit a site that requires an account name and password, when you log in, Safari asks whether you would like to save your password, as shown in Figure 19-5.

Would you like to save this password?

To review or remove passwords you have saved, open Safari preferences, and then click AutoFill.

Never for this Website   Not Now   Yes

Figure 19-5: The easy way to add to your keychain in Safari.

Migration Assistant

 This is pretty much a one-trick pony, but that pony is a prize winner. You use the Migration Assistant to transfer your account and other user information from another Mac or another volume on the current Mac to this one. You need to authenticate as an administrator to use it, but it's a pretty handy way to transfer an account without having to re-create all the preferences and other settings. When you first installed Lion (or when you booted your nice new Lion-based Mac for the first time), the setup utility asked you whether you wanted to transfer your information from another Mac. If you answered in the affirmative, it ran the Migration Assistant.

It's not just for new Lions. You can launch this puppy any time to transfer all or some user accounts, applications, settings, and files from another Mac or PC to this one.

 Lion's Migration Assistant is the first to import user accounts, applications, settings, and files from Windows PCs as well as Macs.

System Information

 System Information (The App Formerly Known as System Profiler) is a little program that is launched when you click the More Info button in the About This Mac window (⌘⇨About This Mac). It provides information about your Mac. (What a concept!) If you're curious about arcane questions such as what processor your Mac has or what devices are stashed inside it or are connected to it, give this baby a try. Click various items in the Contents list on the left side of the window, and information about the item appears on the right side of the window. Feel free to poke around this little puppy as much as you like; it's benign and can't hurt anything.

 If you ever have occasion to call for technical support for your Mac, software, or peripherals, you're probably going to be asked to provide information from System Information, so don't get rid of it just because you don't care about this kind of stuff.

Terminal

 Mac OS X is based on Unix. If you need proof — or if you actually want to operate your Mac as the Unix machine that it is — Terminal is the place to start.

Because Unix is a command-line-based operating system, you use Terminal to type your commands. You can issue commands that show a directory listing, copy and move files, search for filenames or contents, or establish or change passwords. In short, if you know what you're doing, you can do everything on the command line that you can do in Mac OS X. For most folks, that's not a desirable alternative to the windows-and-icons of the Finder window. But take my word for it; true geeks who are also Mac lovers get all misty-eyed about the combination of a command line *and* a graphical user interface.

You can wreck havoc upon your poor operating system with Terminal. You can harm your Lion in many ways that just aren't possible using mere windows and icons and clicks. So — before you type a single command in Terminal — think seriously about what I just said. And if you're not 100 percent certain about the command you've just typed, don't even think about pressing Return or Enter.

20

Troubleshooting Mac OS X

In This Chapter

▶ Facing the ol' "My Mac Won't Boot" blues

▶ Dealing with the prohibitory sign

▶ Recovering from startup crashes

*A*s a bleeding-edge Mac enthusiast with over a quarter century of Mac experience under my belt, I've had more than my share of Mac troubles. Over those years, I've developed an arsenal of surefire tips and tricks that I believe can resolve more than 90 percent of Mac OS X problems without a trip to the repair shop.

Alas, if your hardware is dead, then, sadly, neither you nor I can do anything about it because it is now a job for your friendly Mac repairman — and your fat checkbook or high-limit credit card.

But if your hardware is okay, you have a fighting chance of using the suggestions in this chapter to get your machine up and running.

About Startup Disks and Booting

Although you usually see a stylish Apple logo when you turn on your computer, once in a blue moon, you might not. You might instead see a solid blue screen, a solid gray screen, a solid black screen, or something else entirely, as described in the next section.

...e a permissions problem with a file installeᵈ ...
...ir Disk Permissions.

☑ Show details

Verify and Repair volume "Lion HD"
Checking file system
Checking Journaled HFS Plus volume.
Checking extents overflow file.
Checking catalog file.
Checking multi-linked files.
Checking catalog hierarchy.
The volume Lion HD appears to be OK.

Verify Disk Permissions

Repair Disk Permissions

Capacity : 99.11 GB (99,109,
Mac OS Extended (Journaled)   Available : 57.52 GB (57,516,
Used : 41.59 GB (41,592,
Number of Files : 364,993

The point is that your Mac isn't starting up as it should. When this happens, it usually indicates that something bad has happened to your Mac. Sometimes, it's a hardware component that has bitten the dust; at other times, Mac OS X itself has somehow been damaged.

Rest assured that these occurrences are rather uncommon — most Mac users go an entire lifetime without seeing one. If you ever have a Mac that won't boot, don't despair immediately. Before you diagnose your Mac as terminally ill, here are some things to try.

When I talk about *booting,* I mean using a particular disk or disk partition as your startup disk.

I bet you have a copy of the ultimate startup disk right there on your computer table — the installation DVD (or the first disc if you received more than one) that came with your computer.

For the entire history of OS X, I've advised my readers to keep their OS X installation disc close at hand . . . the one that came in the boxed retail copy they bought. At the time I'm writing this chapter, I can't repeat that advice for Lion. Apple has announced that only App Store purchases will be available for people upgrading to Lion. In other words, unless Apple changes its policy between now and the time you read this, you won't have a Lion Install DVD from which to work. So whatever else you do, make backup copies of the Lion Installer file that you receive from the App Store. The lack of a bootable installer disc solution should do wonders for the sale of external hard drives and high-capacity flash drives.

With Lion, however, because there is no bootable DVD, the Installer creates a bootable partition named Recovery HD on that disk when you first install Lion.

Explaining how to create a bootable recovery disk is beyond the purview of this book, but I hope you'll take it upon yourself to figure it out and make one. The Recovery HD partition is a good concept, but if your hard disk dies, the Recovery HD partition dies too. Which is why I recommend a making a bootable clone of your startup disk as soon as possible, just in case.

A good place to start is Carbon Copy Cloner (www.bombich.com), a donationware app that lets you create a clone of your boot disk with a minimum of fuss. Just add a hard disk as large as or larger than your boot disk, and you'll be good to go.

They call it a prohibitory sign for a reason

When you turn on your Mac, the first thing it does (after the hardware tests) is check for a startup disk that has Mac OS X on it. If your system doesn't find such a disk on your internal hard drive, it begins looking elsewhere — on a FireWire or Universal Serial Bus (USB) disk or on DVD.

If you have more than one startup disk attached to your Mac, as many users do, you can choose which one your Mac boots from in the Startup Disk System Preferences pane.

At this point, your Mac usually finds your hard drive, which contains your operating system, and the startup process continues on its merry way with the subtle Apple logo and all the rest. If your Mac can't find your hard drive (or doesn't find on it what it needs to boot Mac OS X), you encounter the dreaded prohibitory sign.

Think of the prohibitory sign as your Mac's way of saying, "Please provide me a startup disk."

If Apple can figure out a way to put a prohibitory sign on the screen, why the heck can't the software engineers find a way to put the words *I need a startup disk* on the screen as well? The curtness of these icons is one of my pet peeves about the Macintosh. I know — you're clever and smart (because, of course, you're smart enough to find help reading *Mac OS X Lion For Dummies*), so *you* know that a prohibitory sign means you should insert a startup disk. But what about everyone else?

If you encounter any of these warning icons, shown in Figure 20-1, go through the steps I outline later in this chapter. You can try different options, such as using Disk Tools and First Aid, zapping the parameter RAM (PRAM), and performing a Safe Boot. Try them in the order listed, starting with Step 1. Then, if one doesn't work, move on to the next.

Figure 20-1: Any of these means it's trouble-shooting time.

Recovering with Recovery HD

If you see a prohibitory sign (top left in Figure 20-1), spinning-disc cursor (top right), or kernel panic alert (the text in four languages that appears below the other two images) that doesn't go away when you start up your Mac, the first thing to do is attempt to repair hidden damage to your hard drive with the Disk Utility program's First Aid feature. And to do that, you'll have to boot from the Recovery HD partition. That's because you can't run Disk Utility's First Aid feature on your startup disk.

To start up from this magical disk (actually, a disk partition), here's what to do:

1. **Restart your Mac.**

2. **Press and hold ⌘+R until you see the Apple logo.**

If your Mac doesn't boot from the Recovery HD after Step 2, hold down the Option key while booting to display the built-in Startup Manager (see Figure 20-2).

If you press Option after the startup chime instead of ⌘+R, the built-in Startup Manager appears. From this screen, you can click the Recovery HD icon (see Figure 20-2) and then click the arrow below it or press Enter or Return to boot from it. Or, if you're going to boot from a disk other than the Recovery HD, you can select it here.

Figure 20-2: The built-in Startup Manager.

Pressing Option during startup displays icons for all bootable volumes it sees and allows you to select one (including the Recovery HD partition).

Click the disk you want to start up from (Lion HD in Figure 20-2) and then click the arrow below it or press Return or Enter to start up your Mac from it.

This technique is quite useful if your usual startup disk is damaged or having an identity crisis during startup and the ⌘+R trick isn't working to boot from the Recovery HD partition.

If you can boot from the Recovery HD partition (or a, external startup drive, clone, DVD-ROM, or other disk)

If you see the Mac OS X Utilities window after booting from the Recovery HD partition, hope flickers for your Mac. The fact that you can boot from another volume indicates that the problem lies in one of two places: your startup volume and/or Mac OS X itself.

Regardless of what the cause is, your Mac will probably respond to one of the techniques I discuss throughout the rest of this chapter.

Please skip to Step 1.

If you can't boot from the Recovery HD partition, (or a, external startup drive, clone, DVD-ROM, or other disk):

If you can't get your Mac to boot from the Recovery HD partition or another bootable disk, please skip to Step 5.

Step 1: Run First Aid

In most cases, after you've booted successfully from the Recovery HD or another bootable disk, the first logical troubleshooting step is to use the First Aid option in the Disk Utility application.

Every drive has several strangely named components such as B-trees, extent files, catalog files, and other creatively named invisible files. They're all involved in managing the data on your drives. Disk Utility's First Aid feature checks all those files and repairs the damaged ones.

One last thing: If you booted from a disk other than the Recovery HD partition, you'll have to find and launch Disk Utility on that disk before you can follow these instructions.

So with no further ado, here's how you make First Aid fix your hard disk:

1. **Boot from the Recovery HD volume by restarting your Mac while pressing the ⌘ and R keys.**

   The Mac OS X Utilities window appears.

2. **Select Disk Utility, and click Continue (Recovery HD).**

3. **When the Disk Utility window appears, click the First Aid tab to select that function of Disk Utility.**

4. **Click the icon for your boot hard drive at the left of the Disk Utility window (Lion HD in Figure 20-3).**

   Your boot drive is the one with Mac OS X and your Home folder on it; mine is called *Lion HD*.

5. **Click the Repair Disk button.**

   Your Mac whirs and hums for a few minutes, and the results window tells you what's going on. Ultimately, First Aid tells you (you hope) that the drive has been repaired and is now okay, as shown in Figure 20-3. If so, go back to work.

Figure 20-3: First Aid has repaired the disk and gives it a clean bill of health.

6. **Quit Disk Utility by choosing Disk Utility⇨Quit Disk Utility or by pressing ⌘+Q.**

7. **Reboot without holding any keys down.**

If First Aid finds damage that it can't fix, a commercial disk-recovery tool, such as Alsoft's DiskWarrior (my personal favorite) or Prosoft's also-excellent Drive Genius, might be able to repair the damage. And even if First Aid gave you a clean bill of health, you might want to run DiskWarrior or another third-party utility anyway, just to have a second opinion. Make sure you're running a current version; older versions might not be compatible with Mac OS X Lion boot disks.

DiskWarrior has resurrected more dead and dying hard drives for me than any other disk-repair utility I've ever tried — more than all of them combined. If you're going to buy only one utility, make sure that it's DiskWarrior. It's almost like magic.

If everything checks out with First Aid, restart and try to boot from your hard drive again.

If you still get the prohibitory sign, proceed to the next section to try a little dance called booting into Safe Mode.

Step 2: Safe Boot into Safe Mode

Booting your Mac in Safe Mode might help you resolve your startup issue by not loading nonessential (and non–Mac OS X) software at boot time. You do it by holding down the Shift key during startup.

If your Mac is set up so you don't have to log in, keep pressing the Shift key until the Finder loads completely. If you do log in to your Mac, type your password as usual, but before clicking the Log In button, press the Shift key again and hold it until the Finder loads completely.

You know you held the Shift key long enough if your Login Items don't load (assuming that you have Login Items; you can designate them in the Users & Groups System Preferences pane, although some programs create them for you).

Booting in Safe Mode does three things to help you with troubleshooting:

- ✓ It forces a directory check of the startup (boot) volume.

- ✓ It loads only required kernel extensions (some of the items in /System/Library/Extensions).

- ✓ It runs only Apple-installed essential startup items (some of the items in /Library/Startup Items and /System/Library/Startup Items). Note that the startup items in the Library folders are different from the Login Items in the Users & Groups System Preferences pane.

Taken together, these changes often work around issues caused by software or directory damage on the startup volume.

Some features don't work in Safe Mode. Among them are DVD Player, capturing video (in iMovie or other video-editing software), using an AirPort card, using some audio input or output devices, or using a USB modem. Use Safe Mode only if you need to troubleshoot a startup issue.

If your Mac boots in Safe Mode, you might be able to determine what's causing the issue by moving the contents of your Preferences folder (in Home/Library, which you can make visible by pressing the Option key when opening the Go menu) to the Desktop temporarily or by disabling Login Items (in the Users & Groups System Preferences pane). If either of these things resolves the issue, you can put preferences files back in Home/Library/Preferences a few at a time, or you can re-enable login items one at a time until you figure out which preferences file or login item is causing your problems.

If your Mac still has problems, try Step 3.

Step 3: Zapping the PRAM

Sometimes your *parameter RAM* (PRAM) becomes scrambled and needs to be reset. PRAM is a small piece of memory that's not erased or forgotten when you shut down. It keeps track of things such as

- Time-zone setting
- Startup volume choice
- Speaker volume
- Any recent kernel-panic information
- DVD region setting

To reset (a process often called *zapping*) your PRAM, restart your Mac and press ⌘+Option+P+R (that's four keys — good luck; it's okay to use your nose) until your Mac restarts itself. It's kind of like a hiccup. You might see the spinning-disc cursor for a minute or two while your Mac thinks about it — then the icon disappears, and your Mac chimes again and restarts. Most power users believe you should zap it more than once, letting it chime two, three, or even four times before releasing the keys and allowing the startup process to proceed.

Now restart your Mac without holding down any keys.

If the PRAM zap didn't fix your Mac, move on to "Step 4: Reinstalling Mac OS X."

Remember that your chosen startup disk, time zone, and sound volume are reset to their default values when you zap your PRAM. So after zapping, open the System Preferences application to reselect your usual startup disk and time zone, and set the sound volume the way you like it.

Unlike previous versions of the Mac OS, Mac OS X doesn't store display or network settings in PRAM. If you're having problems with video or networking, resetting PRAM won't help.

Step 4: Reinstalling Mac OS X

I present the procedure to reinstall the system software as a second-to-last resort when your Mac won't boot correctly because it takes the longest and is the biggest hassle. I detail this procedure at length in the appendix.

Read the Appendix, and follow the instructions. If you're still unsuccessful after that point, you have no choice but to consider Step 5. . . .

Step 5: Things to try before taking your Mac in for repair

To get your Mac up and running again, you can try any of the following:

- ✔ **Call the tech-support hotline.** Before you drag it down to the shop, try calling 1-800-SOS-APPL, the Apple Tech Support hotline. The service representatives there may be able to suggest something else that you can try. If your Mac is still under warranty, it's even free.

- ✔ **Ask a local user group for help.** Another thing you might consider is contacting your local Macintosh user group. You can find a group of Mac users near you by visiting Apple's User Group web pages at www. apple.com/usergroups.

- ✔ **Try Dr. Mac Consulting.** Shameless plug alert! You can check out my consulting services at www.boblevitus.com or call 408-627-7577. My team of expert troubleshooters does nothing but provide technical help and training to Mac users, via telephone, e-mail, and/or our unique Internet-enabled remote-control software, which allows us to see and control your Mac no matter where in the world you are.

✔ **Check whether you have RAM issues.** Here's a common problem: If you have problems immediately after installing random-access memory (RAM) — or any new hardware, for that matter — double-check that the RAM chips are properly seated in their sockets. (***Warning:*** Don't forget to shut down your Mac first.) With the power off and your Mac unplugged, remove and reinsert the RAM chips to make sure they're seated properly. If you still have problems, remove the RAM chips temporarily and see whether the problem still exists.

Follow the installation instructions that came with the RAM chips — or the ones in the booklet that came with your Mac. But even if they don't say to get rid of the static spark, you should — either by using an anti-static strap (available from most RAM sellers) or by touching an appropriate surface (such as the power-supply case inside your Mac) *before you handle RAM chips.*

If none of my suggestions works for you, and you're still seeing anything you shouldn't when you start up your Mac, you have big trouble.

You could have any one of the following problems:

✔ Your hard drive is dead.

✔ You have some other type of hardware failure.

✔ All your startup disks and your system software DVDs are defective (unlikely).

The bottom line: If you still can't start up normally after trying all the cures I list in this chapter, you almost certainly need to have your Mac serviced by a qualified technician.

If Your Mac Crashes at Startup

Startup crashes are another bad thing that can happen to your Mac. These crashes can be more of a hassle to resolve than prohibitory-sign problems, but they are rarely fatal.

You know that a *crash* has happened when you see a Quit Unexpectedly dialog, a frozen cursor, a frozen screen, or any other disabling event. A *startup crash* happens when your system shows a crash symptom any time between the moment you flick the power key or switch (or restarting) and the moment you have full use of the Desktop.

Try all the steps in the previous sections *before* you panic. The easiest way to fix startup crashes (in most cases) is to just reinstall Mac OS X from the Recovery HD partition. I detail this procedure at great length in the Appendix. Read the Appendix, and follow the instructions. If you're still unsuccessful after that point, come back and reread the "Step 5: Things to try before taking your Mac in for repair" section.

Part VI
The Part of Tens

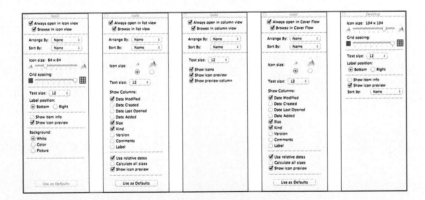

Detect Displays

Color LCD

✓ 1440 × 900
  1344 × 840
  1280 × 800
  1152 × 720
  1024 × 768 (Stretched)
  1024 × 768
  1024 × 640
  800 × 600 (Stretched)
  800 × 600

Number of Recent Items ▶
Open Displays Preferences...

In this part . . .

These last chapters are a little different — they're kind of like long top-ten lists. Although I'd like for you to believe I included them because I'm a big fan of Dave Letterman, the truth is that Wiley always includes The Part of Tens section in its *For Dummies* books. This book continues the tradition. And because Wiley pays me, I do these chapters how I'm asked. (The truth is, I think it's fun.)

First, I tell you how to speed up your Mac experience. I then move on to a subject near and dear to my heart — awesome things for your Mac that are worth spending money on. Last but not least is a collection of great Mac-related websites.

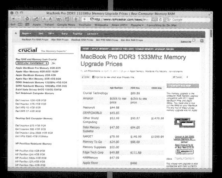

Almost Ten Ways to Speed Up Your Mac Experience

This chapter is for speed demons only. At some time in their Mac lives, most users have wished that their machines would work faster — even those with new Macs with multiple processors. I can't help you make your processors any faster, but here's where I cover some ways to make your Mac at least *seem* faster. Better still, at least some of these tips won't cost you one red cent.

Because this is the infamous Part of Tens, the powers that be require the word *ten* in the chapter title. But try as I might, I couldn't come up with ten ways to speed up your Mac. The nine tips that follow were the best I could do. So if you think of another one (or two) great ways to speed up your Mac, please send them to me at Lion4Dummies@boblevitus.com. If your suggestion is really good, I'll include it in the next printing and give you full credit for thinking of it!

Use Those Keyboard Shortcuts

Keyboard shortcuts (see Table 21-1 for a nice little list of the most useful ones) can make navigating your Mac a much faster experience compared with constantly using the mouse, offering these benefits:

- If you use keyboard shortcuts, your hands stay focused on the keyboard, reducing the amount of time that you remove your hand from the keyboard to fiddle with the mouse.

- If you memorize keyboard shortcuts with your head, your fingers will memorize them too.

- The more keyboard shortcuts you use, the faster you can do what you're doing.

Trust me when I say that using the keyboard shortcuts for commands you use often can save you a ton of effort and hours upon hours of time.

Make a list of keyboard shortcuts you want to memorize, and tape it to your monitor or somewhere where you'll see it all the time when using your Mac. (Heck, make a photocopy of Table 21-1!)

Table 21-1		Great Keyboard Shortcuts
Keyboard Shortcut	*What It's Called*	*What It Does*
⌘+O	Open	Opens the selected item.
⌘+. (period)	Cancel	Cancels the current operation in many programs, including the Finder. The Esc key often does the same thing as Cancel.
⌘+P	Print	Brings up a dialog that enables you to print the active window's contents. (See Chapter 15 for info on printing.)
⌘+X	Cut	Cuts whatever you select and places it on the Clipboard. (I cover the Clipboard in Chapter 6.)
⌘+C	Copy	Copies whatever you select and places it on the Clipboard.
⌘+V	Paste	Pastes the contents of the Clipboard at the spot where your cursor is.
⌘+F	Find	Brings up a Find window in the Finder; brings up a Find dialog in most programs.
⌘+A	Select All	Selects the entire contents of the active window in many programs, including the Finder.
⌘+Z	Undo	Undoes the last thing you did in many programs, including the Finder.
⌘+Shift+?	Help	Brings up the Mac Help window in the Finder; usually, the shortcut to summon Help in other programs.
⌘+Q	Quit	Perhaps the most useful keyboard shortcut of all — quits the current application (but not the Finder because the Finder is always running).
⌘+Shift+Q	Log Out	Logs out the current user. The login window appears on-screen until a user logs in.
⌘+Delete	Move to Trash	Moves the selected item to the Trash.

Improve Your Typing Skills

One way to make your Mac seem faster is to make your fingers move faster. The quicker you finish a task, the quicker you're on to something else. Keyboard shortcuts are nifty tools, and improving your typing speed and accuracy *will* save you time, plus you'll get stuff done faster if you're not always looking down at the keys when you type.

As your typing skills improve, you also spend less time correcting errors or editing your work.

The speed and accuracy that you gain has an added bonus: When you're a decent touch typist, your fingers fly even faster when you use those nifty keyboard shortcuts. (I list a gaggle of these in the preceding section, in Table 21-1.)

An easy way to improve your keyboarding skills is by using a typing tutor program such as Ten Thumbs Typing Tutor ($25.95 at www.tenthumbs typingtutor.com) or aTypeTrainer4Mac (free at http://homepage.mac.com/typetrainer4mac/Menu1.html).

Resolution: It's Not Just for New Year's Anymore

A setting that you can change to potentially improve your Mac's performance is the resolution of your monitor. Most modern monitors and video cards (or onboard video circuitry, depending on which Mac model you use) can display multiple degrees of screen resolution. You change your monitor's display resolution in the same place where you choose the number of colors you want: the Display System Preferences pane. Select your resolution choice from the Resolutions list on the left side of this tab.

In Displays System Preferences, select the Show Displays in Menu Bar check box to change resolutions and color depth without opening System Preferences. You can then select your resolution from the Displays menu that appears near the right end of your menu bar, as shown in Figure 21-1.

Here's the deal on display resolution: The first number is the number of pixels (color dots) that run horizontally, and the second number is the number of lines running vertically. It used to be that fewer pixels refreshed faster. But with LCD and LED (flat-panel) monitors and notebooks, this isn't always true. I have to admit that the speed difference between resolutions these days is a lot less important than it used to be. In fact, I can almost never tell the difference between one and the other. Furthermore, because you can see more on-screen at higher resolutions, a higher resolution reduces the amount of scrolling that you have to do and lets you have more open windows on the screen. Finally, the highest resolution is almost always the "native" resolution of that display, which means it will usually look the sharpest. So you could just as easily say that higher resolutions can speed up your Mac experience as well.

Bottom line: Choose a resolution based on what looks best and works best for you. That said, if your Mac seems slow at its current resolution, try a lower resolution, and see whether it feels faster.

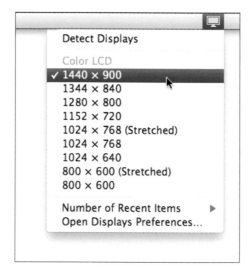

Figure 21-1: The handy Displays menu.

Although you can use Mac OS X at resolutions of less than 1,024 x 768, Apple has designed the OS X windows and dialogs on the assumption that your resolution will be *at least* 1,280 x 800. So if you choose a resolution lower than that, some interface elements in some windows or programs may be drawn partially (or completely) off-screen. Just keep that in mind if you choose a resolution below 1,280 x 800.

A Mac with a View — and Preferences, Too

The type of icon display and the Desktop background that you choose affect how quickly your screen updates in the Finder. You can set and change these choices in the View Options window. From the Finder, choose View➪Show View Options (or use the keyboard shortcut ⌘+J).

The View Options window, like your old friend the contextual menu, is . . . well, contextual: Depending on what's active when you choose it from the View menu, you see one of four similar versions (shown in Figure 21-2). From left to right, the figure shows folders in icon view, folders in list view, folders in column view, folders in Cover Flow view, and the Desktop.

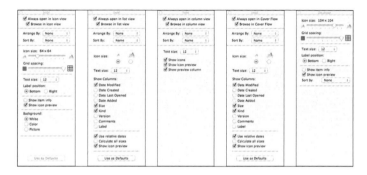

Figure 21-2: Your choices in the View Options windows for icon view, list view, column view, Cover Flow view, and the Desktop.

A handful of settings can affect the speed of your Mac or your ability to see what you want quickly:

✔ **Icon size:** The smaller the icon, the faster the screen updates, especially if the folder has many graphic files with *thumbnails* (those little icon pictures that represent the big picture the file contains).

In the icon view of the View Options window, moving the Icon Size slider to the left makes icons smaller and faster; moving it to the right makes them bigger and slower. In list view, select one of the two Icon Size radio buttons to choose smaller (faster) or larger (slower) icons. The difference is greater if you have an older Mac.

✔ **Calculate All Sizes:** I recommend that you deselect the Calculate All Sizes check box in the View Options window for list view. If you activate this option, the Finder calculates the size of every folder of every open window in list view and displays that number in the Size column. At least to me, the screen feels as though it redraws faster with this feature turned off.

If you want to know how big a folder is, you can always just click it and choose File➪Get Info (or use the keyboard shortcut, ⌘+I).

✔ **Show Columns:** When it comes to speed, don't worry about the Show Columns check boxes in the View Options window for list view — Date Modified, Date Created, Size, Kind, Version, and Comments. The effect of these items on screen updating is pretty small these days, so your choice should probably be made according to the specific information you want to see in Finder windows, not on whether choosing them slows down your Mac.

The Use As Defaults buttons at the bottom of the icon and list View Options windows set the default appearance for *all* Finder windows of that type. If you don't click the Use As Defaults button, any changes you make apply only to the active window (bobl in Figure 21-2). Note that column view windows and the Desktop don't have a Use As Defaults button; in both cases, any changes you make automatically become the defaults.

Get a New, Faster Model

Apple keeps putting out faster and faster Macs at lower and lower prices. But some Mac models still ship with a paltry 2GB of RAM. Yes, it's officially enough RAM to run Lion, but I say it's not enough to run it at its best.

Check out the latest iMacs and MacBook minis — they're excellent values. Or if you crave portability, MacBooks, MacBook Airs, and MacBook Pros are rocking good computers and have never been less expensive. You might even consider a used Mac that's faster than yours. eBay (www.ebay.com) has hundreds of used Macs up for auction at any given time. Shopping on eBay might just get you a better Mac at an outstanding price. Give it a try!

Another excellent option is to visit the Apple web site and search for refurbished equipment. You can frequently save hundreds of dollars by purchasing a slightly used Mac that has been refurbished to factory specifications by Apple. Another advantage to refurbs is that they come with an Apple warranty. If you're on a tight budget, definitely check it out.

You Can Never Have Too Much RAM!

You get a lot of bang for your buck when you upgrade your Mac's RAM. Get an additional 2GB or 4GB; you can never have too much. Your Mac will run better with at least 4GB of RAM, which will cost you under $100 in most cases and can be installed by anyone. Yes, anyone — the instructions are right there in your User Guide booklet, or you can find them at the Apple Technical Support pages (www.apple.com/support; search for *RAM upgrade* and your Mac model).

Unless, that is, you own a MacBook Air. The MacBook Air is exceedingly difficult to open, and Apple frowns upon users opening their MacBook Air. You might want to opt for the services of an authorized, certified Mac cracker-opener to perform your MacBook Air RAM upgrade. Or not.

Get an Accelerated Graphics Card

An accelerated graphics card is designed to speed up one thing: the screen-update rate. They're extremely popular with graphic-arts professionals and with gamers. Accelerated graphics cards blast pixels onto your screen at amazing speeds. And because the OS X Quartz Extreme imaging architecture hands off part of its load to the processor on an accelerated graphics card, it might even make your Mac's other tasks faster because it does some of the work that your Mac's main processor (CPU) used to do.

That's the good news.

The bad news is that you can use a graphics accelerator only if your Mac has an *accelerated PCI slot* for it, which is where you install these suckers. Currently, only the Mac Pro models are capable of graphics-card upgrades.

Again, visit www.macworld.com for information on the various graphics cards available and how they compare with one another. Cards start at around $100 and go up from there. And remember, the older your Mac, the greater the performance boost you'll see.

Get a New Hard Drive

Depending on how old your Mac is, a faster hard drive could provide a substantial speedup. Because you have a Mac with an Intel processor ('cause Macs with older PowerPC processors can't run Lion), the internal hard drive that came with your Mac is probably pretty fast already. Unless you also need more storage space, a new hard drive is probably not the best way to spend your bucks.

On the other hand, if you have an older model, a faster (and larger) hard drive — whether FireWire, USB, or Thunderbolt — could be just the ticket.

FireWire and Thunderbolt are the fastest *busses* (data pathways) you can use for external devices on most Macs.

FireWire, considered (until quite recently) the state of the art in connecting devices that need fast transfer speeds, is used to connect devices that require high-speed communication with your Mac — hard drives, CD burners, scanners, camcorders, and such. It's also the fastest bus that many Macs support natively.

Note that all current Mac models that *do* have FireWire have a type called FireWire 800. It uses a different type of cable from FireWire 400, which was found on older Macs. If you get a device that has FireWire 400, and your Mac has only FireWire 800 (or vice versa), it'll work as long as you get a FireWire 400-to-FireWire-800 adapter cable, available at the Apple Store and many other places.

Thunderbolt, which is available only on the newest Mac models, is the fastest bus around by far. That said, there are few Thunderbolt peripherals at this writing, and I've yet to see a single device with Thunderbolt cross my desk for testing. So while Thunderbolt shows much promise, I can't tell you much more about it at this juncture.

If you must use USB, make sure you get USB 2 and not plain old USB (Universal Serial Bus). Plain ol' USB might work, but it's as slow as molasses by comparison. (Plain ol' USB runs at about 3 percent of the speed of FireWire.)

USB 2, on the other hand, transfers data at roughly the same speed as FireWire. So if you have the need for speed, be sure you opt for a FireWire, USB 2 or Thunderbolt-equipped external hard drive and not an old, stale, plain ol' USB model.

The good news is that whatever you choose, you can usually just plug it in and start using it. Ninety-nine percent of the time, there's nothing more to it!

Get a Solid State Drive (SSD)

The latest and greatest storage device is called a Solid State Drive or SSD. It uses flash memory in place of a mechanical hard drive's spinning platters, which means, among other things, that there are no moving parts.

Another benefit is that they perform most operations at up to twice the speed of mechanical drives.

The bad news is that they're expensive — ten or more times more than a mechanical hard drive with the same capacity. That said, many users report it's the best money they've ever spent on an upgrade.

I'm definitely getting one in my next Mac.

Ten Ways to Make Your Mac Better by Throwing Money at It

*T*his is one of my favorite chapters. I love souping up my Macs. I live to find ways of working smarter, saving time or hand motion, and coaxing my Mac to do more work in less time. So it gives me great pleasure to share in this chapter my favorite top ten things that you can buy for your Mac to tweak it and make it faster, easier to use, and (I hope) more fun.

The items listed in this chapter are things I have, use every day, love dearly, and would (and probably will!) buy again.

RAM

RAM, or *random-access memory,* is your computer's primary working memory. The more you have, the smoother your Mac runs — period. If you have only 2GB in your Mac, you'll like your Mac *a lot* better if you upgrade to 4GB or more. If you like to do more than a few things at the same time, more RAM will make you a much happier camper. (For what it's worth, RAM has never been cheaper than it is today — and it's worth every penny.)

I know I mention it in the previous chapter, but in addition to speeding up your Mac, more RAM makes using your Mac better in other ways. For example, when you have plenty of RAM, you can open many programs at the same time without a performance penalty. I have 16GB in my Mac Pro. I almost always have the 15 or 20 programs I use most open at all times. Then all my favorite applications are available instantly, and I don't have to wait while a program launches.

Right this moment, for example, I have 17 programs running, as shown in Figure 22-1. And even so, Activity Monitor tells me I've still got more than 6GB of RAM available, and my Mac is still quite fast and responsive.

Figure 22-1: Here's what my Dock looked like a few seconds ago.

It's also easy as pie to install RAM in most Macs made this decade. Chances are good that the manual for your Mac includes step-by-step instructions simple enough for a 9-year-old to follow. I know, because I once asked my (then) 9-year-old son to do it. Which he did — and with no trouble, either.

Backup Software and/or Hardware

Only two kinds of Mac users exist: those who have lost data and those who are going to. If your work means anything to you, you had better back it up before it's too late. If you have a spare hard drive, by all means use the cool (and free) Time Machine software that comes with Mac OS X Lion. If you want to create multiple backups to several different devices or types of media (DVD-R, CD-R, Tape, and so on), invest in the appropriate hardware and software.

In case you missed it, you can find a lot of info about backup software and hardware in Chapter 18.

A Better Monitor (Or a Second One)

If you have a tiny monitor, get a bigger one. With a larger monitor, you spend less time scrolling and rearranging windows, and more time getting actual work done — which is a good thing, right?

The best thing about it is that current Macs let you use two monitors as though they were a single display. For example, my main computer setup is a Mac Pro with one 30-inch and one 24-inch flat-panel LCD displays. It's an awesome setup — one that I highly recommend. With two monitors, I keep the menu bar and most windows I'm working with on the big display. Then, with programs like Adobe Photoshop (which has lots of floating palettes), I put some (or all) of the palettes on smaller monitor so I can see more of the document I'm working on. And so on.

Another thing Macs can do with two monitors is mirror what's on one display on the second one. So you can work with one display facing you and point the other one (or a projector) at the audience so they can see what you're doing, too.

Flat-panel LCD displays have come down dramatically in price over the past few years. If you can afford a bigger display, or a second one, I promise you'll love it.

A Fast Internet Connection

Not all DSL and cable Internet connections are equal. In my opinion, a faster Internet connection equals a better experience. Check the prices for higher-speed digital subscriber line (DSL) or cable modem connections. Or threaten to switch and see what kind of deal you can wrangle for a faster connection.

Once you do, web pages that took a while to load appear on-screen almost instantly. And streaming audio and video play with few, if any, hiccups.

If you can afford a faster tier of cable/DSL (from around $30–40/month in most places) and live in an area where you can get faster cable modem or DSL (not all places can yet), it will change the way you use the Internet. For more on setting up an Internet connection, see Chapter 10.

I pay a bit more for the fastest premium cable Internet access offered by my cable operator. It's up to twice as fast as the "standard" speed package — and it's worth every penny.

Games

Gaming on the Mac has never been better, and the game developers are getting better and better at coaxing even more performance out of Mac OS X.

Some of the games I love include *Bejeweled 3, Angry Birds,* and every pinball game LittleWing (www.littlewingpinball.com) has ever created. Try one — you'll be amazed at how far computer gaming has come.

Multimedia Titles

Many great games, references, and educational titles come on CD-ROM or DVD-ROM these days. My favorite is *World Book,* which makes use of many Mac features to deliver an encyclopedia that's both authoritative and fun to use. You'll love it, and so will your kids. Remember, your Mac is more than just a computer — it's a full-blown multimedia player. Enjoy it.

Don't forget that all Macs (but the MacBook Air) can also play video DVDs like those you rent at Blockbuster or NetFlix.

Some Big Honking Speakers with a Subwoofer

Face it: Macs have crummy speakers (or, worse, only *one* crummy speaker). With a decent set of speakers, games are more fun, music sounds like music instead of AM radio, and the voiceovers in your multimedia titles suddenly become intelligible. If you're into sound, you'll enjoy your Mac much more if you add a set of window-rattling speakers, preferably with a massive sub-woofer to provide that booming bass that sound lovers crave. So crank it up! I'm partial to Blue Sky's EXO 2.1 Stereo Monitoring Speaker System (`www.abluesky.com`), which is totally awesome but not cheap (around $450). But any good speakers kick the stuffing out of the speakers built into any Mac.

A killer set of speakers makes watching movies on your Mac a zillion times better.

A New Mouse and/or Keyboard

If you don't really love the mouse or keyboard you're using, do yourself a favor, and beat them to death with a hammer. Then buy a mouse or keyboard that suits you. You'll be so much happier if you upgrade to a mouse that's easier to move around, more comfortable to use, and maybe even has extra buttons and/or a scroll wheel. Or consider Apple's Magic Trackpad so you can enjoy gestures like your laptop brethren and sisteren.

My favorite keyboard is an old Microsoft Natural Ergonomic Keyboard 4000. It's big and strangely shaped, but no other keyboard is as comfortable for my fat fingers.

You'll be amazed at how much easier it is to work with a mouse, trackpad, or keyboard that fits your hand size and needs.

Most third-party mice and keyboards work flawlessly on a Mac.

Also consider ditching the silly little keyboard that came with your iMac, Mac Pro, or whatever. Third-party Mac keyboards on the market today are a huge improvement over what came with your Mac.

I'm partial to third-party keyboards and mice because I can't stand any of the bundled Apple mice or keyboards. They're aesthetically pleasing but not very good compared with almost all third-party mice and keyboards.

I'm partial to so-called ergonomic keyboards, which I find more comfortable for prolonged writing sessions. I also think I type faster with this kind of keyboard. My current axe is a Microsoft Natural Ergonomic Keyboard 4000. Even though it's a Windows keyboard and the modifier keys are mislabeled (the ⌘ key says *Alt,* and the Option key says *Start* and has a Windows logo on it), Microsoft offers excellent Mac OS X drivers for it.

A MacBook or MacBook Pro

You need a laptop because one Mac is never enough. With a portable Mac, you can go anywhere and continue to compute. And MacBooks, MacBook Airs, and MacBook Pros come with Apple AirPort Extreme wireless networking, so you can surf the Net, print, and share files from the couch, the pool, the airport (the kind with airplanes and a lowercase *a* and *p)* — or Starbucks, for that matter.

Ten (Or So) Great Websites
for Mac Freaks

A s much as I would love to think that this book tells you everything you
need to know about using your Mac, I know better. You have a lot more
to discover about using your Mac, and new tools and products come out
every single day.

The best way to gather more information than you could ever possibly soak
up about all things Macintosh is to hop onto the web. There, you can find
news, *freeware* and *shareware* (try-before-you-buy software) to download,
troubleshooting sites, tons of news and information about your new favorite
OS, and lots of places to shop.

The sites in this chapter are the best, most chock-full-o'-stuff places
on the web for Mac users. By the time you finish checking out
these websites, you'll know so much about your Mac and
Mac OS X Lion that you'll feel like your brain is in danger
of exploding. On the other hand, you might just feel a
whole lot smarter. Happy surfing!

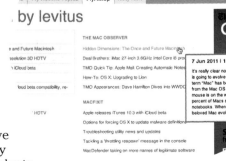

MacFixIt

www.macfixit.com

Long ago, on an Internet you'd hardly recognize
today, troubleshooting guru Ted Landau created an
excellent troubleshooting site to help Mac users solve
common problems and keep current on compatibility
issues with new system software and third-party products.

It's now an arm of web behemoth CNET, but it's still a good resource when you have a problem with your Mac. Chances are pretty good that you'll find a solution at MacFixIt.

Fortunately, though no longer affiliated with MacFixIt, Ted still writes regularly for *Macworld* and *The Mac Observer,* which are both on my Top Ten list. Read on.

Macworld

www.macworld.com

This site describes itself thusly: "News, info, and opinion by Mac users, for Mac users."

And it's true. Macworld is perhaps the best and most comprehensive source of product information for Mac (and other Apple device) users. It's especially strong for comparative reviews of Mac and iPhone/iPad products. For example, when you want to know which inkjet printer or digital camera is the best in its price class, Macworld.com can almost certainly offer guidance. And, you won't merely find product information here; you'll find it accompanied by expert opinions and professional fact checking.

Put another way, I trust the writers and editors at Macworld more than I trust the writers and editors of any other Mac-oriented website. Any other Mac-oriented site, that is, except for . . .

The Mac Observer

www.macobserver.com

The Mac Observer gives you Mac news, views, reviews, and much more.

Disclosure: I write a column — "Dr. Mac's Rants & Raves" — whenever the mood strikes me. I'm also a reviews editor and contribute the occasional review. But I loved The Mac Observer long before I wrote a word for it.

I love that The Mac Observer offers thoughtful opinion pieces in addition to tons of news and product reviews. The quality of the writing by many (if not most) of The Mac Observer staff is a cut above what you'll find at most other sites.

CNET Downloads (formerly VersionTracker)

www.versiontracker.com or http://download.cnet.com/mac/

For free software or shareware, check out the CNET Downloads Mac Download section. It's one of the best sites in the world for software to use with Lion (or any version of Mac OS, for that matter). It's also terrific for getting the latest version of any kind of software: commercial, shareware, and/or freeware. VersionTracker is a virtual treasure trove of software and updates, and it's worth visiting even when you aren't looking for anything in particular.

I love this site and try to visit it several times a week. (I know — I should get a life.)

MacInTouch

www.macintouch.com

For the latest in Mac news, updated every single day, check out MacInTouch. Authored by longtime *MacWeek* columnist Ric Ford and his staff of newshounds, along with a legion of knowledgeable readers, this site keeps you on the bleeding edge of Mac news — including software updates, virus alerts, and Apple happenings. It also offers extensive and unbiased reviews of most Apple hardware and software soon after its release.

I consider MacInTouch essential for keeping up with what's new and cool for your Mac, and have since its inception in 1994.

Alltop

http://mac.alltop.com

Alltop aggregates news from a variety of websites and then serves them up in an appealing format that allows you to scan a large number of headlines and summaries from a wide variety of sources in a very short time. This is a case where a picture is worth 1,000 words, so check out Figure 23-1.

Figure 23-1 shows the custom Alltop page I created at my.alltop.com/levitus so I could scan the headlines of my favorite websites quickly and easily. My cursor is hovering over a story ("Hidden Dimensions: The Once and Future Macintosh"), which is one of those Mac Observer opinion pieces I mention earlier in this chapter.

Figure 23-1: Hover the cursor over any headline, and Alltop provides a concise summary of the story.

Notice the little summary, which appears only when I hover my cursor over that story, which is in the little box with "7 June 2011 | 11:20 am" as its headline in Figure 23-1. That's Alltop's killer feature, at least in my humble opinion.

You can build your own customized Alltop page at `http://my.alltop.com`.

Alltop isn't just for Mac news. There are Alltop pages for hundreds of subjects, including

Marketing: `http://marketing.alltop.com`

Science: `http://science.alltop.com`

Gadgets: `http://gadgets.alltop.com`

Filmmaking: `http://filmmaking.alltop.com`

. . . and literally hundreds more. Alltop has become one of my favorite places to get the information I need quickly and easily.

Apple Support and Knowledge Base

`www.apple.com/support`

Do you have a technical question about any version of Mac OS or any Apple product — including Mac OS X Lion? March your question right over to the Apple Support and Knowledge Base page, where you can find searchable archives of tech notes, software update information, and documentation.

The Knowledge Base is especially useful if you need info about your old Mac; Apple archives all its info here. Choose among a preset list of topics or products, and type a keyword to research. You're rewarded with a list of helpful documents. Clicking any one of these entries (they're all links) takes you right to the info you seek. The site even has tools that can help narrow your search.

The site also offers a section with user discussions of Apple-related topics. Although not officially sanctioned or monitored by Apple, it's often the best place to gain insights, especially on slightly esoteric or obscure issues not covered in the Knowledge Base.

Ramseeker

www.ramseeker.com

One of the best ways to make your Mac better is to buy more random-access memory (RAM). RAM is the readily available memory that your computer uses; the more you have, the smoother programs run. Although Mac OS X might run on a Mac with less than 512MB of RAM, it works much better and faster with more than that — at least 1GB, in my opinion. As cheap as RAM is today, the price that you pay for it can still vary quite a bit. The best way I know to get the lowdown on RAM prices is to use the Ramseeker feature of this site, which surveys multiple vendors daily and then organizes current memory prices by Mac type.

Figure 23-2 shows how it works.

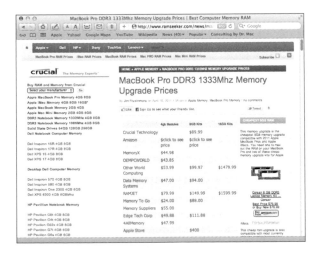

Figure 23-2: Ramseeker serves up prices for RAM upgrades from 11 vendors, including Apple.

Other World Computing

www.macsales.com

Other World Computing has become the "go to" place for Mac peripherals. Whether you need RAM, hard drives, optical drives, video cards, processor upgrades, cables, discs, or anything else you can think of, Other World Computing probably has it at a reasonable price. Because of its inexpensive and reliable delivery and a solid guarantee of every item, you can't go wrong buying from OWC.

EveryMac.com

www.everymac.com

The author of this site claims that it's "the complete guide" to every Macintosh, Mac-compatible, and upgrade card "in the world." You can't argue with that (unless you've done a staggering amount of research). Check out the Forum and Q&A sections (recently updated for Lion) for answers to Mac-related questions.

Inside Mac Games

www.imgmagazine.com

Inside Mac Games is the best of the Mac gaming sites on the web (at least in my humble opinion). Order CDs of game demos, download shareware, check out game preview movies, or shop for editors and emulators. Find forum camaraderie and troubleshoot gaming problems, too.

dealmac

www.dealmac.com

Shopping for Mac stuff? Go to dealmac ("How to go broke saving money," this site boasts) first to find out about sale prices, rebates, and other bargain opportunities on upgrades, software, peripherals, and more.

Dr. Mac Consulting

www.boblevitus.com

Dr. Mac Consulting is (in all due modesty) my cool new troubleshooting, training, and technical-support site, designed just for Mac users. With several expert technicians on staff, Dr. Mac Consulting provides jargon-free expert technical help at a fair price, regardless of your physical location — and usually on the same day. Let one of our experts (or even me) provide high-quality Macintosh troubleshooting, technical support, software or system training, prepurchase advice, and more! We do our thing via phone; e-mail; iChat; and/or our unique web-enabled, remote-control software (or Lion Screen Sharing), which lets us fix many common Mac ailments in less than an hour, controlling your mouse and keyboard remotely as we explain everything we're doing to you on the phone.

The next time you need help, and none of the aforementioned sites does the trick, why not let Dr. Mac Consulting make the mouse call? (So to squeak.)

Note: This crass commercial message is one of two places in the whole book where I blather on about my day job. So if there's something you want to know about your Mac or something you would like examined or fixed, we can probably help you in less than an hour. I hope you'll give it a try.

And now, back to your regularly scheduled programming.

Appendix

Installing or Reinstalling Mac OS X Lion (Only If You Have To)

*I*f Mac OS X Lion came preinstalled on a new Mac, you'll probably never need this appendix.

If you're thinking about reinstalling because something has gone wrong with your Mac, know that a Mac OS X reinstallation should be your last resort. Be sure you've tried all the stuff in Chapter 20 before even *thinking* about reinstalling OS X. If nothing else fixes your Mac, reinstalling Mac OS X could well be your final option before invasive surgery (that is, trundling your Mac to a repair shop). You don't *want* to reinstall OS X if something easier can correct the problem. So if you have to do a reinstallation, realize that this is more or less your last hope (this side of the dreaded screwdriver, anyway).

In this appendix, you discover all you need to know to install or reinstall OS X, if you should have to. I say reinstalling is a hassle because although you won't lose the contents of your Home folder, applications you've installed, or the stuff in your Documents folder (unless something goes horribly wrong or you have to reformat your hard drive), you might lose the settings for some System Preferences, which means you'll have to reconfigure those panes manually after you reinstall. And you might have to reinstall drivers for third-party hardware such as mice, keyboards, printers, tablets, and the like. Finally, you might have to reregister or reinstall some of your software.

It's not the end of the world, but it's almost always inconvenient. That said, reinstalling OS X almost always corrects all but the most horrifying and malignant of problems. And as you soon see, the process in Lion is (compared with root-canal work, income taxes, or previous versions of Mac OS X) relatively painless. I stay with you through it all, though; don't you worry about a thing.

How to Install (or Reinstall) Mac OS X

In theory, you should have to install Lion only once, or never if your Mac came with Lion preinstalled. And in a perfect world, that would be the case. But you might find occasions when you have to install/reinstall it, such as

- ✔ If you get a Mac that didn't come with Mac OS X Lion preinstalled
- ✔ If you have a catastrophic hard-drive crash that requires you to initialize (format) your boot drive
- ✔ If you buy an external hard drive and want it to be capable of being your Mac's startup disk (that is, a bootable disk)
- ✔ If you replace your internal hard drive with a larger one
- ✔ If any essential Mac OS X files become damaged or corrupted, or are deleted or renamed

The following instructions do double duty: They're what you do to install OS X for the first time on a Mac, and they're also what you do if something really bad happens to the copy of OS X that you boot your Mac from. The instructions offered here describe both the process for installing and the process for reinstalling OS X.

Here's how to install (or reinstall) OS X, step by step:

1. **Boot from your Recovery HD partition by restarting your Mac while holding down the ⌘+R keys.**

   The Mac OS X Utilities window appears. Select Reinstall Mac OS X, and click Continue. The Mac OS X Lion splash screen appears. Click Continue.

   The Language Chooser window appears. Here's where you begin the process of installing or reinstalling Mac OS X.

2. **Unless you want to use a language other than English for the main language of Mac OS X, click the Continue button (which looks like an arrow).**

   If you do prefer another language, select the language by clicking its name and then click the Continue button.

   If you're not connected to the Internet, choose a Wi-Fi network from the AirPort menu in the top-right corner.

3. **When the Mac OS X Utilities screen appears, choose Reinstall Mac OS X and then click the Continue button.**

A sheet drops down, asking whether you agree to the terms of the license agreement. If you don't, you can't go any farther, so I advise you to go ahead and click the Agree button.

4. **Choose the disk on which you want to reinstall Mac OS X by clicking its icon once in the pane where you select a disk.**

5. **To begin the installation, click the Install button.**

The operating system takes 30 to 60 minutes to install, so now might be a good time to take a coffee break. When the install is finished, your Mac restarts itself. If you were reinstalling Mac OS X on a hard disk that it had been installed on previously, you're done. You can now begin using your new, freshly installed (and ideally trouble-free) copy of Mac OS X.

If you're installing Lion on a hard disk for the first time, however, you still have one last step to complete. After your Mac reboots, the Setup Assistant window appears. You need to work your way through the Setup Assistant's screens as described in the following section.

Getting Set Up with Setup Assistant

Assuming that your installation (or reinstallation) process goes well and your Mac restarts itself, the next thing you should see (and hear) is a short, colorful movie that ends by transforming into the first Setup Assistant screen, fetchingly named *Welcome*.

To tiptoe through the Setup Assistant, follow these steps:

1. **When the Welcome screen appears, choose your country from the list by clicking it once and then click the Continue button.**

If your country doesn't appear in the list, select the Show All check box, which causes a bunch of additional countries to appear.

After you click Continue, the Select Your Keyboard screen appears.

2. **Choose a keyboard layout from the list by clicking it once; then click Continue.**

If you're an American (or want to use an American keyboard setup), click the U.S. listing. If you prefer a different country's keyboard layout, select the Show All check box, and a bunch of additional countries' keyboards (as well as a pair of Dvorak keyboard layouts) appear in the list. Choose the one you prefer by clicking it — and *then* click Continue.

The Migration Assistant (also known as the Do You Already Own a Mac?) screen appears next. If this is a brand-new Mac or you're installing Mac OS X Lion on a Mac and have an older Mac nearby, you can transfer all your important files and settings by following the on-screen instructions and connecting the new and old Macs via FireWire or Ethernet cable. Just follow the instructions given by the Migration Assistant and then chill for a while; it'll probably take an hour or more to transfer your files and settings from the old Mac to the new one.

The Select a Wireless Network screen appears.

3. **Click the name of the wireless network you use to connect to the Internet; then click Continue.**

   If you don't see the network you want to use, click Rescan. If you don't use a wireless network, click Different Network Setup and then choose one of the available options, or choose My Computer Does Not connect to the Internet. Click Continue.

   The Enter Your Apple ID screen appears.

4. **If you have an Apple ID, type it (such as** stevejobs@me.com**) and your password in the appropriate fields and then click Continue; if you don't have an Apple ID, just leave the fields blank and click Continue.**

   Click the Learn More button to find out more about an Apple ID and what it can do for you. In a nutshell, it lets you make one-click purchases at the iTunes Store, iPhoto, or the Apple Store. If you get one now, you also get a free, limited 60-day trial account with MobileMe. When you're finished reading, click OK and then click Continue.

   The Registration Information screen appears.

5. **Fill out the fields (name, address, phone number, and so on) and then click Continue.**

   If you're interested in what Apple will and won't do with this information, click the Privacy button on this screen and read the Privacy Policy.

   The A Few More Questions screen appears.

6. **Choose an option from the Where Will You Primarily Use This Computer and What Best Describes What You Do pop-up menus.**

7. **Select the Stay in Touch check box if you want to receive news, software updates, and other information from Apple and then click Continue.**

   The Create Your Account screen appears.

8. **Fill in the Full Name, Account Name (sometimes called Short Name), Password, Verify Password, and Password Hint fields; then click Continue.**

This first account that you create will automatically have administrator privileges for this Mac. You can't easily delete or change the name you choose for this account, so think it through before you click Continue.

You can't click the Continue button until you've filled in the first two fields. Because a password is optional, you can choose to leave the last three fields — Password, Verify Password, and Password Hint — blank if you like. If you do, your Mac warns you that without a password, your Mac won't be secure. If that's okay, click OK. If you change your mind and want to have a password, click Cancel.

The Select a Picture for This Account screen appears.

9. **Select one of the two radio buttons: Take a Snapshot or Choose from the Picture Library.**

If your Mac doesn't have a built-in camera, you don't have a choice; your only option is Choose from the Picture Library.

If you choose to take a picture, click the Take Photo Snapshot button. When the picture appears, you can change its size by using the slider control directly below the image and/or move it around in the frame by clicking your face and dragging. If you're not happy with this snapshot, click Retake a Video Snapshot. When you're happy with it, click Continue.

If you choose a select a picture from the picture library, click the picture you want to represent you — the butterfly, dog, parrot, flower, or whatever — and then click Continue.

The Thank You screen appears.

10. **Click Go.**

The Mac OS X Finder's Desktop appears.

That's it. You're done.

Index

• Symbols and Numerics •

– (minus sign), identifying tri-state check boxes, 32
32-bit mode, opening applications in, 118

• A •

About Finder, Finder menu, 107
About This Mac, 39–40
accelerated graphics card, 429
access and permissions, 323–338, 338–340
accessibility features, 366–369
Action button, 26–27, 100–101
actions, 362
Activity Monitor, 394–396
Add This Page button, 215–216
Address Book, 71, 202, 234–240, 247, 379.
    See also e-mail
administrative powers, granting, 325–328
administrative users, 323, 338–339
Administrator accounts, 323, 332
AirDrop, 111, 319
AirPort, 320–321, 396
alerts (beeps), 68, 203, 365–366
aliases, 92–96, 186. *See also* icons
All My Files command, 110–111
Alltop, 439–440
Angry Birds, 435
antialiasing, 58
antivirus programs, 384–385
App Store, 71, 366
Apple Key. *See* Command key
Apple menu, 39–40. *See also* menus
Apple online support, disabling, 20
Apple Support and Knowledge Base,
    440–441

Apple Time Capsule, 376
AppleScript, 359–361
application icons, 70, 90–92
Application Support folder, 133
applications. *See also* Launchpad; widgets;
    specific applications
  access and permissions, 330
  adding to Launchpad, 181
  App Store, 364
  launching from the Dock, 75
  open windows, displaying, 171–174
  opening documents, 143–144, 147–149
  removing from Launchpad folders, 181
  uninstalling, 181
Applications command, 111
Applications folder, 111, 127
appointments. *See* iCal
Arrange button, 100
arranging windows, 34–35
audio chat, 227–228
Auto Save, 134–139. *See also* backing up
    data; Versions
Auto-Click, enabling, 218
automatic login, disabling, 369–370, 391
automatic visual help cues, 22
automation, 361–366
Automator, 360, 361–364

• B •

Back button, 26–27, 99
Back command, 110
Back/Forward buttons, Safari, 215–216
backing up data, 18, 271–273, 376–382, 434.
    See also Auto Save; restoring data;
    Versions
Baig, Edward C., 196
beeps (alerts), 68, 203, 365–366
Bejeweled 3, 435

Bento application, 234
black triangle symbol on menus, 39
blind users, VoiceOver technology,
    357–358
blue/black/gray screen of death, 13–14
Bluetooth, 64, 314, 348–350, 369
bold fonts, 289
Bonjour, 229, 319
Bookmark Bar, 216
bookmarking, 216–218, 277. *See also*
    Reading List; Top Sites page
Boot Camp, 370–371
boot disks, 407–408
bootable partitions, 408
booting, 15, 407–408, 410–411, 413–414
bootstrapping a computer, 15
borders, printing, 309
Bove, Tony, 11
bringing windows to front, 35
build number, displaying, 40
burn folders, 192
burning CDs/DVDs, 185–192, 268–269
business cards, virtual, 235
busses, performance enhancements, 430
buttons, customizing, 55–58. *See also*
    specific buttons

• C •

Calculator, 393–394
calendars, 198–200
calibrating monitors, 397
camcorders, importing video from, 283.
    See also digital cameras
capitalization, keyboard shortcuts, 41
Carbon Copy Cloner, 410
case sensitivity, keyboard shortcuts, 41
CDs/DVDs, 185–192, 268, 331, 347. *See also*
    disks; DVD player
Chambers, Mark L., 2, 196
character viewer, 59–61
chat. *See* FaceTime
chats, access and permissions, 331
chatting. *See* iChat
check boxes, in dialogs, 31–32

circle with slash through it. *See*
    prohibitory sign
ClamXAV, 385
clicking with a mouse. *See* Control+click;
    double-click; single-click
Close button, 26–27, 28
CNET Downloads, 438
color
    ColorSync Utility, 396–397
    DigitalColor Meter, 400
    matching, for printing, 309
Color Management For Dummies, 397
ColorSync Utility, 396–397
Command key, 41
command line interface, 406–407
comments, in icons, 118
compressing files, 164
Computer command, 111
Computer folder, 126–127
Computer level, displaying, 111
conditionals, 361–362
Connect to Server command, 112
contacts. *See* Address Book
contextual menus, 36–38
Control key, 42
Control+click, 19, 37
copy, keyboard shortcut, 42
copying. *See also* burning CDs/DVDs
    a boot disk, 408
    disk icons, 185–186
    documents, files, and folders, 158–160
    files and folders, 158–160
    icons, 158–160
Cover Flow view, keyboard shortcut, 106
cover page, printing, 310
CrashPlan, 382
currency conversion, 394
customizing. *See also* Setup Assistant;
    System Preferences; *specific features*
    buttons, 55–58
    disk menus, 85–87
    folder menus, 85–87
    fonts, 58
    keyboards, 58–62
    Launchpad, 181
    Mail, 248–249

menus, 55–58
mouse behavior, 62–64
number of recent items, 57–58
printing, 307–310
scroll bars, 56–57
title bars, 56–57
windows, 55–58
cutting icons, 159
cycling through windows, 35

● *D* ●

dancing Dock icons, 77
Dashboard, 51–54, 71, 177
dealie-boppers, 31–32
dealmac, 442
deleting. *See specific items*
deselecting icons, 162
Desktop. *See also* Dock; Finder; menus;
windows
background, performance enhancements,
425–426
check boxes, customizing, 114
definition, 24
icons, 24–25, 96–98
illustration, 24, 97
image well, 49
pictures on, 47–49
screen savers, 47–51
status bar, 98
toolbar, 98–101
Desktop & Screen Saver pane, 48–51
Desktop command, 111
Desktop folder, 111, 131
diagnostic and usage data, sending to
Apple, 392
dialogs, 31–32
digital cameras, 280–282. *See also*
camcorders
DigitalColor Meter, 398
disabled (grayed out) menu items, 38
disabled users. *See* accessibility features;
specific disabilities
disclosure triangles, 104
discs versus disks, 184. *See also* CDs/DVDs
disk drives, 17, 398, 427–428

disk icons, 70, 91–92, 150, 184–186
disk images, 400–401
disk menus, customizing, 85–87
disk partitions, 399–400. *See also*
troubleshooting, Recovery HD
partition
disk repair, 411–413
disks
aliases, creating, 186
versus discs, 184
displaying in the Dock, 85–87
ejecting, 193–194
formatting, 185
sharing, on local computers, 332–337
sharing, on remote computers, 340–344
Windows, on a Mac, 186–187
DiskWarrior (Alsoft), 413
DJ, iTunes, 270–271
Dock, 40, 78–87, 152
Dock (submenu), 40
Dock icons, 69–72, 75–81, 85–87. *See also*
specific icons
document files, displaying, 110–111
document icons, 70, 90–92
documents. *See also* printers; printing
opening, 143–149
saving, 134–140
templates, creating, 118
Documents command, 111
Documents folder, 72, 111, 131
double-click, 18, 62–63, 65
Downloads command, 111
Downloads folder, 111, 131
Dr. Mac Consulting, 415, 443
dragging with a mouse, 19
DriveGenius (Prosoft), 413
drivers, printer, 303
drop box, access and permissions, 337, 339
DropBox, 384
duplex printing, 309
duplicate, keyboard shortcut, 42
Duplicate command, 159
duplicate file names, 159
DVD Player, 275–278
DVDs. *See* CDs/DVDs

• E •

educational videos, 264
ejecting disks, 193–194
electrical power, 12, 16–17
e-mail, 227, 239–240, 331, 379. *See also*
    Address Book; Mail
emoticons, 59
emptying the Trash, 74, 116, 164
Enclosing Folder command, 110
encrypting files, 390
Energy Saver features, 17, 59, 367–369
Energy Saver pane, 50
Erase tab, 398–399
Ethernet networks, 316, 320
Ethernet ports, 316
events, 200–203, 379
EveryMac.com, 442
everyone, access and permissions,
    334–335, 337–338
EXO 2.1 Stereo Monitoring Speaker System
    (Blue Sky), 434
Exposé & Spaces pane, 171. *See also*
    Mission Control pane

• F •

FaceTime, 71, 231–232
favorite Web pages. *See* bookmarking;
    Reading List; Top Sites page
fax modems, 313–314
faxing documents, 313–314
file icons, identifying, 150
File menu, customizing labels, 115–116
file sharing. *See also* folders, sharing
    access and permissions, 323–340
    AirDrop, 111, 319
    Bonjour, 319
    icons, 119
    IP addresses, 332
    permissions, 119
    remote connections, 340–344
    setting up, 321–322
    startup disk, 333
file transfer, 229

file type, assigning to an application,
    147–148
FileMaker, 234
filename extensions, 116
files. *See also* folders; icons
    compressing, 164
    copying, 158–160
    creation date, displaying, 118, 119
    deleting, 323
    duplicate names, 159
    encrypting, 390
    extension, displaying, 119
    finding, 165–171
    versus folders, 149–150
    labels, 118
    locking, 390
    modification date, displaying, 118, 119
    moving, 160–161
    name, displaying, 119
    opening, 77–78, 143–149
    organizing, 93, 149–152
    path, displaying, 118
    previewing, 100, 119
    restoring, 379
    size, displaying, 118
    type, displaying, 118
    version, displaying, 118
FileVault, 390
filmmaking, online resources, 442
Finder, 24, 26–30, 71, 89–92, 107–116, 166–168.
    See also Desktop; windows
finding
    Dock icons original, 78
    files and folders, 100, 165–171
    new music for playlists, 269–270
finger movement, 62. *See also* gestures
firewalls, 385–388
FireWire, performance enhancements, 430
First Aid, 398, 411–413
flagging e-mail messages, 245
flash drives, performance enhancements,
    429
flashing-question-mark disk. *See*
    prohibitory sign
Flight Tracker widget, 54–55
flights, tracking, 54–55
folder icons, 70, 91–92

folder menus, customizing, 85–87
folders. *See also* files; icons; *specific folders*
 adjoining triangles, 104
 copying, 158–160
 creating, 42, 153, 181
 displaying in the Dock, 85–87
 versus files, 149–150
 finding, 165–171
 frequently used, on the Dock, 152
 moving, 160–161
 navigating to, 112
 nested, 125–126
 opening, 115, 143–149, 153–154
 organizing, 93, 149–152
 path, displaying, 109–110
 previewing contents, 105
 renaming, 181
 sharing, 118, 331–337, 340–344. *See also*
  file sharing
 Smart, 154–157
 spring-loading, 115, 153–154
 structure, 124–133
 subfolders, 150–152
Font Book, 293–294
fonts
 antialiasing, 58
 bold, 289
 customizing, 58
 deleting, 294
 disabling, 293
 enabling, 293
 Font Book, 293–294
 Fonts folder, 133
 formatting, 289
 installing, 133, 293, 294
 italic, 289
 Library folders, 127–129
 OpenType, 293
 outlined, 289
 PostScript Type 1, 292–293
 printer, 293
 selecting, 287
 suitcase files, 293
 TextEdit, 287, 289
 TrueType, 292
 types of, 292–293

 underlined, 289
 viewing, 293
Fonts folders, 133, 292, 294
footers/headers, printing, 309
Force Quit, 40
Ford, Ric, 440
foreign languages, keyboards, 59–61
formatting disks, 185, 398–399
formatting fonts, 289
Forward button, 26–27, 99
Forward command, 110
forwarding e-mail messages, 244
freeware/shareware, 440
function keys, customizing, 59
Fusion (VMware), 186–187

gadgets, online resources, 442
games, 433, 442
GarageBand, 284
General pane, 55–58
Genius, iTunes, 269–270
gestures, 67. *See also* finger movement
get information, keyboard shortcut, 42
glowing dot, Dock icons, 77
Go menu items, 110–112
Go to Folder command, 112
Google, searching in Safari, 222–225
Grab, 401
grammar check, 290
Grapher, 402
graphic equalizer, 259
graphic files, 279–280
graphics cards, accelerated, 427
graphics in documents, 290–291
gray screen of death, 13–14
grayed out (disabled) menu items, 38
grouping calendars, 199–200
groups, access and permissions, 324, 334
Guest Account, 324
guests, access and permissions, 324
gumdrop buttons, 26–27

• H •

handwriting recognition, 369
hardware. *See also specific hardware*
    information, System Profiler, 39–40
    information about, 126–127. *See also*
        Computer folder
    startup failure, 13–14
    upgrades, performance enhancements,
        426
    zoom, 365
headers/footers, printing, 309
Help Center, Safari, 225
Help program, 12, 19–22
Hide Finder, 107–108
Hide Others, 109
highlight color, customizing, 56
Home command, 111
Home folder, 111, 130–131, 341–344
home office networks, 317–318
Hot Corners, 174–175
"How to remove Mac Defender," 384
hubs, network, 317, 320–321

• I •

iCal, 72, 196–205, 379
iChat, 225–231
iCloud service, 213. *See also* MobileMe
    service
Icon view, keyboard shortcut, 104
icons. *See also* aliases; files; folders;
        specific icons
    alias badge, 94–95
    aligning to a grid, 104
    arranging, 104
    available actions, displaying, 100
    comments, 118
    copying, 158–160
    cutting, 159
    deleting, 131, 164
    deselecting, 162
    Desktop, 24–25
    displaying, performance enhancements,
        425–426

Dock, 69–72
    file sharing, 119
    getting information about, 116–119
    labeling, 115–116
    moving, 160–161
    renaming, 163
    resizing, 26–27, 103
    selecting multiple, 161–163
    sharing, 119
    in this book, 5
iDisk, 111
iLife, 284
iLife All-in-One For Dummies, 11
illumination, keyboards, 59
image well, 49
iMovie, 284
importing
    contacts, 236
    pictures from digital cameras, 280–282
    video from camcorders, 283
incremental backups, 272, 383
index sheets, opening documents in,
        144–145
Info window, 116–119
initializing disks. *See* formatting disks
Ink, 369
Inside Mac Games, 442
Inspector window, 201
installing
    fonts, 133, 293, 294
    Mac OS X, 404, 446–449. *See also*
        reinstalling Mac OS X
    Windows on a Mac, 371
instant messaging. *See* FaceTime; iChat
Internet connection, 210–213, 348–349, 433.
        See also Web
Internet radio, 264–265
inviting event attendees, 202
IP addresses, obtaining, 332
iPhoto, buying, 284
ISPs (Internet service providers), 211
italic fonts, 289
Item Arrangement menu, 26–27
iTunes, 72, 257–273

• J •

junk-mail, filtering, 244. *See also* kill files; spam

• K •

kernel panic, 14, 412
Keyboard pane, 58–62
keyboard shortcuts, 3, 41–42, 61, 421–422. *See also specific shortcuts*
keyboard viewer, 59–61
keyboards, 30, 58–62, 366, 434–435
keychain, passwords, 402–403
kill files, 249–250. *See also* junk-mail, filtering; spam filters

• L •

labeling icons, 115–116
labels, files, 118
Landau, Ted, 437
landscape orientation, 305
laptops, benefits of, 435
Launchpad, 71, 180–181
Library folders, 127–129, 131–133
light show, iTunes, 259–260
lightning, danger to your computer, 16–17
line wrap, TextEdit, 287
List view, keyboard shortcut, 104
LittleWing, 433
local devices, definition, 316
local user groups, troubleshooting resource, 415
location services, enabling, 392
locked items, moving to Trash, 119
locking files, 390
log out, 344, 391, 422
login, 369–370, 391
login screen, disabling, 13
look and feel, changing. *See* System Preferences

• M •

Mac news, 438–440
The Mac Observer, 438
Mac peripherals, 442
Macbook, benefits of, 435
Macbook Pro, benefits of, 435
MacFixIt, 389, 437–438
Macintosh computers, advantages of, 11
Macintosh System 7.5 For Dummies, 1
MacInTouch, 389, 438
macro viruses, 383–385
Macs For Dummies, 196
MacScan, 385
Macworld, 389, 438
Magic Trackpad, 65
magnification, Dock, 84
Magnifier tool, 312
magnifying-glass icon, 168
Mail, 71, 240–256. *See also* e-mail
mailboxes, 245, 250–253
malware, 383–385
Managed accounts, 323, 332
manual backups, 380
margins, TextEdit, 289
marketing, online resources, 440
Mason, Don, 397
memory. *See* RAM
menu bar, 36
Menu Extras, 43
menus. *See also* Apple menu; submenus
   black triangle symbol, 39
   contextual, 36–38
   customizing, 55–58
   disabled (grayed out) items, 38
   highlight color, customizing, 56
   keyboard shortcuts, 41
   pull-down, 35–36
   selecting items, 19, 35–36
   special purpose, 43
Microsoft Word, 286
migrating Lion to another computer, 404
Migration Assistant, 404
Minimize button, 26–27, 28
minimizing windows, 35, 84

minus sign (-), identifying tri-state check boxes, 32
Mission Control pane, 171–180. *See also* spaces
mnemonics for keyboard shortcuts, 42
MobileMe service, 213. *See also* iCloud service
modems, 210–211, 314
monetary conversions, 394
monitors. *See also* screen
  adding, 432–433
  brightness, 368
  calibrating, 397
  cleaning, 18
  energy-saver settings, 368
  resolution, performance enhancements, 423–424
  upgrading, 434–435
mouse. *See also* scroll wheel
  accessibility features, 366–367
  behavior, customizing, 62–64
  Bluetooth, configuring, 64
  clicks, 18–19, 37, 62–63
  customizing, 62–64
  dragging, 19
  moving content by finger movement, 62
  multibutton, 38
  pointing, 18
  primary button, specifying, 63
  right handed versus left, 63–64
  selecting menu items, 19
  speed, setting, 62
  tracking speed, setting, 62
  upgrading, 434–435
Mouse pane, 62–64
movies, 275–279, 284. *See also* video
Movies folder, 131
moving
  files and folders, 160–161
  icons, 160–161
  widgets, 53
  windows, 34, 178
MP3 format, 268
multibutton mouse, 38
multimedia, 434. *See also specific media*

Multi-Touch trackpads, 67
music. *See also* iTunes
  Audio MIDI Setup, 396
  EXO 2.1 Speaker System, 434
  GarageBand, buying, 284
  QuickTime Player, 278–279
  speaker upgrades, 434
Music folder, 131

• *N* •

nested folders, 125–126
network administrators, 318
Network command, 111
networks, 111, 316–321, 389. *See also* sharing
New in Lion icon, 5
News button, 216
No Access, 337, 338
No Name icon, 282
notes, e-mail, 244

• *O* •

Office 2011 For Mac For Dummies, 287
OmniCleanz cleaning solution (RadTech), 18
opening
  documents, files, and folders, 77–78, 143–149, 153–154
  widgets, 52
  windows, 33
OpenType fonts, 293
operating systems, purpose of, 10–11
Option key, keyboard shortcuts, 42
orientation of printed page, specifying, 305, 308
OS X Lion All-in-One For Dummies, 2, 196
Other World Computing, 442
outlined fonts, 289
owner permissions, 333–334

• p •

packages, 149–150
Padova, Ted, 397
Page Setup sheet. *See* printers
Page Up/Page Down keys, scrolling
    windows, 29
Pages, 285
paper handling, 310
paper size, specifying, 304, 308
Parallels Desktop, 186–187
parent alias, locating, 96
parent icon, 94
Parental Controls, 329–331
Partition tab, 399–400
partitions, 399–400. *See also*
    troubleshooting, Recovery HD
    partition
Party Shuffle. *See* DJ, iTunes
passwords
    changing, 331, 344–346
    consolidating, 402–403
    keychain access, 402–405
    login, disabling, 13
    screen savers, 50
    setting, 325–328
    sleep mode, 50, 391
    System Preferences access, 391
paths, displaying, 118
PDFs, 279–280, 310–312
performance enhancements, 421–429
permissions, 323–338, 338–340
photographs, 280–282, 284, 379
pictures, 47–49, 226, 280–282. *See also*
    screen savers
Pictures folder, 131
playlists, 266–271
podcasts, 263–264
pointing with a mouse, 18
Popular button, 216
pop-up menus, 31–32
portrait orientation, 305
ports, printers, 300
PostScript Type 1 fonts, 292–293
power, electrical, 12, 16–17

PPoE (Point-to-Point Protocol over
    Ethernet), 212
PPP (Point-to-Point Protocol), 212
PRAM, zapping, 414–415
preferences. *See* customizing; System
    Preferences
Preferences, Finder menu, 107
Preferences folder, 133
Preview, 72, 279–280, 311
previewing
    document contents, 144–145
    files, 100, 119
    folders, 105
    graphic files, 279–280
    PDFs, 279–280
    pictures in e-mail messages, 255–256
    printing, 310–312
Print sheet. *See* printers, Print sheet
printer fonts, 293
printer settings, access and permissions,
    331
printers
    borders, 309
    color matching, 309
    connecting, 298–299
    cover page, 310
    custom settings, 307–310
    description, 303–305
    documentation, 297
    downloading software for, 300
    drivers, 303
    expanding, 307
    first-time setup, 299–302
    headers/footers, 309
    layout, 309
    number of copies, 308
    options, 304–305
    orientation, 305, 308
    page range, specifying, 308
    Page Setup sheet, 298, 303–305
    pages per sheet, 309
    paper handling, 310
    paper size, 304, 308
    ports, 300
    print settings, 310

printers *(continued)*
  Print sheet, 298, 305–310
  printing documents, 305–306
  removing, access and permissions, 331
  scale, specifying, 305
  selecting a printer, 306–307
  sharing, 302, 348
  TextEdit options, 309–310
  two-sided printing, 309
  variations across printers, 298
  wireless, 299
printing, 298, 306–307, 310–312
processes, monitoring, 394–396
processor type, displaying, 39
product reviews, online resources, 438–439
profanity restrictions, 331
profile information. *See* System Profiler
program icons. *See* application icons
prohibitory sign, 14, 408–409
protocols, 212, 317. *See also specific protocols*
proxies, 212
Public folders, 131, 332
pull-down menus, 35–36

• *Q* •

Quick Look button, 100
Quick Look command, 144–145
Quick Look/Slideshow button, 26–27
Quick Look feature, 255–256
QuickTime Player, 278–279

• *R* •

radio buttons, 31–32
RadTech (OmniCleanz cleaning solution), 18
RAID (Redundant Array of Individual Disks), 400
RAM, 39, 416, 427, 431–432, 441
Ramseeker, 441
Rant & Rave icon, 5

Read & Write permissions, 337
Read Only permissions, 337, 339
Reading List, 218–219. *See also* bookmarking; Top Sites page
Recent Folders command, 112
Recent Items, 40
recently used items, 57–58, 75, 112
Recovery HD partition. *See* troubleshooting, Recovery HD partition
reinstalling Mac OS X, 415, 446–449. *See also* installing, Mac OS X
Remember icon, 5
reminders, 203–204
remote computers, sharing, 229–231, 340–344, 347
remote devices, definition, 316
remote infrared receiver, disabling, 391
removing. *See specific items*
renaming
  folders, 181
  icons, 163
Rendezvous. *See* Bonjour
resizing
  the Dock, 81, 84
  icons, 26–27, 103
  windows, 26–27, 33–34
Restore tab, 400–401
restoring data, 379. *See also* backing up data
restoring factory settings, 400–401
Resume, 134–139
Rhodes, Cheryl, 11
right-click, 37
rotating printed pages, 310–312
routers, 320–321
RSS feeds, 221–222
rules, e-mail, 249–250

• *S* •

Safari, 214–225
Safari icon, 71
safe downloads list, updating, 391
Save a Version, 135–142

Save As, 139–142
Save As sheet, 140
Save sheet, 135–140
saving documents, 134–142. *See also* Auto
    Save; Versions
scaling printed pages, 305
scanners, sharing, 348
science, online resources, 440
screen. *See also* monitors
  capturing, 350, 401
  flashes on alerts, 365–366
  security lock, 393
screen of death, 13–14
screen savers, 47–51
scroll bars, 26–29, 56–57
scroll wheel, 29, 63–64
scrolling, 29–30, 66
Search box, Finder window, 166–168
Search button, 100
Search field, 26–27
searching
  for files or folders, 100
  with Google, in Safari, 222–225
  mailboxes, 245
secure Trash emptying, 164
security. *See also* backing up data; file
    sharing, access and permissions;
    passwords
  diagnostic and usage data, sending to
      Apple, 392
  encrypting files, 390
  firewalls, 385–388
  location services, enabling, 392
  locking files, 390
  logout after inactivity, 391
  macro viruses, 383–385
  malware, 383–385
  remote infrared receiver, disabling, 391
  restricting network connections, 391. *See
      also* access and permissions
  safe downloads list, updating, 391
  screen lock, 391
  viruses, 383–385
select all, keyboard shortcut, 42
selecting
  icons, 161–163
  items from menus, 35–36
  text in TextEdit, 288–289

serial number, displaying, 40
servers, connecting to, 112
Services, Finder menu, 107–108
setting up your computer. *See* customizing
Setup Assistant, 211, 446–449. *See also*
    customizing; System Preferences
Shared folders, 332
sharing. *See also* file sharing; folders,
    sharing; networks; remote computers,
    sharing
  Bluetooth, 348–349
  CDs/DVDs, 347
  disks on local computers, 332–337
  disks on remote computers, 340–344
  icons, 119
  Internet, 348–349
  movies, 279
  printers, 302, 348
  scanners, 348
  Web, 348
Sharing Account, 324
shopping for Mac products, 441-442
Show All, Finder menu, 109
shuffling windows, 34–35
Shut Down command, 16
Shut Down options, 41
shutdown. *See* turning off your computer
Sidebar, 26–27, 98–99, 113
signatures, e-mail, 253–254
single-click, mouse, 18
Sites folder, 131
slash through circle. *See* prohibitory sign
sleep mode, 17, 50, 370, 391
Slideshow option, 255–256
slow keys, 366
smart
  folders, 154–157
  groups, 237–238
  mailboxes, 252–253
  playlists, 267–268
smiley faces, 59
Snapz Pro X utility (Ambrosia Software),
    401
software. *See specific software*
software information, System Profiler,
    39–40
Software Update, 40
songs. *See iTunes*

sound, 67–68
Sound pane, 67–68
spaces, 171–180
spacing, end of sentence, 287
spam filters, 247–248. *See also* junk-mail,
    filtering; kill files
speaker upgrades, 434
special characters, inserting, 288
speech recognition, 351–356
spell check, 249, 290
spinning-disc cursor, 410
Spotlight, 165–169
spring-loading, 115, 153–154
SSDs (Solid State Drives), 431
Standard accounts, 323, 332
starting your computer. *See* turning on
    your computer
startup crashes, troubleshooting, 416–417
startup disk, 39, 333, 407–409
startup screens, 12–13
stationery, e-mail, 245–246
Stationery Pad, 118
status bar, 98–99
Stickies, 205–206
sticky keys, 366
storage devices, information about, 126–127.
    See also Computer folder
streaming radio, 264–265
subfolders, 150–152
submailboxes, 251
submenus, 39
suitcase files, 293
SuperDuper, 382
switches, 320–321
System folder, 129
System Information, 404. *See also* System
    Profiler
System Preferences icon, 72
System Preferences menu item, 40
System Preferences panes, 45–51, 55–68,
    83–87, 171–180, 323, 391. *See also*
    Setup Assistant; *specific preferences*
System Preferences window, 46–47
System Profiler, 14–15, 39–41. *See also*
    System Information

• T •

tablets, 371
tabs (in dialogs), 31–32
tabs (word processing), 62, 289
talking to your Mac, 351–356
TCP/IP, 212
Technical Stuff icon, 5
technical support, 415, 437–438, 440–441.
    See also troubleshooting
templates, creating, 118
Terminal, 404–405
text, converting to speech, 357–358
text editing. *See* TextEdit
Text to Speech, 358–359
TextEdit, 285–291, 309–310
text-entry fields in dialogs, 31–32
32-bit mode, opening applications in, 118
Thunderbolt, 430
time limits, setting, 331
Time Machine, 18, 72, 376–379
Tip icon, 5
title bars, customizing, 56–57
to-do lists. *See* iCal; Stickies
toolbar, 26–27, 98–101. *See also specific
    buttons*
Top Sites page, 219–221. *See also*
    bookmarking; Reading List
tracking speed, setting, 62, 65
Trackpad pane, 65–67
trackpads, 30, 37, 58, 65–67, 366–367
translating languages, 54
Translation widget, 54
Trash, 73–74, 116, 119, 164, 193–194
Trash icon, 72
tri-state check boxes, 32
troubleshooting
    boot disks, 407–409
    bootable partition, 408
    booting, 407–408
    copying a boot disk, 408
    Dr. Mac Consulting, 415
    DVD Player settings, 278
    formatting disks, 398–399
    kernel panic alert, 412

local user groups, 415
opening documents, 146–147
prohibitory sign, 408–409
RAM issues, 416
remote computer sharing, 229–231
repairing disk drives, 398
spinning-disc cursor, 410
startup crashes, 416–417
startup disk not found, 408–409
startup disks, 407–408
tech-support hotline, 415
tools for, 398–401, 408, 413
troubleshooting, Recovery HD partition
  basic recovery steps, 410–416
  booting from, 410–411
  booting in Safe Mode, 413–414
  definition, 408
  disk repair, 411–413
  reinstalling Mac OS X, 415
  running First Aid, 411–413
  zapping the PRAM, 414–415
TrueType fonts, 292
turning off your computer, 16, 40
turning on your computer, 12–15. *See also*
  power, electrical
two-finger swipe, 30
two-sided printing, 309
Type 1 fonts, 292–293
typefaces. *See* fonts
typing skills, performance enhancements,
  423

• *U* •

underlined fonts, 289
undoing
  calendar deletions, 200
  formatting disks, 399
  Trashed files, 164
uninstalling applications, 181
Universal Access, 364–367
unplugging electrical power, 17
updates
  checking for, 40
  installing, 388–389

upgrade cards, online resources, 442
URLs (Uniform Resource Locators)
  adding to the Dock, 79–80
  typing, auto-completion, 215–216
USB 2 performance, 428
user accounts, 323–324
users, file sharing, 323–331, 338–339
Users folder, 129–130
Utilities command, 111
Utilities folder, 111

• *V* •

vCards, 235
version
  files, 118
  Mac OS, 14–15
Versions, 134–142. *See also* Auto Save;
  backing up data
VersionTracker. *See* CNET Downloads
video, importing from camcorders, 283.
  See also movies
video cameras. *See* camcorders
video chat, 227–228. *See also* FaceTime;
  iChat
videos, 263–264
View buttons, 26–27, 99
virtual business cards, 235
VirtualBox, 186
VirusBarrier, 385
viruses, 383–385
Visualizer, iTunes, 259–260
visually impaired users, VoiceOver
  technology, 357–358
VoiceOver technology, 357–358

• *W* •

Wacom, 369
Warning icon, 5
Web. *See also* Internet
  access and permissions, 330
  sharing, 348

Web addresses. *See* URLs (Uniform Resource Locators)
Web browsing. *See* Safari
What You See Is What You Get (WYSIWYG), 290
Widget Bar, 53
widgets, 51–55. *See also* applications
windows
  active versus inactive, 30–31
  arranging, 34–35
  bringing to front, 35
  closing, 33
  creating, keyboard shortcut, 33
  customizing, 55–58
  cycling through, 35
  definition, 25
  description, 25–26
  hiding, keyboard shortcut, 109
  illustration, 24
  managing, 175–177
  minimizing, 35
  moving, 34
  opening, 33
  resizing, 26–27, 33–34
  shuffling, 34–35
  spring-loading, 115
  title bar, 26–27
  views, 99–106
  zooming, 35

Windows, running on a Mac, 186–187, 371
wireless
  AirPort Utility, 396
  backups, 376
  Internet connection, 211
  printers, 299
Word (Microsoft), 286
word processing. *See also* TextEdit
  Pages, 285
  Word (Microsoft), 286
workflows, 362
World Wide Web. *See* Web
Write Only permissions, 337, 339
WYSIWYG (What You See Is What You Get), 290

• X •

x, identifying tri-state check boxes, 32

• Z •

zapping the PRAM, 414–415
zoom, trackpads, 66
Zoom button, 26–27, 28
zooming windows, 35